ESTABLISHING A PURE LAND ON EARTH

Topics in Contemporary Buddhism
GEORGE J. TANABE JR., EDITOR

Establishing a Pure Land on Earth: The Foguang Buddhist Perspective on Modernization and Globalization
STUART CHANDLER

Buddhist Missionaries in the Era of Globalization
LINDA LEARMAN, EDITOR

TOPICS IN
CONTEMPORARY
BUDDHISM

Establishing a Pure Land on Earth

The Foguang Buddhist
Perspective on Modernization
and Globalization

STUART CHANDLER

University of Hawai'i Press
Honolulu

© 2004 University of Hawai'i Press
All rights reserved
Printed in the United States of America
09 08 07 06 05 04   6 5 4 3 2 1

Library of Congress Cataloging-in-Publication Data
Chandler, Stuart
Establishing a Pure Land on earth : the Foguang Buddhist perspective on modernization and globalization / Stuart Chandler.
p. cm. — (Topics in contemporary Buddhism)
Includes bibliographical references and index.
ISBN 0-8248-2746-5 (alk. paper)
1. Buddhism—Taiwan. 2. Foguang shan si (Kao-hsiung hsien, Taiwan) I. Title: Foguang Buddhist perspective on modernization and globalization. II. Title. III. Series.
BQ649.T32C42 2004
294.3'926—dc22
2004003461

University of Hawai'i Press books are printed on acid-free paper and meet the guidelines for permanence and durability of the Council on Library Resources.

Designed by Elsa Lee
Printed by The Maple-Vail Book Manufacturing Group

To Stephanie, Evan, and Eddie

Contents

Series Editor's Preface		ix
Preface		xi
Acknowledgments		xv
Introduction		1
1	A Mountain Monastery in an Urban Society	8
2	Master Xingyun: Foguang Patriarch	28
3	Foguang Humanistic Buddhism	43
4	Humanistic Buddhism in Practice	78
5	Cultivating Talent through Education	118
6	Cultivating Faith through Discipline	137
7	Institutionalizing Buddhism	191
8	Perpetuating Traditional Modernism	236
9	Globalizing Chinese Culture, Localizing Buddhist Teachings	260
10	Globalizing and Localizing: Three Case Studies	275
Conclusion: Global Homelessness		301
Appendix: Chronological Table: Master Xingyun and Foguangshan		307
Notes		315
Glossary		345
References		353
Index		365

Series Editor's Preface

Once confined to Asia, Buddhism has in the last century become a conspicuous part of the religious landscape in countries the world over. From the severest levels of ascetic practice to media images in daily culture, its forms and expressions are recognizably Buddhist even in Buddhism's immense variations. As well as an ancient religion, Buddhism is a modern phenomenon. *Establishing a Pure Land on Earth* is the first volume in Topics in Contemporary Buddhism, a series that provides a forum in which the phenomenon of modern Buddhism can be examined from a variety of perspectives.

Taiwan has produced some of the most innovative and dynamic Buddhist movements of modern times. These groups have transformed the lives of many on the island as well as among overseas Chinese communities. Rising to the challenges of modernization, they have developed a creative set of interpretations and strategies that constitute what one of its early pioneers called "Humanistic Buddhism." Humanistic Buddhism developed in reaction to a prior understanding of a Buddhism that placed greater emphasis on the maintenance of tradition than on people and their needs. At the forefront of this movement is the Foguangshan community, the focus of Stuart Chandler's in-depth study.

On the basis of extensive fieldwork and an examination of a wide variety of textual materials, *Establishing a Pure Land on Earth* explores the themes of modernization, globalization, gender roles, the ordination of women, relations with other religious traditions, cultural and national identity at home and abroad, ethnic tensions, and moral dilemmas. These are familiar issues of our time, and, because Stuart Chandler deals with them in the context of Foguangshan, his work is most appropriate as the inaugural entry in our series.

George J. Tanabe Jr.
SERIES EDITOR

Preface

Any time a study relies heavily on material gathered ethnographically, there is the problem of how to document the sources of one's data. Public meetings, conferences, and ceremonies as well as formal interviews do not pose much of a problem since they can be listed as part of the References section, as I have done in this book. The dilemma arises in determining whether to indicate one's source when the information was given as part of an informal conversation. Over the two years of my stay at Foguangshan I had hundreds of such interactions, some no more than a few minutes in duration, others lasting several hours. Often, my conversation partners would very likely lack a clear recognition that what they revealed could become part of a public document. Despite the fact that I took every opportunity to indicate the nature of my project, even during the closing weeks of my stay in the community, it was quite evident that many of the monks, nuns, and laypeople had little understanding of the purpose of my stay and simply assumed that I was a Foguang devotee. Those who came to know me well also seemed with time to forget my status as academic researcher. Such friends were likely to reveal attitudes or information that did not necessarily accord with Foguangshan's public stance. For this book, I have, therefore, not given the names of people who provided information during informal conversations if, in my opinion, there is any chance that such disclosure could cause difficulties for them.

Another problem that occurs when writing a book about Buddhism is that of deciding on the language in which to give certain terms. Since the present study is about a Chinese Buddhist organization, one could argue that it makes most sense to utilize transliterations of Chinese pronunciations for names and concepts. Conversely, because Sanskrit and Pali are generally recognized as pan-Buddhist textual languages, the vast majority of Buddhist words that have entered English (as evidenced by their inclusion in *Webster's Third New International Dictionary Unabridged* and the *Random House Unabridged Dictionary*) derive from these languages, especially Sanskrit. One could, therefore, argue that employing such standardized terminology is the better approach since it facilitates the further development of a common discourse for English-language Buddhist studies.

I have chosen to follow the latter path. Hence, in this book, rather than finding reference to "Shijiamouni Fo," "Jile Jingtu" and *"kong,"* one will find mention of "Shakyamuni Buddha," "Sukhavati Pure Land," and "sunyata" (although the

Chinese pronunciation appears parenthetically after a term appears for the first time). Because the words are being treated as part of English vocabulary, diacritics associated with the original Sanskrit do not appear. Very few Chinese pronunciations of the Buddhist lexicon have gained currency in English; the word "Chan" is increasingly being used instead of "Zen" when referring to that tradition in its Chinese context. Also, along with "Avalokiteshvara" the *Random House Unabridged Dictionary* lists "Guanyin" as the Chinese name for the Bodhisattva of Compassion. I therefore refer to "Chan" and "Guanyin" in this book.

Buddhist words that function as proper nouns and that have not yet found their way into common English discourse are referred to in an Anglicized Sanskrit: Maitreya Buddha, Tushita Heaven, etc. For other terms that have not yet become current in English, I have either followed an English-language translation that is commonly found in scholarly works (e.g., "pure land," "patience") or utilized a transliteration of the Chinese or Sanskrit pronunciation, depending on the context (when employing an English translation, I show Chinese, then Sanskrit, in parentheses).

The terms "monastic," "cleric," and "venerable" are my translations for the terms *"chujiazhong"* and *"fashi." "Chujiazhong"* literally means "those who have left home." *"Fashi"* signifies a teacher (*shi*) of the Dharma (*fa*). Both refer to those who have taken monastic vows, that is, bhikshus (*biqiu*), bhikshunis (*biqiuni*), shramaneras (*shami*), and shramanerikas (*shamini*). The term "disciple" is equivalent to *"tudi"* and, as such, includes not only ordained monastics but also "lay monastics," my awkward term for *shigu* and *jiaoshi*, those laywomen and -men who have vowed to remain celibate and serve Foguangshan for life. "Master" is a translation of *"dashi,"* "great teacher." The English term "laity" means essentially the same thing as the Chinese *"xintu"* or *"zaijiazhong"* (lit., "those who remain at home"). The term "devotee" corresponds to *"dizi"* and, hence, designates all the master's followers, both monastic and lay.

In this book, I follow the standard academic practice of employing the pinyin system of transliteration for Chinese terms. I make an exception only for proper names that are already well-known by their Wade-Giles or Yale transliteration: for example, Taipei; Kaohsiung; Hsi Lai Temple; Nan Tien Temple; Nan Hua Temple. Because I have chosen the pinyin system, my spelling of Foguang names usually differs from that used by the organization itself. Foguangshan generally employs the Wade-Giles and Yale systems to transliterate Chinese terms into English. It should be noted that Foguang devotees are far from consistent in this matter since they utilize various systems and frequently switch from one to another, having no clear understanding of the differences between them. A particular term or name may, therefore, be spelled a variety of ways from one document to the next (and sometimes even within the same document). The transliteration for Master Xingyun's name, for instance, is typically spelled using Wade-Giles, that is, "Hsing Yun." There are times, however, when it has appeared in the pinyin "Xingyun," and the master himself employs the Yale style, "Shing Yun." Transliterations of temple names also vary, including the spelling of "Foguangshan," which usually appears as "Fo Kuang Shan" but in recent years has increasingly been transliterated in pinyin.

The basic monetary unit for the Republic of China (ROC) is the New Taiwan dollar. In the latter half of the 1990s, the exchange rate fluctuated between NT$26 and NT$32 to U.S.$1. When computing the approximate value of Foguangshan's endeavors, I have, therefore, used an average exchange rate of NT$30 to U.S.$1.

Acknowledgments

The material utilized in this book was gathered through fieldwork conducted from 1996 to 1998. I spent most of that period at the Foguang headquarters in Kaohsiung County of the Republic of China, although for four months I escaped southern Taiwan's brutal summer heat to live at Nan Tien Temple, the Foguang branch in Wollongong, Australia. I also spent a month at Hsi Lai Temple, just outside Los Angeles, and several days in the fall of 1999 at Nan Hua Temple in Bronkhorstspruit, South Africa. At all four locations, my time was devoted to interviewing and having informal conversations with Foguang clerics and lay devotees, observing or participating in Dharma functions, lectures, meetings, and conferences, reading Foguang literature, and generally becoming as immersed as possible in the community's daily life.

As with any study based on fieldwork, the list of people to whom I am indebted is very, very long. Innumerable monastic and lay devotees graciously took the time to answer my questions, solve my problems, suggest or even locate relevant materials, and generally reveal to me what it means to be a Foguang Buddhist. First and foremost, I must thank Foguangshan's founder, Master Xingyun. Not every monastic community would be open to allowing an unknown scholar, along with his wife and four-year-old son, to live in their midst. Master Xingyun made sure that I and my family had everything we needed for a comfortable and rewarding stay: we were provided a two-room apartment in the Foguang senior citizen home; my son attended the kindergarten run by the monastery for local children; and a nun was assigned to tutor my wife in Chinese. The monastery's openness extended to my research as well. When I indicated that I hoped to be permitted to attend meetings and planning sessions to which only monastics were normally invited, Master Xingyun immediately let it be known that I was welcome to observe any meeting. He also took time out of his very hectic schedule on several occasions so that I could interview him or ask specific questions. The master's warm hospitality made fieldwork run about as smoothly as it can.

Master Xingyun was not the only high-ranking member of the Foguang community to set aside time to help me. The Venerables Cizhuang, Cihui, Cirong, Xinding, Yikong, Huikai, and Huiri and other members of the Veterans Council and Religious Affairs Committee sat down with me for interviews, and all showed great concern about my family's well-being.

On a day-to-day basis, it was the office staff of the International Buddhist Progress Society (IBPS) who made sure that my family was properly cared for. I will never forget Ven. Juemen's straightforward yet gentle manner, Ven. Yi'en's playfulness with my son, Evan, Ven. Juezhong's quiet kindness, Ven. Miaoqi's sense of humor, Ven. Huishang's concern for my wife's comfort and happiness, and Zhou Pingzheng's patience in helping me read through many of Master Xingyun's lectures. Most of all, I would like to thank Ven. Manhua, the general secretary of the IBPS office during most of my stay at Foguangshan. I had never known that anyone could show such compassion for stray cats, homeless dogs, and itinerant doctoral students.

I also must thank the dean and teachers of the Foguang kindergarten for the wonderful care they took of my son. Our neighbors in the senior citizen home, especially Ven. Huida and Mr. Han, truly made us feel part of an extended family, as did the staff of the Great Mercy Children's Home and the faculty and students at Pumen High School. Others at Foguangshan who aided my research include Vens. Jiankuan, Yilai, Yi Heng, Yifa, Yihua, Yiquan, Manqian, Manhe, Jueji, Juehui, Miaoru, and Miaohong as well as the laypeople Jijin, Miaohong, Meixuan, Madeline Wheeler-Gibbs, and Gordon Gibbs. The list could go on and on.

Equally important in guiding me in this project have been advisers and friends within the academic community. Special thanks go to the Rocky Foundation, without whose two-year grant fieldwork would have been impossible. I would also like to express my gratitude to my thesis adviser, Professor Tu Wei-ming, and to Professors Diana Eck and Robert Gimello, who served on the reading committee for the dissertation from which this book eventually evolved. Kenneth Tanaka, Charles Prebish, Christopher Queen, Martin Baumann, and Julia Huang all provided insightful feedback on portions of the text. I have also benefited greatly from the work on modern Chinese Buddhism that has been done by Holmes Welch and, more recently, by Jiang Canteng. Another vital source of information and feedback as I worked through a succession of drafts has been my colleagues in the Department of Religious Studies at Indiana University of Pennsylvania; one could not ask for a more engaging group of people with whom to teach and conduct research.

Earlier versions of portions of this book have already appeared elsewhere. Parts of chapters 2 and 4 were first published in "The Dharma of Wealth: The Foguang Perspective on the Role of Capitalistic Enterprise in Buddhist Cultivation" (*Contemporary Buddhism: An Interdisciplinary Journal* 2, no. 1 [fall 2001]: 39–53). Parts of chapters 8–10 originally appeared in "Globalizing Chinese Culture, Localizing Buddhist Teachings: The Internationalization of Foguangshan" (*Jour-*

nal of Global Buddhism 3 [spring 2002]: 46–78). My thoughts in chapters 8 and 9 on the intricacies of identity issues were initially expressed in "Chinese Buddhism in America: Identity and Practice" (in *The Faces of American Buddhism,* ed. Charles Prebish and Ken Tanaka [Berkeley and Los Angeles: University of California Press, 1998], 14–30). Finally, an earlier version of the description of the Hsi Lai Temple donations controversy offered in chapter 10 appeared in "Placing Palms Together: Religious and Cultural Dimensions of the Hsi Lai Temple Political Donations Controversy" (in *American Buddhism: Methods and Findings in Recent Scholarship,* ed. Christopher Queen and Duncan Williams [Surrey: Curzon, 1998], 36–56). The feedback on each of these articles that I received from peer reviewers and editors was invaluable in refining my arguments.

George Tanabe, Patricia Crosby, and Ann Ludeman, my editors at the University of Hawai'i Press, have shown unflinching support for this project. I greatly appreciate their patience, suggestions, corrections, and constant encouragement. I am also grateful for the copyediting skills of Joseph Brown; his comments and queries provided a wonderful lesson in English grammar, usage, and literary style.

I reserve my greatest thanks for my family. My son, Evan, was a very good sport about adapting to a constant flow of new experiences and cultures. His flexibility and openness were surpassed only by those of my wife, Stephanie. Not every spouse would consent to quitting a good job and leaving behind family and friends to spend two years living in a cramped apartment in a Buddhist monastery in a foreign country.

Introduction

Master Xingyun, the founder of the Foguang Buddhist order, frequently announces to his devotees: "I am a global person" (*wo shi guojiren*). This book explores the historical background, cultural context, and social implications of that deceptively simple comment. The master began to refer to himself in this manner around 1990, just as his organization undertook an ambitious campaign to expand beyond its base in Taiwan and establish branch temples around the world, an effort that by the close of the millennium had resulted in the opening of nearly one hundred centers on five continents. For the master and his followers, this has been the first step in the "globalization" (*guojihua*) of "modernized" (*xiandaihua*) Buddhism. From another perspective, it can be seen to be the culmination of a vigorous attempt by an affluent community to protect and promote what its members regard as the best of their traditional culture in response to the Westernization and homogenization that are perceived to have heretofore predominantly shaped the nascent "global village."

The strategy adopted by the master to ensure the continued vibrancy of Chinese Buddhism has been, not to resist modernity, but to embrace many of its pivotal concepts and institutional mechanisms, thereby bringing about a dynamic synthesis of the old and the new. Underlying this approach is the assumption that those elements of modernity conducive to well-being have in fact long been present, at least implicitly, in the Buddha dharma. Tradition can persist and flourish through modernity because the spirit of modernity was already operative in tradition. Or, to restate the issue, modernity neither replaces nor supersedes tradition; it creates a new rendition of it. Master Xingyun's method of selective appropriation has led him to speak of the Buddhist versions of democracy (*minzhu zhuyi*), capitalism (*ziben zhuyi*), equality (*pingdeng*), women's rights (*nuquan*), modernization, and, most recently, globalization.

Because the Foguang thrust to internationalize is in direct response to wider processes of globalization, to understand the Foguang phenomenon we must first place it in this context. The term "globalization" as it has entered late-twentieth- and early-twenty-first-century discourse refers to the modern trend toward both a greater interdependence of all societies and an accompanying heightened consciousness of the world as a single arena. Long-distance transcultural contact and interchange have taken place for centuries, mainly impelled by political ambition, economic incentive, and missionary zeal. To appreciate this fact, one need only recall the empires built by Alexander the Great and Chinggis Khan, the explorations of Marco Polo and the Chinese admiral Zheng He, the remarkable trade of goods from Europe and Africa to China along the silk route, and the vast spread of Christianity, Islam, and Buddhism. Globalization as we know it today, however, having matured over the past century, significantly differs from its earlier manifestations in magnitude. Never before have virtually all segments of all societies been so intertwined with one another or so conscious of transnational and cross-cultural connection. The scale of international tourism, commerce, and migration and the sophistication of global communication and transportation are unprecedented.

The current condensing of the world to one global village is also driven by a new strain of economic forces and motivations that was unknown in former days, namely, modern capitalism. The sociologist Immanuel Wallerstein has forcefully argued that what he called today's "world-system" has evolved directly as a result of market forces that first developed in sixteenth-century Europe (Wallerstein 1974, 1980, 1984). In Wallerstein's neo-Marxian model, the various values that are associated with global capitalism (e.g., faith in progress, democracy, and human rights) have played no significant role in determining the evolution of the world system, having arisen merely as epiphenomena of market forces. From this, one can see that Wallerstein considers the cultural implications of globalization to be of secondary importance. In fact, in his only article specifically dealing with this issue, he states that the concept "culture" is of negligible heuristic use and, in its social function, serves primarily as an ideological mechanism to legitimate the inequities in distribution present in the world system.[1]

Others have found the cultural ramifications of humankind's ever-increasing contact and interdependence to be of great and, in certain respects, troubling significance. Because the international spread of modern capitalism had its origins in Western Europe, a variety of nineteenth- and twentieth-century intellectuals believed that, as other groups were subsumed into the growing market system, they would increasingly assume the cultural traits of the West as well. Economic globalization was, hence, regarded as triggering widespread Westernization. In more recent years, the language has shifted. The presupposition continues to be that the differences in worldviews and values that heretofore distinguished various civilizations will inevitably wane as the same economic forces impinge throughout the world. Instead of seeing the result as merely the monolithic diffusion of Western values, however, observers now describe the emerging "world culture" as a homogenized synthesis that draws its elements from diverse sources.

The sociologist Peter Berger has identified four processes of cultural globalization (Berger 1997). First, there is what he has dubbed "the Davos culture." This "yuppie internationale" of business elites shares particular patterns of dress, conduct, humor, and leisure activities. Another global network of elites is the "Faculty Club International," which represents the global dissemination of values and ideologies originally developed by Western intelligentsia. Notable expressions of this are the worldwide feminist and environmentalist movements. Globalization has occurred on popular levels as well. There is "the McWorld Culture," that bricolage of pop entertainment, fashion, and fast food that carries with it such ideals as self-expression, spontaneity, and defiance of authority. Alongside this has been the rapid spread of Evangelical Protestantism and the concomitant transformations in attitudes toward traditional hierarchies, relations between men and women, and upbringing of children.

Berger is not the only scholar with a budding interest in the relation between cultural factors and globalization. As the topic has gained currency, three issues have proved especially nettlesome. First, there are those who, remaining unconvinced by Wallerstein's dismissal of culture, counter that communal values, concepts, and worldviews jointly constitute an autonomous variable that significantly guides the trajectory of globalization. One of the most vocal advocates of this view is Roland Robertson, who has written extensively on the role of such symbolic constructs as "nation," "civilization," and "world system" in determining the direction of the globalizing process (see, e.g., Robertson 1978, 1992).

Irrespective of whether cultural factors help set the projection of globalization, the question arises as to the degree of convergence that will occur with increased contact and interaction. Will the coalescence of a world system result in the attenuation of cultural differences, a homogenization? Or can a variety of cultural models coexist with participation in the international economic system? In other words, will various societies mobilize indigenous resources so that "multiple modernities" develop? Robertson (1992, 69) foresees the continuation of several dominant and alternative constellations of presuppositions. The anthropologist Jonathan Friedman (1994) has laid out a detailed model indicating that, with the decentralization of capital accumulation inevitably occurring with the global expansion of capitalistic enterprise, cultural balkanization also takes place. The homogenizing trends that have accompanied the modern West's economic predominance will, therefore, naturally recede as semiperipheral and peripheral regions disproportionately accumulate capital through their greater productivity. In fact, in Friedman's opinion, there are signs that such pluralization is already under way.

Beyond disagreements about the role of culture in globalization and about the future status of cultural diversity, scholars vary in the place that they foresee religion holding in the emerging global village. Does the modernization process that attends globalization inevitably breed secularization, or can there be religious expressions of modernity? Some argue that the rise of fundamentalistic religious movements has amply demonstrated the resilience and vitality of religion (e.g., Hadden and Shupe 1989); others claim such extreme expressions to be the last paroxysms of an inevitable demise. In general, arguments for cultural homogenization see that process occurring along secular lines, while pluralists predict continued vibrancy among religions.

Scholarly discussion of the role of culture or religion in modern globalization to this point has tended toward the abstract and general. Research concerning the relation between particular religious traditions and globalization is especially scarce. The collection *Religion and Global Order* (Robertson and Garrette 1991) includes brief articles on Islam, Pentecostalism, and Soka Gakkai. Books on fundamentalism, such as Marty and Appleby (1991, 1993a, 1993b, 1995), the series published through the University of Chicago's Fundamentalism Project, scrutinize the more virulent traditionalist forms of religious resistance to globalization, although they typically do so without directly addressing the process of globalization itself. Furthermore, these data deal only with what are essentially negative reactions against the world's growing interconnection. To employ Robertson's (1992, 68) terminology, they are "anti-systematic movements which attack the worldsystem within the constraints of traditional presuppositions." The sociologist Peter Beyer (1994) has offered a balanced analysis of both traditionalist and modernist religious responses to modernization and globalization, although his monograph remains largely theoretical.

The winter 2000 issue of *Daedalus* has provided the most concrete treatment thus far of how diverse religious (and secular) traditions are imprinting their own, unique stamps on modern global culture. In an introductory essay in that issue, S. N. Eisenstadt argues that the case studies on the Christian, Islamic, Hindu, and Confucian traditions that follow provide clear evidence that modernization has not resulted in hegemonic Westernization or homogenization. Rather, the encounter between Western modernity and the various cultural traditions has spawned what Eisenstadt calls "multiple modernities." By this, he means that, as various groups encounter the economic, institutional, and cultural challenges of modern times, they inevitably reappropriate and redefine the discourse of modernity in their own, new terms. Hence, there is continual reinterpretation of the cultural program of modernity, a reinterpretation that is significantly shaped by each group's history and traditions yet much more than a mere continuation of them.

Furthermore, the major arenas of contestation in which new forms of modernity are taking shape are not just the nation-state but increasingly other social spaces in which alternative constellations of cultural forces are interacting (see Eisenstadt 2000, 24). The studies that follow give substance to Eisenstadt's assertions. Because each deals with at least one entire tradition and is only article length, however, depth of evidence for the observations made is limited. To date, there has been no sustained inquiry into how one particular modernist religious group has understood and adapted to globalization.

This book takes a small step toward filling that gap by analyzing the Chinese Buddhist organization Foguangshan in the light of global studies. I show how Master Xingyun endeavors to make Pure Land and Chan practices relevant to contemporary life by structuring them according to a modernist educational and institutional framework and by creating a synthesis of them and a Buddhist reconstruction of the Enlightenment values of democracy, equality, liberty, justice, and fraternity. Through presenting this material, I argue that cultural factors—specifically, religious beliefs and practices—influence modern globalization either by inhibiting or, as in the case of Foguangshan, encouraging patterns of behavior conducive to capitalist enterprise. Because there are definite similarities in the types of behavior favorable to prosperity through participation in the marketplace, and because communication on the global scale requires a common vocabulary, modern globalization has led to significant cultural convergence. Yet, because the global lingua franca is evolving in dialectical interaction with a variety of cultural frameworks, in each case the significance of various ideals—such as those of "prosperity," "progress," "modernity," "democracy," and "equality"—is given unique coloration. Furthermore, the increase in contact with members of other cultural groups that occurs with globalization sparks questions about identity that act to reaffirm distinctions and boundaries. Hence, modern globalization sustains cultural difference and encourages divergence of interpretation of the modernist conceptual apparatus.

The Foguang material also gives some interesting insight into the question of secularization. It could be argued that Master Xingyun has in many respects secularized Buddhist practice by giving a more this-worldly interpretation of the dharma and by breaking down the boundaries between monastery and general society. Alternatively, these same conceptual and institutional moves could be read as expedient means for the sacralization of mundane spheres. The important point is that any attempt to employ the sacred/secular distinction in a dualistic fashion proves unsatisfactory. The sacred and the secular are polar opposites on a continuum of mutual interpenetration, one gradually transforming into the other. The same relational logic that holds true for the pair tradition/modernity adheres for this dyad as well.

On the spatial plane, globality and locality similarly exist only through one another. Foguangshan represents an instance of the globalization of a local version of Buddhism's universalistic message. This very observation indicates the limitations of using the local/global vocabulary. As a group sharing important similarities with all Buddhists, especially other Chinese Buddhists, can Foguangshan be said ever to have been representative of local tradition? Does the term "local" designate the level of village, region, or nation? Conversely, what does it mean to say that Foguangshan has become global in scale? Geographically, it has spread considerably. Ethnically, its diffusion has remained fairly circumscribed. Such ambiguities in the syntax of locality and globality have become accentuated in a postmodern world in which regional, national, and other forms of imagined communities are finding their geographic anchors increasingly giving way. The language of homeland for a particular people is becoming more and more hazy as migration and international commerce have spawned multiple ties and allegiances. Martin Heidegger has observed: "Homelessness is coming to be the destiny of the world" ([1947] 1977, 219). As one who long ago voluntarily "left home" (*chujia*), Master Xingyun has employed his status of professional wanderer to show that this destiny is by no means lamentable, for, in the Buddhist view, it holds vital, positive import for spiritual cultivation.

My choice of Foguangshan as a case study allows this book to make a contribution as much to Asian studies as to globalization theory. Research into contemporary Chinese religions had until recently seemed irrelevant, if not futile, to many, given the requiems sung on its behalf by Chinese intellectuals and political elites and by such Western scholars as Holmes Welch and Arthur Wright.[2] Only over the past few years have books and dissertations on the current status of Daoism, Buddhism, Confucianism, Christianity, Islam, and a variety of folk traditions enjoyed something of a revival. In the case of Buddhism, Jiang Canteng has been a leader in researching the tradition's resurgence in Taiwan, although all his work is in Chinese (see, e.g., Jiang 1989, 1996, 1997, 2001a, 2001b). English-language studies include Charles Jones's *Buddhism in Taiwan* (1999), Don Pittman's *Toward a Modern Chinese Buddhism* (2001), and a flurry of dissertations.[3]

The material of this book differs from what has been furnished by Jiang, Jones, Pittman, and others in that it focuses more on the interaction of Buddhist and modernist discourses. My goal has been not so much to lay out Foguangshan's organizational structure, or to describe Foguang thought as it has been developed by Master Xingyun, as to show how these two converge with certain dominant institutional and intellectual trends impinging on contemporary Chinese life as it is evolving in Taiwan and the Chinese diaspora. As I have worked toward that objective, I have also uncovered certain aspects of Chinese Buddhist practice that have shaped the tradition's worldview, not only in modern times, but through the centuries yet have garnered insufficient attention from the academic community. My discussions of *jieyuan* in chapter 2 and "monastic filial piety" in chapter 8, for instance, are relevant to a much longer historical scope than just the modern context. By revealing the complex interrelation of continuity and innovation, I hope to give an indication of what it might be like to look at the world through the eyes of a Foguang Buddhist. To the extent that I have succeeded, I believe that this book will be of service to anyone with an interest in Buddhism or Chinese society.

1 A Mountain Monastery in an Urban Society

FOGUANG HEADQUARTERS

When in 1967 Master Xingyun first viewed what was to become Foguangshan (lit., "Buddha's Light Mountain"), the area was covered by impenetrable stands of bamboo and thick jumbles of vines and underbrush. The journey from Kaohsiung along small country lanes and narrow dirt tracks had taken several hours. The lay devotees who accompanied the master were not at all impressed by the site, even refusing to leave their small van to explore the area. Master Xingyun, however, saw great potential in the dense tangle and soon announced that he had found a new campus for his Buddhist college. Today, only a few pockets of bamboo remain, the rest having been replaced over the years by a succession of ever larger and more ornate buildings, gateways, and pavilions. What had once been bucolic lanes winding through a few isolated rice paddies have evolved into crowded thoroughfares; from atop Foguangshan one can even see a newly constructed major expressway jutting across the flat plain.

ENTRY SECTION

For the steady stream of motorists journeying between Kaohsiung and Pingdong Cities, Foguangshan's most prominent structure is the eight-story-tall statue of Amitabha Buddha (Amituo Fo, the Buddha of Light who presides over the Western Pure Land of Bliss). The golden image gazes down on the plain, with both palms facing outward at waist level, the fingers of the right hand turned up to the sky, and those of the left pointing down to the earth, thereby making the mudra of light and wisdom. Although Amitabha usually stands with his back to the rest of Foguangshan, there are reports that, on several occasions, especially during land and sea dharma functions, he has twisted his torso to glance over the monastery itself.

Just below Amitabha, the seven halls of the Longevity Funerary Complex are set into the steep slope in such a fashion as to mimic the architectural design of a pagoda. The complex's lowest level includes Completion Hall (Yuanman Ting) and Lotus Hall (Hualian Dian), where, under the guidance of clerics, bereaved recite sutras to transfer merit to the recently deceased. Next-door is Foguangshan's medical clinic, including its fleet of vans that daily journey through southern Taiwan's mountainous region to dispense care to the poor and housebound. The second level includes a temporary memorial hall for Ven. Xinping, Foguangshan's second abbot, who died in 1995. His remains will eventually be removed to Transmission Hall, the columbarium specifically for high-ranking Foguang venerables that is soon to be constructed atop the mountain. Also on the second level are four hospice accommodations (each with a bedroom, bathroom, and funerary parlor), where Foguang clerics and benefactors may pass their final hours surrounded by constant chanting and prayers. The entire third level has been set aside as a memorial hall for Chen Cheng, vice president of the Republic of China in the 1940s and 1950s and the father of Chen Lü'an, also a prominent player in Taiwan politics. The fourth and fifth floors of the complex remain vacant, although they will eventually house memorial halls for other prominent devotees. Filling the top two stories of the "pagoda" is the Hall of Rebirth (Wangsheng Tang), another location for funerals. Services are conducted here every morning and afternoon on behalf of those whose remains have found their final resting place on Foguangshan. An image of the Reclining Buddha dominates the temple. Behind this statue and along the walls of the upper story are tablets for those deceased whose descendants for one reason or another cannot keep the tablet at home or wish to have a second tablet placed in this auspicious location under the care of monastics. To either side of the shrine are three doors that open to narrow hallways, each of which is lined with storage spaces for cinerary urns, fifty thousand in all, including two thousand that have been donated to the Kaohsiung government to be used for indigent citizens of the county.

All seven levels of buildings are surrounded by row on row of individual stupas that contain urns within which are the ashes of deceased devotees. Along the uppermost row are slightly more ornate stupas, reserved for those who during their life had accumulated an especially large amount of merit. Here are the remains, for instance, of the master's mother, Liliu Yuying.[1] Next to the stupa for Liliu Yuying is that for Sun Muzhang, who arranged for the release of Master Xingyun and three hundred other monks from jail after they had been detained for a month in 1949 by the Nationalist government as suspected Communist spies.[2]

To the left of Longevity Funerary Complex is Kshitigarbha Hall (Dizang Dian). All day long, the deep, resonant ringing of the large bell that hangs just outside this shrine reverberates around the mountain. With each strike of the bell, the vow is made to ease the sufferings of those currently incarcerated in hell. Kshitigarbha Hall looks down over the main driveway to the mountain. A high wall running the length of the avenue blocks from view a cluster of typically drab Taiwan housing, in the midst of which is the very ornate Kunlun Hall, a Daoist temple that serves for many in the surrounding community as a kind of declaration of independence from their wealthy Buddhist neighbor. Just behind Kunlun

Hall are the dilapidated remains of a small amusement park, the failed venture of a local businessman who had hoped to capitalize on the constant stream of tourists to Foguangshan. These two structures, the thriving Daoist temple and the abandoned recreation area, poignantly signify the fragile, uneasy relation between one of Taiwan's largest Buddhist pilgrimage sites and its immediate neighbors, all of whom recognize the monastery's importance for the vicinity's economy, but many of whom still regard the clerics as intruders.

Only under special circumstances are people permitted to drive into the compound. Usually, visitors must park at the base and walk up. Maitreya (Mile Fo) looks down beatifically over the front security gate from atop a twenty-foot-high pedestal. It is fitting that this rotund, jovial bodhisattva of prosperity and hope welcomes visitors to Foguangshan, for this is an order that rejoices in wealth and plenty. Originally, the patined reclining image was at ground level. The story is that, when the statue was first brought to the mountain, the plan had been to locate it opposite Great Heroes Hall (Daxiong Baodian), the main shrine situated near the mountain's summit. On arriving at the entryway, however, Maitreya refused to move farther and could not be budged from his place, even by cranes. The general understanding is that he preferred to be in closer proximity to everyday people so as to more effectively beckon them to visit the monastery.[3] He did allow himself to be moved in 1997, apparently knowing that the intent was merely to raise him onto a perch from which he could, henceforth, gaze serenely down on those entering the temple grounds.

Visitors soon pass through the monastery's front gate. Straight ahead is Bodhisattva Way, which cuts straight up to the mountain's top, where the most important religious structures and administrative offices are located, including Great Heroes Hall, the meditation hall, the recitation hall, and all monastic lodgings. The road trailing off to the left first passes the Visitors Welcoming Office (Xunshan Zhike). All guests must register here on entering the monastery. Just across the street from this office is the Guanyin Release Pond, filled with carp and turtles. In the middle of this man-made pond is a small island on which Guanyin in her white robe stands astride a dragon. She faces Nonduality Gate (Bu'er Men). In years past, most visitors to the mountain strolled under this large archway, then through a shaded courtyard surrounded by statues of the 108 arhats *(luohan)*, finally mounting a broad staircase to Pilgrim's Lodge (Chaoshan Huiguan). This changed in 1997 when the monastery was closed to all tourists. On 16 May of that year, Master Xingyun presided over a solemn ceremony in which the large doors of Nonduality Gate were shut and bolted closed. Since then, groups have been allowed to visit only by special application or to participate in the weekend cultivation retreats (*jiari xiudao hui*). Nonduality Gate itself remains shut. Placed on the staircase before it are a large statue of Shakyamuni Buddha (Shijiamouni Fo) as well as flowers spelling out the year's motto: "Freedom and Wholeness" *(Yuanman Zizai)* in 1998.

On either side of Nonduality Gate are the entrance and the exit of Pure Land Cave (Jingtu Tongku), a Buddhist equivalent of the Disneyland ride "It's a Small, Small World." (In fact, Master Xingyun was inspired to have this constructed after viewing the Disneyland attraction in 1976.) This sprawling horseshoe-shaped "cave" provides a kitschy introduction to the beauties and wonders of Sukhavati (Jile Jingtu), Amitabha Buddha's Western Pure Land. Two large intimidating door gods stand guard at the entrance. Within, there are images of buddhas, bodhisattvas, and arhats, a description of the nine grades of people reborn in the Pure Land, moving figures that play instruments or dance, and a "lotus pond" where one walks on lotus petals to a small wishing pond. Just before exiting, one may turn a large wheel on which is inscribed: "The brilliance of the Buddha daily increases; the wheel of the dharma is forever turned" *(Fo ri zeng hui, falun chang zhuan)*. The Pure Land Cave is one of the few facilities on Foguangshan that over the years has required an admissions fee, indicating that, despite its religious theme, it is regarded more as a recreational attraction than as a place of spiritual cultivation. Since the closing of the mountain, it has essentially remained unused.

A more important recreational facility for the resident monastic community is the Water Drop Teahouse (Dishui Fang), located on the far side of the Guanyin Release Pond. This teahouse opened six months after the cloistering of the mountain and has become quite popular as one of the few places where clerics can gather to chat informally. With the 16 May 1997 ceremony, not only were tourists no longer welcome on the mountain, but Foguang venerables were also instructed to stay within the temple compound as much as possible. Furthermore, around the same time as Water Drop Teahouse opened, the monastery instituted the rule that all monks and nuns were to take their main meals in the central refectory, where eating is to be regarded as a form of meditation and silence is, therefore, strictly enforced. With all the smaller, less formal dining halls closed down, the teahouse became an important place for socializing.

SOCIAL-SERVICE SECTION

The front gate, Longevity Funerary Complex, Visitors Welcoming Office, Pure Land Cave, and Water Drop Teahouse constitute the entry area, or threshold, of the monastery. Everything uphill of Nonduality Gate is part of the mountain's religious section. Beyond Water Drop Teahouse is the monastery's social-service section. This section has a relatively secular tone in the sense that Buddhist teachings and practices are not directly promoted, serving instead as an underlying foundation for educational and charitable enterprises.[4]

The largest of the social-service institutions on Foguangshan's premises is Universal Gate High School (Pumen Zhongxue), which enrolls some sixteen hundred teenagers in its junior and senior high schools and tourism department. Most of the students live in the pair of dormitories located on either side of the activity center and track, going home only two weekends per month. Buddhist influence is decidedly muted at the school. Only the headmaster, Ven. Yiquan, is a monastic. All the teachers are members of lay society and are not even necessarily Buddhists. The students too need not follow the Buddhist faith. The school's objective is to provide a well-rounded education to develop moral, capable citizens. Some Buddhist teachings are present: sayings by Master Xingyun can be found posted around the campus, and, during the daily evening assembly, Ven. Yiquan often mentions Buddhist masters and beliefs. Such references, however, are provided chiefly with the view of instilling ethical values. Students are also exposed to meditation: between each class there is a five-minute session of quiet, and there is a Chan hall in the school's class building. The degree to which students actually engage in meditation is difficult to determine. The between-class sessions seem mainly to be viewed as an opportunity for a quick nap. Similarly, the hall remains largely unused.

The Universal Gate school system also includes a preschool, in which local children attend classes Monday through Friday and two Saturday mornings per month. Buddhist themes are more evident here (and in Foguangshan's three other kindergartens, located in Kaohsiung, Yilan, and Tainan) than in the high school. The fifty or so children say brief prayers before lunch and the twice-daily snacks. After lunch, they walk in two large circles for fifteen minutes while chanting "Reverence to Guanyin Bodhisattva" (*Namo Guanshiyin Pusa*) in accompaniment to a cassette tape. On the first and fifteenth days of the lunar calendar, the children also intone a longer prayer while Lin Meiyue, the lay monastic in charge of the school, makes an offering before the Guanyin statue that stands just uphill from the small campus.[5] Vegetarian fare is provided for lunch on those days. Students are also requested to participate in the processions for large dharma functions, for example, strewing flowers before the small images of the Buddha on his birthday or donning costumes as Buddhist attendants to march in the Chinese New Year parade held annually on the mountain. The school curriculum itself, however, includes no Buddhist stories and utilizes standard textbooks and lesson plans.

Next to Universal Gate Preschool stands the five-story Great Mercy Children's Home (Daci Yuyouyuan). Typically, sixty to seventy children, aged five to eighteen, live here. Some are orphaned or abandoned, but most come from broken homes. These latter spend important holidays and summer vacations with their parents or grandparents and return to them permanently once the family situation has stabilized. The majority of Great Mercy's wards are from around the island of Taiwan, although, since its founding in 1970, children have also come from Hong Kong, Indonesia, India, Malaysia, Singapore, and Thailand. The facilities are wonderful, and the staff, headed by several lay monastics, enthusiastically carries out its work. Buddhism is more present in the lives of the children who reside at Great Mercy Children's Home than it is in those of their neighbors in the Universal Gate school system. Just inside the building's main entrance is a large statue of Guanyin. Each day begins and ends with chanting in the recitation hall on the second floor, and every meal is preceded by prayer. Unlike the orphanages found in mainland China at the beginning of the twentieth century, however, Great Mercy holds no expectation that its wards will join the Buddhist order.[6] In fact, over the institution's three-decade history, only 7 of the 483 children who have found shelter there have taken monastic vows. The goal is simply to provide a nurturing environment to help children from troubled backgrounds develop into upstanding members of society.

Across the street and uphill from Great Mercy Children's Home are four large dormitories. The first of these, Miaohui Hall, houses laywomen who are working long-term on Foguangshan. The other three are jointly referred to as the Hermitage (Jingshe). They constitute Foguangshan's senior citizen home for retired lay devotees and those monastics who renounced very late in life. Also residing here are two dozen or so lay monastics. By continuing farther up this slope, one soon passes a vegetable garden and then arrives at Samantabhadra Hall (Puxian Dian). This marks the edge of Foguangshan's property. Beyond, groves of litchi trees cover the surrounding hills. Samantabhadra Hall affords a beautiful view across to Foguangshan's main ridge. Dominating the view is the towering statue of Amitabha, although farther up along the crest one can also catch glimpses through the foliage of Great Heroes Hall and Tathagata Hall (Rulai Dian).

Religious Section

Even before Foguangshan was sealed off to outsiders, few tourists or devotees visited the social-service section of the mountain. After strolling through the Pure Land Cave at Nonduality Gate, either they would follow a small walkway leading to the Museum of Buddhism and then continue to climb the path to the Welcoming Buddha (as the eight-story Amitabha statue is also called), or they would ascend the broad staircase through Luohan Park up to Pilgrim's Lodge. The exterior of the

Museum of Buddhism replicates Indian Buddhist architecture. Within are moldering displays of Buddhist art from around the world, including paintings, *thangkas* (meditative wall hangings), and a room of *sariras* (relics).

Until the closing of the mountain, Pilgrim's Lodge served vegetarian meals to the general public and, for those staying overnight, could house (in dormitory and private rooms) up to 330 people. The bedrooms continue to be filled during the weekend cultivation retreats, but the dining facilities, no longer necessary after the opening of an even larger refectory in Cloud Residing Hall, have been gutted so that the stairway from Nonduality Gate can now pass under a great arch through the lodge and continue up to Great Heroes Hall. To the right of Pilgrim's Lodge is Bamboo Thicket Garden (Mazhu Yuan), which offers dining space and rooms for another 880 people as well as conference rooms. Just to the left of Pilgrim's Lodge is Devotees' Hall (Tanxin Lou), with its several conference rooms, two small meditation chambers, dining room, and 1,080-seat auditorium. Behind Devotees' Hall, a steep gully filled by a small pond acts as a natural barrier preventing visitors from intruding on the women's college, Great Compassion Hall (Dabei Dian), and the four dormitories of the nunnery. The women's campus of the Foguangshan Monastic Academy and Great Compassion Hall are the oldest buildings on the mountain. Within this compound, two hundred lay and monastic students spend two to four years receiving a free education in Buddhist doctrine and practice. Absolutely no visitors are allowed to enter this part of the mountain. At night, a pack of dogs roams the campus, trained to attack any stranger, especially males or anyone not wearing arhat slippers.

Great Compassion Hall shelters a tall, slender, plain white image of Guanyin. Lining the walls are more than six thousand niches, each with its own image of the bodhisattva. The shrine's overall atmosphere is of peace and tranquillity. Just up the hill, Great Heroes Hall has a much different feel. Here, Amitabha, Shakyamuni, and Bhaisajya-guru (Yaoshi Fo) also stare down serenely in meditative trance, but the massiveness of their gilded forms and the ornate woodwork of the ten thousand smaller Buddha images that fill the surrounding walls of the hall project an almost overpowering sense of grandeur. Before the three main statues are long marble altars, on each of which sit two huge candles and an incense urn. To avoid being swamped with offerings, some of which may not be appropriate (i.e., may include meat or tracts with teachings contrary to those of Foguangshan), the monastery does not allow people to bring offerings to this or any other of its shrines. In the back corners of the hall sit a gigantic bell and drum. It is in this hall and on the wide courtyard leading up to it that Foguangshan holds its large-scale dharma functions, such as birthday celebrations for buddhas, land and sea dharma functions, and triple altar ordinations.

Behind Great Heroes Hall are the Exhibition Hall (Zhanlan Guan), Jade Buddha Hall (Yu Fo Lou), Gold Buddha Hall (Jin Fo Lou), and Tathagata Hall. The Chinese Buddhist calligraphy, painting, and sculpture displayed in the Exhibition Hall constitute only a small percentage of Foguangshan's permanent art holdings. The entire collection is spread out among a total of nine galleries and includes works by such famous artists as Zhang Daqian, Li Zijian, and Shi Guoliang (now known by his dharma name, Ven. Huichan).[7]

Gold Buddha Hall and Jade Buddha Hall house the bhikshuni and bhikshu meditation facilities for the Foguangshan Meditation College. Tathagata Hall is the administrative nerve center for Foguangshan. Located within are the abbot's chamber, information center, computer center, and a variety of departmental offices. On the building's second floor may be found a small exhibition hall showing Foguangshan's history. Among the displays on view are a variety of articles that have been used by Master Xingyun—a robe, a walking stick, a traveling bag, socks, arhat slippers, a slide projector, and a sewing machine (which he jerry-rigged as a desk). There are also a host of photographs of the master with such world leaders as the dalai lama, the pope, and U.S. vice president Al Gore. The museum further provides biographical sketches of Master Xingyun's most important disciples, displays of Foguang literature, charts tracking the order's charitable activities over the years, and maps of its worldwide network of temples and BLIA (Buddha's Light International Association) chapters.

One floor above the exhibition hall is Foguangshan's meditation facility for lay devotees and large-scale retreats. As one visiting monk quipped, this is truly a "five-star meditation hall." Along the four outer walls are the office space for the meditation center staff, dormitories for men and women, and laundry and shower rooms. The meditation chamber itself is quite open and spacious, with very little in the way of furnishings. In the middle is a small kiosk in which an image of Shakyamuni sitting in a meditative pose gazes out toward the front door. On either side of the Buddha are full sets of Foguangshan's edition of the Chan canon. Behind Buddha, a picture of Linji, the founding teacher of the Linji Chan school, faces the back doors. Surrounding the booth is a large open area for walking meditation (*paoxiang*). Benches furnishing space for eighty-four people to engage in sitting meditation run along the north, west, and south walls. By placing an extra row of benches just in front of these, and by setting cushions on the floor, the facility can accommodate as many as three hundred people at a time. Along the east wall are the main entrance and two small booths used by the abbot and the Chan masters when they give guidance *(kaishi)*.

Foguangshan is justifiably proud of its meditation hall. The air-conditioning, washing area, and lighting all make for a comfortable, pleasing setting so that those who come for retreats can concentrate on their practice. Some, however, have found it all too modern, preferring the simpler furnishings of more traditional temples, such as Zhongtaishan (a large monastery in northern Taiwan known for its Chan instruction). As one informant explained, although air-conditioning makes for comfort, this may not be desirable; for one's *qi* (vital energy) to be harmonized it must be attuned, not only within, but also with the surrounding environment, especially the seasonal climate. By creating a hermetic setting, concluded this individual, Foguangshan has inadvertently adversely affected the very process that it is trying to nurture. Foguang monastics disagree with such an argument, countering that most retreat participants are only beginners at meditation and, as such, require optimum conditions so that they can focus purely on the workings of the mind. The two halls used by the Foguangshan Meditation College do not have air-conditioning.

The Venerable Huiri, the monk in charge of the Foguangshan Meditation College, observes that the location of the meditation hall concretely represents Foguangshan's attitude toward Chan. Rather than being placed in a tranquil setting apart from the headquarters' other facilities, the hall is located on the middle floor of the central administrative building. Meditation is not a passive enterprise separate from daily life, he asserts; to be truly effective it must be an integral part of everyday activity.

The two stories above the meditation chamber are occupied by the main floor and balcony of Foguangshan's largest auditorium, which has a capacity of 1,809 people. It is here that Master Xingyun holds meetings with the full mountain community. These sessions are, for many clerics, among the few opportunities to interact with the master directly. The organization has simply become too big and spread out for Master Xingyun to even know the names of all his disciples, much less give them one-on-one guidance.

Foguangshan's latest and largest structure is Cloud Residing Hall (Yunju Lou), a somewhat ponderous six-story high-rise completed in the spring of 1998. The four upper floors provide lodging for two thousand devotees. Most rooms are simple, but on the sixth story is a very spacious presidential suite. The ground floor is Foguangshan's refectory. Master Xingyun proudly observes that, at 6,312 square feet, this is the world's largest room with no pillars to support its vast ceiling. Forty-two hundred people can eat here at a time. On the second floor is an equally large chamber, also without supporting pillars. This serves as the recitation hall for weekend cultivation retreats and is the inner altar *(neitan)* for land and sea dharma functions.

Most visitors fail to notice the small walled-in compound next to Cloud Residing Hall. It may be argued, however, that this is the most important corner of the mountain, for it is Master Xingyun's office and residence. Very few have the opportunity to meet privately with the master in his office, and even fewer are granted the privilege of viewing the inner residential area. The master's house was built for him by Ven. Xinping, who took over as abbot of Foguangshan in 1986. On the first floor is a simply but elegantly furnished living room. The master's living quarters take up the second floor. The dwelling is surrounded by a beautiful yard with several fountains and gardens. In the back is a small basketball court. The Venerable Xinping had this installed so that the master could practice his favorite sport whenever he desired. Since breaking his leg in 1991 and having had heart bypass surgery in 1995, the master has had to give up this pastime. Just beyond the basketball court, a squirrel lives in a large cage. The cage has housed a number of injured small animals that Master Xingyun has rescued, nursed back to health, and then set free, but the current resident apparently refuses to leave the compound.

The back gate of Master Xingyun's residential area leads to Lamp Transmission Hall (Chuandeng Lou), home to Foguangshan's small contingent of bhikshus, including Ven. Xinding, the monastery's current abbot. This abuts the men's campus of the Foguangshan Monastic Academy. Approximately one hundred students study here. Within the campus is Manjushri Hall (Wenshu Dian), within which is a relatively small image of the bodhisattva Manjushri. Towering above the classrooms is the Welcoming Buddha, although he faces in the opposite direction.

Cloud Residing Hall, Master Xingyun's residence, Lamp Transmission Hall, the men's college, and the Welcoming Buddha run along the edge of the escarpment just above Longevity Funerary Complex and overlooking Dashu County. On the occasional clear day, Taiwan's central mountain range is visible to the west. More typically, haze and smog completely obliterate the peaks from view. Below the escarpment can be seen the many restaurants and gift shops opened by local entrepreneurs to cater to the tourists and devotees of Foguangshan. Since the closing of the mountain, such shops have lost nearly all their business.

THE CLOISTERING OF FOGUANGSHAN

For the first thirty years of its existence, especially after the completion of the Welcoming Buddha statue in 1975, Foguangshan was regarded as one of the premier recreational sites of southern Taiwan. Several thousand tourists would come each weekend to stroll around the mountain, enjoy the view from the base of the Welcoming Buddha, visit the Pure Land Cave and Museum of Buddhism, offer incense at Great Heroes Hall, and have a vegetarian lunch at Pilgrim's Lodge. During the month following Chinese New Year, as many as one million visitors would make the pilgrimage to view the lamps festooned around the mountain. The constant stream of tourists was a significant source of revenue for both the mountain and the local community.

All this changed in 1997. On 16 May, the first day of Foguangshan's thirty-first year, the gates to the mountain were bolted closed. Uninvited visitors were no longer welcome. For six months, even Foguang lay devotees were barred from coming to the monastery. Thereafter, they and other Buddhists could come only after registering at a branch temple to join a group pilgrimage to the headquarters. By February 1998, these organized trips had evolved into a weekly opportunity to select one of ten "weekend cultivation activities": meditation; chanting; repentance; scripture copying; walking meditation; pilgrimage (one prostration for every three steps up the mountain); dharma talks; youth camp; parent-and-child camp; and volunteer work. The mountain was, therefore, still open to Buddhist devotees for organized religious functions, especially on weekends, but it was now closed to those simply wanting to come for recreation. The general population was permitted to wander about the mountain on only three occasions: the two weeks of the Chinese New Year; Buddha's Birthday (the eighth day of the fourth lunar month); and Sangha Offering Merit Day (the twenty-second day of the seventh lunar month).

The ceremony marking the mountain's shift in policy was very solemn. A procession of nearly one thousand clerics coursed their way slowly from the high school to the wide staircase leading up to Nonduality Gate. Master Xingyun, shielded from the bright sun under a large parasol, mounted the top step, then sat before a large image of Shakyamuni Buddha that had been placed just the other side of the gate. The monastics recited from a sutra, then assumed the lotus position on meditation pads as the approximately ten thousand people in attendance were seated. Ten lay members gave speeches about the significance and wisdom of the mountain's closing. About halfway though these presentations, two government helicopters swooped just overhead, landing on the parade ground in front of the high school's activity center. Sung Chuyou, governor of the province of Taiwan, was guided to the podium by his team of bodyguards. He gave a brief speech thanking Master Xingyun and Foguangshan for their great contributions to the island, then immediately returned to his helicopter to fly to another engagement. After Master Xingyun and Ven. Xinding made speeches, the clerics stood to recite a sutra before slowly filing past the master and through Nonduality Gate. Last of all to pass beyond the gate was the master himself, who stood immediately before the image of Shakyamuni and continued to look out over the assembled crowd as the newly constructed doors slowly shut. Many of the lay devotees rushed forward in a symbolic last-ditch effort to keep the doors open.

The closing of the mountain altered Foguangshan's relationship with the local populace, the general public of Taiwan, even its own lay devotees. Ever since the monastery had developed into an important recreational site, tourism had become an integral part of the local economy. Restaurants, gift shops, and inns sprouted up around the mountain's entrance, many incorporating "Foguang" as part of their names even though most had no formal connection with the organization. On the weekends, and during the month following Chinese New Year, local farmers opened stalls vending vegetables or snacks.

The relationship between Foguangshan and its neighbors, however, has not always been harmonious. Locals have regarded the monk with an unusual accent and his contingent of monastics as outsiders. A variety of disagreements have heightened the tension. For example, on several of the occasions when Foguangshan has attempted to purchase surrounding land, the monastery and its neighbors were unable to agree on a price. In the 1980s, an argument arose over whose responsibility it was to maintain a small road skirting the temple and the degree to which locals could have access to that road. In the spring of 1996, an even greater controversy erupted when it became known that Foguangshan's garbage was being dumped right next to the Gaoping River, which flows not far from the mountain. Master Xingyun explained that the monastery had contracted out the work of garbage collection and had had no idea where the company carting off the refuse had dumped it, but residents complained that this was just one more instance of the monastery's lack of concern for others in the area.

Foguangshan has had its grievances too. The clerics have felt that the local people have not appreciated all that the monastery has contributed to improving their lives. Foguangshan played a key role in upgrading electrical and water service in the region. The mountain had also opened a post office, a preschool for local children, and a public library. Every Chinese New Year, the monastery would hold a party and raffle for its neighbors, giving away thousands of New Taiwan dollars worth of goods. The boost to the local economy from the steady stream of tourists could not be denied. Instead of being grateful, grumbled the Foguang venerables, the residents simply became greedy, trying to get as much from the mountain as possible without appreciating its positive role in their community. Certain town and county politicians antagonistic to the monastery had employed a variety of tactics to obstruct Foguangshan's ability to receive necessary permits for its building projects. A few locals had apparently even gone so far as to sneak onto the temple grounds at night to steal fish from the Guanyin Release Pond.

When Master Xingyun closed Foguangshan's gates to outsiders, many locals believed that he did so to force Dashu County to back down from its attempt to redefine portions of the mountain as a tourist rather than a religious site and, thereby, collect property taxes. The Foguang leadership denies this, saying that the monastery's for-profit enterprises already paid taxes and that such a change would have had no significant effect. The Venerable Xinding nonetheless admits that poor relations with the local community may have played a role in the decision to curtail the tourist business. Since residents found that the added crowds and traffic caused problems, he told Jody Duffy of Prime Television, the monastery felt that it had the responsibility to help alleviate such inconveniences (see Duffy 1997). The best way to do so, of course, was no longer to allow tourists to visit the monastery grounds. He insisted, however, that this issue played only a very minor role in the change in policy.

The closing of Foguangshan had ramifications beyond the local community. As 1997 drew to an end, several of Taiwan's television stations included this event as one of the island's top ten news items for the year. According to Jiang Canteng, a specialist in Buddhism in Taiwan, Master Xingyun shut the monastery's doors in order concretely to symbolize his retreat from worldly concerns (Jiang 1997, 12–16). In the years leading up to the mountain's closure, states Jiang, the master had experienced several embarrassing political setbacks, and his organization had probably declined in financial power as well.

As far as Master Xingyun's involvement in politics is concerned, many felt that he had entered too deeply into the electoral process when, in 1996, he publicly endorsed his devotee Chen Lü'an, who was running for the presidency. This adversely affected the master's standing in four ways. First, a variety of Buddhist practitioners and political analysts considered it inappropriate for a religious leader to participate in campaign politics so directly. Second, the news media reported that, during the elections, Master Xingyun had put Chen in contact with the powerful underground figure Chen Yonghe (no relation) so that the latter could act as a mediator between Chen Lü'an and President Li Denghui. Such a disclosure led critics to wonder why the master would associate with such a well-known mobster and engage in political maneuverings with him (Hu Zengfeng 1996).[8] Third, the master's public support for Chen Lü'an certainly must have upset the Kuomintang, perhaps causing some difficulties in the short term in gaining necessary permits etc. Finally, the poor showing of Chen in the election (he garnered only 8 percent of the vote) led many to conclude that the master had little leverage over his followers or society in general.

The spate of criticisms that Master Xingyun was too much a "political monk" (*zhengzhi heshang*) came at a time when Foguangshan may very well have been experiencing a downturn in its finances. In the 1970s and 1980s, the expanding economy and growing interest in Buddhism resulted in a flood of donations for Foguangshan's many large-scale projects. The number of prominent Buddhist organizations multiplied through the 1990s, however, while the economy stagnated, resulting in greater competition for resources. Since donors tend to be attracted to what they view as the most cutting-edge projects, Master Xingyun continually initiated ever more ambitious undertakings, most notably a satellite television station and a tuition-free liberal arts university. Foguangshan therefore needed, not just to maintain its donor base, but to increase it, an even more difficult task to accomplish as editorials and commentaries led many to consider the master and his organization as too secular, political, and commercial.

If Foguangshan was already feeling financial strain, it may seem strange that the master would close the headquarters to tourists, thereby cutting off an important source of revenue. In fact, tourist dollars may not have accounted for much income. Non-Buddhist visitors to the monastery tended merely to saunter about without making any donations or buying any souvenirs or lunch. Furthermore, in recent years, other monasteries have constructed similar ornate structures, and the number of recreational sites on the island has increased considerably. The flow of tourist dollars into Foguangshan had, therefore, most likely leveled out or even fallen off over time. Certainly, the month-long Chinese New Year activities no longer drew the crowds they once did. On the other hand, the perception of Foguangshan as a tourist site exacerbated criticisms that the mountain was too secular and commercial, thereby threatening its much more important root of support: Buddhist donors.

Cloistering the monastery so that only devotees could visit, and even they under close supervision, served to reassert the mountain as a sacred place. According to Jiang Canteng, with the clarification of membership through the formation of the BLIA, the distinction between member and nonmember has become much clearer than it had been formerly. Because of this, along with Foguangshan's internationalization, "the pressure to sacralize [*shenghua*] Foguangshan, making it into a sacred place, has steadily increased with time." Jiang emphasizes the economics underlying this trend: "It has been necessary to raise the level of faith by sacralizing the mountain; otherwise, the feeling of dissatisfaction would deepen among devotees, thereby increasing the attrition rate" (Jiang 1997, 15, 16).

Master Xingyun would agree with Jiang's assertion that resacralization is the reason for closing the mountain, but he would discount political or financial factors as the underlying motivation. From the fifth BLIA World Conference (held in Paris in August 1996), when the cloistering of Foguangshan was first announced, the master steadfastly asserted that the shift in policy was being made for purely religious reasons, that is, so that the mountain could regain a solemn and tranquil atmosphere, thereby providing Foguang clerics and lay devotees with the most suitable environment for spiritual cultivation. In the past, according to the master, Foguang headquarters was the principal place where venerables would meet with devotees and others to promote Humanistic Buddhism.[9] Once the organization had successfully established branch temples worldwide as well as a satellite television station and a website, these could assume responsibility as contact points with the general public. The headquarters itself could, therefore, return to its original focus, namely, the cultivation of Buddhist leadership, both monastic and lay.

Regardless of the degree to which financial and political factors may have entered into the decision to close the mountain, religious considerations do seem to have played an important role. "Humanistic Buddhism" serves as the Foguang rallying cry to make Buddhist teachings relevant for modern-day problems and to bring Buddhist values into everyday life. Such a program accentuates a challenge felt by all religious groups: how to reinterpret one's inherited teachings and values so as to make them pertinent without diluting their content. For its first thirty years, Foguangshan offered its openness to all as a symbol of the accessibility of the dharma. The underlying theory was that many of those who initially came for entertainment would leave with a greater understanding of and interest in Buddhism. Recreation, in other words, was considered a legitimate expedient means (*fangbian; upaya*) to attract people to the dharma. In more recent years, Master Xingyun has determined that this particular expedient means is no longer efficacious, that, in fact, its disruptive effects on monastic life overshadow whatever usefulness it might have had.

The shift in policy can also be traced to Foguangshan's greater accessibility. Twenty years ago, when Taiwan's public transportation system was not well developed and few people owned cars, the journey to Foguangshan was, while not terribly arduous, a trek nonetheless. Furthermore, the mountain looked out on woods and small farms, and a sense of separation from urban society was inherent in its location. Today, it is surrounded by highways and condominiums, and there is little, if any, sense of physical isolation. Cloistering the mountain reestablished a boundary, thereby marking it off as sacred space.

This renewed sense of separateness was emphasized by certain physical changes made to the monastery itself. A guard booth was built and a metal gate installed at the very base of the entryway, just below the statue of Maitreya. Only those with special permission may take their cars beyond this point. All others (including teachers at the high school) must park below and, after showing their identification badge, walk up the side path. Also, the jovial image of Maitreya, which for so many years had from its ground-level position seemingly beckoned all those passing by to come join in the festivities, was, as we have seen, raised atop a twenty-foot-tall pedestal. From this new position, Maitreya seems more removed, and the distance between this world and his current abode in Tushita Heaven is brought more to mind.[10] Finally, the wall along the other side of the main driveway was erected, thereby emphatically segregating the monastery from the ramshackle houses and Daoist temple just the other side.

The separation of secular and sacred also was more clearly delineated within the monastery compound. This delineation was accomplished by closing the gate on the path linking the preschool to the women's campus of the Foguangshan Monastic Academy and instituting the rule that neither high school nor monastic students could venture through it to each other's campus. In the past, some of the college students used to go sit on the swings in the preschool yard after dark, and a few used to play basketball on the outdoor courts of the activity center in the cool of evening. Even such indirect mingling with the secular world was, henceforth, to cease.[11] Master Xingyun has indicated that he hopes eventually to make this separation of Foguangshan's secular and religious endeavors even more pronounced by relocating the high school, preschool, children's home, and senior citizens' home elsewhere in Taiwan.

The closing of the mountain to the general public does not appear to have had any long-term effects. In the year following the cloistering, the local community certainly felt a financial pinch. Several restaurants closed, and others drastically cut down on staff. The monastic community also felt the loss of tourism dollars. The decision to return to a much simpler medicine meal in the evening, for instance, may have been motivated as much by financial reasons as by religious ones. The weekend cultivation retreats appear to have been instituted at least partially as a means to recoup revenue since those who participate generally give a donation of at least NT$1,000 (approximately U.S.$33). The mountain averages one thousand visitors per weekend, which translates into an annual income of NT$52 million (U.S.$1.73 million).

The master, ever the optimist, told the monastic community shortly after the mountain was cloistered that, even if the closing would mean greater financial hardship, overall it would prove a boost for self-cultivation. Monks and nuns must learn to be *zizai*, that is, easygoing regardless of circumstances; to become attached to prosperity is very dangerous. Also, he continued, the closing of Foguangshan would provide both the time and the serenity for the resident clerics to spend the greater part of their day engaged in self-cultivation. It appears that this has been the case; many monastics have taken advantage of the increased number of meditation and recitation retreats that have been organized. A larger proportion of the daily schedule also appears to be devoted to self-study. Foguangshan had long been proud of its reputation as one of Taiwan's top recreational sites. As this reputation became more of a liability than an asset, the master decided to sacrifice the benefits of such a reputation to preserve and strengthen the mountain's standing as a place of cultivation.

SECULARIZING THE SACRED, SACRALIZING THE SECULAR

Foguangshan's location is symbolic of its philosophical stance toward the relation between Buddhist cultivation and society. It is neither nestled away in remote mountains, as are many of Taiwan's temples, nor situated in the midst of a city. Rather, it is located where mountain and city meet. The area that thirty years ago was undeveloped is today filled with orchards and residential housing. The two-lane road that passes by the base of Foguangshan makes it easily accessible to such urban areas as Pingdong (thirty minutes away by car), Fengshan (forty-five minutes), and Kaohsiung (slightly over one hour). As metropolitan sprawl has reached the monastery, the monastery has retreated, closing itself off to outsiders. Yet, concurrent with its symbolic separation, the organization has also made itself more widely accessible through technology, establishing a satellite television station and launching a website.

What does the cloistering of Foguangshan teach us about the concepts of sacrality and secularity? Scholars of religion have generally employed the term "sacred" to describe those objects, times, and events that are experienced as manifesting an extraordinary, mysterious force.[12] Such "hierophanies," as Mircea Eliade (1959, 11–13) designated instantiations of sacrality, are highly paradoxical in nature: they attract yet repel, vivify yet endanger, heal yet defile, and hold a power that is somehow utterly transcendent yet radically immanent. Opposed to the sacred is the profane, all those relatively effete articles, periods, and activities of the mundane world that people experience in their daily lives. The particular contours of the existential boundaries distinguishing the sacred and the profane modes of being and the means of mediating between them constitute each culture's religious life, although, in premodern societies, none of this was thought of as specifically "religious" in content since the concept of religion as a distinct cognitive and institutional sphere had not yet evolved.

By "secular" scholars have meant those segments of modern society that are neither guided by religious beliefs nor under the control of religious institutions. The classification of the "secular" differs from that of the "profane" in that the latter is itself a religious category while the former is opposed to that entire construct. In other words, the concept "religion," which has the dyad sacred/profane as one of its most fundamental structural features, is dialectically paired with the notion of secularity. Scholars have tended to confuse the issue by using the terms "secular" and "profane" interchangeably since both designate an absence of sacrality. The two differ significantly in tone and intensity, however, for secularity implies that a much greater cognitive leap—in fact, a radical transformation in the organization of consciousness—must occur for sacrality to be experienced.[13]

The nominalization "secularization" therefore refers to the process through which activities formerly with a transcendent, sacred referent no longer have any such association. Peter Berger defines "secularization" as

> the process by which sectors of society and culture are removed from the domination of religious institutions and symbols. When we speak of society and institutions in modern Western history, of course, secularization manifests itself in the evacuation by the Christian churches of areas previously under their control or influence—as in the separation of church and state, or in the expropriation of church lands, or in the emancipation of education from ecclesiastical authority. When we speak of culture and symbols, however, we imply that secularization is more than a social-structural process. It affects the totality of cultural life and of ideation, and may be observed in the decline of religious contents in the arts, in philosophy, in literature and, most important of all, in the rise of science as an autonomous, thoroughly secular perspective on the world. Moreover, it is implied here that the process of secularization has a subjective side as well. As there is a secularization of society and culture, so is there a secularization of consciousness. Put simply, this means that the modern West has produced an increasing number of individuals who look upon the world and their own lives without the benefit of religious interpretations. (Berger 1969, 107–108)

Berger goes on to say that such secularization is not merely a Western phenomenon but may be viewed as a global trend affecting all modern societies. It is a process of social-structural, cultural, and subjective significance with repercussions for people's understandings of politics, education, entertainment, the arts, literature, philosophy, and cosmology.

As distinct boundaries of religious and secular provinces have been laid out, each has developed along particular trajectories with particular methods. The two have never been hermetically segregated, however. At times, religious and secular institutions have borrowed techniques from one another or have entered an arena generally recognized as within the other's sphere. A simultaneous secularization and sacralization takes place every time that occurs. When a secular organization appropriates language or a modus operandi identified with a religious tradition, it has secularized that vocabulary or technique while it has itself undergone a degree of sacralization. Conversely, a religious organization that appropriates a method regarded as coming from secular society has sacralized that method and secularized itself.

In Master Xingyun's view, such creative interchange between the secular and the religious worlds provides an extremely effective expedient means for bringing people to Buddhism. Once Foguangshan adopted techniques associated with the entertainment industry to become a tourist site (especially when the master borrowed from Disneyland, arguably the world's most poignant symbol of secular entertainment), the headquarters was secularized, losing some of its sacred aura. At the same time, recreation and tourism were sacralized, given potent significance as Buddhist activities. The line differentiating these from pilgrimage and worship blurred; just who was a tourist and who a pilgrim, who a spectator and who a devotee, was difficult to assess. The same can be said, mutatis mutandis, about those instances in which the master has entered the worlds of politics and liberal arts education. The sacred and the secular have become much more difficult to demarcate.

Buddhists who disagree with Master Xingyun's methods voice the fear that he and others like him who secularize their practice remain religious only in name, having taken the sacred out of religion. On the other hand, one could argue that, through resacralizing particular instances of activities within putatively secular sectors, Foguangshan acts to transform the general understanding of those entire sectors in all their instances: they are no longer apprehended as secular but rather as more or less profane. Distinctions remain, but the overall cognitive framework has shifted, transforming subtly in nature. The end of religion and the end of secularity as they have been conceptualized in modern times can occur only in tandem, a metamorphosis into postmodern versions that are, in fact, similar in structural character to the premodern distinctions between the sacred and the profane. In other words, even though the language of "religion" and "secularity" will most likely remain for the foreseeable future, the concepts to which these terms point appear already to be undergoing a reversion to the former senses of "sacrality" and "profaneness."

A perpetual attraction between the sacred and its opposite (whether that be the profane or the secular) seeks to fuse them. There also, however, invariably persists a tension between the polarities: each repels the other. As Foguangshan appropriates secular methods and enters the secular arena, it ipso facto jeopardizes its status as protector and mediator of the sacred. For this reason, as Master Xingyun and his organization have in recent years delved more deeply into secular political and educational endeavors, the need to reconsecrate the headquarters with sacrality through a symbolic withdrawal asserted itself. Given this larger picture, the decision to cloister Foguangshan makes perfect sense.

2 Master Xingyun: Foguang Patriarch

"To know Foguangshan," Master Xingyun advised me during an interview, "you must know me" (Chandler 1996b, 6). What the master meant in this blunt assessment was that Foguangshan as place and Foguangshan as institution are so closely associated with him that it is impossible to speak of either without reference to his activities, values, and ideals. The master's presence is continually felt by his disciples: his photograph invariably will be found in the main office of every Foguang temple around the world, and at the headquarters a desk is reserved for him in each department, a constant reminder that it is he who is in charge of even daily affairs. When one speaks of Foguang thought or the Foguang perspective, one is essentially describing the philosophy and views of Master Xingyun. In this chapter, I consider how this remarkable, if somewhat controversial, man has been able to garner the support of so many people, thereby allowing for the emergence of Foguangshan as one of Taiwan's most influential Buddhist organizations.

"Renjian Fojiao," the phrase translated in Foguang literature as "Humanistic Buddhism," means literally "Buddhism in the midst of people." It aptly points to one of the chief ingredients leading to Master Xingyun's success as a leader: his ability to mobilize large numbers of people and operationalize an effective organization by engendering in each individual a sense of deep respect and personal loyalty to him. In Chinese Buddhist terms, Master Xingyun is unusually adept at *guangjie shanyuan*, "broadly creating links of affinity" (*jieyuan* for short).[1] Because this particular genre of skillful means has been such a key element in the master's modus operandi, we must consider its derivation and current connotations in some detail.

CREATING LINKS OF AFFINITY (*JIEYUAN*)
The *Foguang Encyclopedia [of Buddhism] (Foguang da cidian)* states that, when the term *jieyuan* first developed in Tang dynasty China, it was used to refer to situations in which, "although cultivation in this life can in no way result in liberation, there is an initial point of contact for fruition sometime in the future" (Shi Xingyun 1988a, 5190). In other words, a particular person may have no hope for enlightenment in the present life span, but, by having the seed of the dharma planted in his or her consciousness, he or she will find enlightenment in a subsequent rebirth. Historically, *jieyuan* has been used to describe those undertakings that serve to attract new devotees to Buddhism: building a temple or pagoda; donating funds:

printing scriptures, books, or tracts. Over time, the term has come especially to characterize any activity that establishes or strengthens a personal relationship in such a way as to spread the dharma.

A very important element in forming and sustaining these nurturing conditions is the fostering of a relationship of trust and mutual admiration between the two parties. *Jieyuan* relies on and augments the spontaneous creative energy that arises through direct interaction between people. It is, one could say, a Buddhist manifestation of the Chinese proclivity to conduct affairs through personal contacts, or *guanxi* (although without any of the negative connotations that often adhere to the latter term). In explaining the concept, Master Xingyun observes: "When positive energy is applied to friendship, untold good forces are released. There is nothing in the world more beautiful than the positive energy that can be generated between people and among friends. This kind of energy is like water that can wash away bad karma. It is like an oil that smooths the progress of good karma. Positive energy among people is the single greatest force for bringing good into this world" (Shi Xingyun 1997b, 4).

Because *jieyuan* typically relies on the giving of a small gift to symbolize the creation or strengthening of the dharma relationship, it is helpful to compare it with *dana (bushi)*, the Buddhist virtue of generous giving. The *Foguang Encyclopedia* notes that the Buddha used this latter term to designate the furnishing of clothes, food, and other material necessities by lay devotees to the sangha or the poor. Ever since, it has been regarded as a key means for laity to keep in check greed and selfishness while simultaneously accumulating merit (*gongde*) for a better rebirth. By the time the Mahayana tradition was introduced into China, this virtue's scope had been expanded to encompass the less tangible gifts of preaching the dharma and instilling courage. *Dana* was included as one of the four all-embracing virtues (*si shefa*) and six paramitas (*liu boluomi*), indicating that its ultimate goal is the material, emotional, and spiritual well-being of all creatures (Shi Xingyun 1988a, 1901–1903).

Jieyuan differs from *dana* in two ways. First, particularly when employed in reference to the giving of material goods, the latter is typically considered to be a virtue of special relevance and importance to laity. Lay devotees gain merit through providing the necessary material resources to the sangha, which reciprocates by teaching the dharma. *Jieyuan*, by contrast, is much more likely to describe an act of giving by a cleric, either to a layperson or to another cleric who has not progressed as far along the path to enlightenment. When used in reference to an act of generosity by a layperson, it generally relates to the giving of material goods to children or non-Buddhists, not to monastics. The giver has traveled farther along the bodhisattva path than has the recipient. Second, *jieyuan* has a stronger relational connotation than does *dana*. One gives specifically to establish a close relationship with a person so as to benefit both the recipient and Buddhism. *Jieyuan* is, therefore, a hybrid of *dana* and *guanxi*.

As are forms of *dana*, *jieyuan* is regarded as an important means of attaining merit, and the degree of merit that accrues depends on three components: the gift; the recipient; and the giver. The most precious gift of all is the dharma itself, but, if such a gift would not yet be appreciated by the recipient, more mundane presents will serve the purpose better. The level of merit is determined not so much by the monetary value of the gift as by its appropriateness, that is, its effectiveness in attracting the recipient to Buddhism. *Jieyuan* is often accomplished by drawing people, especially children, to Buddhist practice through distributing candies, treats, or money. It is said that the Tang dynasty Pure Land master Shaokang (eighth century C.E.) first attracted followers by giving children one coin for each invocation of Amitabha Buddha. Within a month, many people had taken up the practice, so he reduced payment to one coin for every ten recitations. By year's end, all in the region were following the practice with no expectation of monetary reward (Yu 1981, 43). The Venerable Yikong, currently head of Foguangshan's Culture Council, tells how, at age four or five, she initially went to Master Xingyun's Leiyin Temple solely to enjoy the "gifts of affinity" (*jieyuanpin*) that were inevitably offered. At first she may have come for these snacks of peach-shaped longevity buns or small "Buddha hands" made of flour, but, as she participated in the various temple programs, she found herself increasingly drawn to the dharma (Fu 1995, 71).

This understanding of *jieyuan* emphasizes that, to plant the seed of the dharma effectively so that it will flourish in the future, one must first create appropriate conditions (*yuan*). The goal of creating links of affinity is to instill a positive predisposition toward Buddhism so that later, when the time is ripe, people will be that much more likely to find resonance with its teachings. Even after such resonance has occurred, one may continue to *jieyuan* with that person, the goal being ever deepening the affinity. Hence, Master Xingyun frequently engages in *jieyuan* with his disciples, giving them books, supplying them with red envelopes at Chinese New Year, and personally providing money to help those who are traveling or studying abroad.[2]

The degree of merit accrued also depends on the relative virtue of the recipient. In instances of *dana* by a lay devotee to a monastic, the latter's relatively high degree of virtue is self-evident. In the case of *jieyuan*, the recipient's virtue becomes fully manifest only subsequently. Master Xingyun and the devotees who provided Ven. Yikong with small treats gained great merit for such acts, for they created the nurturing conditions leading to her renunciation in this life. Significant merit may result even if the recipient does not become a cleric, for it also accrues to the extent that the person benefits Buddhism. This is the reasoning behind Master Xingyun's emphasis on establishing ties of affinity with the elite of society, whether in the business or the political worlds. When a leader becomes a Buddhist, especially an active Buddhist, others follow. If the act of *jieyuan* with a member of the elite does not lead to the person taking the triple refuge, it still may trigger significant merit, for the recipient is in the position to aid the tradition even as a non-Buddhist. A politician, for instance, may help pass legislation advantageous to the religion, or a wealthy person may donate considerable funds to a charity drive.

The third component determining the amount of merit gained through *jieyuan* is the motivation of the giver in providing the gift. The purity of his or her intention is of utmost importance if merit is to accrue. He or she must have no selfish aim in establishing a relationship with the recipient. Chinese Buddhists therefore distinguish *jieyuan* from *panyuan*, which generally signifies the clinging of the wayward mind to external phenomena and, as the opposite of *jieyuan*, refers specifically to providing favors or establishing ties with some ulterior motive in mind (Shi Xingyun 1988a, 6665). In the unsullied giving of *jieyuan*, whether the recipient of the gift can assist the giver in some fashion in the future is of no concern. In fact, those who practice *jieyuan* in its highest form are said to do so with no concept of giver, recipient, or gift; all are regarded as radically interrelated aspects of ever-changing reality. According to his devotees, Master Xingyun has attained this level of compassionate wisdom.[3]

Only the master himself can truly know the degree of his wisdom and the purity of his motivations. It is plain for all to see, however, that he certainly has an unusual capacity to engender in people a sense of special relationship and that he can instill this even in those who come into his immediate presence only rarely. The feeling of mutual commitment is so strong that those who do come into his presence act as conduits, each conducting the resulting interpersonal energy to others, thereby binding together an exponentially vast interpersonal network in what is felt to be one large "family." At the center of this Foguang family is the patriarch: Master Xingyun. Surrounding him are his most senior disciples: Vens. Cizhuang, Cihui, Cirong, and Xinding and others who have renounced for over thirty years and who interact with the master on a daily basis. Just beyond this inner circle are two groups: the remaining thirteen hundred Foguang monastics, who provide the master's workforce, and Foguangshan's chief lay benefactors, who supply the financial and logistic support necessary to maintain the sangha and to carry out the organization's many religious, educational, and philanthropic initiatives. These groups in turn provide the link between the master and his millions of lay followers.

THE MASTER'S MANY ROLES
The nature of the master's interchange with his adherents is multifaceted, depending on the particular devotee and the needs or conduct of the devotee at a certain time. As circumstances warrant, Master Xingyun assumes such roles as wise teacher, stern father, caring mother, doting grandfather, or compassionate bodhisattva. Most lay devotees know him primarily as spiritual teacher and charismatic bodhisattva. For those in a position to know him on a more intimate, personal basis, the familial qualities also come to the fore.

"OUR MASTER, OUR TEACHER, OUR SPIRITUAL GUIDE"
The Chinese term translated as "master" is *dashi*, which means "great teacher." Xingyun is regarded as a master precisely because he is a superlative religious mentor for both monastics and laity. As Ven. Xinding said after being elected Foguangshan's third abbot in 1997: "Master Xingyun may no longer be the abbot, but he will always be our master, our teacher *[laoshi]*, our spiritual guide *[jingshen zhidao]*" ("Foguangshan Benefactors Meeting" 1997). Elevating Buddhist education, especially the training of clerics, has always been a top priority for the master. Up through the early 1990s, he regularly set aside time to teach courses in the Foguang college system, although in recent years his ever more hectic schedule has prevented him from doing this as consistently as he had in the past. Master Xingyun employs three primary pedagogical techniques: lecturing; one-on-one mentoring; and personal example.

When relating the difficulties and setbacks that he encountered after assuming the abbotship of Leiyin Temple in Yilan in 1954, the master often describes the utter disappointment that he felt when it looked as though no one was going to show up to listen to his first dharma talk, despite all the announcements that he had posted. Those days are long gone. Thousands of people fill stadiums to hear him lecture. Every year for more than a decade, he has given talks before capacity crowds at Sun Yat-sen Memorial Hall in Taipei, the Chiang Kai-shek Stadiums of Linkou (outside Taipei) and Kaohsiung, and Hunghom Coliseum in Hong Kong, all of which seat over twenty thousand. In 1996, he lectured before 70,000 people in Shah Alam Stadium, Shah Alam, Malaysia.[4]

That lecturing has played such an important role in Master Xingyun's success is remarkable considering that he does not speak Taiwanese and even his Mandarin can be difficult to understand because of his strong Jiangsu Province accent. He has been fortunate in finding excellent interpreters through the years. The first was the lay devotee Li Juehe, whose linguistic skills and many connections played a vital role in launching the master's career in northeastern Taiwan in the 1950s. Li was fluent in Taiwanese and Mandarin and had considerable knowledge of the Buddhist scriptures, making for lively translations.[5] After the master moved down to Kaohsiung in 1964, Ven. Cihui was most often called on to assume this critical task. Taiwan's citizens have become more comfortable with Mandarin in recent years (through compulsory education as well as television and radio, both of which until 1978 could by law use only Mandarin), allowing Master Xingyun to forgo using translators altogether. Those in the audience who find it difficult to understand him now rely on reading summaries of his talks simultaneously projected onto large screens.

Since the early 1970s, all the master's dharma talks have been carefully recorded to be reproduced as articles and pamphlets. Fifty thousand copies of such pamphlets are printed annually by Foguangshan's Culture Council. For the past decade, the master's more significant lectures have also been made available as audiocassettes and videotapes. Master Xingyun has done a large number of radio shows and television programs. In fact, according to Foguang literature, he was the first Chinese Buddhist monastic to take advantage of such modern technology to spread the dharma to the widest possible audience.

When instructing his disciples on public speaking, the master emphasizes the importance of "matching principle with capacity" (*qili qiji*), by which he means adapting one's talk to the interests and abilities of one's listeners:

> Those who teach Buddhism today must express the highest, most sublime principle in such a way as to match the capability of their audience. Only by using all their wisdom so as to explain the profound in an accessible manner will they get the desired results. For instance, in talking with farmers, going into the subtleties of Cartesian philosophy is not as good as discussing methods of planting. When the Buddha was alive, he used the example of music when teaching musicians, instructing them to tune the strings of their nature in a way neither too taut nor too slack. With shepherds, he used tending a flock as an example, telling such disciples how to train their mind to follow its natural course. Given his adeptness in clarifying profound principle so that it would accord with the minds of his audience, one can say that the Buddha was the best educator in the task of delivering sentient beings. (Shi Xingyun 1995a, 10:444)

One's presentation must be entertaining, both in content and in style. For too long, laments the master, Buddhist clerics have sat before their audience like lifeless sticks, droning on in monotonous voices about abstract concepts little connected with people's daily needs. To be effective, a talk must draw from living examples. Humorous anecdotes can also be included from time to time. Just as recreation can serve as an expedient means to introduce the dharma, so can learning about the dharma be an enjoyable form of cultural entertainment. Hence, in 1953 Master Xingyun became the first monk in Taiwan to use slide projectors in dharma talks so as to illustrate and enliven the presentation. In more recent years, larger-scale lectures have even been accompanied by laser shows and dry-ice displays. For Foguangshan's critics, such displays vulgarize the dharma, just as the master's simplification of the teachings renders them too superficial truly to affect a person's life. Master Xingyun counters that his large-scale lectures "vulgarize" the teachings, but in a positive way; that is, they make the dharma accessible and appealing to the general population. He believes, not only that the showy aspects of his lectures are harmless, but also that his own success has proved them to be an effective means of attracting large numbers to Buddhism. The presentation brings joy; the content associates this joy with the wisdom of the dharma. There are plenty of other opportunities for deepening people's knowledge once the initial interest and commitment have been sparked.

The master's second pedagogical method is one-on-one mentoring. Only his most senior disciples and closest lay devotees have the opportunity to benefit from such personal encounters regularly. Even the majority of clerics posted at the headquarters rarely, if ever, get the chance to speak privately with the master. They usually see him only during large meetings at which anywhere from a few dozen to hundreds of monastics are in attendance. Monks and nuns stationed around Taiwan are in little better position than are the millions of lay devotees: all count themselves fortunate if they see the master in a public setting even a few times in a year. For those who are abroad, such meetings are even more rare. Lack of opportunity for individual audience does not, however, prevent private guidance, for the master is a prolific correspondent. Countless monastic and lay devotees write to him of their worries, fears, hopes, and dreams. For disciples, such letters are the most secure way of confidentially reporting complaints and problems, for they know that the master will personally open the letter and reply.

The third teaching technique employed by the master, and the one that appears to strike an especially resonant chord among his devotees, is personal example. Many Foguang Buddhists, especially clerics, report that they find every aspect of Master Xingyun's conduct to be instructive for their own self-cultivation. His simplest acts—how he sits, eats, relates with others—are regarded as holding profound truths through actualizing the supramundane potential of daily life. This is, in a sense, the Foguang interpretation of Chan mind-to-mind transmission. The vast majority of devotees, who rarely have the opportunity to witness the master's movements, rely on verbal and written accounts of his paradigmatic acts. In general, Xingyun leaves it to others to extol his wisdom and compassion, although he will from time to time incorporate into his talks anecdotes in which he portrays himself as a paragon of Buddhist (and Confucian) virtue. Most of these stories eventually find their way into special Foguang anthologies.[6]

From 1989 to 1997, an even more important mechanism for transmitting this form of teaching was the master's daily diary, which was recorded in Foguangshan's monthly periodical *Universal Gate (Pumen)*. While the entries included references to lectures given and important events that occurred, the emphasis, as the master himself has noted, was on relating his "inner feelings" as a means of giving insight into his "mind" (*xin*) and "nature" (*xing*).[7] The importance of this journal for maintaining a sense of personal connection between the master and his worldwide monastic corps cannot be underestimated. As one cleric wrote:

> I have been Master Xingyun's disciple for thirteen years. In that time, I have had little direct, personal contact with Master, especially since having been stationed in California, Texas, and New York in the United States. I often have not even known Master's whereabouts. I am very grateful for the "Daily Diary" in *Universal Gate*, for it provides overseas disciples with valuable spiritual sustenance. It makes it so you don't feel alone, and it gives guidance for self-cultivation. As soon as I get *Universal Gate*, the first thing I do is read the diary. I read every word carefully; I do not want to miss a single sentence, not even a single phrase. I mark off passages that are especially moving or necessary to remember. I and others often discuss the content. I encourage all devotees to read this diary, for, despite the fact that we reside overseas, through the diary we are able to "touch hearts" [*jiexin*] with Master. It is as though one were listening to him give explanations, receive guests, travel, etc. Reading the diary is an indispensable part of my life. (Shi Xingyun 1994, vol. 3, n.p.)

These comments characterize the attitude of virtually all Foguang clerics toward the master's diary. The entries would be read and reread, not only to savor the master's various successes and to learn from his example, but also to discover books that he recommended or changes in rules that he had made. In those instances recording a conversation between the master and a particular disciple, definite messages were being sent to the entire sangha about his expectations of them all. Personal, intimate mentoring, of a sort that influenced even the smallest details of everyday life, was, thereby, maintained.

"We Monastics Have Just the Same Feelings in Our Hearts as Mothers and Fathers"

As can be seen from the preceding discussion of the master's pedagogical style, his relationship with disciples and certain lay devotees goes much deeper than does that of an academic teacher with his or her pupils. To this mentoring role he also brings an intimacy more analogous to that of a parent. Once, when the master's own mother commented that she felt bad for those disciples whose parents had already passed away, a nun quickly replied: "Grandmother! We have Shifu; we are not at all unfortunate" (Shi Xingyun 1994, vol. 3, entry for 20 February 1990). The traditional term *shifu*, which is often used by lay devotees or by lower-ranking monastics as an appellation for a senior-generation venerable, explicitly brings together the role of spiritual teacher (*shi*) with that of surrogate father (*fu*). In this capacity, Master Xingyun is the stern, authoritarian taskmaster who berates and punishes his disciples when he believes that their misconduct has warranted it. He has been known to scold, chide, and rebuke even relatively senior clerics before the assembled monastic community and is said to have slapped disciples from time to time for impertinence.[8] As father figure, the master's decisions are not to be questioned. One simply obeys. When a woman who had lived at Foguang headquarters for many years as a volunteer worker had begun to consider leaving the organization for a job in secular society, the master told her that this decision was completely up to her. If she were to stay, however, she would have to let him determine her future with no argument or backing out. After wavering for several weeks, the woman decided to leave Foguangshan.

Two things must be kept in mind when discussing the authoritarian streak in the master's leadership style. First, Chan masters, especially those of the Linji (Japanese: Rinzai) school, are expected to treat disciples with severity at times, if for no other reason than as a means of testing their mettle. In fact, Linji chronicles are replete with instances in which a sudden yell or slap has even been the catalyst for an enlightenment experience. Second, the master's attitude is not really so rigid as the anecdote related above makes it sound, and stories of him physically hitting a disciple all date from two or three decades ago. Master Xingyun characterizes his relationship with his disciples as one of "mutuality": "There is a constant two-way communication of ideas and flow of thoughts on the subject of enlightenment. I never once ask them to blindly obey and follow my orders. . . . It is never my style to use my authority to force any of my disciples to agree and accept my point of view" (Shi Xingyun 1997d, 276). Even in the case of the woman about to leave the organization, when she had initially said that she would remain at the headquarters, the two had consulted together as to what her job would be and for how long.

Master Xingyun's moments of strictness are far overshadowed by his displays of warmth toward his devotees and of sincere concern for their welfare. One cleric confided in me that she would not mind if he were to see her eating an ice cream cone (which is against the rules), for "he is so compassionate and young at heart that he would understand." (She did fear, however, some of the senior disciples seeing her doing so, for they would be much less likely to be lenient.) "Sometimes," the young nun continued, "when I am feeling depressed or confused by events happening around me, I look at his picture. This immediately revives my spirit." Devotees, especially disciples, are loyal to the master because they feel that he is devoted to each and every one of them. Balancing his role as stern father is the perception that he acts as a warm, caring surrogate mother, sustaining and nurturing his devotees. The master as mother figure is especially noticeable when he personally tends to the daily needs of those under his charge. Scattered throughout Foguang literature are stories telling of instances in which the master cooked for devotees or made their lives easier by attending to details overlooked by others. In a typical example, one time when he heard that a department store near the newly opened Hsi Lai University (Rosemead, California) was having a 40 percent discount sale, he immediately went to buy pens, stationery, hand cloths, and all sorts of other small items for the college students (Shi Xingyun 1994, vol. 1, entry for 19 September 1989). Master Xingyun also relates a time when a student in the college told her classmates that she planned to renounce, but only after she could have the chance to wear nylon stockings. The master soon thereafter journeyed to the United States, where he had someone buy a pair of panty hose, which he then carried back to Taiwan in his luggage. As he went through customs, the officer, noticing the stockings, looked at him with a very puzzled expression. The story concludes: "I felt like saying . . . 'Mister, how could you possibly understand that we monastics have the same feelings in our hearts as mothers and fathers'" (Shi Xingyun 1998b, 306).

As can be seen from the last anecdote, the master's concern for disciples includes at times indulging their harmless whims. Third-generation Foguang monastics call the master, not *shifu*, "teacher-father," but *shigong*, "teacher-grandfather." As Master Xingyun has aged, his interactions with his younger disciples have become much more like those of a doting grandfather who leaves discipline to others while he simply enjoys gently passing down his wisdom. At times he even bends the rules in his desire to ease his disciples' lives and bring them joy. He has been known to patrol campus grounds with late-night snacks for the students and once found an excuse and the money for a student to go to Kaohsiung so that she could watch the Ice Capades (Shi Xingyun 1995a, 10:604). Students are not the only ones to benefit from the master's indulgences. It was he, for instance, who lifted his own ban against clerics eating pizza, having initially rescinded the rule to reward a group of Hsi Lai Temple disciples who had worked late into the night preparing a mailing for an upcoming devotees' meeting. By relating this occurrence in his diary, the master let all monks and nuns know that, under special circumstances, such as when working unusually late or when traveling away from the monastery, they too could partake of this treat (Shi Xingyun 1994, vol. 1, entry for 5 October 1989).

"I Vow . . ."
Such anecdotes emphasize the master's great compassion, a virtue that is also highlighted in a cycle of stories that relate how he has nursed back to health a variety of small animals, including dogs, squirrels, mice, birds, and even a monkey (Shi Xingyun 1995a, 10:600, 657, 659, 667). These episodes show the master to have a special relationship with creatures, one built on an usual ability to empathize and communicate with them so that they are neither afraid nor likely to misbehave. Here, we see Master Xingyun as a bodhisattva, caring not just for his own devotees but for all beings, no matter how insignificant. According to many Foguang Buddhists, the master is not just any bodhisattva; he is, in fact, a manifestation of Guanyin, although others say that he is Maitreya. Identifying the master as either of these great bodhisattvas signifies that he is not merely a leader in the ordinary sense but one who radiates supramundane, charismatic power.[9]

Master Xingyun's ability to communicate with animals is regarded as evidence that he has *abhijña (shentong)*, the form of magical, supernatural power that Buddhists say occurs on the cultivation of high levels of meditative concentration *(chanding)*. In addition to understanding all speech, both human and animal *(tianertong)*, such supernatural power manifests itself in the abilities to see everywhere in the universe, including the heavens and hells *(tianyantong)*; know others' thoughts *(taxintong)*; transform into various shapes and sizes and travel anywhere, even through mountains and under the seas *(shenzutong)*; know the specifics of others' past and future lives *(sumingtong)*; and attain the wisdom to cut off afflictions so that one will no longer be reborn in samsara *(loujintong)*. The master makes no overt claims of possessing any of these powers and downplays their importance, doing so in two ways. First, he deaccentuates the uniqueness of such forces, reminding his audiences that all life is miraculous; even the simplest, most mundane acts can be seen, if considered deeply, to have magical qualities—the capability of water to quench thirst and people's abilities to walk and swim, for example. Second, the master notes the ethical ambiguity and spiritual limitations of even the most spectacular paranormal powers. The first five forms of *abhijñas* may arise through any form of meditation as well as through the recitation of certain incantations. Hence, not only buddhas, bodhisattvas, and Chan masters but sorcerers and even ghosts may practice these arts. Furthermore, such powers do not in themselves lead to ultimate liberation. Those who practice them but do not cultivate their discipline, wisdom, and compassion will remain within the wheel of transmigration (Shi Xingyun 1995a, 8:251–263).

The master apparently wishes to deflect attention away from such matters for several reasons. First, claims of magical abilities have, on occasion, been used in Taiwan by charlatans to dupe gullible followers and defraud them of considerable sums of money. Second, discussions of paranormal skills do not mesh well with the Foguang assertion that Buddhism conforms with a scientific worldview. The master and his devotees do not discount the existence of such skills, for, in their view, science simply cannot explain certain aspects of the world. Yet, because they recognize that there are those who consider belief in such powers as no more than a superstitious vestige of the past, they prefer to downplay the topic. Third, claims that an individual possesses supernatural ability tend to lead to an assumption of his or her infallibility, and this may easily undermine faith rather than buttress it since any mistake or weakness displayed could place his or her legitimacy in doubt. Even the simplest incidents can be interpreted in a negative light. For instance, because the master broke his leg while climbing out of a bathtub in 1991, a lay devotee questioned whether this did not reflect poorly on his level of concentration since he was hurriedly grabbing for a ringing telephone at the time. "Shouldn't a Chan master always remain calm and be able to foresee trouble?" the man asked at the conclusion of a lecture on Chan (Hsi Lai Temple, 16 February 1998). In a similar vein, during a conversation a nun admitted to me that she was troubled by the political-donations controversy that had followed Vice President Gore's visit to Hsi Lai Temple in 1996. Her concerns were not over the master's innocence, of which she was certain, but, rather, over how someone with the wisdom to know others' motives and to foresee the consequences of any act could have allowed himself to be so taken advantage of.

Master Xingyun's devotees attribute supernatural abilities to him but believe that he chooses not to activate them because, under present circumstances, they prove not to be appropriate expedient means. Rather than marveling over the wonders of supernatural power, the master and his followers are more likely to speak of *ganying*, or "cosmic resonance." In Chinese cosmology, *ganying* refers to the fact that, when a phenomenon of a particular kind arises *(gan)*, this will trigger a concordant response *(ying)* by other phenomena of the same kind. Specifically, *yin* phenomena attract one another, as do *yang* phenomena: with darkness also come sleep and sickness, all *yin* in nature; with light come activity and health. In imperial China, the fall of a dynasty was said to be foreshadowed by various inauspicious, *yin* portents, such as earthquakes, droughts, or floods. The reign of a benevolent ruler or the advent of a new dynasty, on the other hand, would enjoy felicitous weather. Because a small trigger set off at the right time in the appropriate fashion can create a spectacular response, Daoist adepts have long sought to harness such cosmic power so as to be able to control the weather or perform seemingly supernatural feats.

Chinese Buddhists have provided their own interpretation of *ganying*. Resonance, they observe, is merely one manifestation of the law of cause and effect *(yinguo)*. A certain cause *(yin)* invariably leads to a particular effect *(guo)*, although the specifics of the outcome will be modified more or less by contingent conditions *(yuan)*. Foguang Buddhists emphasize that *yinguo* is a natural law and accords with science. Unlike physicists, however, Buddhists extend the law of cause and effect to ethics, asserting that a moral action will bring about beneficial results and immoral acts will inevitably bring eventual suffering on the actor, although it often takes more than one lifetime for the law to work itself out. When speaking of *ganying* as an indigenous Chinese conceptualization of *yinguo*, Master Xingyun underscores the potency of faith *(xin)*, especially when it has been strengthened by a vow *(yuan)*, as a triggering cause, one that can create a magnificent responsive effect. This explains the efficacy of sincerely invoking the name of a buddha or a bodhisattva or chanting a mantra. Guanyin is said to be especially responsive to calls of faith made during times of distress. As evidence, Foguang literature cites incidents when those caught in catastrophic circumstances, such as being trapped in a collapsed building after an earthquake, have survived their ordeal by reciting this bodhisattva's name. Guanyin has also answered sincere cries for help recovering from grave disease, psychological illness, or debilitating handicap (Shi Xingyun 1995a, 8:265–273).

Faith and wisdom send reverberations throughout the cosmos, triggering auspicious responses. This is said to explain why extraordinary phenomena regularly occur in Master Xingyun's presence, such as the time during the groundbreaking ceremony for Foguang University in Yilan in 1992 when "Nine Dragon Water" immediately spouted forth where he had just struck the earth with a shovel. This also provides an explanation for why the master seems to have such extraordinarily good luck, especially when it comes to the weather. Members of the Foguang community commented for months afterward about the sudden break in the rain on the master's arrival in Hualian in June 1998. Although it had been pouring for several days, devotees later reported that, as soon as the master's plane touched down, the deluge ceased and, wherever he went, it was dry. After he left, the downpour renewed.

Extraordinary happenings are asserted to have accompanied the master his entire life. According to his mother, while in labor with him she dreamed that a little gold man and a graying elder approached her bed. After the golden figure pulled out a stalk of rice *(dao)* from her mattress, the elder announced: "This Way *[dao]* shall be fruitful." There were other unusual signs as well: when he was a baby, he was rosy cheeked on one side of his face yet pale on the other, and a pair of reddish lines ran from his nose to his upper lip. His appearance was strange enough that his family kept him indoors to avoid gossip by the neighbors about the "little monster who was born into the home of Li Chengbao [the master's father]" (Fu 1995, 10).

While such strange dreams and markings may have been auspicious portents of an unusual life, Foguang devotees do not find them as remarkable as they do the master's early displays of spontaneous generosity and compassion. *Passing Down the Light (Chuandeng)*, the hagiographic biography of the master, records that he never fought with other children, at age three gave away the family candy to neighborhood friends, by age four had become a vegetarian (following the example of his grandmother), a year later patiently nursed back to health a chick that had been badly burned, and two years after that spent many a day reading to his ill, bedridden mother (Fu 1995, 13–16). It is stories of compassion, not those of supernatural power or even of penetrating insight, that are the hallmark of the master's career. Hence, there is very good reason that he is usually identified as an incarnation of Guanyin rather than some other bodhisattva.

The picture painted of Master Xingyun by his devotees indicates that his charisma derives not so much from supernatural powers as from an extraordinary ability to resonate with others and, thereby, tap into a deep spring of communal energy. One can say that the master's charisma is one of immanence rather than of transcendence. This is a more subtle form of power, one that lacks spectacular display. Yet a type of energy does become manifest through the master's presence. This energy reaches particular intensity during ceremonial occasions, when Master Xingyun presides over meticulously orchestrated communal performances. It persists, however, even in relatively informal settings. So long as the master is interacting with others, so long as there is relationship, the power of resonance abides.

THE DYNAMICS OF RELATIONSHIP IN A GLOBAL ORGANIZATION

It is the master's charisma that holds Foguangshan together. Certain centrifugal forces, however, are constantly at work in such a large organization, especially one that, having grown so fast, has no well-established institutional mechanisms for assuring cohesion. Clerics in particular already feel a strain as the sense of personal relationship with the master has become more abstract with the order's growth, exponentially and geographically. Furthermore, the master must rely on his monastic disciples as his surrogates in order to attract and retain followers. A degree of commitment to that monk or nun must be nurtured in the local devotees for interpersonal energy to vibrate. If loyalty to the master's deputy becomes too strong, however, it may threaten devotion to the master himself and, thereby, undermine commitment to the organization as a whole.

Master Xingyun recognizes that relying on personal relationship to maintain organizational cohesion over space and time is a catch-22. Jiang Canteng and other observers of Taiwan Buddhism cast doubt on the ability of his senior disciples to engender the same deep loyalty among monastic and lay devotees. The master has done several things to rationalize charisma and, thereby, it is hoped, forestall problems of transition. In 1986, he retired as abbot, handing the post over to his chosen successor, Ven. Xinping. He has also put into place a variety of institutional mechanisms designed to encourage loyalty to the entire sangha rather than to any single individual, himself included. Monastic rotation and promotion, set terms for all posts (including Foguangshan's abbotship), and elections for the Religious Affairs Committee (the highest official seat of authority) are all designed to enhance group identity, unity, and cooperation. Ultimately, however, the long-term viability of Foguangshan will depend on the persistence of loyalty to and faith in Master Xingyun without the benefit of his immediate presence.

3 Foguang Humanistic Buddhism

In the last chapter, I focused on the master as personality. Here, I shift my attention to consider him as a creative and persuasive advocate of a new vision of Chinese Buddhist teachings. The key term that the master uses to designate the form of practice at Foguangshan is "Renjian Fojiao," which translates into English as "Humanistic Buddhism."[1] My discussion will, therefore, be structured around this phrase.

Master Xingyun did not coin the term "Renjian Fojiao," nor is he the only contemporary Chinese Buddhist cleric in whose lexicon it plays a central role. Master Taixu (1889-1947), widely regarded as the most influential of the Buddhist modernizers during the Republican era, was the first to employ the concept, although he usually referred to it as "Rensheng Fojiao." In Taixu's opinion, Chinese Buddhism had over the last several centuries suffered a great decline, a deterioration due mostly to an overemphasis on funerary and other rites devoted to transferring merit for the benefit of the deceased. He therefore devised the term "Rensheng Fojiao" to remind people that, as it is the living *(rensheng)* who are in the best position to cultivate the necessary merit and wisdom to attain enlightenment, Buddhists should devote their energies to maximizing this opportunity, both for themselves and for others (Pittman 2001, 169-181). The general preference for the term "Renjian Fojiao" has come about through the work of Master Taixu's most famous disciple, Ven. Yinshun (b. 1906). He preferred *"renjian"* over *"rensheng"* to give even more emphasis to the fact that Buddhism should not just focus on the living but participate actively in human society *(renjian,* "in the human domain," "in the midst of people"). It should not be inordinately devoted to worshiping buddhas as though they were deities, a tendency that, in his opinion, has plagued the Mahayana tradition since its inception (Shi Yinshun 1993, 1-63).[2]

Both Master Xingyun and Ven. Zhengyan (the very influential nun who founded Taiwan's largest lay Buddhist association, Ciji Gongde Hui) have followed Ven. Yinshun's terminology. Taiwan's most famous Chan master, Ven. Shengyan, has preferred to maintain the wording "Rensheng Fojiao," both to show his indebtedness to Master Taixu and to distinguish himself from Taiwan's other leading proponents of Humanistic Buddhism. All five clerics qualify "Buddhism" with adjectives approximating the English "humanistic" so as to redirect people's attention back from other realms and lifetimes to present existence in this world.

Shakyamuni Buddha, they remind people, was no spirit or god but a person who was born in this world, cultivated himself in this world, and attained enlightenment in this world. Buddhists should, therefore, model their practice on him and not devote so much of their time and energy to abstract discussions, performing rites on behalf of the deceased, or seeking a better rebirth in some far-off pure land. The assertion that Buddhists should emulate Shakyamuni begs the question of what exactly it means to do this. To follow in the footsteps of the Buddha, avers Master Xingyun, means simply to tread the middle path, neither succumbing to the temptations of desires nor stubbornly insisting on rigorous asceticism. One will not find at Foguangshan such practices as sealed confinement, long-term vows of silence, or the use of one's own blood to copy sutras. The difference between the attitudes at Foguangshan and those at Zhongtaishan, the monastery that houses Taiwan's second largest sangha but whose master, Ven. Weijue, advocates a "traditional" rather than "humanistic" form of Buddhism, is striking on this point. Foguang monastics would never dream of requesting to be confined alone in order to attend completely to their own cultivation. At Zhongtaishan, being permitted by Master Weijue to enter confinement is regarded as a very high honor, and clerics lament publicly that conditions permitting this have not yet coalesced.[3]

Along with avoidance of asceticism, Humanistic Buddhists believe that treading the middle path implies a certain openness to altering aspects of Buddhist practice, especially those aspects of monastic life that, having been rendered outmoded by current circumstances, have become obstacles to benefiting others. Foguang monks and nuns are emphatic that to base one's conduct on that of the Buddha does not entail sedulously aping everything he did. Just because the Buddha walked everywhere, says Master Xingyun, does not mean that twentieth-century monastics must forgo travel by automobile, train, or airplane, as some clerics have insisted. Such a literalist interpretation in fact contradicts the founding teacher's exhortation that individuals are to think for themselves so as to respond appropriately to every new situation.

This understanding of how to emulate the Buddha has the advantage of flexibility. The hermeneutical challenge is to determine the degree to which such flexibility is permissible, especially concerning the vinaya. What Foguang monastics claim to be acceptable adaptation of precepts and custom in the light of current conditions other venerables assert to be feeble excuse for lax practice. Those advocating Humanistic Buddhism are, hence, accused of undermining Buddhist monastic ethics. Foguang clerics counter that it is easy proudly to claim for oneself complete purity when one remains behind shut doors and, therefore, has almost no interaction with others. As one nun explained to me, purity is a matter of intention and suitability of action. Furthermore, she continued, the middle path requires that one balance the cultivation of wisdom (*zhi*) with the accumulation of merit (*gongde*) and blessings (*fu*). Those who do not follow Humanistic Buddhism have become so engrossed in nurturing the former that they have forgotten that the latter can occur only through helping and nurturing others and that this requires flexibility.[4]

Advocates of Humanistic Buddhism argue that, far from vitiating monastic ethics, their more pliant interpretation has buttressed the Buddha's instructions on morality, not only for those who have "left home" (*chujia*), but for laity as well. Much attention is, therefore, given to broader Buddhist ethical teachings, for example, the four all-embracing virtues, five precepts, and six paramitas. The manual *Foguang Studies* (*Foguang xue*) provides the following categories with which to classify excerpts from the Buddhist canon that are said to have a particularly strong humanistic tone: "generosity"; "discipline"; "patience"; "diligence"; "concentration"; "wisdom"; "repentance and confession"; "gratitude and compassion"; "the Buddha and sangha"; "ethics" (*renlun*); and "practical application" (*shiyong*) (Shi Xingyun 1998b, 237–299). Humanistic Buddhist cultivation is seen to be first and foremost about learning how to be fully human: "Relying on the Buddha, perfection lies in human character; 'humanness' perfected is buddhahood attained. This is called true reality" (Shi Xingyun, n.d.-b, 6). This phrase, often intoned by Master Taixu, is similarly a favorite of Master Xingyun's.

The this-worldly pragmatism that serves as the focal point of Humanistic Buddhism affects Master Xingyun's attitude toward and interpretation of Chan and Pure Land practice. Although a forty-eighth-generation holder of the dharma scroll, the master has only in recent years encouraged monastic and lay devotees to make formal meditation an important part of their cultivation. Up through the 1980s, he considered Pure Land recitation a more suitable expedient means to attract lay followers, given their busy lives, relatively low education level, and scant understanding of the dharma. Clerics were dissuaded from spending too much time in the Chan hall, for to do so was regarded as contrary to the bodhisattva spirit of serving all beings, not just attending to one's own liberation. Only in the early 1990s, when many lay Buddhists (and even non-Buddhists) were turning to meditation as a means to relieve stress, did Master Xingyun more actively discuss the benefits of such practice, backing up his rhetoric by constructing Foguangshan's beautiful Chan hall.

Both before and after he elevated the place of meditation in practice, Master Xingyun remained emphatic that Chan must be integrated into everyday living if it is to have any relevance. As he phrases it, formal sitting is worthless unless one is able to experience "a taste of Chan in daily life." For him, Chan is much more a way of seeing and acting in the world than a particular form of practice. "Grinding a tile will not make a mirror," he quotes from the Chan chronicles; "sitting in meditation will not make a person a buddha" (Shi Xingyun 1979, 7). Not that Master Xingyun totally ignores the specifics of *gong'an* (Japanese: *koan*) study etc.—in fact, he has given numerous dharma talks on Chan since at least the 1970s—but such matters do not have nearly as important a place in his instructions to devotees as does the more mundane concern of mindfully attending to one's relations with others.

The form of meditation practice that Master Xingyun considers to be most compatible with Humanistic Buddhism is "active Chan" (*dongzhong Chan*). Master Baizhang's maxim "A day without work is a day without food" has been broadened radically so that, rather than justifying only farmwork as suitable for monastic life, at Foguangshan it has become a paean exalting all forms of industriousness as an essential part, and potentially the highest form, of religious practice. "Work is nutrition" (*mang jiu shi yinyang*), exclaims the master, while "the most miserable person in this world is one who does not have any work; the greatest privation in life is the loneliness of boredom" (Shi Xingyun 1979, 738). In the view of Foguang monastics, it is they, and not those clerics who sit in absolute silence for hours on end in some isolated monastery, who practice in such a way as to attain the most profound level of Chan realization.

The Humanistic Buddhist perspective has led Master Xingyun to regard Pure Land teachings in a new way as well. Following Vens. Taixu and Yinshun, he has made "establishing a pure land in the human realm" (*renjian jingtu*) a central slogan for the Foguang community.[5] In Chinese Buddhist tradition, a pure land, in the broadest sense, is any place where one may engage in unhindered spiritual cultivation. Drawing from various sutras, Master Xingyun often describes the remarkable features of such pure lands as Sukhavati, the Vaidurya Pure Land, and the inner court of Tushita Heaven. Those reborn in such realms suffer no deprivation or distractions; their surroundings of beauty and peace afford an optimal setting for learning the dharma. None of these pure lands, however, can perfectly serve the soteriological needs of all beings. In line with the Chinese predilection to think in terms of polarities rather than dichotomies, each pure land is relatively advantageous for certain types of people as they journey on their particular paths to liberation. Master Xingyun therefore not only enumerates the benefits afforded by each of the pure lands and the practices associated with rebirth in them but also discusses the shortcomings of each. The inner court of Tushita Heaven, for instance, has the advantage of relative ease of access and is, therefore, available to any Buddhist, yet it is flawed in that it lacks the opportunity for "one-life completion." In other words, anyone who follows basic Buddhist practices and has made a vow to be reborn under Maitreya's aegis will attain rebirth in the inner court even if he or she has yet to cultivate a stable mind that is no longer under the sway of various emotions. As a resident of a heaven, however, he or she will still be within the cycle of rebirth and, thus, must retrogress to this world before attaining final salvation.[6] Those who are reborn in Sukhavati need not worry about having to go through the trials and tribulations of yet another birth in the Saha world; on the other hand, because rebirth in the Western Pure Land depends on reciting Amitabha's name with complete concentration, unadulterated by any conflicting desires, it proves too difficult for many to attain.[7]

According to Master Xingyun, whether a person finds himself or herself in a pure land ultimately depends on the degree of that person's own inner purity of intention and thought. A place rife with defilements for one person remains fully compatible with self-cultivation for someone else farther along the bodhisattva path. "Where the mind is pure," quotes the master from the *Sutra of the Teaching of Vimalakirti (Weimoqi suoshuo jing)*, "the land is pure" *(xin jing ze guotu jing)* (Shi Xingyun 1983, 512). Hence, even our Saha world can be a serene pure land so long as the mind is tranquil. Moreover, tranquillity of mind actively transforms and purifies the surroundings through dependent recompense *(yibao)*. There is, according to this view, no need to await rebirth to experience the bliss of a pure land; one need only fully realize the ultimate sanctity of mind and, hence, of all reality. Not surprisingly, there are qualities and degrees of purity in such "mind-only" pure lands. Those who achieve nirvana through Hinayana practices, for instance, have gained self-liberation and are freed from birth and death, but they have not attained the highest form of realization since their practice is too individualistic.

Master Xingyun's call for people to establish a pure land in the human realm (or "to build a pure land on earth," as the phrase *renjian jingtu* is translated into English in Foguang literature) assumes that optimal spiritual cultivation relies on purifying both external environment and internal intention. Because the purity of mind necessary for meditation and recitation depends on the satisfaction of certain basic material needs, attending to those needs for oneself and others is an ineluctable part of Buddhist practice. Master Xingyun does not want people passively to accept their present conditions while awaiting rebirth. He states: "Today there are many Buddhists who wish to be reborn in the Sukhavati Pure Land, but I think that that is not as good as putting one's energies to changing today's world into a Buddhist pure land" (Shi Xingyun 1995a, 10:413). The Western Pure Land does exist, but, since for the time being we live in this world, this is where we should concentrate our energies (although Sukhavati certainly acts as a perfect model for our activities).

In "The Prospects for Buddhist Youth" ("Fojiao qingnian de zhanwang"), Master Xingyun lays down a tripartite progression in which the world is envisioned as evolving first into a heaven *(tian)*, then into a pure land on a par with Sukhavati, and ultimately into the Lotus World (Huazang Shijie). After describing the ideal lives led by celestial beings in the twenty-eight heavens, the master observes that, in fact, people have already made significant advances toward transforming our own world into such a place of convenience and happiness. He notes that, if several hundred years ago someone had suggested that roads could be paved so that they were smooth and clean or that a person living high up in a building could have running water, no one would have believed it, yet today such things are commonplace. We have air-conditioning in hot summers; automobiles, trains, and airplanes that will take us to far-off places for work or recreation; delicious food; and radio and television broadcasts that can be heard around the world instantaneously. "Truly, we can have whatever we want and do whatever we wish. Hence, on the material level this world of ours is gradually developing such that it is virtually indistinguishable from a heaven" (Shi Xingyun 1983, 511).

According to Master Xingyun, the global trend toward democracy and human rights also fosters the conditions of equality, brotherhood, and peace required for cultivation. The notion of humanity's steady progress through history to ever-higher levels of comfort, freedom, ethical consciousness, and rationality is a central feature of the master's philosophy. He asserts that history can be divided into three eras, each of which has characteristic technical, political, social, and religious forms (Shi Xingyun 1983, 514–518). He calls the earliest phase "the divine power era" *(shenquan shidai)*. At that time, humankind was nomadic, and technology was still rudimentary. Because people were still largely at the mercy of natural forces, anything with an element of *mysterium tremendum* was attributed with divine potency. Eventually, bands joined together and settled down to form agricultural societies. In this second stage of history, "the king power era" *(junquan shidai)*, a few fortunate and usually ruthless men ruled; the vast majority of people had little choice but to do as they were bid. The consolidation of earthly power was paralleled by a concentration of sacred power in specific beings so that religious activities focused on honoring gods and propitiating ghosts.

Over the last two centuries, states Master Xingyun, industrial society has superseded its agricultural predecessor, and democratic governments have increasingly replaced totalitarian regimes. Because the most significant trend of this period is the adoption of constitutions that assure universal rights for all citizens, the master refers to the present historical epoch as "the people power era" or "the human rights era" (*minquan shidai*). The celebration of human dignity and potential has also been reflected in changes in religious worship. The honor once bestowed on gods is now bestowed on those persons who have performed great feats. In other words, religion has been secularized to become a form of hero worship. This is by no means deplorable, the master assures his audiences, for the shifting of emphasis from other worlds and supernatural beings to the actions of real people in our own world has rid humanity of much superstition and has caused people to take more responsibility for their actions. Hence, the current social, political, and religious arrangements allow people to enjoy greater freedom than ever before. Not surprisingly, in the master's view Buddhism represents the earliest and highest expression of such modern thinking.

Humankind can by no means rest on its laurels, for industrial society has created more than its share of problems. Modernization is characterized by progress, but the two are not synonymous. Not all aspects of the modern world are as they should be. As humans attempt to improve their lives, unanticipated and often harmful side effects inevitably occur. In certain respects, then, changes in the name of progress bring no real progress at all or may even be seen as retrogression. For instance, the master observes that the materialism that has accompanied advances in technology has increased distrust among people, thereby preventing relationships from developing in real freedom and equality. While industrial society has unquestionably enriched our lives materially, its effect on spiritual development has been equivocal, and perhaps it has even corrupted and impoverished it.

Fortunately, says the master, as the disparity between material and spiritual progress becomes ever more apparent, people increasingly seek a balanced inner life. "Because of the industrial development of society," he asserts, "people will gradually recognize the necessity of a life of cultivation" (Shi Xingyun 1983, 518). This tension between material wealth and spiritual poverty will usher in the culminating stage of social organization: "the ethical society" (*daoye shehui*). Only with the advent of this form of human community will our moral standards and spiritual lives reach their fulfillment, thereby establishing a pure land on earth. This final stage of Humanistic Buddhism requires people to extend their compassion beyond even the human sphere to encompass all sentient beings. Master Xingyun wonders: "This modern era of human rights gives people a lot of freedom and rights and safeguards their welfare, but is it the ultimate? Is this where people's ideals stop? Those who are knowledgeable all realize that from this 'human rights era' will emerge a 'life power era' [*shengquan shidai*]" (Shi Xingyun 1983, 515).

In this future life power era all living beings will have an equal right to existence. People will extend their knowledge and expertise to benefit all living creatures. After observing that animals have basically the same physical composition as people and all feel pain and happiness, the master continues: "From the higher animals to the lower life forms, such as ants and insects, all show the same desire for survival and dread of death, all wish to escape pain and seek happiness. Hence, as the era of human rights progresses, we can certainly in the future enter into the era of 'life power' that was promoted by the Buddha when he said, 'All living beings have buddha nature'" (Shi Xingyun 1983, 516). Once people have realized the promise of such a life power era, there will be no need to pray for rebirth in a pure land, for the Lotus World itself will have been actualized. Dualisms of here and there, life and death, purity and impurity, will no longer apply.

FOGUANG PURE LAND SOTERIOLOGY IN HISTORICAL PERSPECTIVE

As we have seen, the version of Humanistic Buddhism promoted by Master Xingyun has had repercussions for his interpretations of Chan meditation and Pure Land devotionalism. The master's treatment of the former needs little further explanation, for, despite references to "Foguang Chan" as a unique school, neither the master nor any of his disciples has contributed new insight that significantly transforms Chinese Buddhist meditation tradition.[8] Master Xingyun's attention has been directed much more toward promulgating a version of Pure Land practice that is simultaneously traditional and modern. Specifically, he has sought to harmonize the more conservative depiction of *jingtu* cosmology and soteriology defended by Ven. Yinguang (1861–1940) with the radical reinterpretation advocated by Ven. Yinshun.

The following subsection therefore places in historical context the master's rendering of Pure Land thought, doing so by comparing his version, not only with these two recent predecessors, but also with earlier monks whose writings significantly influenced how the concept of pure land has been understood in Chinese Buddhism.[9] I argue that the very fact that he has borrowed heavily from Vens. Yinguang and Yinshun has required that Master Xingyun contribute some unique hermeneutical moves of his own so as to overcome the incompatibilities of their treatments of the subject. Hence, although he follows Ven. Yinshun's lead in advocating the establishment of a pure land in the human realm, his reasoning for doing so is slightly different and draws from precedents in the Pure Land, Tiantai, and Chan schools. I begin with an explanation of the notion "buddha field" since it is of crucial importance to all conceptualizations of pure land. I then turn to a discussion of the role that the notion of *jingtu* has played for a variety of thinkers, some closely identified with the Pure Land school, others not.

THE CONCEPT "PURE LAND" IN CHINESE BUDDHIST THOUGHT

The term "buddha field" *(fotu; buddhaksetra)* denotes the area where a buddha guides sentient beings toward enlightenment. The buddha field has developed into its pristine state through the compassionate deeds of the buddha during his former lives as a bodhisattva. According to such texts as the *Sutra of the Teaching of Vimalakirti*, there are an infinite number of such fields, and each has particular qualities so as to meet the spiritual needs of beings with different capacities. Hence, the fields vary in their degree of purity, reflecting the level of attainment of the resident beings. The Chinese Buddhist tradition therefore speaks of three types of buddha field: pure; impure; and mixed. Our world is the buddha field under the aegis of Shakyamuni Buddha. As is evident from the omnipresence of suffering, immorality, and inferior teachings (i.e., non-Mahayanist schools of thought), it is an impure field.

To explain the imperfections of this world despite the presence of Shakyamuni by deeming it to be an impure buddha field reflects badly on him since the persistence of such suffering and ignorance indicates that both his purifying activity and his compassion are lacking. Chinese Buddhists have dealt with this issue in three ways: (1) Shakyamuni is said to have been but a transformation body *(huashen; nirmanakaya)*, and his salvific activity was meant to be effective only during his brief stay in this world. Since then, the influence of his teachings has gradually lessened, but there are other fields where a buddha is still present—most notably Amitabha's Sukhavati—so one should focus on being reborn in one of these. (2) Ultimately, just as all buddhas are but manifestations of the one dharma body *(fashen; dharmakaya)*, so too are there no fundamental differences among the buddha fields; all are empty and interpenetrate one another. This Saha world is not impure; it merely appears so to our unenlightened minds. (3) The notion that buddhas first purify their field in their former lives as bodhisattvas is rejected. Those buddhas such as Shakyamuni who choose impure areas as their fields are, therefore, no less effective than other buddhas; they simply have a more difficult task and, hence, are especially compassionate. Shakyamuni's influence is, therefore, ongoing, although the work that he began is in a sense unfinished (Williams 1989, 225–227; Thurman 1976, 86–88).

Those associated with the Pure Land school have typically adopted the first of these tacks to explain how suffering could occur in Shakyamuni's buddha field. According to the doctrine of the three periods of the dharma, after the death of

Shakyamuni, humanity's power of concentration, adherence to the Buddhist precepts, and aspiration to seek enlightenment have steadily declined. At first, during the "right dharma age" (*zhengfa shi*), the Buddhist teachings were still practiced with such purity that enlightenment could be realized. The "semblance dharma age" (*xiangfa shi*) marked a decline in teaching and practice so that enlightenment in this world was exceedingly difficult, although remotely possible. Finally, in the present "last dharma age" (*mofa shi*), the wholesome, nurturing circumstances necessary to actualize the dharma are no longer present. The teaching still exists, but the immediate realization of enlightenment is virtually impossible.[10]

This framework has significant repercussions for the school's soteriology. Because our own weaknesses and tarnished surroundings curtail any lofty aspirations for immediate liberation, the goal for this lifetime is more humble: to be reborn in surroundings that are more conducive to Buddhist practice. And what better place could there be than a pure land such as Sukhavati, where all needs are met and the dharma is constantly preached and practiced? Furthermore, in our degenerate age, the corrupted state of both Buddhist teachings and human nature undermines the traditional methods of cultivation. Not only are these techniques unable to spark enlightenment; they are not even sufficient for attaining rebirth in Sukhavati. In the *Gatha in Aspiration of Rebirth [in Sukhavati] with an Interpretation of the Sutra of the Buddha of Immeasurable Life (Wuliangshou jing youpotishe yuansheng ji jie)*, Ven. Tanluan (476–542 C.E.) distinguished between the "difficult path" (*nan dao*), which is based on "own power" (*zi li*), and the "easy path" (*yi dao*), which relies on "other power" (*ta li*), observing that, in the last dharma age, it is almost impossible to attain any high level of enlightenment through the former.[11] The Venerable Daochuo (562–645 C.E.) agreed, flatly stating in his *Essays on Sukhavati* (*Anle ji*): "To follow the holy path of study, meditation, and other traditional practices in order to attain enlightenment in this world of ours is no longer realistic" (Williams 1989, 259–260).

The only possible recourse under such conditions is to take refuge in the other power of a buddha so that, through sharing in the immense merit of his wisdom, compassion, and vows, one can be reborn in circumstances more suitable to conventional forms of cultivation. The Sukhavati Pure Land provides especially ready access since, in accord with Amitabha's vow, anyone who at the moment of death is wholeheartedly mindful of Amitabha will be born there, regardless of what the person may or may not have done in his or her lives to that point. The goal of religious cultivation is, therefore, to channel in the mind the correct habits of thought so that at the crucial instant sincere reliance on Amitabha naturally wells forth.

With this as his aim, Ven. Huiyuan (334-416), who would ultimately be regarded as the first patriarch of the Pure Land school, led a small group known as the Lotus Society in the mental visualization of Amitabha.[12] The Venerable Tanluan also engaged in this practice, but as only one of five "gates" (nianmen) that he found in the *Sutra [of the Buddha] of Immeasurable Life (Wuliangshou jing)*: worshiping Amitabha (bai fo); praising his name (koucheng nianfo); vowing resolutely to be reborn in Sukhavati (yuan); contemplating the attributes of Amitabha and Sukhavati (guan); and "turning toward" sentient beings (huixiang, i.e., transferring merit attained through the first four methods to benefit all beings).[13] Of these five, he laid particular emphasis on the virtues of praising the name of the Buddha Amitabha, an emphasis perpetuated by Ven. Daochuo and the second Pure Land patriarch, Ven. Shandao (613-681 C.E.).[14] The Venerable Daochuo assured his followers that, so long as one either invokes Amitabha (nianfo) or recites his name with an undivided mind (koucheng nianfo), one will be reborn in the Western Pure Land regardless of past transgressions. Ever aware of our defiled nature, Ven. Shandao stressed that the act of invoking Amitabha is one of confession and repentance, laying oneself bare so that in his compassion the buddha will transfer some of his limitless store of merits and, thus, save us.[15]

Other Chinese Buddhist philosophers incorporated the concept of pure lands into their metaphysics without sharing the emphasis on either the three-period doctrine or the devotional worship that so dominated the Pure Land school's soteriology. Such thinkers as Sengzhao (375-414 C.E.) and Zhiyi (538-597 C.E.) did not want to rule out the possibility of enlightenment here and now. They therefore adopted the assertion found in *The Sutra of the Teaching of Vimalakirti*: "The fact that some living beings do not behold the splendid display of virtues of the Buddha-field of the Tathagata is due to their own ignorance. It is not the fault of the Tathagata.... [T]he Buddha-field of the Tathagata is pure, but you do not see it.... [T]hose whose minds are impartial toward all living beings and whose positive thoughts toward the Buddha-gnosis are pure see this Buddha-field as perfectly pure" (Thurman 1976, 18). In his *Commentary on the Vimalakirti Sutra (Zhu Weimoqi jing)*, which is, in fact, the earliest extant treatment of Pure Land cosmology and soteriology, Ven. Sengzhao took this passage to be central, arguing that, for those who have the dharma eye (fayan), the distinctions between pure and impure are transcended. Such an assertion indicates that, ultimately, there is no difference between such pure lands as Sukhavati and our own world.

Two centuries later, Ven. Zhiyi, the founder of the Tiantai school, expanded on this approach, providing an in-depth discussion of pure lands in his *Inquiry into the Vimilakirti Sutra (Weimo jing wenshu)*.[16] In this work, he states that there are four kinds of pure lands: lands where commoners and saints live together (*fansheng tongzhu tu*); lands of expediency with a remainder (of ignorance) (*fangbian youyu tu*); lands of true reward without obstruction (*shibao wu zhang'ai tu*); and the land of eternal tranquillity and illumination (*chang ji guang tu*). Of particular interest here are Ven. Zhiyi's discussions of the first and fourth of these. Each of the "lands where commoners and saints live together" he subdivides into a defiled land (*huitu*) and a pure land (*jingtu*). Our own cosmos is such a realm, and Ven. Zhiyi implies that our world and Sukhavati represent its two aspects (Li, n.d., 300–301). The land of eternal serenity and illumination, on the other hand, is the dwelling place of the dharma body. Here, such dualistic notions as pure and impure no longer apply. In fact, the very notion of such a land is figurative, for the buddha nature of suchness has no body and no land: manifestation (*shi*) and principle (*li*) have merged into one. As David Chappell (1977, 34) observes, such a cosmology implies that this fourth pure land refers simply to all reality when it is seen without illusion. Since we are already in the pure land but merely do not realize it, the "land" is not some paradisiacal abode but enlightenment itself. The way to attain it is to purify one's mind. According to Ven. Zhiyi's model, the devotional worship of the Pure Land school is not wrong; it merely represents a preliminary stage of understanding since such a pure land (as well as the second and third pure lands) remains within dualistic conceptualization.

The main point pertinent to the present discussion is the differences in attitude toward the possibility of attaining enlightenment in our own world. As Chappell has discerned, the fundamental distinction between the early Pure Land school, on the one hand, and other Chinese Buddhist philosophies, on the other, is not the conceptual framework but the degree of confidence in humanity's ability to actualize the Buddhist experience effectively in the present age. Chappell (1977, 48) notes: "The Pure Land devotees felt compelled to look to another place, the Pure Land, and to another time when they would be reborn there, as the best occasion for the realization of these principles. On the other hand, the nondevotees gave limited value to the pure lands because they could see these same principles illuminating the landscape of their present existence." It is not so much a question of belief or disbelief in the existence of particular pure lands as it is a question of the relative emphasis given to rebirth in such realms as an immediate goal of practice.

The Venerable Zhiyi's synthetic paradigm served as a basis for later assertions that Pure Land and Chan methods are compatible and mutually beneficial. Those with a stronger orientation toward Chan maintained Zhiyi's hierarchical ranking. Others, such as Vens. Yanshou (908–975 C.E.) and Zhuhong (1535–1615), who would ultimately be designated as the sixth and eighth Pure Land patriarchs, respectively, argued that recitation, especially the mindful invocation of Amitabha's name and attributes, was itself a profound means of generating the "feeling of doubt" (*yiqing*) essential to *gong'an* practice.[17] Under the degenerate conditions of current times, Ven. Zhuhong averred, this was, in fact, the most effective such method.

The interpenetration that developed between Pure Land devotion and Chan meditation points to the complex understanding in Chinese Buddhism of the relation between faith and practice. Although Chinese Jingtu devotees have continued to employ the rhetoric of needing to rely on "other power," they have not given as central a place to this concept as have their Jodo Shu and Jodo Shinshu counterparts in Japan. Instead, achieving rebirth in the Western Pure Land is generally attributed to attaining resonance (*ganying*) with Amitabha through activating the three soteriological elements delineated in the *Amitabha Sutra* (*Amituo jing*): faith (*xin*); vows (*yuan*); and practice (*xing*). First and foremost among these three criteria is faith, for, without absolute confidence in the saving power of Amitabha, neither vows nor any form of practice has any efficacy. The vows to be reborn in Sukhavati and to transfer to all beings the merit that one accumulates through acts of devotion, however, serve to give direction and intensity to one's faith, just as a magnifying glass concentrates light rays. Finally, faith can be sustained only when enacted.

The most important form of practice is the mindful invocation (*nian*) of Amitabha's name. As was observed by the ninth Pure Land patriarch, Ven. Zhixu (1599–1655), Amitabha's wisdom and compassion are so great that simply vocalizing his name (*chiming*, lit., "keeping the name" or "holding to the name") spontaneously generates incalculable merit and, hence, this is in itself sufficient for rebirth in the Western Pure Land. Nonetheless, other forms of practice should not be neglected. For one thing, it is possible that, lacking good roots (*shan gen*), one may die under circumstances in which it is impossible to call Amitabha to mind with full sincerity. Engaging in meritorious acts ensures that one will have established the roots for continued faithful practice in a future life. Furthermore, even if one does attain rebirth in the Western Pure Land, the degree to which one has accumulated blessings determines in which of Sukhavati's nine grades one is reborn and, hence, the ease with which one will attain full enlightenment once there. The *Sutra on the Contemplation [of the Buddha] of Immeasurable Life* (*Guan wuliangshou jing*), therefore, lists the following as practices that create blessings: being filial to one's parents; honoring one's teachers; having a merciful heart that harms none; taking the triple refuge; keeping precepts; following decorum; generating bodhi-cita; keeping deep confidence in the law of cause and effect; and reciting Mahayana sutras (Yamada 1984, 23). For Chinese Pure Land devotees, various forms of practice are, therefore, at least indirectly necessary but certainly not sufficient for rebirth in Sukhavati. Faith is primary, vows secondary, practice tertiary.

This brings us to the final strategy employed to explain why there is still so much suffering in Shakyamuni's buddha field and how that suffering is to be overcome. As with the degenerative three-period time line of the Pure Land school, this tactic emphasizes that the world is in a pitiable condition. The *Lotus of Compassion Sutra (Beilian jing)*, which is a principal text for this viewpoint, does not, however, attribute the sufferings of the Saha world to the waning power of Shakyamuni's teachings. Instead, it asserts that the very fact that he came to save beings in such a horrible place proves the depth of his compassion. This conceptual frame intimates that, while our world is far from perfect, through the beneficent acts of the Buddha there is now at least a glimmer of hope for salvation and, thus, that it is a better place than it was before his arrival. His influence is incomplete but ongoing. In other words, the relative optimism felt by Ven. Zhiyi has been made possible only through the wisdom and compassion showered on humanity by the Buddha. Our world is neither an absolutely pure buddha field nor a hopelessly impure one. Instead, on the mundane level, it is a mixture of the two.

Master Xingyun's Pure Land Philosophy in Historical Perspective

The Venerables Tanluan, Daochuo, Shandao, Sengzhao, Zhiyi, Yanshou, Zhuhong, and Zhixu are among the most important thinkers who collectively set the general perimeters within which subsequent practitioners have understood Pure Land cosmology and soteriology. Chinese Buddhists have, therefore, generally relied on one of three methods of cultivation: single-minded devotional Pure Land practice (hence relying solely on the other-power of Amitabha or another buddha); a synthesis of Pure Land and Chan practice, with more or less emphasis on one or the other; or rigorous Chan meditation (i.e., seeking enlightenment through direct, own-power). These categories of methodological inclination have persisted to this day. Master Xingyun falls into the middle camp, as do the vast majority of practitioners. To better understand his particular reasoning for such a centrist approach, let us first consider two other leading figures of twentieth-century Chinese Buddhism, both of whom have, although in very different ways, influenced the master.

Modern China's preeminent paladin of devotional Pure Land practice was Ven. Yinguang.[18] In this last dharma age, he contended, virtually no one can achieve enlightenment through the self-reliance of Chan practice. Significant progress in cultivation requires the less direct route of rebirth in Sukhavati, a path to be journeyed by relying on Amitabha's vow and set under way through the simple, wholehearted piety first urged by the early Pure Land patriarchs Tanluan, Daochuo, and Shandao. In Ven. Yinguang's view, pure lands should not be described as some kind of metaphor for purity; they must be regarded as concrete goals of practice. Nor is recitation to be thought of as merely an appropriate form of *gong'an* for the present age. To render it as such dilutes the power of faith, leaving the practitioner mired in the ignorance and suffering of samsara for at least another rebirth. Rather than pairing recitation with meditation, Ven. Yinguang emphasized the threefold model of balancing faith, vows, and practice. By the last of these, he meant especially recitation and filial piety. He noted time and again that only those who fulfill their social obligations (i.e., actualize the five Confucian relationships), especially that of repaying the immeasurable dept of gratitude owed to one's parents, could retain the calmness of mind required steadily to practice with untarnished faith (Shi Jianzheng 1989, 57–87).

The Venerable Yinshun has offered a very different understanding of the significance of Pure Land cosmology. For him, the pure lands and their attending buddhas and bodhisattvas function as important symbolic guides for practice. In *Research into Questions on Mahayana Buddhism (Dasheng Fojiao de wenti yanjiu)* he states that the figure of Amitabha was not to be found in the early Buddhist community. As the Mahayana school arose and sought to apply the dharma to the spiritual capabilities of common people, aspects of the worship and iconography of the Brahmanic deity Mitra were absorbed into Buddhism. Certain elements of the Indian sun god's characteristics can be seen in the Buddhist cults of Bhaisajya-guru, Aksobhya, and Amitabha. The first two of these, whose pure lands are both said to be located in the east, are associated with beginnings and life. Amitabha's Sukhavati Pure Land, which is to the west, represents completion and rebirth after death. The first two emphasize practice in the here and now; the third triggers faith in future realization. The Venerable Yinshun pairs Sukhavati with one other pure land as well: Maitreya's Tushita Heaven. Because, like our world, Tushita is within the realm of desire, and because Maitreya will have his next rebirth in our world and lead its beings to enlightenment, the emphasis in this case is on immanence, in contrast to the transcendence and distance of Amitabha's land. By devoting too much attention to Sukhavati, argues Ven. Yinshun, Chinese Buddhists have allowed their practice to become associated with death, blind faith, and otherworldly matters. Rather than merely hoping to be reborn in Sukhavati, Buddhists should model themselves on Amitabha, Bhaisajya-guru, Aksobhya, and

Maitreya, all of whom of created pure lands through their great vows and practice (Shi Yinshun 1992, 30-39).

Despite the radically different viewpoints on Pure Land practice offered by Vens. Yinguang and Yinshun, Master Xingyun has somehow found a way to incorporate elements of both in the Foguang worldview. The influence of Ven. Yinguang is readily apparent in the canonical Pure Land cosmology enunciated by Master Xingyun. The master's depiction of Sukhavati, for instance, is taken directly from the *Sutra on the Contemplation [of the Buddha] of Immeasurable Life*, his only modification being to stress the cleanliness of the paradise, not a particularly surprising emphasis in the light of Taiwan's environmental problems.[19] Furthermore, as we have seen, Master Xingyun's eclectic acceptance of multiple types of pure lands and his acceptance of the compatibility of Pure Land and Chan practices has many precedents. Since the time of Ven. Zhiyi, Chinese Buddhists have employed such an inclusivist tactic of accepting the validity of diverse groups' claims though placing them in some type of hierarchy of efficacy.[20]

Master Xingyun's cosmology is, therefore, squarely within the Pure Land school tradition as championed by Ven. Yinguang. The same cannot be said of his soteriology; the master's recipe for salvation differs significantly from that of Vens. Tanluan, Daochuo, Shandao, and Yinguang. This may not appear to be the case at first. After all, Foguangshan has long emphasized Pure Land devotionalism over Chan meditation, and the master clearly states that invocation of Amitabha is the most important practice leading to rebirth in Sukhavati. The stories that he tells to substantiate this and the elaborations of the subject that he provides are directly from the *Sutra on the Contemplation [of the Buddha] of Immeasurable Life*. Furthermore, chanting the name of Amitabha and reciting the texts of Pure Land sutras play an important part in Foguang ceremonies, many of which are conducted according to the guidelines laid out in Ven. Shandao's liturgies. The monastery's daily cycle of worship and rituals is closely modeled on the *Lingyanshan Temple Breviary* (*Lingyanshan si niansong yigui*), which was compiled by Ven. Yinguang in the 1930s. In fact, as with its prototype, the Foguang breviary omits any reference to Chan lineages or teachings.

Master Xingyun's views on salvation nevertheless differ from those of teachers typically associated with the Pure Land school for two reasons. First, the master's focal point is not how to attain rebirth in some other pure land but how to transform our Saha world itself into such an ideal spiritual realm. His emphasis is, therefore, on mundane rather than supramundane existence. Second, activities based on own-power play a much more important part in cultivation than they have for the Pure Land patriarchs. Following standard Buddhist epistemology,

Master Xingyun states that the dharma can be separated into mundane and supramundane aspects (*shijian fa* and *chushijian fa*, respectively), the former referring to worldly truth, the latter to the absolute truth. An essential component of reviving Buddhism, he continues, is shifting its focus from the supramundane to the mundane.

The master argues this for the simple reason that, as we are all a part of the mundane world, whether we like it or not, so long as we are alive, we cannot escape from it completely:

> When the Saha world is mentioned in the Buddhist tradition, it is described as a bitter sea or flaming house or as though people were in prison. But who among us does not make a living in this world? . . . It is not that we Foguang Buddhists do not think liberation from birth and death important, but, if the problems of our daily lives are unresolved, how is it possible for us to seek liberation from birth and death? For example, if you don't have food to eat or clothes to wear, how are you going to "utilize the false to cultivate the true" [*jiejia xiuzhen*]? How are you going to have the calm mind necessary to contemplate the great problem of birth and death? (Shi Xingyun, n.d.-b, 6–8)

Since the ultimate goal of Mahayana Buddhism is the universal liberation of sentient beings, devout Buddhists must act to provide all with circumstances conducive to cultivation. In fact, only by showing such compassion to the plight of others is complete liberation possible.

For Master Xingyun, the Buddha's disciple Sudatta is a model of this bodhisattva ideal. Soon after he became a follower of the Buddha, Sudatta is said to have made this vow: "From today on, whenever a traveling peddler wishes to have something to eat or tea to drink, I will always provide him with some. From today on, if any bhikshu, bhikshuni, or Buddhist devotee passes by my gate and wants to eat or use my home, I will assuredly not prevent it. Or, if there are elderly people with no one to care for them or orphans without parents, I need only know about them, and I will immediately help solve their difficulties" (Shi Xingyun 1995a, 10:409–410). Working to tend to material needs is not simply a prerequisite to cultivation; it is a vital aspect of the process. The master feels that, by overemphasizing the supramundane, Buddhists have forgotten that enlightenment is to be found in this very world. One is liberated, not by attempting to forsake the world, but by learning to live properly within it.

This shift in emphasis from the supramundane to the mundane results in a corresponding shift from a reliance on other-power to reliance on own-power. Master Xingyun would agree with his predecessors that sincerely reciting Amitabha's name will result in rebirth in Sukhavati. He places even greater stress than did they, however, on the necessity of combining *nianfo* with sustained efforts to purify one's mind and environment through compassionate involvement to better this world. The return to self-reliance is not to the individual, isolated self. Even if they be as compassionate as Sudatta, individuals cannot create a pure land on their own. Rather, the return to self-reliance is the community working as a whole toward universal prosperity and liberation. One might refer to this middle path between other-power and own-power as "communal-power"—although Master Xingyun never uses this wording himself. Hence, his tripartite soteriological methodology equally balances other-power (reciting the name of Amitabha), own-power (purifying the mind), and communal-power (compassionate involvement in society).

The assertion that we should exert ourselves so as to transform our own world into a pure land represents a significant departure from the Pure Land school's focus on being reborn in Sukhavati. Nevertheless, Master Xingyun's shift in focus is not nearly as radical as was Ven. Yinshun's historical analysis of the mythological origins and symbolic functions of pure lands. Furthermore, although the master's soteriological method differs greatly from that of the school's most famous patriarchs, it nonetheless can be justified from within the Pure Land tradition. I noted earlier that the third component of Pure Land soteriology found in the *Amitabha Sutra* is "practice." This indicates a this-worldly component in Chinese Pure Land philosophy right from the beginning. Historically, Pure Land votaries have simply accorded greater attention to the other two methods and have interpreted the third—that is, practice—as especially referring to invoking Amitabha's name. While Master Xingyun maintains the three-point scheme, he chooses to magnify the third aspect so that it becomes central and to broaden its mode of application.

Master Xingyun's focus differs from that of his Pure Land school predecessors because he does not share their pessimistic appraisal of the present condition of the world. He states time and again that Buddhists should have a happy, optimistic, and positive outlook on life, and he has even gone so far as to say: "Buddhism might say that life is suffering, but I personally feel that life is very happy" (Shi Xingyun 1983, 595). Not only does he deem the current circumstances adequate for spiritual cultivation, but, in a sense, he has even inverted the three-period doctrine: the world is not degenerating, on the material level, at least; it is progressing, providing an ever better environment for attaining enlightenment. That we are in the last dharma age is not so important to him as the fact that we are on the verge of creating the ethical society of the life power era. To adapt the terminology utilized by William James, Master Xingyun's views on life are decidedly "healthy minded" in tone, in contradistinction to typical Pure Land thinkers, whose stance toward this world has been from the vantage point of the "sick soul."[21]

Some Buddhists take strong issue with such an upbeat message, certain critics even asserting that Master Xingyun's attitude toward the world is so contrary to the teachings found in sutras that Foguangshan should be regarded, not as a Buddhist organization at all, but as a "new religion" (xinxing zongjiao).[22] Master Xingyun rebuts that the belief that Buddhism is negative and pessimistic stems from a partial and biased understanding in which only the first two noble truths are remembered while the good news of the latter two noble truths is forgotten or ignored. He is especially vexed by those who mistake description for prescription and, thus, believe that one must sacrifice the joys of daily life to truly practice Buddhism, some going so far as to wear tattered clothes and eat coarse food when much better fare is available.

Buddhist teachings, asserts the master, certainly do not tell people to go looking for suffering: "Buddhism does not want people to be like a withered log or dead ashes and to talk about the suffering of this world in a serious manner all the time. Buddhism is a happy religion and hopes that everyone will find supreme peace and happiness." Buddhism places such a great emphasis on suffering, states the master, only because a knowledge of its existence is requisite for finding ways to overcome it: "Unless you know suffering, you will not understand happiness and will not firmly resolve to learn the way." He likens Buddhism to such modern sciences as economics, medicine, and politics since they too highlight specific problems in order to improve living standards and minimize human suffering. Unlike these, however, which provide only momentary relief, "Buddhism not only strives to eradicate our present sufferings but places even more emphasis on attaining liberation from the root causes that keep us in the endless cycle of birth and death" (Shi Xingyun 1983, 510, 592). In Master Xingyun's view, Buddhist teachings neither pessimistically accept suffering nor advocate trying to avoid it. Rather, suffering is something to be overcome and transcended positively.

Master Xingyun's outlook is closer to the relative confidence of Vens. Zhiyi and Sengzhao and of the *Lotus of Compassion Sutra* than to the pessimism of Pure Land masters. Unlike Vens. Zhiyi and Sengzhao, however, Master Xingyun sees the question as being, not whether one has the ability in this life to realize that this world is, in fact, already pure and always has been, but whether we are able to work together in order directly to create a pure land in which undisturbed spiritual cultivation takes place. In Ven. Zhiyi's scheme, the awareness of the world as pure land occurs simultaneously with enlightenment. In Foguang soteriology, the act of creating the physical, social pure land is essential to the process of cultivation. Once the task is completed, all achieve enlightenment simultaneously.

By altering the soteriological methodology of Pure Land Buddhist doctrine, Master Xingyun has reduced a tension that has long been present in that tradition. Pure Land philosophy has been criticized for its inability satisfactorily to explain why people should act morally since to do so is a form of own-power. In other words, how is practice to be fully harmonized with a vow of utter reliance on the grace of Amitabha? While this problem is most evident in the works of the Japanese Pure Land Buddhists Honen and Shinran (since they took the doctrine of absolute devotion to Amitabha to its logical conclusions, thereby accentuating the tension), it nonetheless also exists in a more muted form in mainstream Chinese Pure Land doctrine. Master Xingyun's shift from other-power to what I have termed communal-power resolves this tension. People cannot create a pure land here on earth unless they act morally. When they do not, they create hell instead.

In assuaging this tension within Chinese Pure Land doctrine, Master Xingyun's philosophy has created another: such an optimistic model will resonate only so long as technological, social, and political progress continues. If people deem that the quality of their lives is taking a turn for the worse—if, for example, social and environmental problems in Taiwan continue to mount, as they have over the past decade, or the political situation deteriorates—Master Xingyun's assertions about the establishment of an ethical society in a life power era will ring hollow. Such a healthy-minded religion can speak only to those who feel secure and see promise in the future.

Associated with this limitation is the inability of Master Xingyun's system adequately to explain evil. How is it that political corruption, violent crime, religious terrorism, and ethnic cleansing can persist in a world said to be on the verge of becoming a pure land? The master's philosophy tells us why we should act morally, but it does not adequately address the fact that there is still so much suffering and bloodshed. The vulnerable point of his philosophy is the opposite of that of his predecessors: mainstream Pure Land masters have seen only evil, with little, if any, chance for salvation in this world; Master Xingyun has generally emphasized progress, downplaying the problems and even atrocities that have accompanied it. As does the *Lotus of Compassion Sutra,* the master sees the world as a buddha field with both purity and impurity; unlike that sutra, the master feels that the promise of that buddha field greatly outshines its problems and that we humans jointly have a significant role to play in completing the work initiated by the Buddha. It should be noted that, as crime and pollution have increased in Taiwan, Master Xingyun has gradually moved to a more centrist position, shifting attention from technological advancement to moral development, and replacing talk of transforming the entire world into a pure land with the more modest goal of creating miniature pure lands in specific locations. Foguang temples are publicized as small oases of purity where people intent on practice can find refuge from the turbulence shaking the rest of the world. The master is still very much the optimist, the goal still to transform the earth into a pure land, but the time frame extended and the immediate goals made more modest.

THE CHINESE BUDDHIST REVIVAL

Master Xingyun's optimism concerning the upward trajectory of human evolution naturally encompasses the future of Buddhism. Buddhist history differs from general human history, however, for, as with other Humanistic Buddhists, the master follows Ven. Taixu in asserting that Chinese Buddhism is currently experiencing a remarkable revival (*fuxing*) after having suffered a long period of decline. According to Master Taixu, the number of people, particularly young people, interested in the dharma began to multiply exponentially over the first decades of the twentieth century. The Venerables Xingyun, Zhengyan, and Shengyan all echo their predecessor's heartening appraisal, pointing to the phenomenal growth in the numbers of Buddhists in Taiwan as proof that their tradition truly is undergoing an unprecedented and irreversible resurgence.

There is reason for caution in accepting the glowing account given by Chinese Buddhist leaders of their tradition's return to halcyon days. Through careful analysis, Holmes Welch (1967, 222–269) revealed that Master Taixu's rhetoric of revival lacked any concrete supporting evidence. Neither had the tradition suffered such terrible decline in recent centuries as Taixu and others had depicted, nor did it undergo any substantial growth or revitalization during the Republican era. Master Xingyun and other late-twentieth-century advocates of Humanistic Buddhism indirectly confirm Welch's appraisal, for, while they regard themselves as perpetuating the movement initiated by their mentor, they have subtly altered the time frame for the revival and, consequently, the status of its founder. Master Taixu, it is now said, laid the seeds for the revival through his progressive teachings and plans without experiencing their blossoming. Only with Humanistic Buddhism's transplantation from the mainland to Taiwan have conditions finally coalesced, allowing the movement to shift from hopeful anticipation to actuality. Master Xingyun has, according to his followers, not so much refined the theories that were laid down by Master Taixu and Ven. Yinshun as he has created the institutional framework that allows their ideas to be enacted and practiced. Hence, the revival prematurely proclaimed by Master Taixu is, nonetheless, coming to pass.

Buddhist leaders support this claim by pointing to the large and growing numbers of people associating themselves with Buddhist organizations. When, in 1990, the Ministry of the Interior of the Republic of China (ROC) began collecting statistics on religious affiliation, 2.68 million people in Taiwan indicated that they had taken the triple refuge, and 4.48 million stated that they frequented Buddhist temples (13.3 and 22.2 percent of the population, respectively). Two years later, those numbers had jumped to 3.76 and 4.86 million (18.4 and 23.9 percent of the population, respectively).[23] Foguangshan and Ciji Gongde Hui buttress these statistics by pointing to their own impressive growth rates, with each by the turn of the millennium claiming memberships topping 3 million. Master Xingyun, Ven. Zhengyan, and other prominent monastics attribute Buddhism's increased prestige and affluence to the success of their efforts to render the dharma more accessible. There is some truth to this, for the tradition would not have gained wider appeal without suitable "marketing." The public stature of Master Xingyun, Ven. Zhengyan, Ven. Shengyan, Ven. Weijue, and Ven. Quandao (a vocal leader of Taiwan's green movement over the past decade) cannot be denied, nor can the influx of wealth to Buddhist groups that has allowed for the construction of ornate temples around the island.

Assuming for the moment that Taiwan's Buddhists are correct and that their religion has experienced an upsurge in recent decades, what could have caused such a phenomenon? A repackaging of Buddhist teachings represents only part of the picture. A constellation of sociological, political, and economic factors seems to have spurred on the sense of revival.

Most notably, Buddhism has benefited from the search for appropriate vehicles to symbolize social integrity in the aftermath of the removal of the ROC's seat from the United Nations in 1971 and the severing of official ties by the United States six years later. The decrease in missionary work by Christian organizations since that time, coupled with a search for cultural roots and legitimacy by Taiwan's populace, created for Buddhist organizations and such folk traditions as Yiguandao an opportunity for increased prestige and, hence, growth.[24] These groups therefore profited from an overall trend toward "localization" *(bentuhua)*, that is, toward a higher valuation of indigenous culture.[25] The scholar Jiang Canteng (1997, 2) points to Taiwan's rapid urbanization as another important factor in the skyrocketing popularity of Buddhism and of religion in general, for the isolation of city life increased people's sense of alienation *(shuli gan)*.[26]

The lifting of martial law in 1987 and the promulgation of the 1989 Revised Law on the Organization of Civic Groups may have further contributed to Buddhism's spread. The former meant that restrictions on large public assemblies were discontinued. The effects of the 1989 law were even more significant, for the new legislation served to break the hegemony of the Buddhist Association of the Republic of China (BAROC), the government's semiofficial liaison office regulating Buddhist monasteries. Henceforth, clerics would no longer have to receive ordination at a BAROC-sponsored ceremony or gain permission from that body to study abroad, and associations such as the Buddha's Light International Association (BLIA) and Ciji Gongde Hui could form legally. Supplementing these cultural, sociological, and political factors has been Taiwan's economic boom, which has allowed a wide range of devotees regularly to offer generous donations to build facilities and support monastics.

Contemporary Chinese clerics may, therefore, be on firmer ground for asserting a Buddhist revival than was Master Taixu. Several caveats must, nonetheless, be kept in mind. First, long-term trends cannot be tracked since the ROC Ministry of the Interior began compiling the relevant data only in 1990. Even the statistics available since that time are suspect. It seems very unlikely, for instance, that more than one million people took refuge in a mere two years, so the apparent growth from 1990 to 1992 probably reflects a change in computational methodology or the more efficient collection of data rather than significant growth in affiliation. Care must also be taken in using the statistics provided by individual organizations. If, as they claim, both Foguangshan and Ciji Gongde Hui have at least three million members, that would account for virtually all Taiwan's Buddhists, plus a sizable contingent of overseas Chinese Buddhists.[27] Second, even if there had been an increase, the overall numbers remain small. Less than one-quarter of Taiwan's population regards itself as Buddhist. Furthermore, there is evidence that whatever revival has occurred may already have peaked. Interior Department statistics for 1997 indicate that 4.86 million people identified themselves as frequenting Buddhist temples, virtually no increase from five years earlier. As the 1997 figure is only 22.4 percent of the total population, this actually represents a decrease of 1.5 percent from the 1992 figure.[28]

What then has slowed or even reversed the momentum? The single greatest factor, ironically, appears to have been the tradition's phenomenal success. The proliferation of Buddhist organizations in the late 1980s and early 1990s stretched the resources of devotees. When Taiwan's economy slowed, contributions dropped as well. The revival, which had been as much a financial as a spiritual phenomenon, stagnated. This downward trend was exacerbated by a series of scandals involving Buddhist and folk Buddhist organizations that corroded the tradition's image. The autumn of 1996 was especially hurtful. Zhongtaishan received months of adverse press coverage and criticism after Ven. Weijue tonsured 158 novices without gaining their parents' approval. Just as this scandal was simmering down, it came to light that the popular folk Buddhist master Song Qili had swindled devotees out of millions of New Taiwan dollars. Investigators revealed how he had employed trick photography and other stunts to impress the credulous and had then diverted temple funds into his own bank accounts. Numerous other cases of fraud involving self-proclaimed Buddhist masters soon hit the papers, leading the government tax bureau to review the financial records of all Buddhist organizations. Not surprisingly, donations tumbled. This sudden drop in funding intensified what was already a downward trend in donations.[29]

The significance of the revival may, in fact, lie beyond statistics about membership, finances, or temple construction. Instead, I would argue that its importance derives from what such rhetoric says about late-twentieth- and early-twenty-first-century Chinese Buddhist self-understanding. Discussions of the revival of Buddhism through returning it to its humanistic roots employ two sets of conceptual dyads: modernity/tradition and Mahayana/Hinayana.

Traditionalist and Modernist Perspectives on Tradition and Modernity

Twentieth-century religious leaders who have utilized the rhetoric of history to galvanize public support for their revivalist agendas have generally fallen into one of two camps: traditionalists or modernists. Traditionalists declare that the vast majority of changes in social relations that have occurred as an epiphenomenon of modernity have proved to be unnecessary and detrimental to morality and communal stability. Innovations in worldview or custom that have directly challenged religious symbols and praxis are especially anathema, but even those with no such apparent implications are often viewed with skepticism. Modernists have considered such adaptations as necessary for their tradition's survival and have openly espoused them as holding positive benefits.[30] The difference in perspective between these two groups is not as simple as one may at first think, for both have argued that they are the ones who carry on the work initiated by the religion's founder. To understand how, not only the traditionalists, but also the modernists can make such a claim, we must look more closely at the rhetoric of "tradition."

The noun "tradition" and adjective "traditional" describe practices and doctrines that have been passed down through time. Edward Shils (1981, 15) has observed that persistence for three generations is the minimum requirement for something to be regarded as a tradition. The time scope for various traditions may, therefore, vary widely, anywhere from a few decades to several millennia. A particular cultural group inherits a wide range of such traditions, and the sum total of these elements constitutes that group's cumulative tradition as a singular whole.

Members within the group are rarely clearly cognizant of the relative antiquity of the various components making up their cumulative tradition. In other words, people tend to experience their cumulative tradition as a monolithic mass that they assume has remained largely undisturbed through the flow of history. On the basis of readings of certain passages in canonical texts and observations of the practices, beliefs, and values inherited from their parents' and grandparents' generations, inferences are made about the religion's general character as it is presumed to have been passed down over the centuries. Tradition is typically understood as stable, not dynamic.

Both traditionalists and modernists establish their understanding of their religion's "traditional worldview" in this way. The two differ, however, in the significance that they give to their data. Traditionalists typically assume that, until very recently, all mainstream devotees since the religion's founding viewed the world in essentially the same way. While there have been heterodoxies, these were perpetrated by fringe elements and soon thwarted. Only in recent times have pernicious aberrations threatened to undermine the faith's core structure itself, and these deviations are intimately linked to the modern worldview. In other cases, traditionalists largely ignore the religion's history during those centuries just preceding modernity. The contrast given is between classical authority and modern aberration. In either case, the religion is said to have passed through two main stages of history: traditional, characterized by genuine faith, and modern, characterized by spurious forms of faith and antagonistic secular worldviews threatening the religion's very existence.[31]

Modernists similarly construct their image of "tradition" through reference to personal and communal memory. Unlike traditionalists, however, they are more likely to question both whether certain interpretations and customs associated with inherited practice remain viable and whether certain aspects of the cumulative tradition, even some legitimized in canonical texts, were central elements of, or even date back to, the religion's founding. Hence, they base their view on two arguments: relevance and authenticity. First, while their predecessors' worldview may have been appropriate for their own time, it is no longer deemed adequate for the present, modern world. Reformers therefore wish to shed these perceived fetters. Second, many of the assumptions and beliefs shaping the practice of immediate predecessors are said to date back only to relatively recent periods—even in some cases only to the past several centuries—and, hence, represent an aberration from the original faith. More important, recent forebears are criticized for having strayed away from the dynamic spirit that characterized the early community. Unlike the founder and his or her initial disciples, who recognized the importance of engaging contemporary society, later followers have mistakenly latched onto literal interpretations of certain inherited notions and are, consequently, castigated. It is claimed that, by stubbornly adhering to particular elements, these literalists have lost the creative, vivifying spirit that led to the establishment of such beliefs, practices, and values in the first place. Modernists aver that they are not seeking a revolution, only a revival. Claiming that ancient traditional practice was itself modernist for its time, they argue that, to actualize that tradition, one must also be a modernist. It is a question not so much of following particular practices as of embodying a spirit of engagement. Modernists therefore posit a three-stage historical schema: original, genuine tradition (i.e., that practiced in the early community); spurious tradition (i.e., that promoted in subsequent, especially recent, centuries); and modern tradition (i.e., that which contravenes the false practices of spurious tradition to regain the underlying spirit of genuine faith).

Modernists share with traditionalists this rhetoric of sparking a "revival." In each case, there is an assumption that the tradition has gone through a deterioration that seriously threatens its very existence. After all, without such a downward spiral, there would be no need for revitalization. For traditionalists, this mainly means shedding recent, modern accretions. Modernists push back the time frame during which undesirable elements are believed to have crept in to adulterate the "true, pure, original" message. Hence, they tend to speak of distortions that have tainted the faith over the past few centuries and to celebrate modern innovations as effective means for returning to the underlying intent of the genuine teachings.

The degree to which new elements introduced by another cultural complex should be incorporated into one's inherited religious worldview constitutes an age-old debate. The language of "traditional" versus "modern" to describe a particular manifestation of this dynamic has arisen only over the past century. Employing the term "modernism" in relation to a particular form of religious practice first gained currency at the turn of the twentieth century in European Catholicism when Alfred Loisy used it to describe his theological method, which incorporated the acceptance of modern scientific knowledge and employed historical criticism to understand the Bible. Although Loisy was excommunicated for his efforts, his approach soon found vocal supporters within Protestantism, with such advocates as Shailer Mathews, Newman Smyth, and David C. Torrey calling for a "Protestant modernism." Liberals within other religious traditions subsequently appropriated similar language, typically broadening the discussion beyond the relation between religion and science to associate it as well with concepts of Westernization and secularization. Hence, Syed Ahmed Khan and Dr. Ali Shariati both called for "Islamic modernization," just as Mohandas Gandhi was espousing the modernization of Hinduism.[32]

The Venerables Taixu and Xingyun both follow a typical modernist reading of history. Master Xingyun tells audiences that the Buddha was very innovative and "modern" in his techniques for spreading the dharma. Even the Buddha's living quarters took advantage of the latest technology. "According to archaeological relics found in India," observes Master Xingyun, "the Buddha's place of residence was very progressive, no matter whether in terms of sanitation, ventilation, etc., so it was very 'modern'" (Shi Xingyun 1995a, 10:429). Master Xingyun asserts that the Buddha's immediate successors maintained this spirit of innovation and engagement, as did the early Chinese patriarchs. The social services provided by monasteries during the Northern Wei dynasty (424–532) and the Fields of Compassion Institutes (Beitian Yuan) of the Tang dynasty (618–905) all utilized creative, new methods to fulfill their humanistic mission.

Master Xingyun attributes the start of Chinese Buddhism's gradual and steady decline to specific historical, non-Buddhist sources that date to the advent of the Ming dynasty (1368–1644). He explains the initial catalyst as follows:

> Zhu Yuanzheng, the founding emperor of the Ming dynasty, had been a shramanera as a youth and had been a monk, so he understood the degree to which the tradition had penetrated into society, how easy it was for it to be accepted by the masses, and that it was not a force to be treated lightly. At that same time, some undesirable elements used religion to scheme rebellion. Hence, after the founding emperor took the throne, he instituted a variety of government policies to control all religion, especially Buddhism, in that way diminishing its influence over society. He required that monastics of the empire go to the mountains to cultivate themselves, thereby causing Buddhism to leave society, with no means of maintaining contact with the masses, and to become a refuge for only a small number who wished to cultivate themselves. Hence, the spirit of activism and of entering society to liberate people from their sufferings that characterized Sui and Tang dynasty Buddhism decayed, changing into a Buddhism of isolation and retreat in the mountain forests. The aftereffects of this policy can still be felt today, with the result that Buddhism does not fully put into effect its ability to save all beings and, instead, is a laughingstock among people. (Shi Xingyun 1995a, 10:427–428)

The master goes on to say that, ever since monks and nuns retreated to the forests and mountains, laity have sought their guidance only on the death of a relative, when they have called them in to conduct funerary rites so that the resulting merit could aid the deceased in attaining a better rebirth, perhaps even rebirth in Amitabha's Sukhavati Pure Land. People have, therefore, associated Buddhism with seclusion, escape, self-concern, individualism, otherworldliness, old age, and death. The tradition, in other words, is said to have lost its Mahayana spirit and, by the early twentieth century, to have become lifeless and out of touch.

Fortunately, the master continues, over the course of the twentieth century Chinese Buddhism began to experience a felicitous reversal in fortune. Under the leadership of Master Taixu, a small vanguard of young, progressive monks started actively to bring the Buddha's message to urban society. These monks established publishing houses and monastic colleges and employed other innovative techniques to attract intellectuals and reach the masses. Their slogans were "Open up the mountain gate, enter into society," "Buddhism must come down out of the mountains," and "Buddhism must be directed to the masses; it must be popularized and be made artistic" (Shi Xingyun 1995a, 10:428). Foguangshan regards itself as inheriting the leadership role that these monks carved out for themselves, utilizing the even more effective techniques developed since Master Taixu's time to bring his initial efforts to fruition.[33]

The key to the revival, according to Master Xingyun, has been the balancing of modern techniques with traditional wisdom: "Buddhism must use the most effective means to serve the needs of each age so that Buddha's spirit of compassion can be spread throughout society. This is what is meant by being 'modern' for each age. Hence, the Buddhist modernism that we promote is not something new but, rather, a revitalization of the ancient, carrying on the great heritage of the buddhas and great worthies of the past through methods that will be accepted easily and willingly by modern people" (Shi Xingyun 1995a, 10:429). The Buddhist revival, in other words, is both a modern revival and a revival of modernism. For the spirit to remain constant, the techniques, it is argued, must ceaselessly change. Foguang Buddhists therefore see themselves as instituting a modernization that revives Buddhism's original spirit. Hence, it is a modern revival that requires the perpetuation of genuine tradition, the sloughing off of spurious tradition, and the adoption of those modern innovations that can aid in spreading the dharma. Foguangshan takes great pride in organizing what it considers to be model, canonical dharma functions and in providing orthodox training for monastics. The facilities in which these activities take place and the process through which leaders are selected and decisions made, however, take full advantage of twentieth-century advances.

Master Xingyun's implementation of modernization therefore focuses on two areas: the appropriation of new technology and the institutionalization and democratization of monastic life. Technological innovations are embraced if they are judged to do one of two things: materially improve people's lives or directly facilitate the spread of the dharma. Modern means of communication and transportation, for instance, have been enthusiastically appropriated, Foguang clerics proudly pointing to the fact that Master Xingyun was among the first Buddhist monastics to use an automobile, slide projector, and radio and television transmission.[34] Computers and the Internet have received an especially eager reception, although, in practice, Foguangshan was initially behind Ciji Gongde Hui, Zhongtaishan, and Fagushan in developing websites.

More controversial among Buddhists in Taiwan is the introduction of air conditioners in Foguang temples. Detractors cite this as another example of Foguang monastics succumbing to the easy life. Master Xingyun's response is twofold. First, as we saw above, he claims that the Buddha himself took advantage of the most up-to-date means to provide proper ventilation in his dwelling. If the Buddha could do it, why cannot modern clerics? Second, the master states that the critics have mistakenly assumed that, because Foguangshan's public facilities have air-conditioning and other comforts, so do the monastics' private quarters.[35] This is not the case, he assures people. Living quarters for Foguang clerics are very simple, with neither air-conditioning nor soft beds. If anything, he contends, they are even more Spartan than the monastic lodgings found elsewhere around the island.

The second element of modernization embraced at Foguangshan is the adaptation of contemporary political ideals and administrative techniques to monastic life. Foguangshan has a clearly defined institutional hierarchy with codified guidelines for promotion, transfer, taking leaves of absence, etc. Each year, the headquarters sponsors a three-day conference on temple administration that is attended by several hundred clerics, approximately two-thirds of whom come from temples that are not part of the Foguang network. Integral to modern administration, emphasizes the master, is the democratization of the decisionmaking process, especially through the election of temple leadership. The master and his disciples are very proud of Foguangshan's balloting method for selecting the nine members of the Religious Affairs Committee.

The democratization of the temple leadership is important, Master Xingyun says, because it prevents a small coterie of aged clerics from monopolizing power. Just as the Buddhist revival began in China through the agency of young monks who were not entrenched in the status quo, it remains vibrant today because of the input of such young people. The revival is said to be both for China's young people and by its young people, purposively countering what has been the tradition's focus and power base in recent centuries. The inclusion of young people as

Buddhist leaders is considered, in fact, to revive the situation prevailing during the Buddha's time:

> Buddhism was originally a religion for the young but somehow became mistaken as a religion for the elderly. For instance, some people would like to place their faith in Buddhism but, in moments of irresolution, use the excuse, "I'll think about that in the future when I am old." They seem to think that Buddhism is a religion only for old men and women and that one cannot attain enlightenment until one's hair is white and one's teeth loose. There are even those who believe that Buddhism is a religion needed only at times of death, when sutras are chanted for the benefit of the deceased. All these are serious misunderstandings. In Buddhism, we can see that Shakyamuni Buddha had no facial hair. Only after a person has such facial hair can he be considered to be old. It is the same case with the bodhisattvas Guanyin, Manjusri, Samantabhadra, and Kshitigarbha: they all lacked facial hair. Not one bodhisattva or buddha in Buddhism has facial hair. Only the kami in Shinto have facial hair. Shinto is the religion for the old. Buddhism is not; it is a religion for the young. (Shi Xingyun 1983, 525–526)

This language of youth has posed something of a problem for the master as he and his senior disciples have aged. He has responded in two ways. First, he and other older monastics have retired from official posts of authority, allowing younger monks and nuns to take their place. This is why the master abdicated the position of Foguangshan's abbot in 1985 and why Vens. Cizhuang and Cihui (two of his most senior disciples) stepped down from the Religious Affairs Committee in 1997. On the completion of the 1997 elections for the Religious Affairs Committee, Master Xingyun made a special point of both commending the generosity of these nuns in giving younger members a chance to lead and pointing out the fact that the average age of the nine members on the committee was in the early forties. Despite such moves to keep Foguangshan's leadership youthful, no one either within or outside the organization has any doubt as to who still stands at the helm: Master Xingyun and the senior monastics who sit on the Veterans Council.

The second way in which the master has adapted his strategy for identifying Foguangshan with youth is to use the term, not literally, but to indicate a creative spirit open to change. The point is to be young at heart, regardless of the age of one's body. Hence, in 1978, an already fifty-one-year-old Master Xingyun could include himself when exhorting his audience: "We young Buddhists must resolve, not only to promote Buddhism's real spirit and original quality [lit., 'original face'], but also to establish our young people's Buddhism" (Shi Xingyun 1983, 527). The flip side of this coin is that, just because other Buddhist organizations may have younger leadership and monastic members, this does not mean that they better represent Buddhist youthfulness than does Foguangshan. During a meeting of several hundred Foguang monks and nuns, Ven. Cihui observed: "It is very strange. Many other Buddhist organizations also have many young monastics. Yet these young monastics already talk as if they are old. They close themselves off. Today's young clerics are very strange" ("Foguangshan Pan-Taiwan Staff Meeting" 1997). Youthfulness is equated with the ability to keep a fresh, innovative outlook. Those who are physically young are more likely to have such a creative spirit, but it is not necessarily so.

Reviving the Mahayana Spirit

The language of spirit (*jingshen*) in the sense of attitude or approach plays a prominent role in the Chinese Buddhist rhetoric of revival: returning to the Buddha's spirit of engagement with society; maintaining a spirit of youth in one's practice; and, perhaps most important of all, embodying the Mahayana spirit of compassionately serving all beings. Master Xingyun and his disciples frequently distinguish Mahayana from Hinayana Buddhism as a way clearly to enunciate the character and intent of their own practice. As do other Chinese Buddhists, the master states that the Hinayana (Xiaosheng) or "Small Vehicle" approach to Buddhism suffers from a narrowness of view, with the result that its practitioners are motivated by the selfish desire for their own liberation, with little regard for the terrible suffering of other sentient beings. Master Xingyun and other Chinese Buddhists therefore chide Hinayana monastics for locking themselves away in remote temples and feeding off the *dana* supplied by laity without concerning themselves in the least about others' welfare. Devotees of the Mahayana (Dasheng) or "Great Vehicle" approach take the bodhisattva path, vowing to attain enlightenment, not to escape this world, but to save all within it. Humanistic Buddhists, not surprisingly, are regarded as best fulfilling this Mahayana bodhisattva ideal.

The rhetoric of "Mahayana" versus "Hinayana" as it is employed among typical Chinese Buddhists often incorporates the assumption that the two terms refer to distinct schools within Buddhism, each with its own geographic territory. The Hinayana school is identified with the Theravada tradition, which is practiced in Thailand, Sri Lanka, Myanmar, etc. The Mahayana school, by contrast, is seen as having taken root in China, Japan, Korea, and Tibet. When one discusses with Foguang and other Chinese Buddhists the state of Buddhism in the Theravada countries, it soon becomes apparent that few have had anything more than very superficial contact with any Theravadin practitioners or literature. Employment of the categories "Mahayana" and "Hinayana" therefore says much more about Foguang and other Chinese Buddhists' self-understanding than it does about cross-cultural differences in Buddhism, ultimately revealing little, if anything, about the latter.

The functional import of these categories becomes quite evident when Foguang Buddhists either directly utilize the term "Hinayana" or more subtly employ the characteristics associated with Hinayana to comment on what they see as the inferior practice of other Buddhists in the so-called Mahayana countries. After watching a group of visiting Japanese nuns pass by, one cleric observed that, because they overly emphasize self-cultivation over benefiting society, Japanese Buddhists are similar to Theravadins. "Only in Taiwan, especially at Foguangshan, is Mahayana Buddhism practiced," she concluded. This statement implies that even most Chinese Buddhists are deemed to fall short of the Mahayana ideal. The description of Chinese Buddhism's decline since the Ming dynasty is couched very much in terms of a deterioration from Mahayana to Hinayana goals: retreating to the forests so as to pursue self-cultivation rather than acting on one's vow to save all beings. Master Taixu specifically characterized the Chinese Buddhism of recent centuries as Mahayana in name but actually Hinayana in temperament and practice.[36]

Such language continues to be heard at Foguangshan, not only as a description of the past, but also as a characterization of the deficiency of practice at other Buddhist establishments on Taiwan. Humanistic Buddhism as promulgated at Foguangshan is the epitome of the Mahayana bodhisattva ideal. To the degree that the programs at other organizations fail to correspond to Foguang practice, the cultivation of devotees at such organizations is said to assume a Hinayana character. Foguangshan is by no means the only group to employ the Hinayana/Mahayana rhetoric in this way. One lay devotee at Ciji Gongde Hui observed that, because of Foguangshan's emphasis on monasticism and self-cultivation, its adherents enact the goals of Mahayana Humanistic Buddhism only imperfectly. True Mahayana Humanistic Buddhism can be be found only, the devotee asserted, at Ciji Gongde Hui.

FOGUANG HUMANISTIC BUDDHISM IN CONTEXT

As the three most prominent organizations on Taiwan promoting Humanistic Buddhism, Foguangshan, Ciji Gongde Hui, and Fagushan share important traits, but they also differ in significant ways. Master Xingyun and Ven. Zhengyan, for instance, both emphasize compassionate service over rigorous meditation or abstract study. Meditation plays as little, and perhaps even less of, a role in the daily practice of the several dozen nuns who have tonsured under Ven. Zhengyan as it does in that of Foguang monastics. Each day at Tranquil Thoughts Hermitage begins and ends with half an hour of recitation. Most all the time in between these sessions is devoted to running Ciji Gongde Hui's charitable programs. Master Shengyan, on the other hand, is regarded as one of Taiwan's preeminent meditation teachers as well as a first-rate scholar. In his view, meditation is the most effective expedient means to aid all people, both monastic and lay, in eradicating the deep-rooted afflictions (fannao) that are the sources of suffering. Through purifying the mind, meditation frees it from attachment to ephemeral phenomena, thereby sparking realization of this world as a pure land. As an aid to help people attain this realization, Master Shengyan calls for the preservation of this world's beauty through protecting natural resources. Hence, he is closely associated with environmentalism.

Although Master Xingyun and Ven. Zhengyan share an emphasis on service, they differ in terms of focus and method. The Venerable Zhengyan stresses relieving the physical and psychological suffering of life through organizing medical works. Master Xingyun's efforts have centered more on creating joy through Buddhist education. One can say that, while Ven. Zhengyan specializes in the cultivation of compassion (bei; karuna), Master Xingyun's attention has been focused on mercy (ci; metta).[37] Ciji Gongde Hui members argue that their willingness to confront and alleviate suffering is more in line with the Buddha's teachings. Foguang devotees counter that Ciji Gongde Hui's programs are noble but offer only temporary relief. Ultimate liberation from suffering can occur only through realizing the joy of the dharma, and providing people with this opportunity, they say, is the mission of Foguangshan's multifaceted educational enterprises.

Master Xingyun's exhortations to experience a taste of Chan in daily life and to establish a pure land in the human realm underscore a defining characteristic of all interpretations of Humanistic Buddhism: the secularization of Buddhist practice.[38] In other words, the divisions between the supramundane and the mundane and between monastic life and lay life are blurred. The otherness of buddhas as sacred beings and of pure lands as radically distinct realms is minimized in favor of accentuating the possibility of enlightenment for all and the accessibility of purity even in our Saha world. There has always been a conflict between the otherworldliness of Pure Land Buddhism and the emphasis on "immanent transcendence" in the Confucian tradition.[39] This tension has been accentuated in recent years since modern scientific and humanistic values also have a this-worldly orientation. After asserting that, not only the Pure Land school, but all Buddhism will "fail to adjust to the needs of modern Asian man," Arthur Wright goes on to say: "We should be prepared therefore for a long period of secular faiths, of leadership that talks of economic and political salvation rather than the salvation of souls, of earthly utopias rather than heavenly cities" (1971, 26). Ironically, Wright's prediction describes the approaches of Master Xingyun, Ven. Zhengyan, and Ven. Shengyan perfectly: they all downplay the significance of rebirth in the far-off paradise of Sukhavati and emphasize the transformation of our own world into a utopia. Furthermore, as this approach conforms well with the Confucian orientation, such secularization of Buddhist doctrine does not particularly disturb Chinese spiritual sensibilities.

The softening of boundaries between the mundane and the supramundane affects practice; since everyday activities are legitimate and perhaps even the best forms of cultivation, lay and monastic spheres of performance merge. Clerics are urged to return their focus to this mundane world, primarily by instructing lay devotees how to bring an element of the sacred into their lives. The holy life of monastics is secularized, the secular life of laity sacralized. Foguang Buddhists assert that such convergence of monastic and lay life is an extremely effective strategy for transcending the dichotomy "sacred"/"profane." Their critics contend that all Master Xingyun and his disciples have succeeded in doing is trivializing the supramundane. In tacit agreement that Foguangshan had gone too far in secularizing, the master cloistered the headquarters, symbolically reestablishing an aura of sacrality around Foguangshan and reasserting the distinctiveness of monastic life.

Secularization typically incorporates an element of laicization; namely, religious duties are increasingly placed in the hands of nonspecialists. The existence of the sangha in Buddhism (i.e., of a community of religious specialists that is separated institutionally from the wider society) has always been anathema to the Confucian ideal of all persons being embedded in one harmonious community. Master Xingyun by no means wishes to endanger the special status of monks and nuns, but, by asserting that everyone, sangha and laity alike, must tend to the physical and spiritual needs of society, he has attenuated the difference in social status between the two groups. He asserts that only by working together can we hope ultimately to transform our world into a pure land; doctors, engineers, businesspeople, and laborers all have as much to contribute as does the clergy.

Laicization has occurred at Foguangshan with the establishment of BLIA, the society bringing together monastic and lay devotees as members, with a distinct emphasis on giving the latter a formal means of playing a leadership role in promoting the dharma. There are limits, however, to the degree to which Master Xingyun is willing to hand over the reigns of spiritual leadership to laity. On joining BLIA, all lay members must pledge never to hold dharma functions on their own or to interfere in clerical affairs. For Master Xingyun, although monastic and lay life need not be as radically separated as they are in many monasteries, there are, nonetheless, certain services that can be performed only by clerics. Clerics' special status and lifestyle must, therefore, be honored and protected.

In this respect, Ven. Zhengyan can be seen as having taken a more radical step toward laicization than has Master Xingyun, for, despite the fact that Ciji Gongde Hui has a much larger lay membership than does BLIA, Ven. Zhengyan only has eighty to one hundred nuns to support her efforts, all of whom are stationed at Tranquil Thoughts Hermitage. The Ciji Gongde Hui offices elsewhere in Taiwan and around the world are led by laity. Except for the post of chairperson, which is held by Ven. Zhengyan herself, most leadership positions in the foundation and association are likewise filled by lay members (Huang 2001). Master Xingyun feels that Ven. Zhengyan has gone too far in secularizing and laicizing her organization, and, hence, he has predicted (privately among his disciples) that, in the future, Ciji Gongde Hui will completely lose its Buddhist character, evolving into a secular philanthropic society.

The differences in method employed by Vens. Xingyun, Zhengyan, and Shengyan are a matter of emphasis rather than of clear-cut distinctions. Foguangshan, Ciji Gongde Hui, and Fagushan all engage in charitable and educational efforts. The dharma education activities provided by Ciji Gongde Hui's television station, websites, and magazines rival, if not surpass, those offered by Foguangshan. Fagushan is in the midst of founding a very ambitious Buddhist university that will be open to monastic and lay Buddhists. At the same time, both Foguangshan and Fagushan engage in medical-relief and other social-service enterprises. In fact, Foguangshan's mobile medical clinics predate Ven. Zhengyan's efforts in Hualian. The differences in focus nonetheless set the tone for each organization: Ciji Gongde Hui is the Buddhist group famed in Taiwan for its compassionate service, Fagushan is regarded as the foremost place to learn meditation, and Foguangshan is known for its educational endeavors. Having staked their claims in the spiritual marketplace, these organizations staunchly guard their domains. There is little cooperation or even interaction between the three communities. They are rivals more than allies, generally polite rivals, but rivals nonetheless, for they are all vying to attract a limited population: those Buddhists on Taiwan who find the rhetoric of Humanistic Buddhism appealing.

4 Humanistic Buddhism in Practice

HUMANISTIC BUDDHISM IN COMPARATIVE PERSPECTIVE
The slogan "Humanistic Buddhism" is employed in much the same way by Vens. Xingyun, Zhengyan, and Shengyan as the phrase "engaged Buddhism" has come to be used by a variety of Buddhist practitioners and scholars in Southeast Asia and the United States.[1] "Engaged Buddhism," which refers to those individuals and organizations that have explicitly applied Buddhist values in the attempt to influence contemporary political and social issues, is believed to have been coined by Thich Nhat Hanh in the 1960s, and the nonviolent, nonpartisan antiwar movement that he led in Vietnam is regarded as paradigmatic of Buddhist forays into the political world.[2] The outspoken Thai intellectual Sulak Sivaraksa is another figure closely associated with this trend of Buddhist activism; he is the founder of the International Network of Engaged Buddhists and has long shown himself to be quite willing to challenge Thai government policies, but without allying with any political faction. Both Thich Nhat Hanh and Sulak Sivaraksa have been exiled from their homelands for their efforts (the former living in France since having been granted asylum in 1966, the latter forced to take refuge in Europe, the United States, and Japan for a year beginning in the fall of 1991). Both have also been nominated for the Nobel Peace Prize. The dalai lama and Aung San Suu Kyi, recipients of the Nobel Peace Prize in 1989 and 1991, respectively, are two others often cited as exemplars of engaged Buddhism.

Thich Nhat Hanh, Sulak Sivaraksa, the dalai lama, and Aung San Suu Kyi have garnered fame primarily for their political stances. Other individuals and movements also placed under the rubric "engaged Buddhism" are known more for the social implications of their activities.[3] Dr. A. T. Ariyaratne and the rural development projects that have been initiated by his Sarvodaya Shramadana movement throughout Sri Lanka is one case in point. The efforts of Dr. B. R. Ambedkar and the Trailokya Bauddha Mahasangha Sahayaka Gana to elevate the social standing of India's *dalits* through their conversion to Buddhism have also been touted as exemplifying engaged Buddhism. So too have the nascent attempts throughout Asia to reestablish full bhikshuni ordination for women.

The place of political and social activism in Buddhist practice has received considerable attention from Buddhists in the United States, where such books as *The Path of Compassion* (Eppsteiner 1988) and *Engaged Buddhist Reader* (Kotler 1997) have brought together articles, not only by Thich Nhat Hanh, the dalai lama, Sulak Sivaraksa, A. T. Ariyaratne, and Maha Ghosananda, but also by such prominent American Buddhists as Gary Snyder, Robert Aitken, Joanna Macy, Robert Thurman, and Jack Kornfield. In these volumes, "engaged Buddhism" serves as a rallying cry, galvanizing Buddhists, and encouraging them to apply the wisdom and inner peace gained through their individual practice in such a way that it pervades their everyday lives and concerns and frames their responses to crises near at hand and around the globe.

As indicated above, the phrase "engaged Buddhism" first arose and gained currency within the Buddhist community itself. Subsequently, scholars have appropriated it as a heuristic tool to highlight commonalities in the assumptions, teachings, and methods of those Buddhists who subscribe to the principle of transforming current institutions according to a modernist reading of Buddhist ideals.

Christopher Queen and other Buddhologists who have adopted the concept articulate five broad characteristics shared by the diverse individuals and movements that they regard as falling under this heading. First, engaged Buddhists are reformers; they seek significantly to alter or even to abolish institutions that uphold inequality, spawn violence, or perpetuate other forms of suffering. In most cases, the focus of reform is a political or social entity, but, as in the call for reinstating bhikshuni ordination, the "liberation movement" may have as its goal internal reform within organized Buddhism. Second, the reforms espoused are couched in the language of modernism. Engaged Buddhists have a generally favorable attitude toward technological advancement, scientific progress, and such Enlightenment values as liberty, equality, and democracy. Third, engaged Buddhism secularizes religious practice by collapsing the sense of separation between the supramundane and the mundane and, consequently, shifts the focus away from the former and onto the latter. According to Sallie King (1996, 414), this is "a linchpin in the fundamental conception of engaged Buddhism." Christopher Queen adds that such secularization marks a significant departure from Buddhist practice as it has been passed down through the centuries. As he notes in his introduction to *Engaged Buddhism*:

> A profound change in Buddhist soteriology—from a highly personal and other-worldly notion of liberation to a social, economic, this-worldly liberation—distinguishes the Buddhist movements [to be considered in the volume]. The traditional conceptions of karma and rebirth, the veneration of the bhikkhu sangha, and the focus on ignorance and psychological attachment to account for suffering in the world (the second Noble Truth) have taken second place to the application of highly rationalized reflec-

tions on the institutional and political manifestations of greed, hatred, and delusion and on new organizational strategies for addressing war and injustice, poverty and intolerance, and the prospects for outer as well as inner peace in the world. (Queen 1996b, 10)

Queen continues that such secularization is also expressed in a trend toward the "democratization of spiritual practices" so that laity can actively participate. This laicization, the fourth major attribute of engaged Buddhism, may be seen in the constant exhortations to apply the dharma in all activities of everyday life and in the rise of laity to such positions of authority as meditation teachers. Finally, engaged Buddhists tend to affirm the positive role that other religious traditions can play in advancing spiritual liberation and world peace. They are, therefore, active participants in interfaith dialogue.

The parallels between Humanistic Buddhism and engaged Buddhism are obvious; all five characteristics of engaged Buddhism also pertain to the values and ideals of those who advocate Renjian Fojiao: reform; modernism; secularization; laicization; and interfaith cooperation. The Venerables Xingyun, Zhengyan, and Shengyan may all, therefore, be thought of as representative examples of engaged Buddhism. There are, of course, significant differences distinguishing each of these three from one another and from other figures who also have been placed within the category "engaged Buddhism." To better situate Master Xingyun, in this chapter I look more closely at the ways in which he conforms with and differs from other engaged Buddhists. Specifically, I consider the extent to which he has called for reforms in social and political institutions and the nature of the reforms that he has advocated. Before doing so, however, it will be helpful to begin by examining his usage of modernist language.

The Lexicon of Buddhist Modernism

Modern political and social movements have gained much of their justification and power by drawing on six concepts: human rights; freedom; liberation; equality; democracy; and justice. In the United States, the founding fathers opened the Declaration of Independence by pairing "liberty" and "equality" with what they saw as two other universal rights: "life" and "the pursuit of happiness." The motto for the Jacobins of the French Revolution was "liberty, equality, and fraternity." Six decades later, Karl Marx and Friedrich Engels predicted a coming worldwide proletarian upheaval that would free all people from the shackles of social class, thereby ushering in a fully egalitarian society. Twentieth-century reform movements such as women's suffrage and the American civil rights campaign similarly drew up blueprints of a just society in which all people would be free in the sense of having equal access to political, economic, and educational resources.

Not surprisingly, such rhetoric has found its way into the discourse of those religious leaders who have identified themselves as modernist political and social activists. Many of those at the forefront of the suffrage and civil rights movements in the United States, for instance, were devout Christians whose worldview had been strongly shaped by Protestant modernism and the Social Gospel. Hence, the speeches and articles by Francis Willard and Martin Luther King Jr. were replete with biblical references said to support democratic principles as God's instrument to actualize humankind's freedom and equality. The Indian Muslim Muhammad Iqbal relied on similar hermeneutics to interpret the Qur'an in such a way as to reveal democracy to be a natural expression of the Islamic affirmation of humankind's equality and brotherhood (see, e.g., Iqbal 1964, 1968). Iqbal's countryman Mohandas Gandhi called on Hindus and Muslims to work together toward a "true democracy," one founded on "nonviolence" *(ahimsa)* and "freedom *[swaraj]* of the masses" and in which "all stand on a footing of equality" (Gandhi quoted in Hay 1988, 256–261).

Modernist Buddhist leaders have also relied on such terminology. For Dr. Ambedkar, who found Gandhi's advocacy of a form of equality that maintained the caste system to be disingenuous, the key corrective was "freedom." As Ambedkar wrote in *The Buddha and His Dhamma* (1959): "[The Buddha taught] social freedom, intellectual freedom, economic freedom, and political freedom. He taught equality, equality not between man and man only but between man and woman. It would be difficult to find a religious teacher to compare with Buddha, whose teachings embrace so many aspects of the social life of a people, whose doctrines are so modern, and whose main concern was to give salvation to man in his life on earth, and not to promise it to him in heaven after he is dead" (quoted in quoted in Queen 1996a, 47). The fourteenth dalai lama, Tenzin Gyatso, shares with Ambedkar a deep, personal interest in the human quest for freedom. In his autobiography and other writings, he stresses that political freedom and spiritual liberation are intimately interrelated, the complete actualization of either dependent on the other (see, e.g., Gyatso 1990, 268–269). Such individual and communal freedom requires a realization that, as all people share buddha nature, we are equal and, hence, due the same fundamental rights. The Thai monk Buddhadasa Bhikku employed similar language, asserting: "Freedom, equality, and fraternity—in terms of *siladhamma*—exist fully in Buddhism and in the Lord Buddha's behavior. Buddha already had the character of democracy as understood morally" (quoted in Santikaro 1996, 164). It should be noted, however, that, with time, Buddhadasa began to have reservations about democracy, questioning the efficacy of a system that relied on the cumulative opinions of unenlightened folk (see Santikaro 1996, 173).

Of the Chinese equivalents for the concepts of human rights, freedom, liberation, justice, equality, and democracy, two have received the most sustained attention by Master Xingyun—equality and democracy. He supports movements for human rights (*minquan*), but he finds the term too centered on the self and, therefore, prefers to speak of human responsibility, not just toward other people, but toward all sentient beings.[4] His attitude toward freedom (*ziyou*) remains ambivalent. On the one hand, he recognizes the importance of political and intellectual independence; on the other hand, he, like many of his compatriots, regards an overemphasis on personal autonomy as merely an excuse for greed and indulgence. In other words, because freedom, as does human rights, focuses on the individual, it too must take secondary place to a higher calling: "There is a saying: 'Money is truly precious, life is even more valuable, but, for the sake of freedom, both can be sacrificed.' We Foguang Buddhists should amend this to read: 'Life is truly precious, freedom is even more valuable, but, for the sake of Buddhism, both can be sacrificed.' If we do not place our faith in Buddhism above our self, it is impossible to reap the valuable benefits that the religion has to offer" (Shi Xingyun, n.d.-b, 4). The type of freedom that the master advocates is, therefore, one that comes from letting go of those desires, passions, and ambitions that normally bind people within samsara, a freedom, in other words, of wise, voluntary restraint as guided by the precepts. Such a freedom is not that of the modern notion *ziyou* but that of the traditional Buddhist virtue *zizai*, which, predicated on an experiential realization of impermanence, interdependence, and emptiness, teaches a carefree attitude toward any and all circumstances in which one finds oneself.

"*Jiefang*," the twentieth-century Chinese translation of "liberation," does not show up in the master's writings, most likely because of its association with Communist ideology. The Buddhist term "*jietuo*" (a translation of "*moksha*") appears frequently, but only in the sense of emancipation from karma, and, hence, if anything, is a deliverance to be delayed until the indeterminate future, when conditions are ripe for universal enlightenment. Master Xingyun also speaks from time to time about justice (*gongping* and *gongzheng*), but only in passing, not as a central theme. This is not the case with the concepts of equality (*pingdeng*) and democracy (*renmin zhuyi*), both of which have received much attention from him. I turn now to a consideration of the first of these, focusing on how the master's understanding of equality has influenced the nature and extent of his engagement in tackling social issues. Next, I explore Master Xingyun's views toward the role that he believes leading members of the sangha should play in guiding democratic politics in general society.

ONTOLOGICAL EQUALITY REGARDLESS OF SOCIAL DIFFERENCE
Master Xingyun likes to point out that Buddhists recognized the equality of all people long before Western political and social thinkers took this position. His most comprehensive treatment of the subject, the lecture "Equality and Peace" ("Pingdeng yu heping"), opens by eluding to the following Buddhist sayings: "Sentient beings and buddhas are equal" *(sheng fo pingdeng)*, "Nature and form are equal" *(xing xiang pingdeng)*, "Self and other are equal" *(zi ta pingdeng)*, "Phenomena and principle are equal" *(shi li pingdeng)*, and "Emptiness and existence are equal" *(kong you pingdeng)*. We do not recognize the truth indicated by each of these statements, the master goes on to explain, only because our minds have become befogged by vexations, especially by the ignorance that comes with dualistic thinking. With these afflictions arises the causal chain of karma and, hence, the various forms, abilities, and conditions experienced by beings. Such distinctions, however, are superficial, created by the discriminating mind. Ultimately, "the essential nature *[benti zixing]* of all sentient beings is without duality" (Shi Xingyun 1996a, 1).

The master then provides four methods by which to delve beneath surface differences to once again plumb the depths of equality. He begins by observing that equality requires mutual respect between people: "A fundamental Buddhist principle is that we all should respect and treat one another equally, regardless of nationality, race, social class, gender, or age.... Only if we are able to abandon our prejudices and biases, treat all with respect and equality, and care for one another will we be able to live together in an atmosphere of peaceful joy" (Shi Xingyun 1996a, 2). The master then observes that equality requires the ability to stand in each other's place. To appreciate the hardships of others rather than harshly judging their foibles, and to share in their successes instead of jealously envying them, one must be capable of imagining oneself in their circumstances.

The third way of seeing the world so as to experience equality is to recognize the mutual interdependence of all beings. The master states: "We all rely on one another for our birth and continued existence. In you there is me, and in me there is you. Through conditions are phenomena born, and through conditions are they extinguished; all are mutually interdependent forms. Only on understanding the conditioned arising of all things can one see equality in the midst of difference and find unity among contradictions, hence discovering the true nature of suchness *[yiru]*." Finally, asserts the master, all are equal in that there is no difference between one and many: "Most people desire abundance and dislike scarcity, leading to constant comparisons and contention. This gives rise to delusion and creates karmic effects. It is for this reason that the world is in perpetual turbulence. In truth, according to Buddhism, one is many and many one; there is no difference between these. All are complete and fulfilled in their basic nature. Because the myriad things [*fa*, "dharmas"] are of the same suchness, of one body are they born. Every single thing has an intimate, inseparable relationship with the whole" (Shi Xingyun 1996a, 4–5, 5).

Each of the four methods advocated by the master for realizing equality points to the concept's moral implications. Equality and interdependence are the ontological ground on which the ethical imperatives of respect and magnanimity rest. It is because of its moral implications that Master Xingyun pairs equality with peace. As he says: "Equality and peace are two sides of the same truth" (Shi Xingyun 1996a, 7). By this he means that, ultimately, neither is possible without the other: peace can occur only through respecting the equality underlying any difference, and the recognition of this equality requires a calm, unperturbed mind free of vexations.

The concept of equality has for many thinkers of the modern era been a strong impetus for demanding social change. Such activists have insisted that, because people are equal, they all have a right to equitable access to political and economic power. In "Equality and Peace," Master Xingyun recognizes the potential that advocating equality can have for redressing injustice. At the very outset of that address he notes: "Today, the world is in turmoil: politically, the strong exploit the weak; economically, there is disparity between the wealthy and the impoverished; races and religions are often at odds; and regional and gender inequalities persist. All these problems that we have been unable to solve peaceably result from not treating each other equally" (Shi Xingyun 1996a, 1). The master's strategy for resolving these divers forms of inequality is to initiate ever-expanding movements of moral regeneration. He does not advocate any form of activism that becomes confrontational. In his opinion, campaigns for radical alterations in social structure invariably cause considerable suffering yet only touch the surface of the problem since they fail to penetrate dualistic thinking. He believes that a gradualist approach, one that transforms people's very way of experiencing their social embeddedness, will have a much more long-lasting effect. The danger of such a tactic is that it easily serves merely to legitimate the status quo.

The gradualist tone pervading Master Xingyun's interpretation of equality is evident in the fact that he has chosen to link equality with respect and peace, both of which, while noble virtues, tend toward maintaining the current social and political order. In other words, associating equality with these moral standards creates a much different attitude and approach than does joining it with liberty and justice, for instance. Furthermore, because equality is essentially seen to be a supramundane rather than a mundane truth, its actualization occurs only with progress in cultivation. This means that, for the time being, equality can become manifest only within the monastic community.

This assumption is noticeable in the following story, told by Master Xingyun during a lecture that he gave at the Sun Yat-sen Memorial in Taipei in 1979:

> The fact that Upali, who came from a humble background, could join the sangha founded by the Buddha showed that, once anyone from the four castes renounced, all were simply Shakyamuni's disciples, with no distinction between the eminent and the humble, the rich and the poor. From Upali's accomplishments in renouncing, attaining high levels of awakening, and becoming the arhat most renowned for adhering to the precepts, one can see that the religion promoted by the Buddha is one of true equality, breaking down class and racial barriers. In any other given society or profession, we realize that attaining complete equality is extremely difficult. How can the rich and the poor, the intelligent and the ignorant, and the old and the young, be on an equal footing? As we differ in our circumstances, our professions, and our lives together, universal equality can never be expected to come easily. Yet, before the Buddha's dharma seat, all are equal, and all are the same, regardless of gender, age, or socioeconomic condition. (Shi Xingyun 1983, 292–293)

Social and financial inequality disappear in the sangha. It would be unrealistic, however, to expect this to occur in other "circumstances" and "professions." The sangha serves as a model for all others, but only one that points toward possibility for the distant future, not imminent social transformation.

The moderately conservative tone that subtly shapes the master's treatment of equality is reflected in the lack of any concerted push for social change on the part of Foguangshan. This becomes apparent when one looks more closely at the Foguang perspectives on women's rights, wealth, and politics.

HARMONIZING MALE AND FEMALE

Discussions of women's rights and of equality between the sexes have been quite prominent in recent years at Foguangshan, which has played a leading role in making full bhikshuni ordination available to all women regardless of Buddhist lineage.[5] The high point of this effort thus far came in the spring of 1998, when Foguangshan made it possible for 136 women representing Sri Lankan, Thai, Burmese, Tibetan, and Chinese Buddhist traditions to journey to Bodhgaya, India, for a triple altar ordination. Two years later, an additional seventy women from Sri Lanka joined in another ordination at Foguang headquarters. This initiative has been quite controversial within Buddhist circles. Conservative Theravadins argue that the bhikshuni order cannot be reestablished in their branch of Buddhism because it disappeared there in the eleventh century and, according to the vinaya, ten ordained nuns must be present to confer the precepts. In the Tibetan tradition, where there have never been fully ordained nuns, similar arguments are raised. While the dalai lama voiced support for the ordinations and sent a representative to witness the proceedings in Bodhgaya, he has remained equivocal on the issue of bhikshuni ordination.

The crux of the issue is whether nuns of the Mahayana Chinese tradition can confer vows on Theravadin and Tibetan novices. Foguangshan argues that nuns of different lineages certainly can provide this service. Foguang clerics note that the Chinese bhikshuni order was founded by a group of nuns who journeyed from Sri Lanka to the Middle Kingdom in the fifth century. Chinese nuns are now honored to have the opportunity to return the favor and ordain their Theravadin sisters. Furthermore, state Foguang clerics, ordination is a question, not of doctrinal lineage, that is, whether one is of the Mahayana, Theravada, or Vajrayana tradition, but of following the vinaya. Chinese bhikshuni ordination is conducted according to the Dharmagupta Vinaya. While this is not exactly the same text as those utilized in ordinations conducted in Sri Lanka, Thailand, and Tibet, it agrees with them on all important points.

Making such ordination available to women from the Theravadin and Tibetan traditions is without doubt a significant reform within institutional Buddhism. Two points need to be kept in mind, however. First, this reform has no effect on the status of nuns in Taiwan, for whom the rank of bhikshuni has been available for centuries. Foguang and other Chinese Buddhists are holding themselves up as a model for others to follow. They are, for the most part, justified in doing so, for Chinese nuns generally enjoy prestige and responsibility comparable to that accorded monks. Nonetheless, while the reform being advanced is internal to the Buddhist tradition, it has no transformative effect on the Chinese Buddhist community itself and, hence, is a relatively benign cause for it to champion. It is always easier to ask someone else to change than it is to change oneself.

More important, the call for bhikshuni ordination to advance equality between nuns and monks has not translated into a similar advocacy of social equality between laywomen and -men. The collapse of gender-role distinctions is assumed to be possible only with the higher degree of cultivation that occurs on entering monastic life, and, at this level, distinctions are said to melt away because the nuns have transcended their sexuality, an assertion symbolized by reference to them as "dharma brothers" (*fa xiongdi*). Hence, even at the more rarefied strata of monasticism, the central point is not equality of the sexes. Rather, that entire issue has become irrelevant owing to the symbolic elevation of women to the status of men. Such a view, which has held sway in Chinese Buddhism since the establishment of the bhikshuni order during the fifth century C.E., allows distinctions in gender roles to remain intact for laity.

In lay society, equality is to be expressed through men and women respecting one another and harmonizing their roles so that life can function smoothly and peaceably. In "The Buddhist View of Women" ("Fojiao de nüxing guan"), Master Xingyun describes the differences between men and women as follows:

> According to the general view, men distinguish themselves through their masculine strength and power. Although there are dashing, handsome men, the male appearance cannot compare with natural feminine beauty and attractiveness. . . .
>
> Confronting a problem, men express masculine courage by overcoming the obstacles and marching onward. Women, however, are patient, modest, and able to find peaceful means to resolve problems. Men are sometimes unable to match this. Men are very creative and adventurous. Sometimes the easygoing and harmonizing character of women can compensate for men's rash carelessness so that the two supplement and complete one another. Men are more coarse and lack restraint. Women are careful and attend to details. Behind every successful man is a supportive woman. Men emphasize reason; women emphasize feelings. Men tend toward strength; women are generally tender. Men and women differ in many respects, not only biologically, but in character development as well. Since women have a weaker physique and more biological hindrances, their social position is lower. Hence, it is easier for them to enter a life of faith, and they have a stronger inclination toward religion than do men. Because women care for the children and tend to the family, they are more likely to confront aging, and, hence, therefore it is easier for them to experience the world's impermanence. . . . Men join the workforce, while women are the homemakers, where they experience the difficulties of tending to material resources. Hence, women are more generous than men

and better understand the law of cause and effect. (Shi Xingyun 1995a, 10:258–260)

As can be seen from the foregoing passage, the proactive *yang* element of men and the more passive, yielding *yin* nature of women are understood to complement one another. This translates into separate social functions. The master assumes that the focal point for men is their work. Women, on the other hand, are primarily homemakers. The secrets to being a good husband and a good wife are, therefore, strikingly different. The master gives married men four suggestions for keeping their wives happy:

> 1. Come home for dinner: One often hears the sentence, "Dad is home for dinner." After the hustle and bustle of being out all day, not only should a man return home to eat his dinner, but he should make every effort to do so, for it is an opportunity to promote family unity and harmony. Eating his meals at home will also prevent him from going to entertainment houses or drinking establishments, so turmoil in family life will naturally be avoided.
> 2. Don't keep too much pocket money: Money can build a successful business, but it can also destroy a good future. Refraining from carrying around too much pocket money will prevent a man from gambling, keeping a mistress, or engaging in other unsavory practices.
> 3. Leave messages: Some wives resent the fact that, once their husband has gone out the door, it is as though he vanishes without a trace.... When a couple has reached the state that neither cares about the other's whereabouts, their family life has come to a standstill.
> 4. Socialize together: Many husbands use the socializing necessary as a part of business as an excuse to conceal their objectionable, inappropriate activities from their wives. In the end, the family is in tumult, and feelings are severed. If one truly needs to socialize, one ought to go together with one's wife. Allowing one's wife in this way to participate in one's work as an able assistant can nurture mutual understanding and, moreover, avoid unnecessary family squabbles. (Shi Xingyun 1995a, 10:261–262)

Women "supplement," "support," and "assist" men. They may find employment and to a certain extent are encouraged to do so, but they should not be career minded.[6] Master Xingyun cautions: "Nowadays, many women have ventured into the work world. Working women increase society's wealth and resources, but, when the couple does not cooperate, latchkey children and problem teenagers result. One cannot ignore this issue. There are some women who do not work but spend all their time in frivolities, to the neglect of family matters, so that many family disputes arise. This is even more imprudent." In the master's view, the woman is the key figure to a harmonious family. He provides the following four suggestions for being a good wife:

> 1. Be warm and comforting: The husband works hard all day, having to taste the sweet and bitter of life, see through snobbery, and deal with frustration and failure. He needs to come home to a comforting wife who can help him overcome difficulties and recover from disappointments. The last thing he needs on returning home is to be accosted with, "Where have you been? Only now you remember to come home. Look, our neighbor Mr. Chen has bought his wife expensive jewelry and clothing, but you are so worthless and make so little money. I am so unlucky." Such words will never let the husband raise his head. . . .
>
> 2. Make delicious meals: People say that the way to control a man is through his stomach. It is not easy for a husband to come home for dinner. If the meal is always boring and not to his taste, of course he will find an excuse to eat out. If the meal is delicious, every meal flavorful, so that he does not become used to eating out, he will naturally keep coming home at the appropriate time. Moreover, there is no need to say that balanced meals are necessary to protect the husband's health.
>
> 3. Keep a beautiful house: Contemporary society promotes human beautification. Such beautification includes not merely beautifying one's personal appearance, body, and environment but also beautifying our language, mind, and home. Sweep and dust the living room, place flowers by the window, hang a painting on the wall so that it is pleasant and elegant. When your husband comes home, give him a cup of tea, some reading material. If you make life like paradise, can he have any reason not to come home? . . .
>
> 4. Communicate everything: Women like to keep little secrets—not letting their husband know about that bit of money, storing it away for the unexpected; doing something that they want to conceal from their husband. A husband and wife are a couple. Their relations are warmest when they are both honest and tell each other everything so that there are no secrets at all. In this way, family life will naturally be completely happy. (Shi Xingyun 1995a, 10:265, 263–264)

Despite the fact that the wife herself may have been "working hard all day," she is still expected to make a delicious dinner and keep a tidy house. It is her responsibility to continually draw the husband back home, or else, as we have seen, he may be tempted to carouse. In the name of family harmony, the woman is expected to yield to the husband. Paraphrasing the *Sutra of Lady Yuye (Yuyenü jing)*, the master asserts that a wife must act as the "mother," "assistant," "younger sister," "maid," and "partner" toward her spouse. She must care for, comfort, and encourage him in the same way as did his mother, support him as an able adviser, respect him as a younger sister would her older brother, attend to the myriad household chores without complaint, and share his joys and tribulations (Shi Xingyun 1995a, 10:269–270).

If there are family problems, the wife is regarded as shouldering the brunt of the blame. Women whose husbands are having affairs, for instance, are advised by Master Xingyun to look at their own behavior to determine what has driven the men to look for pleasure and contentment elsewhere:

> Sometime a woman will complain that her husband is fooling around. What is the reason for this? It is because, when he goes to the other woman, he sees a wonderful smile, hears soft, warm words, and receives all kind of kind consideration but, when he returns home, what he gets is a cold look, coarse scolding, as if he is in hell, so he naturally has no mind to go home and thinks only of going to the paradise outside. Women cannot use only their appearance to win over a man's heart. Only through sweet, loving words and considerate attention will you garner a man's eternal devotion. (Shi Xingyun 1995a, 10:263)

Master Xingyun's comments imply that it is in men's nature to have a wandering eye. He does tell them that extramarital affairs are against the precepts, yet he also makes it quite clear that, when men fail in this regard, much of the fault lies in the pestering conduct of their wives.

While Master Xingyun's attitude concerning proper gender relations is on the conservative side, it would be a mistake to exaggerate this: he certainly does not advise women to quit the workforce or to remain submissive to their husbands in all regards. He also provides a variety of lay leadership positions for women through the Buddha's Light International Association (BLIA). On the other hand, neither is he a strong advocate lending a voice for women's concerns and problems in contemporary society. His moderately conservative characterizations about men and women simply reflect mainstream Taiwan society's current understanding of gender roles. As with many Chinese, he believes that feminist ideology as it has evolved in Western countries is too disruptive of familial and social harmony without truly benefiting anyone, including women.

THE DHARMA OF WEALTH

Master Xingyun's understanding of supramundane equality subsisting within social differentiation and stratification is closer to Gandhi's interpretation of equality than it is to Ambedkar's castigation of the entire caste system. The assumed legitimacy of hierarchical social differentiation naturally pertains to economic relations as well. The justification of economic disparity is readily apparent in the following story from the *Sutra of One Hundred Fables* (*Bai yu jing*), which was published in *Awakening the World* (*Jueshi*), Foguangshan's free monthly magazine issued to devotees:

> Once upon a time there was a king whose many possessions included several beautiful castles filled with priceless antiques, famous paintings, countless gems, and many imported rare plants. He was not in the least happy, however, for his two sons continually squabbled with one another over money.
> One day, the king fell ill and died. After the two brothers attended to their father's funeral, they began dividing the estate. Because each hoped to receive the larger share of the property, no matter how the belongings were meted out, neither brother felt satisfied. Finally, the older brother angrily said, "The only way to be fair about this is to divide each thing right down the middle." The brothers thereupon cut in half every gem, antique, painting, and rare plant. As if this were not enough, they then had some workers split the palaces in two.
> From that day on, each brother lived in half a palace. The walls were covered with half portions of various paintings. On the tables were placed half portions of antiques. Each brother ate out of half of a bowl, washed his face in half a basin, and slept on half a bed. Since each had only half of an umbrella, whenever it rained, half the body would get wet. (Shi Juezhao 1997, 46)

Master Xingyun and his disciples find this tale instructive because, as the Foguang commentary observes, its chief lesson is that "manifest equity" (*juedui de gongping*), that is, that which is determined by "calculating everything exactly" (*jinjin jijiao*), is, in fact, a subtle expression of greed and selfishness and, hence, does not establish "true equity" (*zhenzheng de gongping*). This latter arises when each person is given a fair opportunity to cultivate his or her talent and is apportioned a just share of material resources, one depending on need and contribution to society.

In Master Xingyun's view, because capitalism provides opportunity and abundance for all who are willing to work industriously, it has proved to be the most effective sociopolitical ideology for actualizing "true equity." So long as the occupation in which a person is engaged is legal and moral, the master regards both the process of work and the ability to help others through wisely dispensing the resulting resources as potentially serving important roles in a person's self-cultivation.[7] Such an affirmation of the beneficial role that economic activity can have in spiritual cultivation reminds one of Max Weber's provocative thesis that the "this-worldly asceticism" espoused by the early Puritan sects (especially Calvinism) catalyzed instrumental rationality, which in turn was essential to the rise of the "spirit of capitalism." A brief summary of the main points of Weber's argument will allow a better understanding of the dynamics underlying Master Xingyun's version of the "Buddhist capitalist spirit."

Weber explained that, in the Calvinist doctrine of predestination, proof that one had been chosen by God to be among the elect lay in the ability to engage in laboring diligently to promote God's glory in this world and maintaining ascetic self-control in the face of temptation. The moral status of all activities, including those in the sphere of economics, depended entirely on what they revealed about the person's faith: "Wealth is thus bad ethically only in so far as it is a temptation to idleness and sinful enjoyment of life, and its acquisition is bad only when it is with the purpose of later living merrily and without care. But as a performance of duty in a calling it is not only morally permissible, but actually enjoined. . . . To wish to be poor was, it was often argued, the same as wishing to be unhealthy; it is objectionable as a glorification of works and derogatory to the glory of God" (Weber 1958, 163). Giving ethical legitimacy to making and accumulating money, not as a means of obtaining material comfort, but as a sign of a higher calling, set the stage for the creation of a disciplined labor force and for the regularized investment of capital, the two most fundamental requisites of rationalized capitalistic enterprise.

According to Weber, religions other than Christianity lacked the proper balance of worldliness and asceticism to spark the modern capitalistic mode of rationality. Buddhism he saw as being too ascetic. Because its goal of attaining nirvana requires a complete renunciation of all modes of behavior and thinking that tie one to the samsaric world, in Buddhism, Weber held, "all rational purposive activity is regarded as leading away from salvation, except of course the subjective activity of concentrated contemplation, which empties the soul of passion for life and every connection with worldly interests." Weber concluded: "There is no path leading from this only really consistent position of world-flight to any economic ethic or to any rational social ethic" (Weber [1968] 1978, 628–629).[8] Confucianism also failed to encourage capitalism, but, ironically, for the opposite reason: it has simply been too accommodating of the present world order. Lacking any ascetic values, it seeks to align the individual with the intrinsic harmony of the universe. Such adjustment to the world "as it is" could not engender the dynamic instrumental rationality necessary for the evolution of the industrial capitalistic spirit.[9]

The late-twentieth-century financial success of Japan and the four "mini-dragons" (Hong Kong, Taiwan, Singapore, and South Korea) has led scholars to rethink Weber's dour assessment of the compatibility of East Asian ethical systems and capitalism. The part that Confucian values may have played in the region's phenomenal economic boom has been a topic that has garnered the most scholarly attention. In the "post-Confucian hypothesis" proposed by Tu Wei-ming, Gordon Redding, and others, seven features of the Confucian worldview are highlighted as having been particularly important in East Asia's successful implementation of its own cultural style of modern capitalism: the emphasis on personal self-cultivation as a communal act; the perception that the person is not an isolated individual but a center of relationships; the recognition that family cohesion is crucial for "organic" social solidarity; the insistence that education go beyond the transferal of practical knowledge to include character building; the understanding that, although laws are important, even more vital to social unity is the perpetuation of custom and propriety (li); the faith in government authorities as exemplary leaders; and the commitment to an anthropocosmic vision that regards the secular world as sacred.[10] These values, in conjunction with such situational factors as U.S. aid and an eager, plentiful workforce, have given rise to a vibrant form of modern capitalism, albeit one quite distinct from that to be found in Western countries.[11]

Tu Wei-ming suggests that the post-Confucian hypothesis implies that modernization can be understood, not merely as Westernization, but also as a complex cultural phenomenon with pluralistic manifestations. From such a vantage point, Tu sees the Christian West as providing "the genetic rather than the structural reasons for modernity." He continues: "The Confucian case clearly indicated that a non-Protestant, non-individualistic, and non-Western form of modernity is not only conceivable but also practicable. The implications are obvious. The Daoist, Buddhist, Islamic, Hindu, Jain, Sikh, Maori, Hawaiian, or Native American ethic, as a response to the challenge of the modern West, can also create its own unique form of modernity. . . . In a comparative civilizational perspective, this may mean many if not all spiritual traditions can at least in principle creatively transform themselves so that they can provide rich symbolic resources for the modernizing process" (Tu 1992, 10).

Let us consider the relevance of Tu Wei-ming's comments specifically for the case of the Buddhist tradition. Only very recently have scholars begun to delve into the subject of Buddhist resources for spurring capitalistic development. The topic has not been raised before for two reasons. First, economic growth has been uneven across regions in which the Buddhist tradition functions as an important cultural force. Sri Lanka, Thailand, and Myanmar have not as of yet experienced the burst in prosperity already enjoyed by their Buddhist brethren in East Asia. Hence, it is more difficult to construct a convincing argument for a direct relation between Buddhist values and the assimilation of a modern capitalistic lifestyle.

Second, some of the most prominent Buddhist leaders of the contemporary world have been skeptical of capitalism, tending to see Buddhism as more compatible with socialism. Master Taixu, for instance, advocated the establishment of "democratic socialism" since, in his view, capitalism feeds off and nurtures people's greed and selfishness (Pittman 2001, 182, 192–193). Buddhadasa has employed similar reasoning in his call for "Dhammic socialism" (Thai: *dhamma samgamaniyama*) (Santikaro 1996, 166ff.). The dalai lama too is skeptical of capitalism, although he has been equally disheartened by the heavy-handed manner in which communism has been implemented in mainland China and elsewhere. In his autobiography *Freedom in Exile,* he therefore informally allies himself with those environmentalist parties that appear to be blazing a middle path between the promise of Marxism and the more humane implementation of capitalism (Gyatso 1990, 268–269). Soka Gakkai president Daisaku Ikeda follows a similar tack when he employs the language of "humanistic socialism" to describe the ideal, egalitarian society of the future that transcends both free-enterprise capitalism and the system of materialistic socialism (Metraux 1994, 49–52).

Despite these countervailing factors, scholars are beginning to examine how certain Buddhist groups are employing their religion's symbols and resources in such a way as to foster a fruitful interaction between capitalistic modes of operation and dharmic values. Martin Baumann, who has conducted extensive research on the introduction of Buddhism into European countries, argues that the Friends of the Western Buddhist Order (FWBO) has successfully integrated the Buddhist notion of right livelihood with the economic rationalism that Weber saw as essential to modern capitalistic endeavor (see Baumann 2000). He notes that those who work at Windhorse Trading and other FWBO cooperatives view their commercial activities as furnishing multifaceted resources for treading the bodhisattva path:

the daily challenges of the work site are said to afford a perfect setting for applying and extending the positive states of mind induced through formal sitting meditation; the inevitable contacts made with a wide range of people within the business world allow for the subtle promotion of Buddhist teachings; and the commitment to contributing the majority of profits to furthering FWBO's projects in India cultivates nonattachment, generosity, and compassion. The group's objective is not to adapt Buddhist teachings to aid devotees in excelling within the capitalist system, thereby merely buttressing the status quo, but, on the contrary, to employ market strategies in such a way as to create a new society, one that accords with Buddhist ideals.

Baumann assumes that the FWBO's European context has been key in bringing together the ethics of a tradition rooted in Asiatic agricultural societies with the industrial milieu of the modern Western world.[12] If he were pressed further on this point, Baumann would most surely agree that Buddhism has not had to come to the West to feel the impact of modern industrialization and capitalism. It therefore should not surprise us that, in the ideology of the Asian-based organization Foguangshan, one finds an enthusiastic endorsement of the mutually beneficial relation between Buddhist values and the world market system. In other words, Foguangshan can be placed alongside FWBO as a provocative manifestation of the Buddhist capitalist spirit. This can be seen in the following six points: Foguangshan's positive valuation of money; its glorification of diligent work as a form of Chan and a concrete means through which compassionately to serve others; the interpretation of impermanence as both the dynamic principle making progress possible and a call to cherish every moment as a fleeting opportunity for self-cultivation through work; the utilization of the Buddhist concept of karma to motivate the unceasing accumulation of wealth by accentuating the idea that socioeconomic standing reflects past moral virtue and, hence, one's current spiritual level; the fostering of "this-worldly asceticism" through constant admonitions that monks and nuns temper their asceticism by being active in the mundane world and that laity bring an element of monastic austerity into their daily lives; and the offering of the cleric community as an exemplar of those virtues especially conducive to maximizing human fulfillment through capitalistic success. Let us consider these elements in more detail.

Master Xingyun sees nothing wrong with making money or becoming rich, so long as one has done so in a moral way and shares the benefits of one's prosperity with others. At the BLIA Youth Conference of 1–5 January 1997, he explained his position toward wealth:

Are we better off with or without money? Some Buddhists think that disdain for money indicates high integrity. In my opinion, a lack of money does not indicate purity. Most social problems come from poverty. If Amitabha Buddha were poor, how could he possibly build a seven-story complex, pave roads with gold, and cover lanterns with gems in his pure land? Money is not necessarily good or bad. It depends on how you use it. Can you tell me if this fist is good or bad? If I hit you with it, you will sue me in court. But, if you have a sore back and I massage it, you'll say, "Hit harder, harder." Dharma is neither good nor bad; good or bad is dharma. So a fist is neither good nor bad; it depends on how you apply it. Money is the same. Use it in a good way, and it is good. Use it in a bad way, then it is bad. Although some Buddhists regard money as poison, it can also support cultivation. Such money can be regarded as "pure wealth" [jingcai]. In considering things, don't be too rigid, thinking, "This is permissible, this is not." The Buddhist approach is to take a middle path to consider things realistically. Why not regard your personal investments as public investments? Likewise, why not regard your personal possessions as public? Why not invest your present wealth for the sake of the future? Why not make your possessions be the source of enjoyment? Why not make transitory wealth into eternal wealth?

In concrete terms, this positive assessment of money means that Master Xingyun expects people to work diligently, remain thrifty in their expenditures, yet also generously contribute to charitable and religious causes. Because money is inherently neither good nor evil, transforming it into "pure wealth" largely depends on the person's intention, which may be analytically broken down into three aspects. First, the work must be such that it benefits rather than harms others; it must be an instance of "right livelihood" (*zhengming*). Second, the person must have the proper attitude toward carrying out the work, valuing it as a form of service and cultivation rather than merely regarding it as a means to a materialistic end. Third, the proceeds accruing from one's employment must be spent wisely, in a fashion consonant with Buddhist values.

During a talk at Foguangshan's "International Conference of Outstanding Buddhist Women" in October 1996, Master Xingyun suggested that, while still young, women work hard so that they will not be overly reliant on their husbands and that, on reaching old age, they pledge their estate to a worthy cause so as to prevent their children from bickering and becoming lazy. Both this advice and the story related above about the two brothers evince a disapproval of inheritance, which is believed too often to spark greed, to create discord within families, and to undermine the work ethic of those who have received large bequests. Inheritance is also contrary to the master's vision of a truly meritocratic society, in which material affluence follows in accord with each individual's talent. This is how class society is to be transcended even among the laity. Legacies are to go, however, not to the government, which would smack too much of socialism, but to charitable and religious organizations, thereby allowing people a final means of accumulating merit, and buttressing the financial health of mediating institutions such as Foguangshan.

Diligence is not merely extolled for the fruits that it brings about. It is valued in its own right. As the master says: "Industry is nutrition" *(mang jiu shi yinyang)*, and "Industry is cultivation" *(mang jiu shi xiuxing)*. The high level of concentration required in fully productive endeavor is believed to trigger the same calmness and focus of mind engendered through Chan meditation. Formal sitting meditation is, therefore, to be but a preliminary and supportive form of cultivation, achieving real significance only through application in more practical activities. Furthermore, because such "active Chan" has as its goal the liberation of all sentient beings, it avoids the tendency toward selfish preoccupation with only one's own enlightenment that is said to undermine traditional methods so easily.

Along with fostering unperturbed concentration, industry is a form of cultivation in that it both reflects and nurtures patience. The Chinese Buddhist term *renru* (Sanskrit: *ksanti*) emphasizes forbearance in the face of insult, a rendering that Master Xingyun regularly mentions, particularly if Foguangshan has recently received unfavorable press. In addition to using the term in this way, the master also employs it as synonym for "diligence" (Chinese: *jingjin*; Sanskrit: *vyayama*). On one occasion, while discussing his favorable impressions of the United States, describing it as a pure land in which such Buddhist values as the six paramitas are already practiced, Master Xingyun praised the American work ethic:

> As for patience *[renru]*, Americans are very patient *[rennai]*. Patience *[ren]* does not mean that if you yell at me I do not reply or that if you hit me I do not hit back, swallowing my pride and forgetting about it. These are not examples of patience. Patience refers to taking responsibility. Patience refers to having strength. Patience is also a sense of optimism, of striving forward, and of sacrifice about the burdens one must bear. Americans work hard, don't they? They patiently endure such hardships. . . .
>
> Everyone knows about Americans' diligence. Americans are active, dedicated, and hardworking. We believe that America is a heaven. In

truth, Americans are very industrious. They work conscientiously, without laziness or mediocrity. Their work ethic is very much like the Buddhist notion of diligence. (Shi Xingyun 1995a, 10:177)[13]

Concentration, patience, and diligence in secular work do not have the same profound significance as does the self-conscious cultivation of Chan, *ren*, and *jingjin* through engagement in Buddhist practice. The two spheres of activity are related, however, for development of key virtues through secular employment lays the foundation for Buddhist cultivation, and conscientious engagement in following Buddhist teachings will, in turn, increase one's effectiveness in secular endeavors.

Thus far, we have seen that a strong work ethic is supported in the Foguang insistence on meritocracy and in the reading of industriousness as a legitimate method of cultivating three of the paramitas. Diligence is further encouraged through an emphasis on time as a limited and, hence, precious commodity, an understanding that derives from Master Xingyun's interpretation of impermanence. In one anecdote, the master relates:

> As a child, I heard the neighbors, on their way back from school, singing at the top of their lungs, "Time is money, money cannot buy time." The phrase grabbed my attention at once, and I was stricken with fear. At that precise moment, I understood the value of time; it needs to be treasured. I renounced everything and became a monk early in my teens. Once I read in a sutra the four-line verses of Samantabhadra Bodhisattva's caution to all beings: "Life decreases as the days pass, like fish with very little water, how could there be happiness?" I was startled by the words. Thenceforth, I took the bodhisattva's statement as a warning not to waste time and to always value the importance of time. As the enterprise of propagating Buddhism has expanded and developed, I have become increasingly busy. Many have asked me, "Why do you keep such an intense schedule?" They have no way of knowing my aspirations. How I wish I could accomplish a day's tasks in one hour, a year's tasks in one day, and the tasks of many life times in one life. . . . When I have an appointment, I never let others wait, so their time is not wasted. In addition, I make good use of what little time I can manage off my tight schedule to quickly finish matters that require my attention. As for meetings, I gather the heads of all related departments in one place at the same time for consultation in order to solve many problems at once. I never hurry from one place to another just to perform repentance services

or chanting sessions. I also do not waste my time on meaningless social functions. My main focus is to work conscientiously and seriously so as to put forth all my efforts and attention on the building of a pure land. (Shi Xingyun, n.d.-a, 13)[14]

Not a moment can be wasted. Cultivation through work must be a continual, unceasing commitment. When advised to take it easy while recuperating from heart surgery, the master replied that he would have opportunity enough to rest once he passed away. Until then, there was too much to do. During one meeting with his disciples, when it was brought to his attention that a certain person had seemed to take an overly long time to recuperate from the flu, the master announced: "If a person is well enough to watch television, he is well enough to recite Amitabha's name. If a person can eat full meals, then his appetite is healthy enough to return to a full schedule" ("Meeting of Foguang Abbots and Department Chiefs, Taiwan Branch Temples" 1997a). Taking their cue from the master, Foguang monastics proudly work seven days a week and late into the night. Very few take the two days of leave permitted per month. As the monastics like to say, they work whether "tired or rested, hungry or full." They believe that, in so doing, they are fulfilling the bodhisattva ideal, according to which one must be willing to sacrifice everything one has, even one's very body, for the benefit of others. The ability to work despite fatigue is regarded as an indication, not only of a person's devotion, but also of his or her level of cultivation, for it signifies lack of attachment to the self and actualization of the energizing power of the dharma.

Lay devotees frequently praise Master Xingyun's incredible vigor and remark that he is a great inspiration to them as they seek to balance their own hectic schedules. They too are to work diligently toward establishing a pure land on earth, both directly through their engagement in right livelihood and indirectly by contributing the money that they have thereby earned to Buddhist (i.e., Foguang) enterprises. Through such contributions they have, in fact, fulfilled yet another paramita, that of *dana*, generous giving.

The financial and social success that is said assuredly to result from conscientious work is also given religious significance in that a person's socioeconomic station in this life is believed to reflect the religious and moral trajectory of his or her actions in the past:

> Although we have all been reborn as humans, we nonetheless have individual karma. Hence, the karma that has led to us all becoming people is called "guiding karma" (*yinye*), and this indicates that the karma of all

people, having much the same force, has led to us becoming humans and not being reborn as dogs, oxen, or horses. Nonetheless, although we have all transmigrated to become people, among us there are such differences as the worthy versus the foolish and the wealthy versus the poor. These differences are due to the karmic force *(yeli)* created by individuals during their past lives. Those who have been generous become rich; those who have killed others attain a short life span as a result. This type of karma that fills out the specifics of an individual's life is called the "karma of completion" *(manye).* (Shi Xingyun 1979, 555–556)

Hence, there is overlap between the moral/spiritual and material/physical realms. The general connection between past virtue and present material prosperity has an important implication for the symbolic function that money can play: financial success can be treated as a gauge of moral virtue. The ability to accumulate money is interpreted as indicating that one has the sufficient good roots *(shan gen)* to progress quickly in self-cultivation. The more one is able to amass, the deeper and healthier are those roots assumed to be. The roots will sprout, however, only if one expends this wealth wisely, living frugally, and cultivating fields of blessedness *(futian,* i.e., through contributing to Buddhist enterprises): "Mahayana bodhisattvas believe that, the more money one has, the better it is, and that, the higher position one attains, the better it is. As long as they do not make one greedy and are beneficial for promoting Buddhism, are not money and position very useful tools?" (Shi Xingyun 1983, 605–606).

The direct bearing that socioeconomic standing and generosity in providing *dana* have for religious status is expressed in Foguangshan's nine grades of benefactors. Generally, ranking is determined by the amount of money donated to the monastery. Those in the lowest grade have contributed NT$10,000 (approximately U.S.$300), those few in the highest grade millions of New Taiwan dollars. The master and his disciples hope that devotees will contribute generously, but they are careful to dissuade anyone from donating beyond their means and to remind people that they should give in a completely carefree manner *(zizai)* without any ulterior motives of personal benefit.

Many Buddhists in Taiwan, including many Foguang devotees, believe that there is a direct correlation between participation in Buddhist activities, especially dharma functions, and success in business ventures. The merit accrued through donating large sums of money is said to create such favorable conditions, including financial prosperity, that it can be regarded as an investment in personal well-being that will bring a sure, and abundant, return. Master Xingyun discourages such thinking, asserting that it is predicated on a misunderstanding of the law of cause and effect that places too great a materialistic slant on religious cultivation:

> People of contemporary society misunderstand the law of cause and effect. Those who recite Amitabha's name blame him when a problem arises. They say, "I've been cheated out of money and gone bankrupt. Why didn't Amitabha protect me?" "I haven't made any money in the stock market. Where is Amitabha's power?" "I am a vegetarian, but my health is not improving. Why is Amitabha so lacking in compassion?" But where is the connection between reciting a buddha's name or being a vegetarian and wealth, fortune, health, and longevity? The connection between a particular cause and a particular effect must not be confused. How can a person who plants a melon expect to get beans? Chanting and keeping a vegetarian diet are in the realm of religious and moral cause and effect. Amassing great wealth is in the domain of economic cause and effect. For the body to be healthy or to enjoy longevity, there are causes and effects in the domain of health: one must exercise and maintain hygienic practices. How can people push all responsibility onto Amitabha of religious faith? There are too many people today who, having confused the connection between particular causes and effects, are not able accurately to understand the law of cause and effect. (Shi Xingyun 1995a, 10:198)

Note that the master does not employ *dana* as an example, for, in Buddhist tradition, the offering of money and other material goods as a form of religious service links these two realms of cause and effect and, hence, generates merit that will manifest itself in both planes, if not in this lifetime, then in some future birth.

The master's point is that the relation between these spheres is complex and long-term and that any attempt to create immediate material benefits through religious acts is, therefore, misguided. When a person donates an unreasonably large amount of money given his or her financial standing, the result will, in fact, be the opposite of what was intended: because the motive was tainted, the act's religious efficacy will be negligible (perhaps even detrimental), and, by depleting monetary resources so that they are no longer available for reinvestment, the act will produce financial hardship, not prosperity. Master Xingyun therefore frequently reminds devotees that it is better to give regularly in small amounts and that they should always do so within their budget. In his lecture, "The Buddhist Perspective on Wealth" (see Shi Xingyun 1995a, 10:203–228), the master draws from passages in the *Samyuktagama Sutra (Za ahan jing)*, the *Maharatnakuta Sutra (Da bao ji jing)*, and the *Parinirvana Sutra (Niepan jing)* to offer the following financial advice to lay devotees: 40 percent of family income is to be devoted to one's business or career, 30 percent is to take care of family needs, 20 percent should be put away as savings, and 10 percent is to be given away as charitable donations.[15] Foguangshan also has certain institutional safeguards to decrease the likelihood of devotees overextending themselves by contributing more than they can afford. The Foguang policy is to spread financial responsibility among as many people as possible and to receive the pledged amount in small payments over a long period. In this way, no one person gives an inordinately large amount or strains the family budget (i.e., pledges an unreasonably large amount relative to their financial status—some very wealthy devotees donate millions of New Taiwan dollars). By following this method, Foguangshan encourages judicious personal financial planning and extols the greater efficacy and security provided by communal joint investment.

This note of prudence is balanced by a much more assertive attitude toward taking calculated risks in one's business ventures. To encourage such risk taking, Master Xingyun once again draws on the concept of impermanence, which he values as the dynamic principle allowing for improvement and progress:

> I don't know when Buddhism began being colored by pessimism. Whenever Buddhists see each other, they inevitably say such things as, "Life is suffering! Such suffering! All is impermanent! Oh, impermanence!" Buddhism is happy in character and joyful in spirit. It speaks of boundless happiness, endless compassion, and covering all the world with joy....
> The Buddha taught that all phenomena are impermanent. Impermanence is wonderful, for it makes change possible. Hence, the bad can be transformed into the good. Because of impermanence, adversity can be followed by felicity, and bad luck can change for the better. It is because of impermanence that fate is not irrevocably determined. Our task is to disseminate the seeds of joy so that all the world may attain the dharma and everyone can live a complete, fortunate, and joyful life. (Shi Xingyun 1995a, 10:192)

Before there is decay, there is growth, and, in fact, even within decay are found the seeds for future renewal. By seeing only the decay and failing to appreciate the good news implicit in the principle of impermanence, asserts the master, Buddhists have become listless and defeatist. The secret to success is to identify the seeds of growth and to create the proper conditions so that they may flourish. Instead of clinging to the old, one is enjoined to constantly seek out the new, which promises to be even better than its predecessor. This emphasis on impermanence as progress is given physical testimony at the Foguang headquarters, where construction never stops and the already-decaying buildings of a decade or two ago are being replaced by ever larger and better-equipped facilities.

Master Xingyun very much has a pioneer spirit that incorporates both creative adaptation of modern innovations and a drive to beat competitors in exploring new fields. Foguangshan regards itself as being in the vanguard of Buddhist practice. As one nun told me: "The Buddhist world looks to Taiwan for leadership, and Taiwan Buddhists look to Foguangshan." The organization's literature often describes its events as "turning a new page in history." A list of the more than fifty "Foguang firsts" is often proudly displayed. Among these proclaimed innovations are the first employment by a Buddhist master of slide projectors, radio, and television; Foguangshan as the first Buddhist organization to establish in Taiwan a Buddhist choir, sports club, medical clinic, and liberal arts university; Hsi Lai University as the first Buddhist college in the United States (although this is not accurate); and Foguangshan as the first Buddhist group anywhere to sponsor a large-scale international ordination ceremony (at Bodhgaya).

Impermanence is, therefore, not only descriptive of life, but also prescriptive of how to live life to the fullest, that is, by being on the cutting edge in one's particular field. Master Xingyun and his disciples exemplify a can-do spirit. "Only useless people continually say it isn't permissible," exhorted the master at one meeting, "A useful person says everything is possible." Because of this attitude, Foguangshan is very willing to take financial risks, regularly relying on loans, and embarking on projects even before the necessary funds are secured. The key to successful growth is to be driven by creative ideas, not bound by financial restraints. If the ideas are sound, it is assumed that the financing will come. Such steady improvement in service and product through continual expansion certainly provides a noteworthy model of the modern capitalistic spirit for laity to emulate.

In the foregoing analysis, I have repeatedly shown how Master Xingyun in particular and the Foguang monastic community in general serve as a paradigm of Buddhist capitalism from which lay devotees can draw important lessons and, thereby, actualize this lifestyle in their own circumstances. Weber would certainly have been shocked by the assertion that Buddhist clerics can serve in this capacity. In his view, the mendicant lifestyle of monks is the antithesis of economic rationalism (see Weber [1968] 1978, 630). Far from acting as a countervailing paradigm to capitalist society, monastic life at Foguangshan is transformed into a paragon of the entrepreneurial spirit. As one newspaper stated, if Master Xingyun had chosen to enter the business world rather than to renounce secular life, he very well could have become another Wang Yongqing (one of Taiwan's wealthiest citizens) (Shi

Xingyun 1994, vol. 3, entry for 24 January 1990). Foguang clerics exemplify the capitalist work spirit at its very best: they are a highly organized, diligent labor force, remaining frugal in personal life, but daring to expand the horizons of their "occupation." Most important, the dualism between secular occupation and religious cultivation collapses: to practice Buddhist teachings is to serve others productively, and any beneficial service is an expression of dharma.

The master's optimistic attitude toward capitalistic enterprise has been criticized by some within Taiwan's Buddhist world. In certain cases, detractors have questioned Master Xingyun's motives, asserting that his main goal is the acquisition of wealth and prestige. As one visitor to Foguangshan said with evident disgust: "I smell money and power." Master Xingyun therefore finds himself continually, but unsuccessfully, attempting to shed the label "commercial monk" (*jingying heshang*). Others do not dispute the master's sincerity or integrity but do voice serious reservations about the efficacy of the methods that he utilizes. These reservations center on the belief that, although the master may regard the making of money as only a means to actualizing the goal of promoting the dharma and, thereby, transforming the world into a pure land, for those who have not yet reached a sufficient level of cultivation (and this would include, not only laity, but also most monks and nuns) the means can too easily become the end, creating greed and attachment, and serving merely to maintain the inequalities, hypocrisies, and sufferings of the status quo. The debate ultimately comes down to differing attitudes toward presentation and cultivation style. Critics of Foguangshan are wary of the seductive power of wealth and possessions. Master Xingyun and his followers, on the other hand, see the seemingly endless possibilities for improving the human condition afforded by the wise management of financial and material resources.

MONASTICS IN POLITICS

Creating Links of Affinity with the Political Elite

It is well-known in Taiwan that Master Xingyun maintains close relationships with many prominent political figures on the island. Major newspapers regularly display large photographs of him chatting with or posing alongside some of the most influential officials of the Republic of China (ROC). The master's very public role as moral adviser to politicians is a point of pride among his devotees and a source of censure among his detractors. He has not always enjoyed such a cozy relationship with those in power, however. Even before he came to Taiwan in 1949 as part of a medical relief team of clerics, Master Xingyun's relations with the Kuomintang

(KMT) were shaky. Both the Nationalists and the Communists had interrogated him for intelligence about the other two years earlier, while he was running the primary school of Dajue Temple (just outside Nanjing). Shortly after he arrived in Taiwan, a rumor that three hundred of the monastics who had come to the island had been sent by the Communists as operatives led to Master Xingyun and other monks being jailed for twenty-three days. Sometime later, police followed the master constantly after having received anonymous reports alleging that he was in radio contact with the mainland and disseminating pro-Communist literature. Master Xingyun continued to be monitored by the national intelligence bureau throughout the 1950s, especially when he organized large public gatherings or any activities for college students. Suspicions persisted into the late 1960s. Not long after the founding of Foguangshan in 1967, local authorities voiced concern over reports that the fledgling community was stockpiling some two hundred rifles.

Master Xingyun's relations with the government improved as he became better established. Having experienced firsthand the inconvenience and even the danger of being perceived as an outsider and a potential threat, he seems to have actively sought the trust of political authorities. At the same time, KMT officials may have felt that the ability of this monk from Jiangsu Province to gain a devoted following among Taiwanese natives made him a vibrant symbol of cultural unity. The transformation in the perception of Master Xingyun from possible enemy to valued ally occurred in the early 1970s. In 1971, four years after the founding of Foguangshan, Minister of the Interior Xu Qingzhong took part in the ribbon-cutting ceremony for Great Compassion Hall, the mountain's first temple. Two years later, Jiang Jingguo, then premier of the executive yuan, visited Foguangshan for the first time. He would come to the mountain on three more occasions, the last time being in May 1978, during his presidential election campaign. Since then, pilgrimages to the mountain have been made by a vast array of vice presidents, secretaries-general, governors, ministers of government departments, legislators, county magistrates, and city mayors, especially as elections approach. Chen Lü'an and Wu Boxiong, both powerful players on Taiwan's political stage, have publicly identified themselves as the master's devotees. President Li Denghui visited the monastery three times, first in 1992, once again shortly after the 1996 presidential elections (to show that, as a supporter of democratic politics, he held no grudge against the master for publicly endorsing a rival), and for a final time in 1999 (taking the opportunity formally to announce that 8 April, the Buddha's Birthday, would henceforth be observed as a national holiday).

Master Xingyun's close relationship with the government is manifest in other ways as well. He has served on the Central Advisory Committee (CAC) of the

KMT Party since 1988. The post is ceremonial, involving no policymaking; the committee's 210 members attend funerals and weddings on the party's behalf. The master nonetheless apparently feels a bit uneasy about having such a formal association with the island's dominant political party, for he frequently tells people that he has never attended any of the CAC meetings. A year after joining this committee, Master Xingyun accepted another semiofficial post as well, presiding over the board of directors of the ROC Mongolian-Tibetan Cultural Center Foundation. This ad hoc group of several clerics and government officials used NT$10 million donated by General Jiang Weiguo to build a Mongolian-Tibetan Buddhist temple on land provided by the government. The foundation may have had a cultural objective, but the strong political overtones of such a project are readily evident, given the tense relations between the People's Republic of China and Buddhist Tibet. The most recent political committee to which the master has been named is the Overseas Chinese Affairs Commission (OCAC), established in 1997. The government of Taiwan asked Master Xingyun to join the OCAC in recognition of the role that Foguangshan's global network of temples plays in maintaining a sense of community and of loyalty to the ROC among overseas Chinese.

The master has also received numerous awards. For his efforts in promoting theater, he received a government Contribution to the Dramatic Arts Award in 1980. Five years later, he became the first Buddhist leader to gain recognition from the Education Department for meritorious service. In May 1997, both the Ministry of the Interior and the Ministry of Foreign Affairs conferred on Master Xingyun medals of commendation, the highest honor bestowed by these offices on ROC citizens. Three years later, the executive yuan added a National Public Service Award to the master's credentials.

KMT sanction of Foguangshan's activities is also evident in the fact that the party has allowed the master access to government halls to give lectures on Buddhism and to have his disciples perform sutra recitation concerts. The monastery performed a three-day "Concert to Spread the Dharma through Buddhist Chanting" at Sun Yat-sen Memorial Hall in 1990, for instance. Two years later, as part of the "Festival of Traditional Chinese Arts" sponsored by the Taipei municipal government, two hundred clerics from the Foguangshan Monastic Academy chanted Buddhist scriptures in the National Music Hall. Since 1988, Master Xingyun has also been invited to propagate the dharma among and confer the triple refuge on soldiers stationed on Jinmen and Mazi Islands, a task that he has continued to perform periodically at various army bases and military academies. From 1991 to 1996, the BLIA conducted its worldwide Buddhism examination, not only at Foguang temples, but in public schools as well, although this privilege was rescinded as unconstitutional by Taiwan's courts in 1997.

Master Xingyun has long evinced an interest in establishing ties with politicians beyond the borders of Taiwan, an interest that gained momentum as Foguangshan expanded its operations worldwide. As early as 1963, he joined a tour organized by the Buddhist Association of the Republic of China (BAROC) and funded by the KMT that met with Prime Minister Jawaharlal Nehru of India, King Bhumibol Adulyadej of Thailand, and President Diosdado Macapagal of the Philippines. Because his relations with KMT and BAROC officials were quite tenuous at the time, however, the master had little chance of making such international travels a regular practice. Throughout the 1970s and 1980s, he was able to make only a few contacts with political figures outside Taiwan. Prime Minister Li Guangyao of Singapore visited Foguangshan in 1972. Master Xingyun and the king of Tonga, a Pacific island nation, met in 1978. Eight years later, Prime Minister Brian Mulroney of Canada sent a letter to congratulate Foguangshan for organizing the "World Sutric and Tantric Buddhist Conference."

Recognition from a wide spectrum of non-Taiwanese political figures has blossomed only since the founding of BLIA, Foguangshan's lay organization. His Excellency Sir Clarence Seignoret, president of the Commonwealth of Dominica, joined as a non-Buddhist "friend" during the association's 1992 inaugural ceremony. One year later, Santiago Ruperez, director of the Spanish Chamber of Commerce (Spain's unofficial government representative to Taiwan), made the pilgrimage to Foguangshan to take the triple refuge. Vice President Guadalupe Jerezano of Honduras visited the mountain in May 1995. French president Jacques Chirac as well as U.S. president Bill Clinton and vice president Al Gore sent letters congratulating BLIA on the convening of its 1996 World Conference in Paris. That same year, Vice President Gore visited Hsi Lai Temple, and Chancellor Helmut Kohl of Germany invited two members of the Berlin chapter of BLIA to introduce the organization to him during the Berlin International Cultural Fair. Several Australian politicians, including Her Excellency Leneen Forde, the governor-general of Queensland, visited Chung Tien Temple in the spring of 1997 to allay the community's fears in the wake of anti-Chinese sentiment sparked during the previous year's elections. Elizabeth Aguirre de Calderon, the first lady of the Republic of El Salvador, visited Foguangshan in April 1998.

SHOWING CONCERN OR INTERFERING?

Buddhist monastics with a high level of cultivation can interject moral stability into democratic politics. Clerics must be very careful when attempting to do so, however, lest their own purity be sullied by the lure of power and prestige. Contending that such a thing has happened with him, some of Master Xingyun's detractors have saddled him with the pejorative label "political monk" (*zhengzhi heshang*). During the January 1997 BLIA Youth Conference, one of the many times that the master has defended his political involvement, he asserted:

> Politics is not in competition with religion. Politics does, however, play a very important role in society. We cannot neglect its role as a force. After the Buddha attained enlightenment, he acted as an adviser for several kingdoms. Yet no one has ever accused the Buddha of being a "political Buddha." Many sutras also tell rulers how to act and administer their realms. After Buddhism was introduced into China, several Buddhist clerics served as grand masters for the entire kingdom and advised the ruler. There are also records of monastics being involved in various political matters and administration. The current problem of the status of religion in Taiwan is due precisely to the fact that outsiders [*waihang*] with no understanding of religion have been placed in charge of religious affairs.
>
> In Southern Buddhist countries, Buddhism is used to guide politics. For instance, in Thailand, the king prostrates to the head of the sangha. When a king mounts the throne, he will be crowned by the head of the sangha. In Tibet, politics and religion are one. The second law of the Japanese constitution states that everyone should respect the triple gem. . . . As a Chinese, I appreciate Western society because, in China, there has been no respect for religion. The West, however, emphasizes freedom of religion. That is why Chinese Buddhism can survive there.
>
> Generalissimo Chiang Kai-shek invited Master Taixu to establish a Buddhist political party. I can empathize with Master Taixu, for, in that conservative environment, he did not dare to organize a Buddhist party. The best he could do was propose that twenty monastic members be included in the national assembly. Although Chiang Kai-shek wanted to have Buddhists involved, others opposed such involvement, thinking that, if twenty monastic members joined the national assembly, they would have too great an influence. Master Taixu's political philosophy toward politics followed this principle: "Be concerned with politics, but do not interfere in them" [*wen zheng bu ganshe*]. As Buddhists, we should be concerned about society and all beings, but we should not take any formal government position. Show concern, but do not interfere. Master Taixu's ideal, however, has never been actualized over the past forty or fifty years. In

mainland China there is a People's Negotiating Council, which has many Buddhist monastics and laity participating, so they can show their care for the nation. Unfortunately, as we all know, they are no more than "a vase for flowers" [i.e., they have position, but no power].

In Taiwan, only one monastic has served on the national assembly. Strangely enough, no one calls him a political monk. I am the one regarded as the political monk. That monk is terrific. Whenever the other representatives get into a fight or brawl, he starts to recite "Reverence to Bodhisattva Guanyin" ["Namo Guanshiyin Pusa"]. . . . This whole issue doesn't mean much to me. Personally, I do not think that monastics should engage in any political activities. But we can cultivate lay people to be involved in politics. Monastics should emulate Ven. Taixu: show concern, but do not interfere with politics. My whole life I have abided by this idea: care for society and for all beings.

. . . You all know that Buddhist temples have had to pay taxes and that their monastics have had to serve in the military. . . . In order to achieve equality for religion, especially for Buddhism, we need many representatives at the national level to protect our rights. . . . As for politics, Buddha placed the responsibility of spreading the dharma in the government on lay people, especially on those officers serving in the imperial court. In fact, Buddhists all know to follow the principle of being neither too distant nor too close to politics. But, as you know, social progress requires entrance into politics. For example, if you care about social welfare and other matters, then the politics are very complicated. . . . When you see Buddhism involved in politics, don't Protestants and Catholics get involved in politics, don't they have political power? . . . In our nation we should exercise our compassion to all beings without establishing particular ties.

As can be seen from these comments, Master Xingyun wavers in the degree to which he believes that Buddhist masters should participate in government affairs directly. Where exactly does "showing concern" end and "interfering" begin? By "showing concern" he seems to mean that clerics should serve as moral guides so that political leaders will foster the type of ethical society necessary for Buddhists and others to fulfill their spiritual aspirations. Monastics should not, however, actively lobby for the implementation of particular policies. To do so constitutes "interference."

When the master says that clerics "should not take any formal government position," he does not mean this to be a proscription against sitting on ceremonial or advisory committees, for, as we have seen, he himself has served in this capacity on several occasions. In the master's view, the main function of such points of contact between leaders of the Buddhist and the political worlds is to provide opportunities for the face-to-face encounters so important to the sparking and nurturing of friendship, trust, and confidence. They are, in other words, fortuitous occasions for *jieyuan*. To the degree that the official seeks moral or religious guidance from the master, to that extent can he or she be regarded as a devotee, a relationship that may be formalized through the taking of refuge under the cleric, but one that frequently remains casual. These devotee-officials become the lay Buddhists who more or less self-consciously employ the dharma to shape government policy. The role of the Buddhist master is to remind these devotees who hold so much power in the mundane realm to keep an eye on the larger picture even as they remain immersed in the fray of political maneuvering and contention.

Clerics can be especially valuable in dissuading politicians from placing personal power and success over national harmony. Master Xingyun has on several occasions recalled how he helped Wu Boxiong, one of his most prominent devotees, from becoming ensnared in a bitter campaign feud. The master explains:

> The 1994 gubernatorial race was hotly contested. This was the first popular election to be held in the history of China. In the beginning, there were three well-matched candidates: Mr. Wu Boxiong, the minister of the interior, who had entered the campaign without the KMT's approval; the sitting governor, Song Zhuyou, who was the KMT appointed candidate; and Chen Dingnan, the Democratic Progressive Party's candidate. I accidentally ran into Wu Boxiong at the Sun Yat-sen Memorial Hall during a kickoff ceremony for a nationwide antidrug campaign. We went back to Foguangshan's Taipei Branch Temple for a three-hour heart-to-heart talk. I advised him that he should consider the matter in a comprehensive way and not lose sight of the big picture. When two people of power and influence fight each other, it is embarrassing for the individuals, the party, and the country. Wu, a man of wisdom, promptly withdrew from the campaign the next day. Such magnanimity won widespread praise. He won a battle with his own heart and avoided a political war. (Shi Xingyun 1997d, 416)

This was not the first time that Master Xingyun had sought to avert public feuding between politicians. He tells of several other instances in which either the KMT or a particular politician requested his assistance in resolving a dispute. In

1967, for example, the KMT asked for him to help pacify one of his devotees who was undertaking legal action against the party after it had overturned her election victory as a county assembly representative in favor of someone else. "For the sake of local and national stability," states the master, "I promised to try my best" (Shi Xingyun 1997d, 414). He offered the woman a position as director of the Virtue Welfare Center (a charitable organization that he oversaw) and convinced her that she could do more for society in that capacity than as an assemblywoman. She agreed, withdrawing her lawsuit against the KMT. Two years later, the KMT again asked for the master's assistance in averting a nasty legal battle between Kaohsiung mayor Wang Youyun and a provincial assemblywoman surnamed Zhao. Once again, Master Xingyun was able to resolve the conflict, this time by calling the two antagonists to meet together with him on Foguangshan, where they worked out their differences. In 1994, shortly after the master had convinced Wu Boxiong to withdraw from the gubernatorial race, he also resolved an imbroglio involving, not merely two political adversaries, but the military and a local community. The admiral in charge of a navy base in Dashu County (where Foguangshan is located) refused to pay the county government an annual water right fee of NT$10 million for ten wells that had been dug on the base. After the general asked the master to mediate the dispute, the principal players met together on Foguangshan, where a compromise was formulated.

Master Xingyun was called in on two occasions in 1995. First, Taipei mayor Wu Dunyi telephoned him at Hsi Lai Temple in the United States in the hope that he could end a dispute between the mayor and a father-son team surnamed Wang over who should fill the post of deputy mayor. Master Xingyun was more than willing to lend a hand, but, in this case, the adversaries patched over their differences before he had returned to Taiwan. Not long after he had returned, however, a much more contentious altercation occurred that did require his negotiatory services. In early July, an explosion at a dynamite-manufacturing plant not far from Foguangshan had destroyed several nearby farmhouses. Outraged residents of Dashu Township took to the streets, insisting that the factory be closed down immediately. When company and political representatives met at Foguangshan, they still could reach no agreement. Only after the master visited each side separately several times could he convince both to agree on a deal in which the factory would be moved to a more remote site elsewhere in Kaohsiung County within five years.

Certain themes weave through the master's accounts of each of the instances in which he mediated political disputes. First, he strongly believes that such disagreements are best handled through private, tête-à-tête meetings. In public, emotions are more likely to run high, making satisfactory resolution difficult. Second, maintaining social harmony is essential, even if it requires personal sacrifice. Because legal action necessarily involves conflict, it is to be avoided if at all possible, for, in the long term, it can only perpetuate distrust and resentment. Third, harmony is to be fostered through mutual compromise. Each side must give some ground so as to meet at a midpoint, allowing everyone to save face. To do so, the adversaries must be able to place themselves in each other's shoes so as to appreciate the difficulties of the other party's position and the reasonableness of his or her demands. The role of the cleric is to provide a calm example and a neutral, private setting (i.e., a monastery) so that reason can reign over emotion. By remaining above the fray, by taking no sides and making no judgments, the monastic encourages both parties to replace anger and selfishness with compassion and wisdom. This can be said to be Master Xingyun's theory of Buddhist mediation technique, one that he has apparently employed to good effect in Taiwan.

Beyond his behind-the-scenes work, Master Xingyun believes that, as a Buddhist master, he has both the right and the responsibility to play a public political role, which he does by endorsing candidates. With every election since the lifting of martial law, politicians have flocked to Foguangshan so that pictures of themselves alongside the master might appear in the next day's newspapers. Usually, the master's endorsement is silent: the very fact that he has agreed to meet with someone is regarded as a tacit pledge of support. In the 1996 presidential campaign, however, the master sparked considerable debate when he publicly endorsed Chen Lü'an, the former president of the control yuan and a vocal supporter of Foguangshan (see, e.g., "Guai kelian de" 1995; Jiang 1995; and Zhen Songyu in *Lianhe bao*, 23 August 1995, 11). Master Xingyun cited not only Chen's political experience but also his ethical integrity, deep spiritual maturity, and years of self-cultivation as the qualities making him best suited to act as the country's paramount leader. This endorsement caused a flurry of criticism, with some fearing that, if other religious figures followed Master Xingyun's example, the resulting "war of religions" (*zongjiao zhanzheng*) would further exacerbate the already acrimonious political climate. Such accusations were fueled by the fact that Chen frequently visited Buddhist temples as part of his campaigning and explicitly employed Buddhist terminology in both describing his role as a political leader and painting his vision of Taiwan's future.[16]

The debate that arose therefore centered on two issues: to what degree, if at all, religious symbolism should be employed by political candidates and what role, if any, religious leaders should play in campaign politics. Commentators generally applauded the attention given to the ethical dimension of political leadership, but they also lampooned the sanctimonious posturing of Chen and other candidates and looked askance at a Buddhist master taking such a public role in the country's first free presidential election.

Stung by these rebukes, the master toned down his support for Chen, saying that it was natural for him to back one of his own devotees and that, as a citizen, he had a right to do so. In the end, Chen garnered little more than 8 percent of the vote. In both this and other elections, analysts of the ROC political scene have found little correlation between religious affiliation and voting patterns.[17] Yet, at every election, politicians continue to make the pilgrimage to Foguangshan (and other prominent religious centers). They do so, it seems, because the master's endorsement provides a patina of moral respectability and the pilgrimage displays one's respect for Buddhism. Because Foguangshan is interested in the ethical and spiritual renewal of Taiwan's society, Master Xingyun's endorsement signifies that a candidate shares this concern, although his or her method of achieving renewal may differ from that of Foguangshan. The master views his public support for a candidate not as an endorsement of that person's policies or even as an endorsement of his or her qualifications as a politician. Rather, he is publicly stating his belief that the person has the requisite moral character necessary to provide political leadership and has a favorable attitude toward Buddhism. Master Xingyun has even endorsed two opposing candidates with quite different platforms; in a legislative race in 1995, for instance, he supported both Jiang Sheping and Zhao Ning, staunch rivals.

Politicians as Expedient Means to Spread Buddhism

Master Xingyun has no doubt that Buddhist masters of high cultivation can play an important part in purifying politics. He also believes that such contact with political figures can benefit Buddhism as well. During the conference "Religion and Society" held at Hsi Lai Temple, the master told the assembled scholars:

> I am very interested in the relation between religion and society. When religion and society have a close relation, then religion can spread smoothly. Otherwise, it is not easy for it to develop. When Buddhism spread into China, it spread from officials [guanfang] to the people. With this strength to promote from above to below, it was easy to develop within society. When the Buddha was alive, he highly valued the thinking of the Benevolent King Who Protected the Dharma [Renwang Hufa]. The reason why Buddhism enjoyed a golden era during the Tang and the Song [960–1279 C.E.] dynasties is that, in addition to royal patronage, there were many

scholars who studied and practiced it. (Shi Xingyun 1994, vol. 1, entry for 14 October 1989)

The master's remarks were meant to emphasize the important place that scholars hold in the promotion of Buddhism. Of greater interest for the current discussion is his trickle-down theory about the spread of religion from government officials to the general public. To create links of affinity with political leaders is especially efficacious, for, as they lead (even simply by example), others will follow.

ROC government authorities are in a position to serve Buddhism in another, more surprising fashion as well: by legislating laws to better regulate certain aspects of monastic affairs and by creating an office to oversee compliance with those laws. Master Xingyun has on numerous occasions over the years made these recommendations, and he did so again, and quite vocally, in the fall of 1996 in the wake of a series of scandals involving self-proclaimed Buddhist masters who used orchestrated displays of purported supernatural powers to bilk their followers of enormous sums of money. The most serious case was that of a man named Song Qili who, through claims of miraculous abilities supported by fabricated numinous images, defrauded followers of over NT$3 billion. Shortly thereafter, a Master Miao Tian was found to have cheated devotees out of millions of New Taiwan dollars through selling "lotus seats" in his temple's columbarium. The lotus seats, guaranteed to bring good fortune and health to descendants of the deceased, sold for as much as NT$300,000. A variety of controversial religious figures, including Qing Hai, were accused of engaging in real estate scams and other forms of fraud.[18]

In the midst of these scandals, Master Xingyun joined over one hundred of Taiwan's religious leaders, government officials, and scholars of religion in a "Symposium on Religion and Social Trends," sponsored by the executive yuan, to discuss ways to avoid such problems in the future. At the symposium, Master Xingyun announced that he would like to see the ROC's laws regulating religion updated. As do many other clerics, the master thinks that the current statute, that is, the Temple Regulation Law, passed in 1929, is antiquated and unfair, especially since, as far as property matters are concerned, it pertains only to Buddhist and Daoist temples, not to Christian churches. Specifically, he would like to see the adoption of two types of new laws: one set to regulate inheritance of the personal property of monastics and another to standardize the criteria for ordination and for assuming abbotship of a temple (so that only those with the appropriate qualifications could don clerics' robes or run Buddhist organizations).

As far as inheritance is concerned, currently it remains unclear whether a venerable's biological family or dharma family (i.e., monastic community) has the greater claim, a situation that too often leads to squabbles between the two parties on a venerable's death. In the master's view, it is the temple that has the greater right, and he therefore would like to see the passage of a law stipulating that, unless a monastic has written a will that explicitly leaves certain of his or her belongings to family members or other individuals, on his or her death all possessions will automatically be regarded as temple property.

The regulation of admittance to the sangha—the more ambitious of the proposed sets of legislation—is more controversial. What Master Xingyun has in mind is, apparently, an arrangement similar to that devised during the Tang dynasty when Emperor Xuanzong, in consultation with a group of prominent clerics, inaugurated a system of official ordinations sponsored by the state. In the Tang system, before novices (*tongxing*) could take shramanera vows, they had to receive from the Bureau of National Sacrifice (Ci Bu) a certificate showing that they had passed that bureau's examination. In the modern form of the system proposed by the master, rather than attending to the examination of individual candidates, the state would regulate monastic membership by requiring individuals to have graduated from a government-accredited Buddhist college (*foxueyuan*) before renouncing. Accreditation would be granted by a panel composed of government officials and respected Buddhist leaders. This, in the master's view, would prevent charlatans such as Miao Tian from falsely portraying themselves as part of the sangha yet still protect monastic autonomy.

Master Xingyun would also like to see the government upgrade its office dealing with religious affairs from its current status of "division" (*ke*) to that of either "department" (*si*) or even "bureau" (*ju*) so that it could have the necessary labor power and clout to enforce whatever new laws are passed. Once again, he seems to have something in mind similar to the Bureau of National Sacrifice. His one concern in relying on a government agency to regulate religious affairs is that it can too easily be filled by bureaucrats with no knowledge of religion and an unsympathetic or even antagonistic attitude toward it. That is the current situation, as he sees it, the result being that "outsiders are managing insiders" (*waihang guanli neihang*). To prevent this from occurring, the master proffers two recommendations: first, that the civil service examination include questions concerning religion so as to elevate understanding among all government employees; second, that ways be found through which the government's office can work in close communication with clerics. He does not indicate the mechanism through which this latter is to occur, although one would assume that it would entail the creation of some form of advisory commission.

Government and religion are, therefore, not, in Master Xingyun's view, totally separate and independent realms. He takes his cue much more from Ven. Fotudeng than from Ven. Huiyuan in this regard.[19] For Master Xingyun, Buddhist leaders have a definite, if generalized and indirect, contribution to make in purifying the political process. Likewise, government officials and laws can aid in the promotion of authentic Buddhist teachings. Not everyone at the "Symposium on Religion and Social Trends" agreed with the master. While representatives of Buddhism, Daoism, and Yiguandao generally supported his ideas, Catholics and Protestants argued that such legislation would be an infringement on religious freedom as guaranteed in the ROC constitution. Internal self-regulation within each tradition (*zi lü*), they countered, would be the better route to take. After three hours of debate, the gathering decided to put aside the controversial issue of new religious laws and agreed on three recommendations to forward to the executive yuan: the ROC's Division of Religion should be promoted to the status of either "department" or "bureau"; the civil service examinations should include items concerning religion; and religious studies should be integrated into university education through the creation of religion departments and institutes.

Public Voice and Private Practice

In examining Master Xingyun's political views and activities, one finds that, as are other religious leaders at the turn of the new millennium, he is struggling to develop an appropriate strategy for giving his religious tradition a public voice. From time to time, he has attempted to interject himself into the political process by endorsing candidates or participating in government-sponsored committees and conferences. His less direct solutions have been to cultivate close personal relationships with societal leaders and to lead high-profile public campaigns of moral regeneration. Both these latter strategies are based on a premise of the interpenetration of private lives, civil society, and public polity. All people participate in their country's economic and political arenas to a certain degree, and, at those times and to the degree that they do so, the distinction between private and public collapses. The differentiation between the categories becomes most tenuous in the cases of leading business and political figures, for their personal values strongly shape the contours of the policies that they enact. Master Xingyun therefore believes that creating ties of affinity with them is especially effective in improving all people's lives. Ultimately, however, he is convinced that long-term sociopolitical amelioration does not proceed best through manipulating the superstructure since this changes the shape of problems but does not get at their root cause. Instead of advocating a form of activism that alters the nature of political or social relations, Master Xingyun relies on organizing massive campaigns of moral regeneration in which individuals gather together to commit publicly to purifying their intentions and actions. For him, moral, intellectual, and spiritual education is the key to improving people's lives.[20]

5 Cultivating Talent through Education

MONASTIC EDUCATION

THE FOGUANGSHAN MONASTIC BUDDHIST ACADEMY

The first building that Master Xingyun had constructed on Foguangshan was not a shrine, recitation hall, or meditation center. It was the compound for the Eastern Buddhist Academy (Dongfang Fojiao Xueyuan). Such a move was not mere happenstance, for the master has always regarded a systematized, comprehensive education, especially of the sangha, to be the key to the regeneration of society and the revival of Buddhism. For those who are considering renouncing under the master, it is at this campus, or at one of the other half dozen Foguang seminaries, that formal training in monastic practice begins. Master Xingyun founded the Eastern Buddhist Academy in 1967 when the facilities of Shoushan Buddhist Academy, the pilot school that he had established in Kaohsiung three years previously, proved inadequate for the rapidly growing student body. Approximately twenty young women were admitted biennially for the two-year program until 1974, when it became apparent that the burgeoning monastic population needed an expanded training regimen and a school system that could better attend to their differing educational backgrounds. The Foguangshan Monastic Academy (Foguangshan Conglin Xueyuan) was, therefore, added as a two- to three-year program that could draw graduates from the Eastern Buddhist Academy as well as from general high schools. Master Xingyun soon created yet another level, the Chinese Buddhist Research Academy (Zhongguo Fojiao Xueyuan), designed to train teachers, not just for Foguangshan, but also for the growing number of other Buddhist seminaries that had begun to sprout up around Taiwan.

Together, these three levels of training are known as the Foguangshan Monastic Buddhist Academy (Foguangshan Conglin Fojiao Xueyuan) and constitute the religious school segment of the Foguang education system. By the advent of the twenty-first century, somewhere between four and five hundred students were enrolled at the various Foguang campuses each year. The Eastern Buddhist Academy is no longer located at Foguang headquarters, having moved to two new sites: the Yuanfu School in Zhanghua (central Taiwan) for girls and the Shramanera School in Beihai (northern Taiwan) for boys. The Yuanfu School generally caters to approximately twenty junior and senior high school–age students. Those who renounce tend to do so as novices rather than as shramanerikas.[1] The two dozen boys at Beihai are younger, with most of either elementary or junior high school age, and nearly all take the shramanera vows, although there is little expectation that they will persist in the monastic lifestyle into adulthood. For the most part, their parents have sent them to the school in the hope that a solid Buddhist education will provide the guidance necessary for them to develop into moral, capable members of secular society.

The focal point of Foguangshan's monastic education is its network of seminaries, which has grown to ten schools, although most of these are quite small, having only two dozen or so students. Campuses may be found not only in Taiwan but in Malaysia, Australia, and South Africa as well. The two main campuses are those for men and women on either side of Foguangshan, and students who are doing well at other schools (i.e., those who appear to be on their way to renouncing) will often be transferred there. The Foguangshan Monastic Academy has two divisions: the Division of Specialized Cultivation (Zhuanxiu Xuebu) and the Division of International Studies (Guoji Xuebu). All students begin their studies in the Division of Specialized Cultivation, where they gain a general education in Buddhism. At the conclusion of the second year, those students interested in continuing their academic training must take either an examination that covers the five areas offered by the Division of Specialized Cultivation (sangha education, ritual, dharma propagation, monastery administration, Buddhist art) or, if they wish to study through the Division of International Studies, an examination that tests their ability in English or Japanese.

Approximately 70 percent of second-year students continue their studies. The other 30 percent are assigned a post either at the headquarters or at a branch temple. College training is typically terminated after two years for one of four reasons. Sometimes it is a matter of personal choice; the student simply has no interest in academic studies or recognizes that he or she does not have scholastic aptitude. Other times the student is unable to pass the entrance examination. Yet other times the temple leadership decides that the student's skills are needed by the sangha; this is a badge of honor, for it indicates that one is regarded as being especially talented. Finally, the student may be deemed too disruptive of college life, perhaps having "dangerous ideas" that may adversely influence other students. These individuals will likewise be assigned to a work unit, where it is assumed that they will pose less of a threat to communal harmony since their colleagues are further along in their cultivation.

The Division of International Studies has three divisions: the English-Language Buddhist Academy (Yingwen Foxueyuan), the Japanese-Language Buddhist Academy (Riwen Foxueyuan), and the Division of International Students

(Waiji Xuesheng Yanxiuban). The English-language program is designed to train personnel to serve in the growing number of Foguang temples in English-speaking countries—the United States, Canada, the United Kingdom, Australia, and New Zealand. The Japanese-language program lacks a clearly defined mission, as Foguangshan has only two small branch temples in Japan and rarely sends clerics there for graduate work. Hence, most of the Japanese-language school graduates never put their training into practice. Only two or three of the twelve 1996 graduates, for instance, were actually sent to Japan. Most of the others were stationed in temples around Taiwan, with two being sent to Australia.

The Division of International Students provides to those who do not speak Chinese elementary instruction in the Mandarin language as well as classes in English on Buddhist teachings. This constitutes Foguangshan's attempt to broaden its sangha beyond the Chinese community so that it can be international in scope not only geographically but ethnically as well. A smattering of students has been drawn from Indonesia, Malaysia, Hong Kong, Myanmar, Japan, Ladakh (North India), Nepal, Sri Lanka, the Congo, Germany, and Russia. As we shall see in chapter 10, most such foreign imports have soon become discouraged and left the organization. In other words, Foguangshan's efforts at developing a cross-cultural sangha have as yet met with little success.

The Chinese Buddhist Research Academy, the apex of Foguangshan's monastic education system, provides a three-year program that trains teachers to fill Buddhist seminary posts. Areas for specialized study are the same as those in the Foguangshan Monastic Academy—sangha education, ritual, dharma propagation, monastery administration, and Buddhist art. Candidates who hold a degree from a seminary enter the institute as a "research apprentice," said to be equal in status to a master's student in a liberal arts university. Those students who obtain a research apprentice degree and pass the appropriate entrance examination receive another three years of training as a "researcher," the equivalent of a doctoral student. As of 1998, there were twenty-two nuns and two laywomen enrolled in these programs.

FOGUANGSHAN'S PEDAGOGICAL THEORY AND PRACTICE

Foguang literature proclaims that its education system combines the best of traditional monastic life with the most up-to-date equipment and teaching methods in order to give students a thorough intellectual knowledge of Buddhist history and doctrine, as well as in secular subjects, and simultaneously instill in them an existential understanding of the dharma. Students at the college level, for instance, take six hours of classes each day Tuesday through Saturday to learn about the most important sutras and sastras and the span of the tradition's history, with an emphasis on the various Chinese schools. Secular subjects taught include philosophy, psychology, Chinese literature, foreign languages, social studies, statistics, computer science, and monastery administration.

The Venerable Huikai, the dean of the Foguangshan Monastic Buddhist Academy from 1996 to 1998, pressed to raise the school system's academic standards. In his opinion, if the Chinese sangha is to shed its image as a superstitious atavism, it must prove itself fully versed in the latest, most sophisticated knowledge that academe has to offer. This means both staying abreast of technological advances, especially in computer science, and training students to interpret Buddhist teachings in a more scholarly fashion. A monastic academy, however, cautions Ven. Huikai, is not the same as a liberal arts university. The goal of a Buddhist seminary is to train the tradition's future leaders. Intellectual growth alone is, therefore, not sufficient. In order for the students to become society's spiritual and moral vanguard, they must learn how best to tap into their innate religious resources, which they can do only by engaging in various forms of Buddhist practice (Chandler 1998g). Students in the Foguang seminary system therefore find much of their time devoted to four forms of Buddhist practicum—etiquette, ritual conduct, meditation, and manual labor.

Learning Buddhist decorum requires students to recondition some of their most basic habitual behaviors. They must learn to "walk like the wind, stand like a tree, sit like a bell, and recline like a bow," as the proverb phrases it. These fundamental acts are considered to hold a profound significance in a person's religious cultivation, for, unless the body is harmonized both internally and with its surrounding environment, the mind cannot achieve balance. This integration of body and mind finds its highest expression in the enactment of the daily communal services—morning recitation, morning meal service, lunch service, evening medicine meal, and evening recitation. At these times, correctly donning one's robe, walking and bowing in proper sequence, and chanting with alacrity serves to focus personal, communal, and cosmic religious forces. Furthermore, as the students will soon be the ones to lead such services, it is all the more imperative that they thoroughly memorize the most commonly recited sutras and gathas and learn the proper use of the various dharma instruments (bell, wooden fish, drum, miniature gong, cymbals, inverted cymbal, etc.). The third aspect of Buddhist practice to be learned is meditation. This area receives less attention than do the others. Students nonetheless twice annually enter the meditation hall for week-long retreats. The final form of practice is manual labor. In a modern rendition of Baizhang's maxim, "A day without work is a day without food," students perform a variety of menial chores around the mountain—preparing and serving meals, sweeping the grounds, tending to gardens, etc. Even Mondays—officially days of rest—are spent giving the monastery facilities a thorough cleaning.

Balancing classroom studies with religious practice is a difficult task since both are time-consuming. From the moment they rise at 4:30 A.M. until the lights are shut off at 10:00 P.M., the students find every minute of their day planned for them. They must keep to the schedule, including the 10:00 P.M. curfew. Tardiness is regarded as especially improper if it inconveniences others. Hence, if the student responsible for sounding the bell or board that signals a new phase in the daily regimen does so at the wrong time or hits the wrong pattern, he or she must publicly repent, as must those who have been late in preparing a meal. Discipline is strict in other ways as well. There is to be no talking or glancing about during the three meals or the processions to them. Nor may students converse after 7:00 P.M. since this is to be a time of self-study and reflection. Anyone caught breaking silence must wear a placard that reads "talks too much." (In practice, complete silence is not kept in the evening hours. Teachers generally look the other way if a pair of students whispers about homework. Punishment is meted out only if someone talks loudly or several gossip in a group.)

The students attending Foguangshan's seminaries are expected to work seriously toward the ambitious goals that have been set for them by Master Xingyun, Ven. Cihui (the dean of Foguangshan's seminary system until 1995), Ven. Huikai, and subsequent deans. It may be that the goals are too ambitious. Even with rising every morning before dawn, there simply is not enough time in the day to attend the communal services, prepare for the classes, and perform the various chores. The difficulty in fulfilling such expectations is exacerbated by frequent interruptions in the schedule. Students are constantly called away from classes to conduct alms processions, participate in conferences or dharma functions, or supply logistic support for some event. Similarly, the clerics at the Chinese Buddhist Research Academy attend to the large number of lay devotees who come each weekend on pilgrimages to the Nanhua campus of Foguang University.

In constantly barraging students with so much, the Foguangshan Monastic Buddhist Academy runs the risk of sacrificing quality and substance. Some of the mountain's critics claim that its college students are little more than a ready source of labor. The Foguang leadership denies this, arguing that only those who can joyfully provide service regardless of personal sacrifice, tackle multiple tasks simultaneously, and take the initiative to study on their own in free moments have the personality and aptitude to be a Foguang monastic. Whether a person has the mettle to tread the bodhisattva path should, it is felt, be ascertained as soon as possible. Furthermore, it is argued, the Foguang seminary system should be regarded as only the beginning of a person's lifelong religious education. A school setting can go only so far in training clerics. At a certain point, usually two to four years into the process, being a student is not enough; one must serve in a temple.

To become part of the monastic elite, however, a person is increasingly expected to receive a more in-depth education than can be attained through attending a Buddhist college. For some, this means studying at the Chinese Buddhist Research Academy. Even more prestigious is earning a graduate degree at a liberal arts university, for this allows the monk or nun both to introduce the dharma to other intellectuals and simultaneously to acquire the skills and knowledge necessary to keep Buddhism abreast of current social, political, and technological trends. Foguang monastics were first sent to graduate school in Japan in the early 1970s.[2] According to Master Xingyun, many Buddhists, including some of his own devotees, thought it a mistake to send his most senior disciples away for two years of academic training: the lack of proper supervision could be detrimental to the young nuns' self-cultivation, the knowledge gained would be irrelevant to their future duties, and the financial drain of dispatching them overseas would be crippling to the fledgling organization. The master has never regretted his decision and, in fact, has sent over two dozen monks and nuns abroad for graduate work over the past three decades. Among these are Vens. Huikai and Yifa, who received their doctorates in the study of religion from Temple University and Yale University, respectively. Such monastics immediately achieve recognition for their efforts, receiving promotion, awards, and the honor of having their accomplishment prominently recorded in the organization's magazines.

A certain skepticism nonetheless continues to color the attitude toward advanced scholarly research. On the one hand, developing a highly educated sangha is regarded as necessary for elevating Buddhism's status; on the other hand, monastics who devote too much time to their own studies are seen as engaging in pedantic irrelevancies, losing touch with the concrete needs of common people. Master Xingyun's own ambivalence about the necessity of higher education came through in the 1950s when he arranged to go to Japan as a Ph.D. student at Taisho University, then backed out at the last minute, having determined that his fate lay in preaching the dharma directly to everyday folk rather than in academic research. The questionable usefulness of spending many years learning various languages and pinpointing the fine points of Buddhist history and doctrine became a major topic of debate during the "International Symposium of Religion and Higher Education" sponsored by Foguangshan in November 1996. Several younger monks and nuns representing a variety of Buddhist organizations lamented that, having gone abroad for study, on their return to serve in a monastery there was no opportunity to employ the knowledge that they had acquired, and that, by being away so long, they had distanced themselves from the general public.

How best to make graduate work applicable to the practical needs of the sangha also came up for discussion between two of Foguangshan's up-and-coming clerics during the "Meeting of Foguang Monastics Assigned to Taiwan Branch Temples" (1997). The Venerable Yikong, who at the time was studying for a doctorate at Kaohsiung Teacher's College while simultaneously maintaining her responsibilities as head of Foguangshan's Culture Council, argued that it is better to study in Taiwan or someplace near a temple so as to be able to continue to serve the monastic community directly. "Some people just keep studying for years and years, without it having any application," she observed. The Venerable Huikai, who had recently returned to the headquarters after having spent some ten years at Temple University, disagreed. He countered that few people are studying just for the sake of studying: "If the study can't be applied, it is certainly worthless. On the other hand, in-depth study takes time. One studies precisely so that one can serve better. It is not just for one's own sake. Studying is not the goal; it is a very basic method of cultivating the bodhisattva path." The underlying question framing this debate is the relation between self-cultivation (in this case, one's intellectual development) and serving others. As with meditation, academic study is to play a secondary role in the Foguang system, behind organizing activities deemed of benefit to the laity.

The Venerables Yikong and Huikai would agree that, ideally, academic research allows monastics more effectively to guide others to a deeper understanding of the relevance of the dharma in confronting contemporary challenges. The crux to actualizing this ideal successfully is to find ways to infuse Buddhist teachings, practices, and values into daily modern life. This may be accomplished in two ways: providing religious education to Buddhist laity and bringing Buddhist values to bear on the secular education of members of the general public.

LAY EDUCATION

Foguangshan sponsors a variety of programs geared toward attracting people to the Buddhist teachings and then deepening their knowledge of the dharma once they have taken the triple refuge. As we saw in chapter 2 above, an essential component of this undertaking is the dharma talks given by Master Xingyun. To a lesser extent, his more senior disciples also give such lectures. The Venerables Xinding and Yikong have reputations as good speakers (and are fluent in both Mandarin and Taiwanese), so their dharma talks attract as many as a thousand people at a time. Abbots and abbesses of larger Foguang branch temples also lecture regularly. As part of his initiative to give more responsibility to lay devotees, Master Xingyun has instituted a program of lay dharma lecturers (tanjiangshi) and teachers (tanjiaoshi), the former position being open to any devotee who has shown a good understanding of Buddhist doctrine, the latter being reserved for such followers who are also prominent members of society, such as Chen Lü'an and Gong Pengcheng (a former high government official who is the president of Foguang University). As of 1997, there were 112 lay dharma lecturers and 7 lay dharma teachers. None of these speakers, however, can attract audiences as large as those for clerics. Chinese Buddhists, at least those in the Foguang organization, apparently feel that spiritual guidance remains the domain of monastics, regardless of rhetoric concerning the need to develop present-day Vimalakirtis.

Once people's interest in Buddhist doctrine has been sparked by the lectures, a primary means of increasing their knowledge of the tradition's history and teachings is making available a wide range of books and CD-ROMs on the subject. Foguangshan is especially known among Buddhists in Taiwan for its extensive work in the publication of sutras, commentaries, histories, and reference material. Since its inception in 1959, Foguang Publishing House has issued more than six hundred titles, and it continues to print dozens of books annually. Among these publications, three projects have required an especially large amount of time, energy, and resources: the *Foguang Encyclopedia [of Buddhism]* (*Foguang da cidian*) (Shi Xingyun 1988a); the *Vernacular Edition of Selections from the Chinese Buddhist Canon* (*Zhongguo Fojiao jingdian baozang jingxuan baihua ban*) (Shi Xingyun 1997e); and the *Foguang Chinese Buddhist Canon (Punctuated Edition)* (*Foguang Zhongguo Fojiao jingdian baozang*) (Foguangshan Tripitaka Editing Committee 1984, 1995). Foguangshan completed its encyclopedia of Buddhism in 1988. Nine years later, the entire work was also issued on a CD-ROM. According to Foguang literature, this is the first complete Buddhist encyclopedia in modern Chinese. The ten-volume work, which is largely based on a Japanese Buddhist encyclopedia and took eight years to complete, contains twenty-three thousand entries and has seven million words and five thousand photos. Over ten thousand copies are in circulation.

Once the encyclopedia was in print, the Culture Council turned its attention to rendering 132 texts of the tripitaka into vernacular Chinese in editions that include annotations and introductions. Shorter texts, such as the *Heart Sutra* and the *Diamond Sutra*, were provided in full. Longer scriptures, for example, the *Avatamsaka Sutra*, were excerpted. Rather than having the editorial work done by Foguang personnel, Master Xingyun invited one hundred scholars from Beijing and Nanjing Universities in mainland China to undertake the task. He did so both to encourage cultural exchange across the Taiwan Strait and to plant a seed of the dharma among mainland intellectuals.[3] In her preface to the *Vernacular Edition of*

Selections from the Chinese Buddhist Canon (Shi Xingyun 1997e), Ven. Cihui states that this series is designed as a "raft" or "compass" to guide beginning Buddhists so that they can comfortably read the most important sections of the tripitaka's especially profound and influential sutras.

To meet the needs of those with a better background in Buddhist studies, Foguangshan has since 1977 gradually been churning out a punctuated, annotated version of the entire Chinese tripitaka. Thus far, a four-volume Agama collection, *Zhong ahan* (Foguangshan Tripitaka Editing Committee 1984), and a fifty-one-volume Chan collection, *Chan zang* (Foguangshan Tripitaka Editing Committee 1995), have been published. An edition of Prajña literature is currently in progress, and another thirteen such collections are planned (including the *Lotus Sutra*; the *Avatamsaka Sutra*; sutras of the Pure Land, Vinaya, Consciousness Only, and Esoteric schools; Theravada sutras; Jakata tales; histories and biographies, etc.). The Foguangshan Tripitaka Editing Committee includes eight clerics along with close to twenty lay volunteers. The group bases its work on seven versions of the tripitaka: four Chinese editions; one Korean; and two Japanese. The completed series will be the first full version of the Chinese Buddhist canon to have been reedited since the Qing dynasty (1644–1912 C.E.) and the first such edition with modern punctuation.

Foguangshan's publishing empire also includes the daily newspaper *Merit Times* (which has the Chinese name *Renjian fu bao*) and the monthly magazine *Universal Gate* (*Pumen*).[4] The twelve-page newspaper, launched in the spring of 2000, emphasizes positive happenings in society, current events in the Buddhist world, and Foguangshan's most recent accomplishments and upcoming plans. Interspersed with such articles are recipes for vegetarian dishes and advice for self-cultivation. The paper comes out five days a week and has a reported circulation of ten thousand. *Universal Gate* is designed to be more literary and scholarly. Rather than reporting on Foguang activities, its articles often lay out historical or doctrinal background that serves to justify the Foguang position or position it as mainstream Buddhist practice. Other essays have no direct bearing on current events, instead introducing readers to an aspect of Buddhist art, practice, or cultural history. Circulation is slightly over thirty thousand per month.

The vast array of Foguang printed matter is supplemented by an equally impressive array of audiovisual productions. Foguang literature boasts that, in 1957, the master cut the first-ever ten-inch Buddhist record. By the 1970s, he had begun giving short dharma talks on radio and television. Today, Foguang bookstores showcase vast numbers of cassettes, videos, CDs, and CD-ROMs, and one can hardly go into any sizable bus depot or train station in Taiwan without viewing a videotaped image of Master Xingyun on a large-screen television. In 1998, Foguangshan launched its own satellite television station, allowing the monastery a regular venue through which to air its productions and keep devotees apprised of its activities.

Another important component in Foguangshan's lay education system is the various courses of instruction provided at branch temples. Most every temple advertises lectures by clerics and classes on sutra study, meditation, vegetarian cooking, flower arranging, and Buddhist singing and dance. At larger centers with expanded curricula, the night and weekend programs are coordinated as "urban Buddhist academies" (*dushi Foxueyuan*) that grant "degrees" in dharma studies to graduates. Such a format takes advantage of the craze in Taiwan for night schools (*buxiban*) as the best means of advancing one's studies and career. Foguangshan has adopted an academic tone in its lay Buddhist education system in two other ways as well. First, the organization regularly sponsors symposia that focus on Buddhist themes. Scholars from around East Asia (and a few from Europe and the United States) are invited to present papers on such topics as "The Sixth Patriarch and the Platform Sutra," "Religion and Higher Education in East Asia," and "Modern Buddhism." Similar conferences geared for Foguang devotees focus on "Humanistic Buddhism" and "Foguang Studies."

Foguangshan also gives its education system an academic imprint through the Buddha's Light International Association (BLIA)'s annual Buddhism examination, versions of which have been developed for elementary, junior high school, and senior high school students as well as for adults (see "Foguangshan shijie Foxue huikao chengrenzi tiku" 1996; "Foguangshan shijie Foxue huikao manhua tiku" 1996). The two lowest levels, both in cartoon format, require the children to identify elementary Buddhist teachings, virtues, and figures. The 1996 children's test, for instance, included such questions as those reproduced in cartoons 1–4. Buddhist themes remain fairly muted at this level, the emphasis being placed on encouraging filial behavior toward parents, proper respect toward teachers, helpfulness toward friends, and diligent study habits. Of the 150 questions on the 1996 children's test, only 25 had a specifically Buddhist content. The remaining questions were similar in tone to those reproduced in cartoons 5 and 6.

The percentage of questions dealing with Buddhist history and doctrine remains low for senior high school students, with much more attention devoted to health education and acceptable social behavior. Hence, along with being asked to explain why there are so many buddhas and bodhisattvas in Buddhism, students are also asked to list reasons why people become overweight and why one should abstain from taking recreational drugs. The version for adults differs significantly

128 • CULTIVATING TALENT THROUGH EDUCATION

in content from the other tests in that all questions deal directly with Buddhist doctrine, history, and practice. Participants are typically asked to define such terms as *samadhi (sanmo)*, "four immeasurable minds" *(si wuliang xin)*, and *tathagatagarbha (rulaizang)*. True/false and multiple-choice questions test knowledge of the five aggregates, the sundry schools of Chinese Buddhism, famous Buddhist translators and patriarchs, etc. Participants are then ranked into one of four groups on the basis of their scores.

Since Master Xingyun first devised this examination system in 1990, Foguangshan has dedicated considerable energy to developing it. In 1995, the Education Department of the Republic of China (ROC) granted permission for the test to be administered in public schools, thereby boosting participation to over 1.2 million people. That same year, BLIA appended the adjective "worldwide" to the test's name and had it translated into fourteen languages so that it could be given to non-Chinese speakers in overseas branch temples. Foguang literature proudly exclaimed that the examination was held at more than one thousand locations in

CARTOON 1
The Buddha with a jolly countenance, a bellyful of patience, and an optimistic outlook to forge ahead is:
(1) Amitabha Buddha;
(2) Maitreya Buddha;
(3) Shakyamuni Buddha.

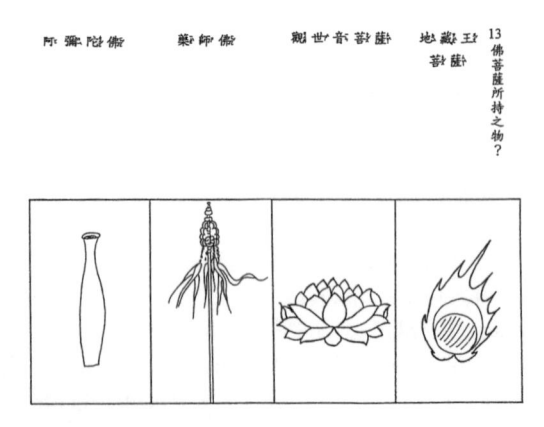

CARTOON 2
Which article is associated with each buddha and bodhisattva? [Students are to draw a line linking the name to the appropriate symbol.] From left to right: Amitabha Buddha; Medicine Buddha; Guanshiyin Bodhisattva; Kshitigarbha Bodhisattva. From left to right: vase of elixir; khakkara staff; lotus flower; mani pearl.

four hundred cities of fifty countries on six continents (Shi Xingyun 1997a, 298). Since then, the scope has diminished, principally because, at the urging of several Christian churches, the ROC Education Department rescinded permission to administer the examination in schools, declaring that doing so contravened the constitutional separation of church and state (Yang 1996, 6).

The impulse to structure Buddhist education in an academic framework partially derives from a desire to counter the characterization of Buddhism as superstitious and anti-intellectual. For Buddhism to survive, believes Master Xingyun, its teachings must garner the same respect as do other fields of knowledge. What better way to validate Buddhist teachings than to make them the subject of secular academic scrutiny and the topic of examination? There is a problem, however, with utilizing an academic model for Buddhist propagation: young people in Taiwan are already burdened with so much pressure to excel in exams that, while on one level they feel comfortable with such a format, on another they would prefer anything other than another test. Foguang headquarters and larger branch temples

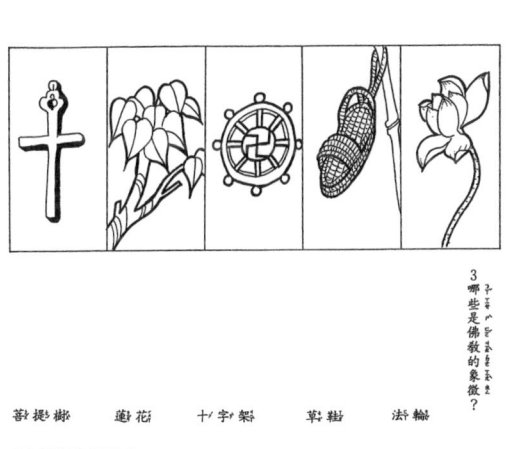

CARTOON 3
Which of these are Buddhist symbols?
[Students are to draw a line linking the name to the picture for those articles that are Buddhist symbols.] Terms from left to right: Bodhi Tree; lotus; cross; straw sandals; dharma wheel.

CARTOON 4
Under what kind of tree did the Buddha attain enlightenment?
(1) papaya tree;
(2) Bodhi Tree;
(3) mango tree.

therefore also sponsor two- to seven-day camps geared toward high school and college students (as well as teachers and families). These camps are meant to be both educational and fun, a brief respite from the usual stress and toil of school life. According to Foguang monastics, theirs was the first Buddhist monastery to institute such camps, which have proved to be an especially effective way of sparking interest in Buddhism among young people. Several clerics, in fact, mentioned that attending such a camp played an important role in their decision to renounce.

As can be seen from the foregoing description, Foguangshan's religious education system for monastic and lay devotees is extensive. No other Chinese Buddhist organization can boast so many students in its seminary system or so many publications issued year after year. The primary pedagogical challenge that Foguang clerics face in both their own education and that of lay devotees is how to make Buddhist teachings relevant and accessible without diluting their profundity and transformative power. In Master Xingyun's view, religious education should serve to guide a person in his or her intellectual, moral, and spiritual development.

CARTOON 5
Filial behavior is:
(1) to study diligently;
(2) to listen to one's parents' instructions;
(3) to help to do things.

CARTOON 6
What kind of attitude should we have when talking with our teachers? (1) looking around; (2) listening attentively; (3) using lame excuses.

Without intellectual and moral cultivation, spiritual life at best remains superstitious *(mixin)* and at worst degenerates into evil faith *(xiexin)*. For those who have not yet generated sufficient merit to tread the bodhisattva path, the first step must, therefore, focus on intellectual growth and moral cultivation. Hence, these are the twin foci of Foguangshan's secular education agenda.

SECULAR EDUCATION

The Foguang secular education network comprises Foguang University, Hsi Lai University, Universal Gate High School, four preschools, and several public libraries. The most recent, and by far most ambitious, foray into secular education is Foguang University, its main campus in Jiayi (northeast Taiwan) having opened its doors in the year 2003. Until then, all students took classes at Nanhua Management College, the university's satellite campus located just outside Nantou (west central Taiwan). Master Xingyun had for many years voiced the hope of founding a liberal arts university. Frustrated by government regulations making it difficult for religious organizations to pursue such projects, he established Hsi Lai University on a small plot in Rosemead, California, in 1989. The ROC government finally granted preliminary approval for the establishment of Foguang University in the early 1990s, at which point the master shifted his energies back to Taiwan. Since then, Hsi Lai University has floundered, lacking both a clear mission and a significant source of revenue. Foguang University, on the other hand, has developed into one of Foguangshan's major undertakings. As of the 1997–1998 academic year, three hundred students were enrolled at the Nanhua campus. The goal is eventually to enroll over one thousand students per year.

Foguang University, asserts Master Xingyun and school president Gong Pengcheng, "is a university founded by Buddhists, but it is not a Buddhist university" ("Nanhua Management College Grand Opening Ceremony" 1996). The goal has nothing to do with training the future Buddhist vanguard; rather, it is to provide talented young citizens with the technological know-how, cultural sophistication, and ethical values that will allow them to develop into society's leaders. The insistence that the university will by no means focus on teaching Buddhism is not in itself particularly remarkable since, according to ROC law, no university *(daxue)* may dedicate itself to religious instruction. Institutes of higher education that do so must be organized as academies *(xueyuan)* or research institutes *(yanjiusuo)*. The oldest universities on Taiwan to have been established by religious organizations (including Fu Jen and Tung Hai Universities, both founded by Christian groups) specifically stipulate in their charters that they are liberal arts academies with no religious agenda. The same can be said about the charters for the other universities currently being opened on the island by Buddhists, most notably Master Shengyen's Fagu University and the Chinese Buddhist Association's Xuanzang University.

The difference between these other institutes and Foguang University, according to Gong Pengcheng, is that the former are still structured in such a way as to sustain a subtle preference for the worldview and values of the sponsoring religion:

> Personal ethics as it is taught in many schools is taken directly from the values of the religious organization with which the school is associated. For example, schools run by Protestants emphasize "faith, hope, and love," and schools run by Buddhists want their students to be "compassionate." They have only offered education from the unique point of view of their own religion, without considering that religion is a matter of individual faith while public education is universal. Of the general student body receiving the education, only a minority take the religion's morals, values, and worldview as their personal faith. For those who have no religious faith or have faith in another religion, the morals and values being taught either have no significance or engender antipathy, being perceived as little more than slogans and creeds. Religious organizations that run schools must be very careful in this regard. (Gong 1996, 7-8)

Foguang University will not give preference to Buddhist teachings in this way, assert both Gong and Master Xingyun.[5] The latter often points out that his choice of Gong to serve as president itself exemplifies the university's commitment to pluralism: before this appointment, Gong had had very little contact with the Buddhist world, being much better known for his scholarly research of the Confucian and Daoist traditions.[6]

Foguang University's pluralistic program is to be accomplished by bringing together the best aspects of the Chinese and Western humanistic traditions. Hence, Confucian resources are to be mobilized to foster in students an appreciation for aesthetics, ritual, ethics, and social responsibility. To counter any tendency toward rigidity, the Daoist love of creativity and spontaneity is also to be cultivated. The bridge between social responsibility and personal creativity is to be provided by the Buddhist teachings of compassion and service. The point is not directly to immerse students in the history and teachings of each of China's cultural systems (although students do have the opportunity to do so if they desire) but, instead, to draw from the wisdom of these traditions so that they may jointly serve as the stylistic framework for the educational enterprise as a whole. Also vital components in the framework are the scientific and democratic worldview and the liberal arts pedagogy first brought to China from the West over a century ago. Gong Pengcheng hopes to introduce these various principles to students, not merely in theory, but in practice as well. Therefore, he says, democratic principles feature prominently in school administration, with committees organized in such a way that administration, faculty, and students work closely together in shaping and implementing policy.

Those outside the Foguang organization (and even some within) remain skeptical about whether this enterprise will succeed. Many wonder whether Foguangshan will be able to raise the huge amounts of money necessary to establish and run a university, especially considering how the organization has already spread its financial resources so thin in creating its worldwide network of temples and its satellite television station. The school's annual budget most likely runs somewhere between NT$2.4 and NT$8 billion (between U.S.$80 and U.S.$266 million) (Gong 1996, 13). Nearly all this must come from donations from Foguang devotees, for Master Xingyun has pledged that, as education should be available to all regardless of economic situation, the university is to charge only a nominal fee for tuition.

Others question why Buddhists should support a project that offers no direct benefit to the promotion of the dharma. Would not the money be better spent in encouraging Buddhist studies, by both monastic and lay scholars? Such people argue that, given limited resources, Buddhists should concentrate their efforts on those programs that are specifically religious in content. This, in the end, would serve all of society best.

Master Xingyun obviously believes (as do many others) that Buddhists serve both Buddhism and general society well by running a liberal arts university and other such secular programs. Four factors seem to have played a prominent role in motivating him to establish Foguang University—religious and cultural pride and Confucian and Buddhist sentiment. He and other Buddhist leaders are well aware that Taiwan's most prominent private liberal arts universities—Tung Hai, Fu Jen, Zhongyuan, and Soochow Universities, to name but a few—were all founded by Christian missionaries. Chinese Buddhists, on the other hand, began to establish seminaries to train monastics only in the 1920s and have never run a liberal arts program for laity. Compounding this, many Chinese are embarrassed by the fact that, despite their long heritage of scholarly academies and general emphasis on education, the world's leading universities are located, not in China, but the West. The vast majority of Taiwan's most prominent academics have been trained in European or American universities. The explicit bringing together of Western and Eastern tradition by Foguang University is a statement that Chinese traditions have a valuable contribution to make to modern discourse, providing vital balance to the Western models of rationality so as to prevent them from degenerating into no more than instrumental logic.[7]

Master Xingyun has also pushed to establish Foguang University out of what can only be called "Confucian sentiment." He has a profound faith in the transformative power of education, regarding education as a lifelong process that inherently develops self-understanding and social responsibility. Society will be healthy only as long as its leaders have been fully exposed to the scientific expertise and humanistic values of a liberal arts education.

The final factor that has strongly shaped the master's educational goals are the Buddhist ideals of giving *(dana)* and creating ties of affinity *(jieyuan)*. Master Xingyun frequently tells his followers that Foguang University is their gift to society. By donating liberally to support this project, devotees embody the Buddhist virtue of selfless giving, having transcended, not only the dualism of self versus other, but even those of religion versus secularity and of Buddhism versus non-Buddhism. Ironically, such generous giving to a secular university creates favorable conditions for the spread of the dharma in two ways. First, the display of such selflessness by Buddhists fosters a positive predisposition toward the tradition by others. Seeing such a generous contribution to society, people cannot but become interested in learning more about the teachings responsible for sparking the virtuous conduct. Second, Master Xingyun has total confidence in the persuasive power of the dharma. He rests assured in the conviction that, given proper education and opportunity, people will very naturally come to the conclusion that Buddhist teachings provide the most accurate description of reality and human potential. Hence, a well-educated general populace is in the interest of Buddhism. One need not attempt to force people to accept the truth of the dharma; given the freedom to seek for themselves and to delve into the lessons taught by the various religious and secular traditions, people will of their own accord join the Buddhist fold. Master Xingyun's characterization inverts the view held by many twentieth-century Chinese intellectuals, who have assumed that greater education would result in a decrease of religious faith. According to the master, education serves to lead people away from superstitious and evil faith. It is not, however, antithetical to authentic faith *(zhengxin)* and, in fact, plays a vital role in leading people to it.

MORAL EDUCATION

The Foguang religious education system strives to develop the intellectual, moral, and spiritual capabilities of tomorrow's Buddhist leaders. The organization's secular education system focuses on the intellectual and moral dimensions in the confidence that such training will inevitably create the proper conditions for spiritual maturation as well. There are other settings in which Master Xingyun sets his sights almost exclusively on nurturing people's moral sensibility. Since the 1980s, Master Xingyun and other Foguang monastics have visited correctional facilities throughout Taiwan to speak with inmates. They introduce the convicts to the Buddhist notion of karma as a means to encourage them to mend their ways and, thereby, secure a happier future. These lessons frequently end with an opportunity to take the triple refuge. Inmates may also participate in Foguangshan's Buddhism examinations. Such chaplaincy therefore certainly has its religious elements. The emphasis is, nonetheless, on self-rectification through commitment to lead a moral life henceforth.

Foguang efforts to cleanse society through the moral regeneration of individuals extend beyond Taiwan's prison population. As already noted, the versions of the Buddhism examination that are prepared for students focus almost entirely on ethical behavior, and the majority of programs on Foguang Television are simply wholesome family entertainment. Furthermore, Master Xingyun periodically has called for large-scale campaigns to raise moral awareness throughout the island, an effort that has intensified in recent years as the crime rate has risen. In response to several high-profile murders involving prominent Taiwan citizens, Master Xingyun initiated the "Campaign of Compassion and Love" (Cibei Aixin Huodong) in the fall of 1997.[8] BLIA organized a rally of eighty-thousand people at the Chiang Kai-shek Memorial in Taipei to kick off the campaign. ROC vice-president Lian Zhan, Justice Minister Liao Zhenghao, and other government officials participated in the gathering, calling all of Taiwan to heed the campaign's slogan: "Purify the mind and spirit, refine morality, recover a sense of conscience, and harmonize society" (*xinling jinghua, daode chongzheng, zhaohui liangzhi, anding shehui*). In the months that followed, BLIA delegates organized smaller rallies and parades in cities around the island, gathering signatures from thousands of people, both Buddhists and non-Buddhists, who agreed to abide by the campaign's seven admonitions, namely, to avoid taking drugs, committing adultery, acting violently, stealing, gambling, drinking excessively, or engaging in abusive speech.

Master Xingyun chose the term "admonition" (*jie*) rather than "precept" (also pronounced *jie*, but written slightly differently) both to emphasize that the campaign was aimed at all Taiwan society, regardless of religious faith, and to give salience to the voluntary character of following such guidelines for conduct. Taking precepts is also voluntary, of course, but it assumes a more serious, long-term dedication to keeping one's vow. In other words, encouraging people to abide by the seven admonitions is but a start, both for the individuals involved and for society as a whole. True regeneration requires a deeper commitment to moral purification as a part of spiritual cultivation. In the next chapter, I turn to a consideration of the Foguang interpretation of the role of precepts in directing spiritual development.

6 Cultivating Faith through Discipline

LAY VOWS

TRIPLE REFUGE

Participants in a triple refuge ceremony openly express that, henceforth, the Buddha, his teachings, and the community that he founded will be the locus of their faith. They do so by reciting the phrases

> I take refuge in the Buddha; I take refuge in the dharma; I take refuge in the sangha.
> I take refuge in the Buddha, revered by humans and devas.
> I take refuge in the dharma, revered by those free from desire.
> I take refuge in the sangha, revered among the multitudes.
> I take refuge in the Buddha realm; I take refuge in the dharma realm; I take refuge in the sangha realm.
>
> I take refuge in the Buddha; I take refuge in the dharma; I take refuge in the sangha.
> Taking refuge in the Buddha, in life after life I will not take refuge in the evil beings [tianmo] of unorthodox ways [waidao].
> Taking refuge in the dharma, in life after life I will not take refuge in the wayward teachings [xiejiao] of unorthodox ways.
> Taking refuge in the sangha, in life after life I will not take refuge in disciples [mentu] of unorthodox ways.
> I take refuge in the Buddha realm; I take refuge in the dharma realm; I take refuge in the sangha realm.
>
> I take refuge in the Buddha; I take refuge in the dharma; I take refuge in the sangha.
> Taking refuge in the Buddha, in life after life I will never fall into hell.
> Taking refuge in the dharma, in life after life I will never be reborn as an animal.
> Taking refuge in the sangha, in life after life I will never be reborn as a hungry ghost.

I take refuge in the Buddha realm; I take refuge in the dharma realm; I take refuge in the sangha realm. ("Sanbao dianli," n.d., 2–3)

According to the sutras, says Master Xingyun, thus taking refuge affords numerous benefits, guaranteeing that the person who does so is assured of being reborn as either a human or a heavenly being, never in hell or as an animal or a hungry ghost; the growth in faith will shine through the person's bearing, bestowing on him or her a refined dignity; the person will be protected by dragon kings and devas; light karmic obstructions will be reduced, leading to a life of success and peace; and, most important, enlightenment will be attained since, even if one does not engage in any further cultivation in this lifetime, the seed of awakening has been planted through one's faith (Shi Xingyun 1995a, 1:6–7).

With the benefits of taking refuge come responsibilities. Devotees will reap advantage only to the degree that they cultivate the seed of faith by dedicating themselves to learning more about Buddhism and to aiding monastics in spreading the dharma. They are expected to develop right understanding and views, especially concerning the law of cause and effect. They are also exhorted to participate in Buddhist activities regularly and to contribute to temples. As we saw in chapter 4 above, Master Xingyun emphasizes that there is much more to making contributions than simply donating money. "Don't think that merit is tied to how much money one gives," warned the master during one triple refuge ceremony. "A person can provide service in many ways. For Foguang devotees it is not a matter of how much money they have or donate but a matter of cultivating their heart and mind. To spend too much money on Buddhism is not good, in fact, for it may make difficulties for one's family. Instead, gradually accumulate merit through regular participation and cultivation and through speaking positively about Buddhism and Foguangshan" ("Triple Refuge Ceremony" 1996).

Master Xingyun almost invariably makes comments to this effect during his explanatory remarks *(kaishi)* just after the vow of refuge has been taken. He typically instructs the audience members in three other matters as well. First, he assures them that taking the triple refuge carries with it no obligation to keep any precepts. The ceremony is simply an expression of dedication to the three gems and, hence, necessitates no major changes in one's daily routine. One need not become a vegetarian, nor is there any pressure for lay devotees to adopt a monastic lifestyle. This does not mean that anything goes, of course, for those who have taken refuge are expected to act morally, but the separation of making this faith statement from accepting precepts makes it easier for such people as butchers and fishermen to become Buddhists.

Second, the master informs the new devotees that they have taken refuge in the three gems, not in Foguangshan. One of the major reasons that Chinese Buddhism remains weak, he insists, is persistent partisanship among devotees. Allegiance must be to the Buddha, his teachings, and the entire community that he founded, not just to one interpretation of the teachings or to one representative or segment of the community. Master Xingyun therefore reminds those taking the triple refuge under his guidance that they may participate in any Buddhist activity at any temple, not just those at Foguang centers. Similarly, those who have taken refuge through other organizations are welcome to join Foguang associations and programs. "Temples are different," observes the master, "but the basic teaching is the same."

Master Xingyun would like to see all Buddhists work together to spread the dharma. So long as they compete with one another to attract devotees, such cooperation will remain limited. Within the Foguang organization, unity is maintained by stipulating that, while any monastic may take in devotees, he or she may do so only as a representative of the most senior cleric, that is, the master. It is Master Xingyun's name that appears on refuge certificates, whether or not he was present for the ceremony.[1]

Such a strategy may work within the Foguang order, but, by creating a sense of identification with that order and its master, it ipso facto creates a distinction over against other organizations and teachers. Devotees may take refuge in the three gems, but they inevitably do so under the guidance of a particular cleric, and through this very act they become a "refuge disciple" (*guiyi dizi*) of that monk or nun. During a conference with his monastic devotees, Master Xingyun told of an incident in which a Foguang branch invited a well-known bhikshu who heads his own organization to give a dharma talk. The monk held an impromptu refuge ceremony at the end of his presentation. Master Xingyun found this very improper and, therefore, warned his disciples against inviting any non-Foguang clerics to give lectures. If devotees were truly just taking refuge in the dharma and not also establishing through the ceremony a special relationship with the presiding venerable, Master Xingyun would not have been so affronted by what the guest speaker had done.

Calls for pan-Buddhist unity cannot overcome the fact that the various Buddhist masters and organizations are in competition with one another for human and material resources. Such competition has become accentuated in recent years as the number of large Buddhist organizations has proliferated and Taiwan's economy has slowed. Foguangshan has certainly felt pressure to find new ways to fund its ambitious projects under such tightening fiscal conditions. During the same triple refuge ceremony in which the master warned against equating how much one donates with the accumulation of merit, all participants were given cards extolling the merit received though making a generous financial contribution to Foguang University. Ideally, how much money devotees give does not matter; pragmatically, it is extremely important.

Foguangshan and other Buddhist organizations have had to be particularly careful in recent years in the degree to which they press devotees for financial assistance. As we have seen, several well-known folk Buddhist masters were indicted in 1996 for bilking their followers of millions of New Taiwan dollars through a variety of scams. Newspapers and officials called for heightened government supervision and regulation of all Buddhist organizations. The scandals not only focused attention on temple finances but also sparked discussion about criteria for determining who ought to be regarded as a trustworthy religious teacher as well as about the degree of faith that devotees should place in such leaders.

Master Xingyun used the opportunity provided by the scandals to remind his devotees that, while they are free to go to other temples, they must be careful to distinguish organizations that promote "authentic faith" (*zhengxin*) from those advocating "superstitious" (*mixin*) or, even worse, "perverted" faith (*xiexin*). In one refuge ceremony he stated: "Distinguish the real from the fake. To get apples, one needs to plant an apple seed. Just because a person has a shaved head does not mean he is a Buddhist monk. When a person is sick, it is dangerous to go to someone who is not really a doctor. It is the same with monks. Don't be fooled or cheated. A monk must have wisdom, compassion, and merit. Once a person becomes a Buddhist, he or she must not place faith in charlatans." Since it is not always easy to differentiate authentic teachers from imposters, devotees are warned to be careful. Hence, while they may participate in other Buddhist organizations, they are discouraged from doing so. Foguangshan is their original *dharmadhatu (fajie)*, so they should consider it as their second family: "Your father and mother have raised you physically; Foguangshan will raise you spiritually" ("Triple Refuge Ceremony" 1996).

The question of authenticity extends beyond internal variations in Buddhist doctrine and praxis to encompass the relation of the dharma to the worldviews and values of other religions. This is the third and final matter in which Master Xingyun typically instructs devotees during refuge ceremonies. Once again, he advocates a cautious, circumscribed openness, stating that Buddhists may worship the deities of other traditions so long as the spiritual being is not evil in nature (i.e., is not a *tianmo*) and such veneration does not result in harm to the worshiper or others. According to the master, there is a fundamental difference between taking the triple refuge (*guiyi*) and engaging in worship (*baibai*): the former is a lifelong faith commitment (*yi sheng de xinyang*), the latter a transient means of expressing respect and courtesy. A Buddhist has, not just the right, but the duty to show such respect to the divinities of other authentic religious traditions. One's lifelong faith, however, must remain only in the three gems (Shi Xingyun 1995a, 1:12). What, then, distinguishes faith from respect and authentic faith from that which is harmful or superstitious?

Master Xingyun identifies four types of faith commitment (Shi Xingyun 1983, 146, 168–169; Shi Xingyun 1995a, 10:435–438). The first is that seen in those people who feel no connection or resonance with any religious faith (*bu xin*). Such a purely secular, atheistic worldview is unfortunate, in the master's view, because it proves to be so shallow, preventing the person from realizing the deep possibilities of his or her full being. On the other hand, to lack faith is better than to have entrusted oneself to a form of perverted or distorted faith, the second type of faith commitment. Those who base their conduct on such a skewed vision of reality (*xiejian*) not only fail to gain any benefit but actually multiply suffering, both for themselves and others. Very often, this is the faith that arises from blind credulity, leaving people open to the chicanery of such charlatans as Song Qili and Qing Hai, both of whom were embroiled in the 1996 scandals. The third type of faith commitment is superstition (*mixin*). Like distorted faith, superstition is based on a misunderstanding of the nature of reality. Unlike distorted faith, however, it is relatively harmless, basically reflecting an unsophisticated, immature stage of cultivation. This is the belief in the efficacy of folk deities, such as Mazi and Guangong, and in such popular customs as geomancy, phrenology, and fortune-telling. On the one hand, such faith is salutary in that it can give people hope and lead them to follow upright, moral lives. Nonetheless, because it is simplistic, its benefits are limited, and the tendency toward extravagance wastes time and resources.

Only authentic forms of faith—the fourth type of faith commitment—allow for long-term cessation of suffering and the fulfillment of human potential. They are able to do so because they are based on wisdom, not ignorance. According to Master Xingyun, such faith is manifested in all the major religions of the world (e.g., Buddhism, Christianity, Islam, and Judaism) as well as the Chinese traditions of Confucianism, Daoism, and ancestor worship. Although they are all authentic expressions of human spirituality, even these traditions differ, the master notes, in the depth and breadth of their sagacity. Not surprisingly, he believes Buddhism to be the most profound expression of religious faith because of its uniquely penetrating and universal nature. He states: "The difference between Buddhism and other religions is not only that Buddhism is replete with faith, precepts, rituals, and other such methods of cultivation but also that these practices are based on a system of thought that is fully rational and objective. The foundational doctrines of Buddhism . . . accord not just with Buddhist logic but with all human logic. Regardless of the era or place, [the dharma] can be applied to human society, and its logical character is even more proved by its compatibility with the advances of science and literary fields" (Shi Xingyun 1995a, 10:430).

Master Xingyun therefore distinguishes Buddhism from other traditions because of its rationality and universal validity and applicability. By "rationality" *(helixing)*, he means that Buddhist teachings may be easily verified by historical, logical, and scientific analysis. Contrary to other religions, which typically ascribe supernatural status to their founders, Buddhism emphasizes the very human origins and capabilities of Shakyamuni. "The process through which the Buddha became enlightened and the record of his teachings," asserts the master, "are recorded in concrete, reliable historical accounts; his was not an empty, ambiguous, miraculous existence" (Shi Xingyun 1995a, 10:430).[2] Buddhist doctrine also accords better with logic than do the worldviews of other traditions in that it need not rely on some mysterious ultimate source impervious to human reason; the notions of cause and effect, impermanence, and emptiness simply explain reality in a more satisfying way than do the Jewish, Christian, Muslim, and Hindu concepts of an eternal soul and creator god. The greater logic of Buddhism, continues the master, can also be seen by its better correspondence with the modern scientific understanding of the world, although he neglects to give any specifics as to the ways in which the two systems correspond.

For the master, the most important point is that the rationality and logic of the dharma renders it more effective in solving the multitudinous dilemmas confronting humans in their diverse cultural and historical settings. Unlike other religions, which are said to have only limited application, the Mahayana Buddhist approach has universal scope. Master Xingyun demonstrates this inclusivism by comparing the world's major religions to the five vehicles of Buddhism. The Confucian emphasis on ethics and interpersonal relations, for example, he equates with the "human vehicle" *(rensheng)*. The focus on heaven and hell found in Christianity is said to be comparable to the "vehicle of heavenly beings" *(tiansheng)*. The Daoist celebration of nonaction *(wuwei)* and radical skepticism, meanwhile, has echoes in the Buddhist *shravaka (shengwensheng)* and *pretyakabuddha (yuanjuesheng)* vehicles, making Daoism essentially equivalent to Hinayana Buddhism. Each of these traditions, in other words, provides significant insight into a particular aspect of the human experience of reality. Only the bodhisattva vehicle of Mahayana Buddhism, however, brings all these together. The other religions are not wrong—they too are versions of authentic faith—they are simply incomplete. As "external teachings" (*waijiao*), they fail to reach the innermost core of reality in its multivalent aspects (Shi Xingyun 1995a, 10:442–443).

Authenticity is not an either/or proposition. In line with the Chinese predilection to think in terms of polarities rather than dichotomies, Master Xingyun has constructed his understanding of faith on a graded scale of comprehensiveness and efficacy. His paradigm of faith is firmly rooted in pragmatic considerations: to the degree that a particular teaching or practice leads to ultimate well-being is it to be deemed authentic. Because the deities of other religions guide people to a high level of well-being, they are worthy of even Buddhists' respect; as the dharma alone can provide the way for all to attain ultimate liberation, however, only the three gems merit faith.

Five Precepts

In South and Southeast Asian Buddhist communities, when a person takes the triple refuge, he or she will simultaneously accept the five precepts: no killing; no stealing; no adultery; no lying; and no intoxicants. Chinese Buddhists have tended to regard the vow to uphold these precepts as separate from taking refuge, although some follow their southern brethren in insisting that the two must go hand in hand. Foguangshan follows a middle course. Triple refuge and five precept ceremonies are often held simultaneously, but there is never any insistence that all participants take the precepts. At other times, triple refuge ceremonies occur on their own, and special retreats lasting several days are held for those taking either the five precepts or the bodhisattva vows.[3]

In his lectures on the precepts, Master Xingyun emphasizes that these are not commandments or rules that must be followed to the letter, regardless of circumstances. Rather, they are guidelines for behavior to aid people in acting appropriately. Failing to observe a precept will almost invariably have repercussions either during this life or during a future rebirth, but, at times, blind adherence will result in even heavier karmic consequences. The master stresses repeatedly that, for the precepts to remain relevant to contemporary problems, their underlying spirit of discipline and compassion must be rigorously maintained while the specifics of their application be enacted flexibly.[4]

The first precept dictates that a person abstain from killing or even harming other lives. The vow encompasses all animals, but, observes Master Xingyun, its primary referent is people. Hence, to murder a human being is an unforgivable violation of the precept (*jizhongzui*; *parajika*), while killing an insect is but a minor transgression (*qinggouzui*; *duskrta*). The extermination of cockroaches, rats, and other pests brings almost no karmic harm when it is done to prevent illness and death among people. The killing of bugs out of simple annoyance or repugnance, on the other hand, carries more severe consequences. In other words, it is as much the intention as the specific act that determines the karmic weight.

The killing of higher animals or fish also has much lighter karmic effects than does the killing of people, but, the less one does so, the better. It is, therefore, strongly advised not to earn one's livelihood in a way that requires the repetitive slaughter of such beings. Even butchers and fishermen can compensate for the evil karma accrued through their occupation, however, if they continually repent for the suffering that they cause. Buddhist monastics have too easily forsaken those who engage in unsavory professions, avers Master Xingyun. The point is to help these people develop their compassion and wisdom so that, if not in this lifetime, at least in a future rebirth they will enjoy circumstances in which such a profession will be unnecessary. This is the same reasoning as that underlying the master's missionary work in prisons.

The act of willfully murdering a human carries such a heavy karmic burden that no amount of repentance can fully compensate for it. There are, nonetheless, certain attenuating circumstances under which even the killing of a person results in relatively light karmic repercussions. Because wars between countries arise from the communal karma between the two groups of people (*gongye*), so long as a soldier acts out of a sense of duty rather than out of malice, the individual karma accumulated will be negligible. On the other hand, to turn one's back on one's country during its time of need indicates an unconscionable lack of gratitude and loyalty.

Capital punishment is also permissible in Master Xingyun's view. In fact, according to the law of cause and effect, executing a murderer fulfills the natural consequence of that person's act. So long as the executioner holds no enmity or grudge against the person being executed, little individual karmic effect will adhere, for he or she is merely carrying out the country's law. Those involved in handing down the death penalty may even accumulate positive karma if their intentions are as pure as those of Shakyamuni Buddha, who, according to the Jakarta tales, had, in one of his previous lives, killed a bandit to prevent him from massacring five hundred merchants.

The karmic consequences of abortion depend on the pregnant woman's circumstances. If she has been raped and the raising of the child would cause her continual distress, aborting the fetus does not result in great karmic backlash. Similarly, if the expectant mother knows that the child will suffer from serious abnormalities, placing a burden on society, ending its life is justified. It is not that the woman will be free of all karmic reverberations but, rather, that the extenuating circumstances *(yuan)* minimize the impact of the cause *(yin)* and, hence, dilute the effect *(guo)*. "Hence," the master observes, "a mother has the right to decide whether it is permissible for her to have an abortion, for she is the one who will have to carry the inevitable burden of cause and effect" (Shi Xingyun 1998b, 325).

Similar reasoning dictates the Foguang perspective on euthanasia. If a patient has reached a vegetative state with no hope of recovery, or if he or she is in constant severe pain, it is up to the family members to determine whether the best course is to end that person's life. The karmic effects of killing may be more than compensated for by the power of the family members' love. "There are no definite rules of permissible or impermissible," asserted Master Xingyun at one meeting (29 January) of monastics in which abortion and euthanasia came up for discussion. "Anything is possible, so long as it is done out of compassion and wisdom" ("Meeting of Foguang Monastics Assigned to Taiwan Branch Temples" 1997).

"Killing" not only means ending the physical life of a sentient being, contends Master Xingyun, but, in its wider sense, includes any act that reduces life. Wasting time is, therefore, a form of killing. Other Chan masters have stated that, whenever one is not mindful of a particular moment but, instead, has allowed one's thoughts to wander into the past, the future, or fantasy, one has ended the chance for life in that duration. Master Xingyun expands on this line of reasoning, arguing that any unproductive moment, any time whiled away rather than devoted to Buddhist cultivation for the salvation of all beings, is so much of life that has been killed. The transgression is even more serious if a person has wasted another's time. Resources, for instance, must be preserved since each such material good represents so much time and effort on the part of the producer. As noted in chapter 4 above, punctuality is highly prized at Foguangshan. There is a great sense of urgency among Master Xingyun and his followers; with so much work to be done and so little time in one's life, every moment must count.

The second precept is that against stealing. Master Xingyun states that this precept is quite straightforward, referring simply to respecting other people's property and wealth. It is, nonetheless, he continues, perhaps the most difficult of the five vows to keep. This is because bribery and corruption have become so pervasive in modern society that those who refuse to go along with coworkers risk ostracism and retaliation.

The third precept, that against sexual misconduct, includes "any sexual activities that occur between the sexes outside a husband-wife relationship—for example, adultery, bigamy, rape, prostitution, sexual abuse, pornography, and pedophilia" (Shi Xingyun 1995a, 1:18). Ideally, states the master, marriage is for life.

This is best for the couple and, especially, for the children. Just as conditions bring people together, however, circumstances also arise at times under which a couple must separate. Divorce is not to be encouraged, in other words, but it is also not necessarily to be condemned. Master Xingyun is vague about his stance toward homosexuality. He does not include it in his list of illicit sexual relations, and, in one reference to homosexuality, he merely states: "According to Buddhism, any emotional involvement, whether homosexual or heterosexual, is a form of attachment [*zhizhuo*] and, therefore, is a source of suffering" (Shi Xingyun 1998b, 324). During a meeting with the Foguang community when there were rumors that two laywomen at the headquarters were lovers, the master spoke more strongly, calling homosexuality a perverted view (*xiejian*) ("Foguang Headquarters Community Meeting" 1998a).

The fourth precept, that against lying, means abstaining from distorting reality, especially in a way that hurts or cheats others. Following the mainstream Buddhist categorization, Master Xingyun divides lies into three types: "major lies" (*da wangyu*); "minor lies" (*xiao wangyu*); and "lies of convenience" (*fangbian wangyu*). The first of these categories comprises any false claim to have achieved enlightenment or supernatural powers and any malicious criticism of Buddhist devotees, especially monastics. The second covers any attempt to bear false witness or to fabricate a story. The third refers to well-intended misrepresentations of the facts, such as a doctor protecting the feelings of a terminally ill patient by keeping back the unpleasant truth.

The fifth precept, against intoxicants, refers specifically to abstaining from drinking alcoholic beverages, but, more broadly, states Master Xingyun, it can be taken as a proscription against ingesting any drug unless it is medically necessary. Unlike the first four precepts, which are collectively called "character precepts" (*xingjie*) because they focus on directly preventing evil behavior, the fifth aims to prevent a loss of inhibition, which may then lead to breaking one of the first four. The fifth precept is, therefore, called the "intervention precept" (*zhejie*). Master Xingyun does not include either cigarettes or betel nut under this category, although he strongly advises against either because of the health risks. He finds the chewing of betel nut especially problematic because of its reported aphrodisiac properties and the recent trend in Taiwan to have the nut sold by teenage girls dressed in provocative clothing.

Bodhisattva Precepts

For those who have vowed to keep the five precepts, the next level of commitment is taking the bodhisattva precepts (*pusa jie*). At Foguangshan, as at other Chinese

Buddhist temples, this means pledging to keep the six primary and twenty-eight secondary precepts enumerated in the *Upasaka Precept Sutra (Youposai jie jing)*. The six primary precepts include the five precepts enumerated above plus a vow not to slander any of the four groups of Buddhists (bhikshus, bhikshunis, upasakas, and upasikas). The twenty-eight secondary precepts cover such issues as regularly making offerings to one's parents, teachers, and elders, abstaining from boisterous, unseemly behavior, avoiding traveling alone in dangerous places, etc. All twenty-eight of these are regarded as elaborations on the six primary vows and, as such, do not necessitate any significant change in lifestyle from what was already required on taking the five precepts.

In explanatory remarks offered during bodhisattva precept ceremonies, Master Xingyun tells the audience that the real significance of taking these precepts is to be found, not in the specific vows, but, rather, in the shift in focus of cultivation. Those who take the bodhisattva precepts pledge wholeheartedly to devote themselves to aiding others by self-consciously following the bodhisattva path of loving kindness *(ci; metta)* and compassion *(bei; karuna)* for all beings. Unlike the five precepts, which focus on cultivating self-restraint, the bodhisattva vows encourage the practice of good deeds in order actively to promote the welfare and liberation of others. These precepts therefore fall under three categories: the codified precepts *(shelü yijie)*; any action that works for goodness *(sheshan fajie)*; and whatever leads to the well-being and salvation of sentient beings *(raoyiyouqing jie)* (Shi Xingyun 1998b, 327).

The commitment fully to devote oneself to benefiting others is most concretely manifested in two practices that are associated with taking the bodhisattva precepts but that are not, in fact, included among the vows. The first is scarification. The same day that preceptees take the vows, they have three "precept scars" *(jieba)* burned on their forearm by moxa. Undergoing such scarification is said to demonstrate both that one has transcended mundane concern for one's body and that, as one follows the bodhisattva path, one is willing to accept any suffering on behalf of all sentient beings. Interpretations of the significance of the three scars themselves vary. Some say that they represent the three gems. Others offer that they symbolize the principal aspects of Buddhist practice—discipline, concentration, and wisdom. Regardless of hermeneutics, on a practical level having incense scars provides a physical sign that one is a deeply committed Buddhist.

The second practice associated with taking bodhisattva precepts is vegetarianism. The vow against killing taken as part of the five precepts is, here, extended to avoid even indirectly causing the death of animals by purchasing meat. Although the karmic consequences of consuming meat are not particularly heavy, the goal is to minimize all such negative karma; one may not have personally killed the animal, but, by eating it, one has contributed to the conditions leading to the animal's demise. Master Xingyun acknowledges that, outside the Chinese Buddhist community, even most Buddhist monastics take meat as food. The Chinese encourage a vegetarian diet, he says, because it nurtures compassion and is advocated in various sutras, such as the *Nirvana Sutra* (see Shi Xingyun 1995a, 1:17; Shi Xingyun 1998b, 328–329).[5] The resolution to abstain from eating meat does not extend to completely avoiding all leather goods. Even the drums in Buddhist temples employed to gather devotees, heavenly beings, and buddhas for dharma functions require leather heads, observes the master. Since the quantity of leather that most people use is slight and the benefits of such products to human well-being readily seen, the negative repercussions of using leather goods in moderation are negligible.

Chinese Buddhist vegetarianism has been questioned on two fronts. Some have argued that plants too have a life and that suffering is, therefore, an inevitable consequence of sustaining one's own existence. A vegetarian diet merely alters the sufferer, without reducing suffering itself. Master Xingyun follows the mainstream Chinese Buddhist response to this, namely, that a plant has only physiological reactions without being conscious, as are animals. A vegetarian diet therefore does not kill *sentient* life. Others have questioned the widespread practice within the Chinese Buddhist community of creating vegetarian dishes that taste and even look like meat: vegetarian "beef," "chicken," "lamb," and "fish." By bringing such associations to the diner's mind, it is argued, such dishes trigger vestiges (*xiqi*) of the anger and ignorance that accompany the killing of actual animals and, therefore, hinder the cultivation of compassion. Master Xingyun explains that ersatz meat entrées are an expedient means to ease the transition to a vegetarian diet. The dishes should not, however, too closely resemble meat in taste or appearance, for this would detract from the underlying intent and could lead outsiders to deride Buddhism. Hence, while the act itself of eating vegetarian dishes closely resembling meat carries few karmic reverberations, because of outside social factors this practice breaks the precept against exposing the sangha to ridicule and, thereby, still has negative karmic implications.[6]

Karmic effect is determined by the act, the intention framing that act, and the attitude toward what one has done. "When upright people engage in a wayward practice, the wayward becomes upright; when wayward people engage in an upright practice, the upright becomes wayward," state Foguang clerics, quoting the Buddhist proverb. Good karmic effects arise in relation to the degree of compassion and wisdom. Compassion alone is insufficient, for, without wisdom, one's noble intentions may lead to an evil outcome.

For this reason, Master Xingyun does not particularly advocate the ceremonial release of animal life. Although this custom has developed as an expression of compassion, he explains, it often results in suffering and death. Too often, people have the wrong motive for engaging in the practice, often doing so in hopes that the attending merit will bring long life. Another problem with the practice is that people release the animal in an unsuitable place. Turtles have been freed in release ponds, for instance, resulting in them eating the fish placed there by others. Animals purchased from a pet shop do not know how to survive in the wild. Doves, a favorite recipient for release, are often trained by unscrupulous store owners to fly back to the shop, so nothing has really been freed at all. As the master says: "Freshwater fish are set free in the ocean, and saltwater fish are released in ponds or streams. People have even released poisonous snakes where they can harm people. . . . To pay such intensive attention to releasing life is not really to release life. It may go by the pretty name 'releasing life,' but, in truth, it is not moral. One ought to promote the release of life according to conditions, not according to prearranged design" (Shi Xingyun 1998b, 327). Good intentions are not enough, and, when perpetuating suffering and evil, they inadvertently result in unfortunate karmic consequences.

SHORT-TERM PRECEPT RETREATS
The bodhisattva precepts are the most demanding of the long-term vows taken by laity. There are two types of precepts that may be taken for a set period of time that provide even more rigorous discipline during their duration: the eight precepts and short-term monastic precepts.

The eight precepts are the vows to abstain from killing, stealing, engaging in any sexual activity, speaking falsehood, imbibing intoxicants, wearing personal adornment (including perfumes and cosmetics), partaking in or watching entertainment (such as singing or dancing), and using a broad bed.[7] The Buddha is said to have advised lay followers to observe these precepts over a twenty-four-hour period on the six fast days of each month (the eighth, fourteenth, fifteenth, twenty-third, twenty-ninth, and thirtieth days of the lunar calendar) as a means both to purify conduct and to gain a taste of monastic life. In contemporary Chinese Buddhist tradition, these vows are usually kept while spending a weekend night in a temple. Participants in such retreats wear the same black robes and brown vestments used during dharma functions by those who have taken the five precepts. They also keep a vegetarian diet and do not eat after noon. According to Foguang literature, one of the primary benefits of undertaking such a retreat is that those who do so with sincerity will have planted the seed to take full monastic vows, if not in this life, at least in some future rebirth (Shi Xingyun 1995a, 1:24, 30). Most of the larger Foguang branch temples offer eight precept retreats once per month, and the headquarters sponsors them weekly as part of the weekend cultivation activities.

Laity may experience a more intensive taste of what it would be like to be a cleric by participating in a seven-day "short-term monastic retreat."[8] These programs are one of Foguangshan's innovative contributions to Chinese Buddhism. Their genesis lies in two sources. First, Master Xingyun began offering week-long Buddhist camps for college-age men and women in 1969. Modeled after the camps sponsored by Christian organizations, the sessions were designed to be both fun and a means to attract young people to Buddhism. In the 1970s, similar camps were developed for mothers, teachers, and senior citizens. Then, after the master traveled to Thailand in 1988, where he saw firsthand how every young man renounces for at least a short stint, he decided to offer such an opportunity to Chinese lay Buddhists, both male and female.

Men participating in the retreat take the ten shramanera vows; women take the six *siksamana* precepts. The ten vows for men include those taken for the eight precepts retreat plus a formal precept against eating after noon and an additional one forbidding the handling of gold, silver, or money. *Siksamanas* take slightly different vows. They abstain from touching any male's body with an impure mind, stealing four units of money or more, ending an animal's life, being untruthful, eating after noon, and ingesting intoxicants. Women are given the *siksamana* rather than the shramanerika vows so that they need not shave their heads.

Men begin the retreat by being tonsured. All participants then spend the afternoon learning the basics: everything from how to wear monastic clothing (i.e., gray cassock, black novice robe, and brown vestment) to how to walk and eat and proper etiquette while in the shrine (e.g., never enter through the central door, never cross directly in front of the main image, etc.). The period from the evening of the first day of the retreat to the morning of the third is largely devoted to rehearsing and performing various ceremonies: altar purification; tonsure; repentance; precept conferral; and puja offering. For the next three days, a variety of lectures take place on such subjects as "theory and practice of Humanistic Buddhism" and "how to develop the bodhi mind." Participants are also taught the fundamentals of Chan, and each day begins and ends with chanting and meditation. Once the precepts are taken, only porridge is served for the evening medicine meal. There is to be no talking throughout the retreat. On the final day, participants hand back their robes, alms bowls, and ritual ground cover (*woju; nisidana*) as they return to lay life. The relinquishment ceremony is very emotional, with tears flowing freely.

Participants in short-term monastic retreats range in age from teenagers to those in their sixties. Older participants engage in the week of monastic cultivation to gain merit and with the expectation that they have thereby planted the seed for full ordination in a future life. Many of the younger participants enroll in the function precisely because they are seriously contemplating renouncing in this life. Shortly after the inaugural program during the last week of July 1989, Master Xingyun noted in his diary that, of the five hundred people who had taken part, more than fifty expressed an interest in studying at the Foguangshan Monastic Buddhist Academy, and thirty-two eventually pledged to matriculate (Shi Xingyun 1994, vol. 1, entries for 29, 31 July 1989). Hence, these short-term monastic retreats, along with the various camps, are important recruiting opportunities for Foguangshan's seminary system. Once in the Foguangshan Monastic Academy, the vast majority of students renounce within one to two years.

MONASTIC VOWS

Motives for Renouncing

What leads young men and women to renounce? What circumstances in their personal or professional lives have impelled them to "leave home" (*chujia*), shave their heads, and submit to the rigors of a monastic career? Clerics voice eight common motives for entering the sangha. First, there are those monks and nuns who have come from devout Buddhist families. Buddhist teachings therefore played an integral role in their upbringing. Furthermore, it may be their parents' wish that they renounce. Such monastics are typically on the younger side when they join the order, sometimes undergoing tonsure before having even reached their twentieth birthday. Family support (and, perhaps, pressure) to become a venerable is especially noticeable when more than one family member has joined the sangha, a phenomenon that has occurred more than two dozen times at Foguangshan. In one case, four sisters have all renounced. In another, two brothers, a sister, and a nephew have taken the monastic vows. In yet another, three sisters were eventually joined by their mother in the Foguang monastic community.[9]

The death or sickness of a parent or some other relative has frequently sparked in an individual a desire both to better understand why such tragedies occur and to aid the deceased to attain a comfortable rebirth. Such circumstances were certainly at work when Master Xingyun renounced at age twelve: it was during the futile search for his father, who had disappeared during the Nanjing Massacre in 1939, that the master resolved to tonsure under Ven. Zhikai. One nun told me that her decision to renounce partially stemmed from having never completely gotten over either the brutal shock that she experienced on learning that her father had been killed in a car accident or the horror of having to identify his body in the morgue. Subsequently, as the oldest child she had had to help her mother support and raise six younger siblings. Another nun related that, as a young girl and teenager, she had been deeply moved by the way in which her aunt had gained solace in Buddhist teachings after having given birth to a boy with dwarfism, struggled with her inability to assuage his suffering, and, ultimately, found herself needing to come to terms with his death at age eleven. Although no members of the extended family had been active Buddhists before the boy's birth, they all increasingly became involved as they witnessed the great peace that both the boy and his mother experienced through reciting the Guanyin Bei Zhou and, after the boy passed away, the depth of the mother's earnestness in engaging in charitable works so as to transfer merit on his behalf.

Yet other monastics cite career dissatisfaction as the catalyst for their leaving secular life. Not surprisingly, these people renounced at a slightly older age, usually in their thirties. One such nun informed me that she had managed an office of over fifty workers before entering the sangha. Although the job had given her responsibility and challenges, she also found it stressful and began to question the worth of what she was doing. She wanted to have a deeper impact on more people. A Buddhist cleric, she stated, can minimize, if not completely eradicate, vexations (*fannao*) while also creating beneficial ties (*jieyuan*) with all sentient beings. Hence, she renounced to cultivate personal well-being and to better serve others.

The decision to don monastic robes is, for some, evidently tied to a quest fully to assert their identity as a Chinese. The nun mentioned above who had become disenchanted with her managerial job did not immediately think of renunciation as an option. Initially, she went to Hong Kong to get a master's degree in philosophy. Then, in 1994 and 1995, she took an extended trip through mainland China. The unexpected lack of resonance that she felt with the people of her homeland accentuated her identity crisis. On returning to Taiwan, she came upon a book by Master Xingyun that profoundly affected her, not only because of its ideas, but also because of the fact that this man from mainland China had been able to strike a deep chord with people in Taiwan. After a six-month stint of volunteer work on Foguangshan, she tonsured.

Actualizing values inculcated since childhood, fulfilling family expectations, coming to terms with the suffering or death of a loved one, fostering personal well-being through eradicating vexations, gaining a sense of meaning through service to others, and establishing a strong sense of one's Chinese identity are motives equally applicable to both monks and nuns. There are two other factors that appear to play a role in the decision to become a nun. First, some bhikshunis readily admit that, having seen what their mothers went through to pacify their mothers-in-law, get along with their husbands, and raise the children, they had no wish to follow in their footsteps.[10] Second, job dissatisfaction as a motivating force for renunciation may be especially acute for women in that they soon recognize that a glass ceiling limits their chances for promotion to positions of leadership. As nuns, they have multiple opportunities for public speaking, teaching, running a temple, and organizing large-scale events. Such openings occur both because monks and nuns tend to have independent, parallel institutional structures (allowing nuns to lead nuns and monks to lead monks) and because the surplus of nuns places them, rather than the monks, firmly in the majority, with the result that their concerns and opinions are much more likely to be heard and taken seriously in the sangha than they are elsewhere.

Assuming that the motives for renunciation proffered by Foguang monastics represent typical explanations for turn-of-the-century Chinese Buddhist monks and nuns, how do these reasons compare to the motives that prodded their predecessors? On the basis of an analysis of interviews that he had conducted with monks who had migrated to Hong Kong from mainland China after the Communist rise to power, Holmes Welch (1967, 259–269) listed eight reasons for renunciation. Thirteen of his interviewees stated or implied that they had renounced in order to escape from the secular world; in other words, they had failed the civil service examination, were army deserters, had been jobless, or had experienced disappointment in love.[11] Six of the monks had fallen ill as children (or their parents had fallen ill) and had vowed that they would join the sangha if the illness abated. Another six had been raised by a Buddhist organization after being orphaned. Yet another six said that they had always liked the monastic atmosphere. Several cited interest in the study or practice of Buddhist doctrine as their primary motivation. Two had been persuaded by relatives already in the sangha. One admitted that he had joined to escape his parents, who "hated him." Finally, one said that he had wanted to gain supernatural powers.

Comparing these answers to those provided by Foguang clerics, we find both continuities and disjunctions. On the one hand, certain themes persist, namely, a fondness since childhood for the monastic atmosphere, an interest in studying and practicing Buddhist teachings, and family encouragement. On the other hand, there are some quite noticeable discrepancies: none of Welch's contacts cited as motives the death of a loved one, the fostering of personal well-being through eradicating vexations, the gaining of a sense of meaning through service to others, or identity issues. Foguang monastics did not mention several of the goals cited by their predecessors: none admitted that they had entered the sangha as the result of some disappointment in the secular world, whether it be failure of college entrance examinations, inability to find work, or the collapse of a relationship; nor did any speak of joining the sangha in fulfillment of a vow to do so after recovering from illness, or as a result of being raised in a Buddhist orphanage; and the cultivation of supernatural powers was never mentioned.

The differences in articulated motives can be attributed to four sources. First, Welch and I were both working with fairly small samples: Welch was drawing from thirty-nine interviews that he conducted with monks who only barely knew him, and I was bringing together comments from some two dozen interviews and conversations. A larger pool may have increased the number of common motives offered. Second, Welch and I could list only articulated motives. That a reason was not mentioned does not necessarily indicate its absence. It very well may be that monastics also had had other motives that were unclear even to themselves, or that seemed so obvious that they did not bother mentioning them, or that they preferred not to reveal. The recognition of particular causes or hopes and the willingness on the part of interviewees to voice such causes or hopes are themselves significant, for they indicate which reasons are acknowledged by the individual and the community as worthy and appropriate. None of the Foguang monastics, for instance, admitted to me that they had entered the sangha as the result of some disappointment in the secular world. This very well may have played a role in the decisionmaking process of certain clerics, but none acknowledged such to be the case, either for themselves or for others.[12] Instead, the emphasis was on leaving successful careers or choosing to renounce while attending a top-notch university. Renunciation is touted as being the positive choice of winners, not some last refuge in response to failure. This rhetoric apparently carries such force that those who came to the sangha out of a sense of personal failure are reluctant to admit it.

Third, sociohistorical changes have rendered certain reasons obsolete while fostering others. The interplay between such broad factors and monastic recruitment can be seen in four instances. First, the decrease in the numbers of orphans and the general access to education have diluted the connection between Buddhist orphanages and monasteries. As noted in chapter 1 above, of the 483 children who had gone through Foguangshan's children's home as of March 1999, only 7 had renounced. Unlike in the Buddhist orphanages established in mainland China during the early part of this century, in Foguangshan's children's home it is not expected that the wards will renounce, and they are not pressured to do so. Second, improved health care appears to account for the disappearance of the practice of vowing to join the sangha after recovery from some illness, having done so by decreasing the frequency of life-threatening childhood diseases. The disappearance of this practice may also indicate that the making of such a vow is no longer seen as efficacious (or, less likely, that the keeping of such a vow is no longer necessary). Third, the rescinding of imperial laws that excused monastics from corvée labor or military service, coupled with improved tracking of the population, has nullified the avoidance of conscription as an important motive for becoming a monk. All young men who have tonsured at Foguangshan before having fulfilled their duty to serve in the military must return to lay life to join the armed forces on reaching age twenty. Finally, the felt need to assert one's Chinese heritage has come to the fore only since the division of mainland China and Taiwan, the expansion of the Chinese diaspora, and recent improvements in communication and transportation technologies, the latter having made renunciation a viable option for members of the diaspora.

Finally, the fact that the cultivation of supernatural powers was never mentioned by Foguang monastics reflects the values of one particular organization. Because Master Xingyun plays down the importance of acquiring such powers, it is unlikely that those hoping to acquire them would join his order (and, if they did join his order and maintained such aspirations, they would at least keep them to themselves).

Tonsure

The first step toward joining the Foguang order is to take up residence at the headquarters, either as a student in the Foguangshan Monastic Buddhist Academy or (especially if one is older) as a volunteer worker. If this experience further strengthens an individual's resolve—not just to be a monastic, but to be a Foguang monastic—he or she then requests to be tonsured as a disciple of Master Xingyun. Foguangshan's bylaws stipulate that, in order to preserve the organization's unity, a person may renounce under no Foguang cleric but the master.

The procedure by which one applies to become a disciple includes supplying a statement of intent to renounce, a certificate of physical health, and a letter of parental approval. The certificate of health ensures that the applicant suffers from neither physical handicaps nor psychological problems, both of which, according to the vinaya, indicate karmic obstacles too severe to attain monastic life. Receiving parental approval to renounce can be an emotional and difficult chore in some cases. Many parents are strongly adverse to one of their children joining the Buddhist order, especially if it is an only child or a son, particularly the eldest son. One young man who had lived on Foguangshan as a lay volunteer for three years had twice unsuccessfully sought permission from his father. Others tell of having received such approval only grudgingly. Renunciation as a Foguang monastic is virtually impossible without such a signed letter from the head of the household, however.

Once the application materials have been received, the Lamp Transmission Committee (Chuandeng Hui, Foguangshan's personnel department) then interviews the applicant to gauge whether he or she has the character, maturity, and commitment to renounce. The notes of this interview, along with the application materials, are forwarded to Master Xingyun, who decides whom among the candidates to accept.

Successful applicants have typically already spent some time studying in a Foguang seminary, although a few have received their training elsewhere and this requirement may be waived for those who are older, especially if they possess notable experience in some occupational field. Until recently, almost all Foguang seminary students who applied to renounce received permission to do so immediately. But the master and the Lamp Transmission Committee have, apparently, decided that a semester or two of study are no longer sufficient. Nearly thirty of the fifty applicants in February 1998 were turned down, including all first- and second-year college students. The reason given for denying these people's request for tonsure was their young age (all were around twenty) and lack of experience in either the secular or the Buddhist worlds.

Tonsure ceremonies occur at least biannually, usually just after the Chinese New Year and during Master Xingyun's birthday celebration in August. The night before the ceremony, Master Xingyun holds a banquet for the incoming disciples and their families. Even when both parents fully support their child's decision to renounce (and often at least one has reservations), this last evening before the son or daughter leaves home is an emotional time for all. Master Xingyun advises all present that those about to be tonsured have this last opportunity to reconsider. Later in the night, clerics will help each novitiate shave his or her head, quoting as they do so the gatha: "I vow to cut off all defilements; I vow to develop goodness; I vow to liberate all beings." (The monastics will, henceforth, silently invoke these same vows as they take their first three mouthfuls of rice at the beginning of each meal.)

The official tonsure ceremony takes place in Great Heroes Hall. As the enormous bell and drum ring out, the novices, now cleanly shaven and dressed in simple black monastic robes, silently file in, their family members and perhaps some friends observing from the perimeters of the hall. Master Xingyun mounts and sits on the dais just before the huge image of Shakyamuni Buddha. "Have your parents heard that you are becoming a monastic?" he asks. "They have!" affirm the new clerics. The master chants a series of formulaic stanzas (*fayu*) praising the monastic life, recites a poem written by Emperor Shunzhi in praise of the sangha, and reads portions of the *Sutra of the Buddha Speaking of the Merit of Renouncing (Fo shuo chujia gongde jing)*. His comments end with some short instructions to his new disciples. "Novices, in vowing to leave home to cultivate yourselves as monastics," he told one group on 6 January 1998, "your faith in the three gems must never waver, your loyalty to the monastic community must never be divided, your studies and practice must continually progress, your support for the dharma must be a constant duty, honoring your teachers' admonitions must be your highest priority, and you must accept the Buddhist teachings with a sincere heart." The master then descends to the initiates and uses a razor symbolically to shave the scalp of a representative monk. The ceremony concludes shortly thereafter, followed by another banquet for disciples and parents. Unlike the previous evening, however, the renunciants eat in the proximity of the master, not with their parents, signifying the transition to their new family.

The tonsure ceremony does not include the taking of any precepts. It is merely a formal means of signifying intent fully to renounce. Once disciples have tonsured, they may wait anywhere from merely a month to as long as four years before receiving their monastic vows, depending on personal choice and the timing of the next triple altar ordination. Monks and nuns who have not yet been ordained are sometimes referred to as "shramaneras" and "shramanerikas," although this is merely from lack of a more suitable term since they have not taken the shramanera/shramanerika vows.[13] Their status is marginal: with shaved heads, they no longer identify themselves as part of lay society, but, having as yet taken no vows, they cannot claim to be full members of the sangha. Most therefore prefer to participate in a triple altar ordination as soon as possible.

TRIPLE ALTAR ORDINATION

Before the passage in 1989 of the Revised Law on the Organization of Civic Groups, only the Buddhist Association of the Republic of China (BAROC) was permitted to hold triple altar ordinations, so, as did all clerics on Taiwan, Foguang monastics participated in the BAROC ceremonies.[14] These ordinations were held once or twice each year at various prominent temples around the island. Foguangshan was the site for BAROC's 1977 ceremony, in which approximately five hundred venerables took their vows. Since the late 1980s, Foguangshan has sponsored five ordinations (see table 1).

Full renunciation is conferred through novices receiving a series of precepts (*shou jie*) over the course of three ceremonies. First, the novices take the ten shramanera/shramanerika vows, that is, the same vows as are taken by male lay devotees for the short-term monastic retreat. At this time all preceptees receive their monastic cassock, alms bowl, and ritual ground covering. Typically two weeks later, the 250 bhikshu and 348 bhikshuni vows of the pratimoksha are accepted. In theory, these determine all aspects of monastic life, from what is worn to how disputes are resolved. As we shall see, in practice the bhikshu/bhikshuni precepts play only a very general role in guiding daily routine. The shramanera and bhikshu vows taken by Chinese clerics are essentially the same as those received by their counterparts in South and Southeast Asia. Two weeks later, the first two sets of precepts are supplemented with the ten primary and forty-eight secondary bodhisattva vows as found in the *Brahmajala Sutra (Fanwang jing)* and the *Yogacaryabhumi Sastra (Yujia shidi lun)*.[15] The bodhisattva vows taken by monastics are very similar to those received by laity, although the version taken by clerics places more emphasis on the responsibility properly to guide and preach to disciples and devotees. Nonetheless, the focus in both cases is on maintaining harmony and unity within the tradition and on benefiting all beings through doing good deeds. Like laity, Foguang clerics receive three precept scars (*jieba*) as part of the ceremony. Unlike laypeople, monastics have their scars burned into their scalp, just above the forehead.[16]

The three altar ceremonies follow the same basic structure: the evening before novices receive the precepts, a repentance rite is held; to begin the ceremony proper, the novices gather, then several representatives request the *shila upadhyaya*

TABLE 1
Foguangshan-Sponsored Triple Altar Ordinations

YEAR	LOCATION	NUMBER OF PARTICIPANTS	DURATION
1988	Hsi Lai Temple	Approx. 300	1 month
1991	Foguangshan	479	10½ weeks
1996	Foguangshan	Approx. 300	1 month
1998	Bodhgaya	150	9 days
2000	Foguanghshan	Approx. 300	1 month

(*dejie heshang*), karma acharya (*jiemo heshang*), and instructing acharya (*jiaoshou heshang*) for guidance; each of these three gives a discourse on the significance of the vows being taken; prayers are offered asking buddhas and other powerful beings for their protection; preceptees are questioned about obstructions or transgressions that would prevent them from receiving the precepts; another repentance rite takes place, then preceptees take the triple refuge; there is another discourse on the significance of the vows; the vows are conferred; final instructions are given; merit is transferred. The sequence of these elements is fairly flexible; not only does it differ slightly between each of the three ceremonies, but it may also be altered or curtailed depending on the circumstances of the ordination.

Of the three ceremonies, the longest and most involved is the second, that is, the taking of bhikshu/bhikshuni precepts. This rite also differs from the other two in that much of it is conducted in private. Each preceptee is individually questioned by the ten ordination acharyas about his or her motives for renouncing and about possible obstructions. No laypersons are to be present during the conferment of the precepts. In fact, according to more conservative readings of the vinaya, the bhikshu precepts should not even be discussed in front of any nonmonastic. The rite is also unique in that the female preceptees must participate in a supplementary ceremony presided over by ten bhikshus and ten bhikshunis in which are conferred an additional ninety-eight precepts over and above those taken by their male counterparts.

The traditional length for a triple altar ordination is said to be fifty-three days, although in practice the duration varies considerably. The 1977, 1989, 1996, and 2000 Foguang ordinations each took one month, apparently the standard timetable in Taiwan. The 1991 series of ceremonies, however, lasted a full seventy-three days. It was, according to Foguang literature, "the longest, most rigorous full ordination in China's history" ("Foguangshan sanshi nian dashi ji" 1997, 11). Financial and logistic considerations kept the 1998 ceremony in Bodhgaya, India, to a mere nine days. The auspiciousness and symbolic import of the location, argued the Foguang leadership, more than compensated for the radically curtailed schedule.

The days leading up to each of the three rites are spent teaching the novices the basics of monastic life and preparing them for the upcoming ceremony so that it proceeds smoothly. The curriculum offered during the training sessions is essentially a concentrated version of the education provided at Foguang seminaries. The syllabus for the 1991 ordination, for instance, included the following four areas:[17]

Precepts:
(1) the shramanera, bhikshu, and bodhisattva precepts;
(2) the gathas that should be used to guide every action of a monastic's life;[18] Buddhist deportment.

Virtue:
(1) sayings of ancient sages;
(2) conduct of great clerics;
(3) Chan instructions;
(4) Foguangshan's history and spirit;
(5) sayings and writings of Master Xingyun.

Wisdom:
(1) teachings of the eight schools, especially Chan and Pure Land;
(2) Buddhist terminology;
(3) the path to buddhahood;
(4) selections from scriptures;
(5) Buddhist history;
(6) the current state of Buddhism;
(7) canonical studies.

Chanting: passages to be memorized for the five daily services, ceremonies of repentance, and various dharma functions.

This is standard fare for Foguangshan's ordination training, although the longer time frame of the 1991 event allowed for these subjects to be treated more thoroughly than is usually the case.

Each of Foguangshan's ordinations has been noteworthy in certain respects. The 1988 ceremony was significant for two reasons. First, it was the first triple altar ordination performed without BAROC sponsorship by a Taiwan-based Buddhist organization. By holding a full ordination abroad and, thereby, circumventing the official ban just months before it was to be lifted, Foguangshan made a clarion statement about its independence from the semigovernment agency (and beat out its competitors in doing so). Master Xingyun's relations with the BAROC leadership had been cordial yet strained ever since he left Taipei in the early 1950s to run first Leiyin Temple in Jiayi, then Shoushan Buddhist Academy and Foguangshan in southern Taiwan, all sufficiently remote to be hidden from the watchful eyes of more senior monks. Conducting his own ordination ceremony both further legitimized his organization and strengthened its autonomy. Second, in holding the month-long ordination at its newly opened Hsi Lai Temple in California, Foguangshan dramatically announced its push for globalization. To amplify this symbolic import, several women of Tibetan and South and Southeast Asian traditions were invited to participate, including an American who practiced within a Tibetan lineage and the German Ayya Khema, who had already spent many years as a *dasa sil mata* in Sri Lanka and had more recently become influential in the European Buddhist community.

The 1991 ordination was notable in several ways. As I observed above, it lasted considerably longer than any other ordination that has been sponsored by Foguangshan or any other Buddhist organization on Taiwan. This extended schedule apparently added an extra strain on the nerves of the preceptees, leading several dozen to drop out. Of the 479 people who initially registered on 30 March, only 438 remained when training for the second altar ordination began at the beginning of May. Of the forty-one who left during that early stage, reasons for dismissal were given in thirty-five cases: five did not pass the initial inspection; fifteen had come only to receive shramanera/shramanerika precepts;[19] five preceptees had health problems; five were listed as unable to adjust to monastic life; and five were asked to leave after displaying inappropriate behavior. Of this last category, two were unwilling to accept instruction, one had "wrong views," another had "continual vulgar thoughts," and one preceptee was said to be mentally unstable, having "spoken wildly" and broken the precept against killing (with hints that she may have attempted suicide).

The 1991 ordination was also of note for its inclusion of a large number of participants from non-Foguang temples: approximately 42 percent had non-Foguang generation names.[20] Furthermore, as in the 1988 ordination, efforts were made to invite preceptees from beyond the shores of Taiwan. Sixty-six people registered from ten countries: four from the United States; one from Germany; one from Portugal; thirty-four from Malaysia; four from Singapore; four from Thailand; nine from Indonesia; three from Vietnam; four from Korea; one from Hong Kong; and one from Nepal. Nearly 50 percent of these participants represented non-Foguang organizations. Only three, however, were of non-Chinese ethnicity.

Comparing these numbers with the initial registration figure of 479, several observations can be made. Overall, 14 percent of participants were from abroad. Foguangshan was especially effective in attracting foreign women to join the Foguang order. Of the 208 nuns who had tonsured under Master Xingyun who participated in the ordination, 35 (or approximately 17 percent) were from overseas. These numbers differ considerably from those for men: of the forty-eight men participating in the ordination who had tonsured under Master Xingyun, only four (or approximately 8 percent) were from overseas. It should be noted that overseas participants were especially likely to drop out: one of the women said to have engaged in wild speech was from Singapore, three of the five initiates listed as unable to adjust to the monastic lifestyle were from Korea, and one of the preceptees with medical problems was an older Euro-American male.[21] Hence, overseas participants had a dropout rate of 7.6 percent, compared to that of 3.9 percent for those from Taiwan. It is likely that those from Taiwan had undergone a longer stint of seminary training than had those from abroad and, therefore, had a clearer idea of what to expect. Furthermore, cultural issues obviously did not come into play for them, as they did for some of the overseas novices.

Foguangshan invited over a dozen clerics from other monasteries to offer instruction to the preceptees. This, coupled with the high percentage of non-Foguang novices involved, led some critics to assert that the ordination was Master Xingyun's attempt to establish Foguangshan as the leading organization of a "southern branch" of Buddhism on Taiwan, in competition with the "northern branch" controlled by BAROC. Master Xingyun denied that he had any such intention. Whatever his objective was, inviting clerics from so many other monasteries to participate in what was certainly a very ambitious ceremony certainly served to upstage the ordinations sponsored by BAROC. Any attempt to organize the diverse range of temples represented in the 1991 ceremony more formally was, however, doomed. Monasteries around Taiwan were exerting their independence from the government's semiofficial agency largely to avoid the political maneuverings that they had witnessed within that organization. They therefore had no interest in again becoming enmeshed in the internecine squabbles that would invariably occur in establishing an alternative network headed by as powerful a monastery as Foguangshan.

Foguangshan narrowed its scope considerably for its 1996 ordination. Nearly all the three hundred novices who received the vows were drawn from within Foguangshan's own ranks. External events, however, caused the Taiwan media to pay greater attention to the ceremony than it might have otherwise. In August of that year, Zhongtaishan, Taiwan's second largest monastic community, had become embroiled in controversy when its master, Ven. Weijue, tonsured 158 new disciples without first receiving consent from their parents. The astonishment and horror expressed by some of the families revived the age-old assertion that Buddhist monasticism undermines the Confucian principle of filial piety that serves as the bedrock of the Chinese moral system. Consequently, both Foguangshan's tonsure rite in September and its ordination ceremony in November were closely scrutinized.

The theme of globalization that was adumbrated in the 1989 and 1991 ordinations gained full salience in 1998, when Foguangshan invited 140 novices from over twenty countries and representing Theravadin, Tibetan, and Mahayana traditions to take full ordination in Bodhgaya, India.[22] In addition to providing women of Theravadin and Tibetan traditions the opportunity to receive the bhikshuni vows, the event was noteworthy on two other counts as well: the site chosen and the international, ecumenical scope of the participants. According to Foguang literature, this marked the first time that a Chinese Buddhist organization ever had held a triple altar ordination in Bodhgaya, the site of the Buddha's enlightenment. The auspiciousness of such a location is obvious. It also provided the perfect setting for bringing together Buddhists from around the world and representing a wide range of lineages. Novices from Taiwan, Japan, Korea, Hong Kong, Vietnam, Thailand, Malaysia, Singapore, Myanmar, India, Nepal, Sri Lanka, Australia, Germany, Belgium, Denmark, England, Spain, the Congo, and the United States gathered for nine days to take the three sets of vows. The list of witnessing acharyas is similarly diverse: eight from Sri Lanka; four from Thailand; two each from India, Nepal, Malaysia, Taiwan, and Great Britain; and one from Cambodia. Of the 150 people who ultimately received the precepts at the ordination (ten women who had walked for five days from Maharashtra but who had not preregistered were allowed to join at the last minute), 55 represented Mahayana traditions, 63 Theravada, and 32 Tibetan lineages.

The international and ecumenical nature of the ordination posed a variety of challenges. Lodging and travel arrangements had to be made, not only for those participating in the ordination, but also for the twenty-one hundred Foguang devotees who came to tour sacred sites in the region and to take the triple refuge and the five precepts. As one of Buddhism's most important pilgrimage destinations, Bodhgaya has facilities to house and feed pilgrims, but not so many at once, so coordinating a suitable timetable proved a daunting task for the planning committee. Preceptees and acharyas were housed in the Myanmar, Sri Lankan, Japanese, and other Buddhist temples of Bodhgaya. Lay devotees came in for two or three days at a time and stayed at hotels and hostels. There were other challenges as well. Ordination participants spoke ten different languages—seventy-one spoke English, fifty-three Chinese, twenty-four Sinhalese, twenty-six Hindi and other Indian dialects (including Ladhaki), sixteen Nepalese, eight French, seven Tibetan, five Korean, three Japanese, and one Thai. Even for Foguangshan it was difficult to muster a sufficient number of disciples from within its ranks to act as translators. There were dietary issues as well since monastics of the Tibetan and Theravadin traditions do not eat after noon and are not vegetarian. As a compromise, nothing was consumed after the midday meal, but only vegetarian fare was provided.

Finally, some clerics questioned whether Theravadin preceptees should have to take the bodhisattva vows since some in that tradition regard doing so as a hindrance to attaining liberation. This concern was allayed in two ways. First, those bodhisattva precepts that can be interpreted as demeaning the Theravadin tradition were deleted, so, instead of taking forty-eight minor vows, preceptees took only forty-one. Second, a form was designed by Ven. Ananda (a Theravadin monk of Dutch heritage) in which preceptees could state whether they would participate in the third altar ceremony and, if so, whether and where (scalp or forearm) they would receive the three incense scars (on the assumption that some monastics might fear reprisal by conservative Theravadins if they had the scars and especially if prominently placed on the scalp). As it turns out, all preceptees took the bodhisattva vows, although many chose to have the incense scars burned into the forearm.

Foguangshan expended a considerable amount of money and energy to ensure that this affair would succeed. The monastery essentially footed the bill for the entire proceedings, paying for the airfare and lodging for all preceptees and acharyas. It also exerted considerable effort to plan and carry out the ordination. In the year leading up to the event, a committee of nuns traveled virtually around the world to garner the support of Buddhism's most prominent leaders, including the dalai lama, Thich Nhat Hanh, the supreme patriarch of Thailand, the chief lama of Mongolia, the chief prelate of Malaysia, and numerous *maha theras* in Sri Lanka. A small contingent of nuns was also stationed in Bodhgaya for the three months preceding the February ordination to make the complicated logistic arrangements. For the ordination itself, several dozen Foguang monastics, led by all the most senior clerics, made the journey to Bodhgaya.

The ordination lasted nine days, with the triple altar and triple refuge/five precept ceremonies taking place at Bodhgaya's Chinese and Tibetan temples. When not presiding over the various rites, Master Xingyun visited all the Buddhist temples in Bodhgaya to thank the abbots for their support and conducted three charitable activities in which he oversaw the giving of clothing and other goods to the poor. The ordination went generally as planned, although there were two unanticipated events. On the third day, a China Airlines plane crashed in Taiwan, killing all 250 people aboard. Master Xingyun called on the preceptees and those taking refuge or the five vows to transfer the merit thereby generated to benefit those who had died in the accident. Three days later, a preceptee by the name of Karma Chopel Dronma died from a heart attack literally under the Bodhi

Tree while chanting a morning service. Both Master Xingyun and Ven. Xinding exclaimed that a monastic could not ask for a more auspicious place to pass away. Karma Chopel Dronma's remains were cremated in Bodhgaya, with one-quarter of the ashes being returned to her native Spain, one-quarter going to Scotland to be placed in the columbarium established by her teacher (Ven. Lama Yeshe Losal Rinpoche), one-quarter going to Foguangshan to be placed in Longevity Funerary Complex, and one-quarter remaining in Bodhgaya. Thus dispensing her ashes both called to mind the dispersal of the Buddha's relics and displayed modern Buddhism's full globalization.

Foguangshan as an important center for global, ecumenical Buddhism and women's rights continued to find expression in the May 2000 ordination, which included seventy *dasa sil matavo* from Sri Lanka. Once again, Foguangshan paid all expenses and offered long-term educational and financial support for the women. The ordination took place as part of a month-long observance of Foguang headquarter's thirty-fourth anniversary, a celebration that also incorporated the annual Buddha's Light International Association (BLIA) World Conference and brought together clerics from diverse traditions for Foguangshan's eighth International Monastic Conference.

MONASTIC VOWS IN DAILY LIFE

THE FOGUANG PERSPECTIVE ON THE FUNCTION OF VOWS

The central, most vital feature of Buddhist ordination is the taking of vows. Over the course of triple altar ordination, Chinese Buddhist monks take a total of 318 precepts and nuns 416: 10 shramanera/shramanerika precepts; 250 bhikshu or 348 bhikshuni precepts; and 10 major and 48 minor bodhisattva precepts. They pledge to abide by these for the rest of their lives, a commitment that is renewed twice each month at the *posadha (busa)* ceremony. One would, therefore, assume that the precepts play a major role in shaping even the most minute details of monastic life. And, in certain respects, they do. Particular orders as well as individual monks and nuns consciously and unconsciously refer to the vinaya as they determine the appropriate way of life for those who have renounced. There are, nonetheless, distinct limitations in the degree to which monastics follow the vinaya. Few, if any, clerics of any Buddhist tradition keep all the precepts to the letter all the time. It can even be argued that each of the traditions, and, in fact, particular organizations within each tradition, bases its assertion that it adheres to the pratimoksha on a strict observance of the more general injunctions as well as of certain key precepts that are compatible with its own style of cultivation. The disjunction between ideal monastic life as structured by the precepts and the way clerics actually live may be traced to four points: some precepts have long been incompatible with the mores of particular indigenous cultures; others have no significance in particular social contexts; sometimes the vinaya does not cover the needs of particular monasteries; and, finally, some precepts are at odds with important strands of twentieth-century thought. Let us consider each of these points as they have played out in the Chinese context.[23]

Ever since Buddhism spread into China two millennia ago, certain precepts have been deemed antithetical to indigenous life and, therefore, ignored or circumvented. Precepts that have long been neglected include those forbidding eating after noon, digging in the dirt, handling money, and engaging in business transactions.[24] Conversely, certain precepts have been quite easily observed since they have been so irrelevant to the contemporary cultural and social context that opportunities for breaking them have rarely, if ever, arisen. The various rules concerning how one is to accept wool when offered as a present, who may be asked to weave it, and the proportions of colors to be kept when making it into a sleeping mat have always had little relevance to Chinese monastic life, as have many of the precepts concerning the acceptance and handling of material for robes. Other vows that may once have been relevant even in China have become obsolete with the passage of time, for example, the injunction against speaking the dharma to someone who is riding a donkey. These precepts are kept, but they have no real significance in guiding modern clerics' lives.

Just as various precepts do not speak to the needs of Chinese culture, specific developments in the evolution of Sino-Buddhism could not have been foreseen by the Buddha, and he therefore did not address them in the pratimoksha. To close such gaps, Chinese venerables refer to the *Pure Rules of Baizhang* (*Baizhang qinggui*) and other such compilations of regulations written by Chinese specifically for Chinese monastery use. As such manuals tend to deal more with ritual than with administration, larger temples have also developed their own bylaws. (As we shall see in chapter 7 below, Foguangshan's bylaws cover such topics as promotion, the election of the sangha leadership, and educational and medical benefits.)

Finally, clerics are having to find ways to interpret those precepts that are considered by at least some to be contrary to modern knowledge or values. One precept, for instance, forbids monastics from drinking water in which they know there to be life-forms. As Master Xingyun has pointed out, science has shown all water to be inhabited by countless microscopic organisms. Were the precept therefore to be followed precisely, monks and nuns could never drink—which would be absurd. Much more controversial are those precepts that serve to limit women's access to knowledge of the dharma and to authority as religious leaders. As we have seen, for the South Asian and Tibetan lineages of Buddhism, the debate has centered on whether it is possible to reinstate full bhikshuni ordination. For Chinese Buddhist nuns, the issue is more one of asserting their equal status with monks as clerics. Some, for instance, find especially irksome the eight *gurudharma* precepts, especially the first, which requires all nuns, no matter how long they have renounced, "to rise, salute, and venerate" any monk, even if he received ordination only that day, and the eighth, which stipulates that "a bhikshu may admonish a bhikshuni, but no bhikshuni may admonish a bhikshu."[25]

Citing the fact that so much of the pratimoksha is irrelevant to or incompatible with contemporary life, Ven. Yifa, a Foguangshan nun with particularly progressive ideas, has called for the formation of a committee bringing together representatives of all the major Buddhist traditions to consider how the vinaya can be updated. Underlying her call for reform is the assertion that, while the dharma is supramundane and, hence, eternal, the vinaya is but conventional truth and, therefore, subject to periodic reevaluation. Shakyamuni had told his disciples that, while they must always keep the major precepts, they could alter minor ones as circumstances demanded. Because the Buddha never enunciated just what he meant by "major" and "minor," clerics have kept all precepts, at least in spirit. The Venerable Yifa believes that the sangha must take more responsibility in openly judging the importance of various precepts for guiding ethical conduct and maintaining communal harmony (Shi Yifa 1998).

Others within the Foguang order are uneasy with such a radical challenge to the authority of canonical monastic discipline. Most apparently prefer to continue the present, unofficial strategy of pledging allegiance to the entire pratimoksha while ignoring much of it in practice. While Master Xingyun does not directly question the authority of the vinaya in toto, he does call on monastics to retain flexibility in their interpretation of specific vows. He often tells a story in which Chan Master Yixiu, who was renowned for his strict adherence to the pratimoksha, broke the precept against having bodily contact with a woman when he helped a young lady ford a river by carrying her on his back. A disciple who was accompanying the venerable was appalled at this transgression but, at first, dared not question his conduct. After three months of silent torment over the incident and what it meant about his teacher's virtue, the disciple finally asked him how he could have done such a thing. Laughing, Master Yixiu replied: "Oh disciple, you are exerting yourself too much. I put that woman down as soon as we had crossed the river. Why do you keep hold of her in your mind? To thus carry her for three months is much too arduous" (Shi Xingyun 1996c, 2). Master Xingyun finds this anecdote instructive because it reminds clerics that abiding by the precepts is a form of practice, not its goal. The more important measure of one's level of cultivation is the degree to which he or she can actualize the "substance of the precepts" (*jieti*). When a person of highly cultivated wisdom and compassion determines that, under the circumstances, it would be better not to follow a particular precept, he or she has not broken the precepts (*fan jie*) but rather "opened" them (*kai jie*).

Master Xingyun himself has on occasion followed a course of action contrary to the codified precepts. He tells of a time when he ignored the prohibition against a venerable eating leeks:

> When in 1949 I brought the Sangha Medical Relief Unit to Taiwan, Ven. Xingru was a member of the team. At the time, he was already in the third stage of pulmonary tuberculosis. He would lie in bed and breathe with difficulty. At that time, tuberculosis was known as the black plague of the twentieth century, so everyone was very afraid and dared not even get near him. The times were very turbulent, and we lacked adequate supplies. Even getting three meals a day was difficult for me, so how could I take him to be cared for in a hospital? Fortunately, I found an unorthodox way to help him in the back of a book written by Master Yinguang. I followed the method, every day patiently scraping a kind of fuzz off the back of loquat leaves to make a thick soup and then spoon-feeding this to him one mouthful at a time.
>
> When he showed signs of slight improvement, I gave him leeks mixed with rice as well. There was some gossiping about this because some people said monks were not supposed to eat leeks. I retorted: "This man came close to death. What does it matter if he eats a few leeks to cure the illness?" After I had cared for him for half a year, Ven. Xingru fully recuperated. He later became abbot of Puji Temple in Beitou. (Shi Xingyun 1995a, 10:626–627)

The master's conduct here was fairly safe from criticism since it fell within the province set by the vinaya for opening precepts. More controversial are those times when the master has taught a disciple about the importance of keeping an ethical injunction by initially allowing that disciple to contravene it. He relates the following incident about one of his nuns:

> When Ven. Yide first entered the monastic order, some of her old habits stayed with her for a while, especially her fondness for eggs. She loved eggs

so much that she often found excuses to go back home to visit her family just so she could have some. Once, I heard that she was planning to go home yet again, so I asked the lay monastic [shigu] Yang Ceman to make boiled eggs, fried eggs, stewed eggs, poached eggs, scrambled eggs—every kind of egg that she could think of for Ven. Yide to eat.

When Yide heard that I was not allowing her to go home, she was upset and came to find me. I instructed her first to go see Yang Ceman and then come back to talk. She went as I had bid, and, on finding Yang Ceman, she also found a whole table covered with eggs. She tasted some of them, but from that day on she saw that she had to attend more carefully to her desire for eggs.

At the time, some people were quite critical, saying I had acted arbitrarily and had set a poor example. After a while, however, everyone came to see that my method was inspired. If doing something like that can really succeed in turning someone around, then it's a good method. I often think that, if we can keep a more magnanimous, open mind, many of the "human" problems in this world could be easily resolved. (Shi Xingyun 1995a, 10:606)

Even in this situation, the master's actions could be justified by recourse to the *Yogacarabhumi Sastra*, which grants exemption from many infractions when the monastic has broken the precept specifically as a skillful means to teach another the importance of not doing so. Furthermore, the proscription against consuming eggs is not to be found in the vinaya, having developed in China as an uncodified injunction. Precepts and ethical proscriptions have been instituted by the Buddha and his disciples through the ages, argues the master, to minimize distractions to cultivation and to aid people in developing their compassion and wisdom. Of course, as the sangha has had very good reasons for laying down the various proscriptions, they should not be ignored or contravened lightly. Hence, those who are just beginning their monastic career should be especially vigilant in abiding by the codified precepts and customary injunctions. To follow any of these, even precepts, blindly, with no thought to present circumstances, however, proves counterproductive, severely truncating compassion and wisdom.

This call for a flexible interpretation of even vinaya rules was given historical foundation in an essay written by Ven. Xinding and distributed to preceptees at all five of the triple altar ordinations sponsored by Foguangshan. In the essay, entitled "The Evolution of the *Posadha* Ceremony and the *Pratimoksha Sutra*" ("Busa yu Buoluotimucha jing de fazhan" (see Shi Xinding, n.d.), Ven. Xinding argues that the evolution of the *posadha* ceremony, the formulation of *siks* (*xue*) and *siksapada* (*xue-chu*), the development of *desanapratimoksha* (*shuo buoluotimucha*), and the recording of the various editions of the *Pratimoksha Sutra* (*Buoluotimucha jing*) represent a gradual shift in monastic ethics from relying primarily on normative guidelines to laying ever greater emphasis on adherence to legalistic rules.

The Buddha, states Ven. Xinding, adopted the *posadha* ceremony from Vedic culture, first utilizing it as an opportunity for lay members to observe the eight precepts, then shifting the emphasis to affirm the purity of the cleric community. In the beginning, the venerables simply recited the "Ovadapratimoksha" ("Jiaoshou buoluotimucha"), a short verse admonishing monastics to guard purity of speech. As the number of disciples grew, the Buddha found it necessary to formulate the one hundred *siks*, that is, guidelines of training, so that his disciples could correctly apply the dharma in particular situations.

The Buddha initially developed no punitive measures to support these ethical norms: "When an individual blatantly overstepped the bounds of proper behavior, *siks* had no power to compel him to correct his actions. All they could do was to exhort and reprimand the offender for his disregard of the teachings. It is similar to the dictates of propriety [*li*] of ancient times that likewise had ethical ramifications but no power to compel" (Shi Xinding, n.d., 18). With the continued increase in the number of disciples, however, the quality of the sangha membership deteriorated, so the Buddha felt it necessary to put forth the *siksapada*, that is, a definite system of rules that the disciples were to follow without exemption and that were buttressed with punitive measures for any transgression.

The Buddha did not decree some carefully crafted, systematic code; rather, he simply created new rules and punishments or amended existing ones to meet particular situations as they arose.[26] Eventually, after he turned over the day-to-day administration of the sangha to some of his more senior disciples, the list of rules (*anapratimoksha*; *weide buoluotimucha*) was organized into categories (thereby forming the *desanapratimoksha*) so that it could be more easily recited and explained at the *posadha* ceremonies. What had been guidelines for behavior derived from specific circumstances had now been transformed into a corpus of 250 rules (348 for nuns) established to regulate the conduct of individuals so as to maintain communal harmony. The Venerable Xinding states: "*Siksapada* is like law (*falu*), for it goes beyond the realm of what one ought and ought not to do to speak of what is and is not permissible. It is enforceable and carries with it the inescapable consequence of punishment. It was established by the Buddha for the sake of maintaining the purity and harmony of the sangha by utilizing the collective strength of the community in carrying out the will of its members. Therefore, offenders are to be punished without exception" (Shi Xinding, n.d., 18). Foguang Buddhists therefore believe that, ideally, precepts function less like laws *(falu)* in a legal system than like rules of propriety *(li)* in Confucian ethics. In the Confucian scheme, such rules are balanced by the virtues of humanity *(ren)* and righteousness *(yi)*. In Buddhism, the balance is between precepts, compassion, and wisdom.

The Venerable Xinding closes his essay by observing that there continue to be both normative and legalistic interpretations of the pratimoksha, some orders allowing a more fluid application of certain precepts, others insisting on strict adherence to specific details of each and every one. Although he never says so directly, he implies that the truly authentic way of interpreting the precepts is to apply them with the same wise flexibility as the Buddha employed when he first formulated them. Strict, legalistic readings of the vinaya may follow the letter of the precepts, but flexible interpretations actualize their true spirit.

Vows, Rules, and Customs Shaping Foguang Monastic Daily Life

Thus far, my discussion of the Foguang perspective on the role of precepts and other ethical injunctions in monastic life has largely remained on the theoretical plane. To show how the vinaya, monastery bylaws, and uncodified Chinese custom interact to structure daily life for clerics, I turn now to a consideration of such topics as money, possessions, dining, bhikshu-bhikshuni relations, travel, and entertainment.

Money

Whether clerics should carry money has been a topic of debate within the Buddhist community since at least the Second Council, which took place in northern India sometime during the fourth or third century B.C.E. The Central Asian Buddhist missionaries who introduced the tradition to China during the early centuries of the common era represented schools that permitted venerables to receive gold and silver. Since that time, the Chinese sangha has generally seen no problem with individual clerics handling money and even keeping personal savings.[27]

At Foguangshan, clerics can receive funds from four sources. First, every monastic is paid a monthly stipend ranging from NT$500 to NT$1,500 (U.S.$17–U.S.$50), depending on seniority and position. Second, monks and nuns may receive gifts of money from their families, although this is discouraged. At one meeting, Master Xingyun said that he strongly dissuaded parents from giving such gifts until the child had renounced for twenty years since, before that time, the level of cultivation may be insufficient to resist the temptations that arise when one has spending money on hand. Third, "red envelopes" *(hongbao)* are provided by devotees, especially during the Chinese New Year. According to the February 1997 issue (no. 417) of the *Foguang Newsletter* (*Foguang tongxun,* the internal journal for Foguang monastics), the following guidelines were established for receiving such monetary gifts: amounts up to NT$2,000 (U.S.$67) can be kept by monastics; of amounts from NT$2,000 to NT$4,000, NT$2,000 can be kept by monastics, the rest going to the monastery; of amounts over NT$4,000, half can be kept by monastics, the other half going to the monastery. Finally, Master Xingyun and other senior monastics can receive payment for the various books, cassettes, radio broadcasts, and television programs that they produce.[28]

Although clerics can receive money, they must still handle it with caution. Foguangshan's rules stipulate that monastics may have personal funds *(yongyou jinqian)* but that they cannot seek to amass savings *(si xu jinqian).* Monks and nuns are also strongly encouraged to keep all moneys in what is called a *futian* (blessed field) account in the temple's own banking system (Shi Xingyun, n.d.-b, 14–15). Several informants told me that they had not bothered to close savings accounts in banks on ordination but that they did not use them much. Others opened such personal bank accounts only when they went overseas, thus making it easier for family members to wire funds as the need arises. The majority, however, keep no personal savings accounts, placing all their assets in Foguangshan's *futian* accounts.

Any money possessed by a monk or nun is to be used for the benefit of the monastic community *(changzhu)* and Buddhism. "Only a person who has a carefree attitude toward money and who knows how to spend it on Buddhism and the general public," observes Master Xingyun, "truly knows how to use money" (Shi Xingyun, n.d.-b, 15). As do other Chinese Buddhists, Foguang practitioners regard such proper dispensation of one's material wealth as a source of merit *(gongde).* Generous giving *(bushi; dana)* is not just a responsibility but a source of joy. Foguang monastics are, therefore, very liberal in donating their personal funds to Foguang enterprises, sometimes contributing considerable sums for the building of a temple or some other such project.[29]

Clerics feel secure in such generosity because the monastery has an obligation to attend to all their financial needs. As Master Xingyun explained during a meeting (20 June 1997) of Foguang abbots:

> When a disciple has given good service in the past, if he or she needs money, the temple provides it. This is a fundamental difference between a Christian church and a Buddhist temple. Christian ministers are paid a salary. The financial obligation of the church to them ends there. For Bud-

dhist disciples, however, the temple is their home. A temple is like a family, with the temple being the parent and the disciples being the children. Without the devotion and sacrifices of the disciples, we would have no temple. So, when a disciple needs to do something for himself or herself, the temple provides the necessary money. ("Meeting of Foguang Abbots and Department Chiefs, Taiwan Branch Temples" 1997)

The master went on to say that any venerable who is continuing his or her studies in a graduate program will have all tuition and expenses paid by the monastery. Similarly, the temple will furnish any funds that a cleric may require to pay for a parent's birthday celebration or funeral.

The line differentiating personal and communal assets is, therefore, very hazy for those in the Foguang monastic community. Temple funds are not so much "corporate" as "communal"; individual moneys are better thought of as "personal" than as "private." In other words, there are distinctions between the categories "personal" and "communal," but they are far from being clearly defined. This ambiguous interrelation holds true for material property (*si zhi chanye*) as well.

Possessions

Master Xingyun does not believe that monastics should possess only three robes, an alms bowl, and a walking staff. He does, nonetheless, advise his disciples to keep belongings to a minimum: "For those in society, the more possessions, the better. For those cultivating the way, however, the fewer possessions, the better. Otherwise, not only do possessions fail to assist one's cultivation; they actually pose an obstacle to it. For this reason, we Foguang Buddhists should never have the selfish intention of acquiring private property. The only property we use is that belonging to the entire monastery. This is because privately acquired possessions give rise to greed and this flood of greed and desire sweeps away the peaceful calm that our body and mind had originally enjoyed" (Shi Xingyun, n.d.-b, 23).

Most Foguang monastics are able to place all their personal belongings in a few suitcases. Other than their robes, they may own prayer beads, a "wooden fish" dharma instrument, some books, a tape recorder and cassettes of Buddhist chanting, a portable computer, and small articles for daily needs.[30] They have usually purchased these things with their own funds, for they are discouraged from receiving such material goods as gifts from their biological families on that grounds that this may spark greed and cause discord within the sangha. Those who do accept presents from their parents (and some have received a car or a house) are encouraged to donate them to the monastery.

All clerics write a will on joining the order. The expectation is that they will leave all or the majority of their assets to Foguangshan, although there is no rule requiring them to do so. The will written by Ven. Xinping, who died of liver cancer in 1996, is regarded as exemplary. The Venerable Xinping was one of the first monks to renounce under Master Xingyun, having done so at age twenty-six in 1963. He succeeded the master as abbot of Foguangshan in 1986, being reelected for a second term six years later. In his will, written after he had been diagnosed with terminal cancer, he apologized to the master for having failed to complete the final two years of his second term. He then dictated that, although he had no savings to pass on, what few possessions he had accumulated had all been provided to him by Foguangshan and were, therefore, to be returned to the monastic community, to be distributed as the Religious Affairs Committee deemed fit. He asked that his body be cremated according to Buddhist tradition, with the preference that there be neither elaborate funeral services performed nor any mortuary mound set aside for his ashes, as these would waste money. Instead, he hoped that his remains would be placed in one of the niches of the Foguang columbarium. He specifically stipulated that his biological family *(sujia)* was to have no say in either attending to his estate or planning his funeral, for, as he was a cleric, such affairs were to be decided by clerics *(seng shi seng jue)*. The will closed with an admonition to Foguang monks and nuns to do all they could to aid Master Xingyun in spreading Humanistic Buddhism. Unable to fulfill his role as a model successor, Ven. Xinping did the next best thing, setting himself as a paragon of monastic service to Foguangshan even in death.

The Venerable Xinping stated in his will that Foguangshan had provided him with all his significant material needs. Let us turn to consider these in more detail, most notably clothing and housing.

Clothing

Manner of dress provides an immediate, substantial signifier of personal and communal values. The tonsured scalp, loose flowing robe, and simple slippers of Chinese Buddhist clerics allow them silently to announce to all who pass that they have left behind the world of vanity, fashion, and class. The identical attire donned by monks and nuns gives sartorial evidence that even the distinction of male and female no longer applies.[31] Chinese Buddhist monastics typically possess four types of robes. Daily wear consists of the *changshan*, a long gown of a single color, although the color itself varies. Black, various shades of gray, and mustard yellow are most often seen, although rust red and brown are also worn. This gown is replaced by the shorter, typically gray *duangua* robe when the monastic is engaged in manual labor. Rituals and formal meals require the *haiqing,* similar in style to the *changshan* but with sleeves full enough to serve as very deep pockets. For especially important events, such as major dharma functions or a visit by a high government official or religious leader, the *haiqing* is partially covered by a vestment, or *jiasha,* which drapes over the left shoulder.

Monastics' clothing is a subtle confirmation of their commitment to compassion, for both silk and leather are avoided, although these prohibitions are not absolute, as is evident by the many monks and nuns who use leather watchbands. Along with a wristwatch, wrapped around the arm of a cleric often will be found a set of prayer beads. These rosaries may be of precious material that has been simply yet elegantly crafted and priced to match. The higher-quality examples in Foguang gift shops are made of crystal, jade, or amber and cost several thousand New Taiwan dollars. Laity who don rosary beads may wear them as they would a piece of fine jewelry.[32] For monastics, the string of beads is to be regarded purely as an aid for religious practice, in accordance with the vinaya interdict forbidding articles of personal adornment. Both because rosary beads are a favorite gift to bhikshus and bhikshunis from lay devotees and because they are one of the few articles that clerics may purchase for themselves, there is need to guard against the arising of greed. Master Xingyun has, therefore, stipulated that Foguang monastics are to have only inexpensive rosary beads, ideally costing no more than NT$1,000.

The final article of clothing by which Chinese Buddhist venerables are identified is the arhat *(luohan)* slippers. As the physical means that expedites one's journey along the way, these cloth sandals are especially imbued with symbolism. The six apertures lining their sides simultaneously remind the wearer of the frailty of existence, the interpenetration of emptiness and being as perceived through the six senses (sight, hearing, smell, touch, taste, and thought), and the importance of enacting the six paramitas with one's every movement. Constantly in motion, arhat slippers represent impermanence and, hence, the need for vigilance in one's practice. "What is a cultivator?" one nun asked the American monk Ven. Huiyong shortly after he had tonsured at Foguangshan on 6 February 1998. "A person wearing worn out sandals," she continued, answering her own question by quoting from a Chan story. "What is their value?" she quoted from the same story. "One would not trade them even for a city."

The arhat shoes and various robes worn by Chinese Buddhist clerics bespeak their common aims and lifestyle. Within this general statement of monastic ideals, however, a closer inspection of apparel reveals subtle distinctions identifying particular communities and ranks within those communities. While virtually all Chinese venerables wear arhat slippers, for instance, not all wear socks. Master Xingyun insists that his disciples don high gray stockings to cover their feet and calves. In his view, those who do not do so look like so many unkempt country bumpkins.

In many of the small monasteries that dot Taiwan, each cleric simply wears the robes offered him or her by a particular devotee, with the result that no sartorial uniformity identifies the group. In larger, better-established sanghas, such as Foguangshan, Fagushan, and Zhongtaishan, clothing for venerables is systematized. Foguang monastics typically wear mustard-colored *changshan* gowns. Only those who have gone through full ordination and who have graduated from the Buddhist college, however, may wear this color; novices and clerics of junior rank wear plain black cassocks. Some disciples who have already completed their novitiate training choose, nonetheless, to continue to don the black attire. For some, the more plain style represents humility; until they have attained a deeper level of cultivation, they feel unworthy to wear the more prestigious color. Others have a more practical reason for keeping to the darker hue: it is easier to clean. No choice is involved in dressing for public events, however; since the mustard cassocks symbolize unity and allegiance to Foguangshan, all wear them.

That even clerics fairly low in the Foguang hierarchy are allowed to wear the mustard-colored gown has been criticized by other Buddhists in Taiwan. One nun related to me an encounter that she once had with an elderly monk who had renounced decades before. The bhikshu made it very clear that he thought a bhikshuni as young and inexperienced as she had no right to wear anything other than a black cassock. For such detractors, the apparel of Foguang monastics is but another instance of the monastery's hubris. Foguangshan's own venerables contend that they have full prerogative to don the mustard-color robes and claim that, if they do have pride in their clothing, it is a statement, not of their own achievements, but of those of their master and of the organization as a whole.

Housing

Just as some take Foguangshan to task for allowing clerics to wear robes considered to be unfitting for their status, there are also some who assert that Foguang monks and nuns live in luxurious circumstances unbefitting to the Buddhist monastic spirit of simplicity. Master Xingyun has emphatically denied this on many occasions. In his view, people who make such claims mistakenly believe that Foguang venerables live in quarters comparable to the plush rooms provided for devotees in Pilgrim's Lodge and Cloud Residing Hall. "Monastics do not have the type of comfortable lodgings that guests enjoy on Foguangshan," he explains. "In fact, the simple and plain conditions, bordering on hardship, found at Foguangshan follow the true traditional spirit of monastic living. This is something that others do not see" (Shi Xingyun 1994, vol. 3, entry for 3 January 1990).

The living quarters for monks and for nuns at Foguang headquarters are on opposite sides of the mountain's religious zone. Monks live in one of three dormitories: students live in the Foguangshan Monastic Academy dormitories; bhikshus in the Foguangshan Meditation College live on the fifth floor of Jade Buddha Hall (one floor below their meditation hall); all other bhikshus, including the abbot, Ven. Xinding, live in Lamp Transmission Hall.[33] There are four residential compounds for nuns: students live in campus dormitories; bhikshunis in the Foguangshan Meditation College live in Gold Buddha Hall; bhikshunis who have already graduated from the Foguangshan Monastic Academy but who are still of junior rank also live in Gold Buddha Hall, but on a different floor; and all other bhikshunis live in one of the four dormitories of the convent area.

Students in the Foguangshan Monastic Academy live in open rooms, each accommodating twelve people. In general, lay and monastic students will be in separate quarters. Each student has a bed and a small area to keep clothing and personal effects. There are no desks provided as students are expected to study in a classroom or library. Accommodations for clerics who have already graduated depend on their rank. Those who have graduated but are still in the lower echelons share a room with five or six others and use a bathroom down the hall. Monastics with a slightly higher ranking have their own rooms but share bathroom facilities. Each private room is just large enough for a bed, desk, and bookcase. Clerics of the highest rank have their own bathrooms and share a telephone on their floor (everyone else uses the single telephone located at the dormitory entrance, although many now circumvent this restriction by carrying a cellular unit). Since lodging is determined by rank, people often move to new quarters every few years as they are promoted. For nuns, this may mean changing to another of the four dormitory buildings since assignment to these reflects rank.[34]

Monastics' living quarters are off-limits to guests. When asked about their accommodations, venerables tend to evade the question, preferring not even to identify the location of the dormitories. As does Master Xingyun, they emphasize that their quarters are much simpler than are the rooms provided for lay visitors. They do not benefit from any air-conditioning, nor are they allowed televisions, mattresses for their beds, refrigerators, or any cooking facilities.[35] In general, their living quarters seem to be comparable to those found in Taiwan's other large Buddhist monasteries. At Zhongtaishan, for instance, every fully ordained bhikshu and bhikshuni is supposed to have his or her own room—although this is not always possible owing to the current housing crunch caused by the community's rapid growth—and shramaneras share facilities, the youngest living in a large dormitory room, and those of high school age sharing doubles or triples.

While the living arrangements of Foguang and other clerics in Taiwan may be considered relatively spartan compared to how members of general society live, monks and nuns today enjoy nicer quarters than did most of their predecessors in comparable institutions up through the first half of the twentieth century. Residents of the Chan temple of Jinshan slept on a raised platform lining the outer perimeter of the meditation hall, having merely a small drawer in which to place their scant belongings (although the precentor [weinuo] and instructors had individual apartments within the compound). At Lingyanshan, the preeminent monastery of Pure Land practice, monks slept in two dormitories adjoining the recitation hall. Conditions at Baohuashan were more comparable to those found at Foguangshan and Zhongtaishan. Novices who came to be ordained stayed in large dormitories, but the teachers who lived there long-term not only had private rooms but even had their own cooking facilities, a practice that Master Xingyun condemns as prompting division within the sangha. Let us turn now to such issues of diet and commensality.

Dining

Every day at 6:00 A.M., 11:00 A.M., and 6:00 P.M., the entire Foguang community files into the refectory of Cloud Residing Hall. This dining room is immense, comprising over sixty rows of narrow tables, thereby providing space for three thousand people to eat at a sitting (and, by squeezing in more tables, as many as forty-two hundred may eat at time). At the center of the back wall, directly across from the main entrance, is the place for Ven. Xinding, or whoever else may be presiding over the meal. Just behind this main seat is the list of five contemplations that monastics are to focus on while silently eating:

> Considering the work required in producing this food, I am grateful for its sources.
> If, on judging my virtues, no faults are found, then I regard myself as worthy of this offering.
> May I guard my mind against faults, especially greed.
> To cure the frail body, I consume this food as medicine.
> To achieve cultivation, I receive this food.

Each meal begins with an offertory prayer. For breakfast and lunch, the two main meals of the day, there are three bowls of food (one each for soup, rice, and vegetables) and a piece of fruit at the edge of the table before each place. All in attendance carefully raise their chopsticks, bring the food toward them, and take three bites of rice, reciting to themselves: "With this bite I vow to eliminate all defilements; with this bite I vow to cultivate all goodness; with this bite I vow to deliver all sentient beings." Talking is forbidden, and all eyes remain fixed straight ahead. To receive more food, the person places his or her bowl at the front edge of the table, where it is immediately refilled by one of the college students serving on the kitchen staff. The meal ends within half an hour, all reciting a final prayer, then filing out.

Foguang clerics keep to a simpler repast in the evening in observance of the vinaya injunction against eating after noon. Strictly speaking, the monastics are not "eating food" but "taking medicine," the "medicine" consumed typically consisting of noodles or rice porridge. Unlike their monastic brethren in Sri Lanka and Thailand, who voice great concern for adhering to the vinaya precept concerning dietary schedule, the monks and nuns of East Asia have never followed this rule to the letter, arguing that their efforts in saving other sentient beings are too strenuous completely to forsake sustenance in the evening.[36] Until the cloistering of Foguang headquarters, in fact, the evening provisions had been as substantial as the two earlier meals of the day, leading some critics to surmise that the move to simpler fare was dictated as much from financial as from religious considerations. Given Foguangshan's overall budget, this is doubtful. The shift in practice was primarily dictated by the general effort at that time to rededicate the mountain headquarters as a model for cultivating sangha leadership.

Foguang monastics take dining etiquette very seriously. Shortly after the rule was instituted that all venerables were to take all three meals in the main refectory in Cloud Residing Hall, Master Xingyun convened a meeting in the refectory to review with his disciples the rules and underlying spirit of monastic dining ("Foguang Headquarters Community Meeting" 1998b). During the assembly, the master instructed servers how to ladle out food most efficiently and reviewed how clerics can silently lift their bowls and chop sticks, holding the former "like a pearl in a dragon's mouth" so that, when they eat, they "dip their head like a phoenix." He also had the monks and nuns practice sitting down and standing up in unison so that they could do so silently and gracefully. During the question and answer period, disciples asked about the proper speed for sounding the board that calls everyone to assemble as well as the order in which they were to line up. As the new, simpler evening fare had just recently been instituted, several monks and nuns argued that this more "ascetic" medicine meal was contrary to the spirit of Humanistic Buddhism as propounded at Foguangshan. Monastics must have plenty to eat since they often work late into the evenings, they asserted, so what was the sense in going hungry? The Venerable Cihui disagreed, stating that Foguang venerables were certainly not starving. A little hardship would do most of them some good, in her opinion. The master closed the meeting by emphasizing that he expected all disciples (except the most senior clerics) always to eat with everyone else in the refectory. "Eating is a form of cultivation," he exhorted. "Work can wait, but eating cannot."

In addition to the three main meals, Foguang disciples regularly eat snacks in midmorning, in midafternoon, and, if working late, at night. The attitude toward eating is far from ascetic: when one is hungry, one should eat; the point is simply to avoid the extremes of either sensual attachment or excessive renunciation. Such communal eating *(guotang)* plays a great role in group bonding. For a person to remain aloof from group meals and snacks indicates an unwillingness to share in temple life. When two monastics enumerated for me the various reasons why a particular non-Chinese cleric had never fit into the organization very well, one of the primary complaints cited was the person's insistence on preparing and eating food separately instead of partaking of the communal pot. Early on, by contrast, Ven. Huijin, a young monk from the Congo, learned to accept his Chinese colleagues' offerings of food. "The clerics are always eating," he told me, a broad smile spreading over his face. "Any time someone studies late at night, for instance, others come around with a snack. If you don't want to eat it, they get all worried, expressing concerns that you aren't adjusting well. Simply saying that you aren't hungry isn't good enough. It is much more difficult to turn down a bowl of soup than to just eat it, so I have given up and eat whatever I am given" (Chandler 1998f).

Eating together represents, not only unity, but also equality. Hence, Master Xingyun has been highly critical of the practice of keeping "small pots" *(xiao guo)*, a convention that was apparently widespread during the early part of the twentieth century in mainland China's public monasteries. In the ordination center Baohuashan, for instance, only initiates ate in the refectory. All permanent residents used their own funds to individually purchase vegetables for their evening meal, which each prepared on a private stove either in his own apartment or adjacent to it (Welch 1967, 112). Master Xingyun considers such preferential treatment contrary to the monastic spirit and, therefore, explicitly forbids clerics from keeping private cooking appliances or food. After Cloud Residing Hall was completed, the master even closed the smaller refectories in the colleges, dormitories, and Tathagata Hall so that all monks and nuns would have to eat together. No longer the abbot of the monastery, however, he rarely personally eats with the monastic community even when he is on the premises. Instead, he and his most senior disciples take their food in his office.

Regardless of the motivations that impelled the Foguang clerics to simplify their evening fare, they and their critics alike would hardly assent to foregoing the evening gathering altogether. Contrary to their counterparts in Southeast Asia, Chinese venerables stress, not the hours of eating, but rather the nature of the food consumed. Meat, fish, and vegetables of the onion family (as well, of course, as all intoxicating beverages) are forbidden.[37] Such abstinence is by no means regarded as a form of self-denial. Foguang devotees and other Chinese Buddhists are justifiably proud of the various ersatz meats and other delicacies served from their kitchens. Expressing compassion to others, they insist, need not require undue, excessive privation for oneself.

Taiwan's Buddhist circles have in recent years begun to change their attitude toward the appropriateness of consuming such dairy products as milk, eggs, and cheese. Clerics who drink milk, as do most at Foguangshan, cite the fact that one of the first acts of the Buddha on forswearing strict asceticism for the middle path was to accept a serving of goat's milk. The reasoning given to justify the consumption of eggs is quite different. Eggs are regarded as becoming sentient only after they have been fertilized. In the past, one could never be sure whether any particular egg had been fertilized. The advent of modern farms has obviated such doubt since laying hens are kept separate from roosters. Knowledge of this fact has led to a slackening in the prohibition against consuming egg products. The force of tradition continues to weigh heavily nonetheless, so many monastics still waver on the issue. As a result, this topic comes up for discussion among Foguang clerics quite frequently. The temple's general policy is that baked goods made with eggs can be eaten but that plain eggs should be avoided. As Master Xingyun joked during a pan-Taiwan conference of Foguang disciples, it would sound like a weak rationalization if, with mouth full of egg, one were to attempt to explain to a devotee that the egg had not been fertilized. Less sophisticated members of the laity may easily misinterpret the change as signifying that monastic discipline is declining, thereby deleteriously affecting their faith in the sangha as moral leaders.[38] Furthermore, non-Buddhists may make denigrating remarks if they see venerables eating eggs when this has for so long been prohibited. Since the pratimoksha prohibits doing anything that exposes Buddhism to ridicule, clerics should abstain from consuming eggs despite their own conviction that it is justified. The premise underlying the proscription against eating eggs has, therefore, shifted from an appeal for compassion to a call for preserving appropriate deportment ("Meeting of Foguang Monastics Assigned to Taiwan Branch Temples" 1997).

The same issues are at work in the question of whether monastics may eat cheese and, more specifically, pizza. Many monks and nuns do not partake of this American treat, both because the process of aging cheese is known to require enzymes from an animal's stomach and because the end product is deemed to be a Western snack food, hence unsuitable for those following the Chinese monastic lifestyle. The modern process for manufacturing cheese relies on synthetic enzymes, so the former compunction is no longer relevant. It is now purely a question of appearance. Pizza has been approved as fare for Foguang clerics since 1989. In his journal entry for 5 October of that year, Master Xingyun says: "In the evening the Hsi Lai disciples sent notices about the upcoming devotees' meeting. Everyone worked past 11:00 P.M., so we bought pizza for all to eat. I had made the rule that no one was allowed to eat pizza because monastics should not crave food [*tan chi*]. Other than the food and drink provided by the temple, monastics should not eat snacks. But, when I saw how hard everyone worked today, I could not but provide this bit of convenience" (Shi Xingyun 1994, vol. 1).

The master ends the anecdote by parenthetically stating two stories that he had heard about the origins of pizza. According to some, the master wrote, pizza dates from the eighteenth century when it was invented by a baker for the royal family in Naples. Others believe that, after Marco Polo returned to Italy from China, he extolled Chinese cooking, and pizza was the result of his inexperienced hand trying to reproduce Chinese cuisine. In other words, the master implies by these stories, such fare is certainly appropriate for Chinese monastics: if it was not originally a Chinese dish, at the very least it was first made for royalty. Pizza continues to be a favorite food, especially among clerics stationed abroad, who order it for many a special occasion, such as when putting in long hours preparing for a big event or while taking a day trip away from the temple.

Similar dynamics underlie monastics' ambivalence about eating ice-cream cones, although the general policy dictates against indulging in this treat. That this is the case became readily apparent one unusually hot January afternoon. I and my family had just attended the opening ceremony for the annual BLIA Youth Conference. As we strolled down Bodhisattva Way with a young nun, my son enthusiastically observed that such weather was perfect for eating ice cream. The bhikshuni readily agreed, but, as we made our purchase at the souvenir shop across from Pilgrim's Lodge, she also looked uneasily around and suggested that we eat our snack under the alcove halfway down the main stairway leading to Nonduality Gate. Once we were safely ensconced in the alcove, the nun explained that monastics are not supposed to eat Popsicles or ice-cream cones, particularly when walking. As with chewing gum, it appears undignified. More progressive monks and nuns think the rule out of date, but conservative clerics still strictly adhere to it and look askance at those who do not.

Just as the nun finished her explanation, she saw to her chagrin several senior bhikshunis ascending the stairs. To save our friend embarrassment, I led my son to the other side of the wide stairway, instructing him to intone the greeting "Amituo Fo" to each passing monastic. Naturally, and to the young nun's relief, all focused their attention on the cute foreign five-year-old who could speak Chinese rather than on the nun standing with the American woman under the arbor.

The Foguang perspective on dietary restrictions is, therefore, very much in line with the community's attitude toward precepts in general: one should be guided by compassion and wisdom to apply such rules appropriately.

Bhikshu-Bhikshuni Relations

The attitudes toward eating ersatz meat, eggs, and ice-cream cones shed light on another aspect of the Foguang interpretation of the precepts: the importance placed on the *shila* prohibiting monastics from exposing Buddhism to ridicule (a rule buttressed by the Chinese abhorrence of losing face, *diulian*). This same vow has also played a role in two other Foguang policies: that regarding monk-nun interaction; and the rules concerning the form of transportation to be employed by clerics.

Foguangshan is very careful to avoid any possibility of a sex scandal rocking the sangha. At the headquarters, dormitories for monks and nuns are on opposite sides of the mountain's religious section. Bhikshus and bhikshunis are stationed together only at those branch temples that have sufficiently separated living areas—Hsi Lai Temple and Nanhua Temple, for instance. Even when traveling, monastics do their best to avoid spending the night in a temple run by clerics of the opposite sex. Monks and nuns were especially keen to avoid even the appearance of impropriety during the spring of 1998, for, apparently, an article in a Taiwan newspaper had claimed that a monk and a nun in another monastery were having an affair and had lambasted Buddhist clerics in general for their lack of morality.[39] For several months thereafter, bhikshus and bhikshunis were cautious about even walking side by side in pairs, especially after nightfall. Although the reason that the pair was walking together could be completely innocent, if a reporter were to see them and, thereby, gather fodder for an exposé, the two would have broken the precept, not against engaging in sex, but against exposing Buddhism to ridicule.

Travel

Master Xingyun believes that monastics should take advantage of all technological advances that can either directly or indirectly facilitate the promotion of Buddhist teachings. He was, therefore, the first Buddhist monk on Taiwan to utilize slide projectors, radio, and television. Similarly, as air travel is faster than any other mode of transportation, the master considers it a valuable tool for spreading the dharma. High-ranking Foguang clerics regularly fly the short jaunts between Taiwan's main cities (Taipei, Taichung, Hualian, and Kaohsiung). Monastics lower in the hierarchy had also been traveling by plane within Taiwan on a steadily increasing basis—until word got to the master that people were criticizing this practice, saying that Foguangshan's monks and nuns were too worldly and were flaunting their wealth. Whether it was truly because of these comments or for financial reasons, Master Xingyun altered the monastery's regulations, allowing low-ranking clerics to fly only when speed was essential. Otherwise, they were, henceforth, to travel by car, train, or bus. Foguang disciples explain that, although there is really nothing wrong with their saving time by flying, since others mistakenly think that they should not be flying and, thereby, defame Foguangshan, the compassionate response is to abstain from that form of travel to save the detractors from creating bad karma for themselves.

Entertainment

Entertainment as Cultivation

Although Master Xingyun may have bent to criticism with regard to low-ranking monastics traveling within Taiwan by airplane, on more than one occasion he has forged ahead with an idea despite adverse reactions on the part of others within Taiwan's Buddhist circles. This has been the case in matters concerning the role of entertainment in cultivation, both lay and monastic. In the 1950s, when the master organized Taiwan's first Buddhist choir, he was accused of breaking the precept forbidding clerics from even attending any form of entertainment, much less writing songs and organizing concerts. The master's response was that music can be a very effective expedient means. By setting Buddhist lyrics to popular tunes, one can attract even those who at first have no interest in the significance of the words. Such people may initially come to enjoy the melody, but, with time, they associate their enjoyment with the dharma and, thus, wish to learn more. The Venerable Cizhuang, Master Xingyun's most senior disciple, relates that this is exactly what happened with her. She had originally gone to Leiyin Temple, not because she was curious about Buddhism, but because she wanted to join a choir. Soon enough, she continues, she found that she gained an even deeper sense of joy through the Buddhist teachings than she did through singing.

Other forms of entertainment can also function in the same way as music to subtly draw people to Buddhism. The Pure Land Cave, the Welcoming Buddha, and other tourist attractions constructed on Foguangshan were designed as recreational facilities with an ultimately didactic objective. The people who enter

Pure Land Cave to see the colorful, moving figures end up learning about the nine grades of rebirth in the Western Pure Land and about the tranquil joy that comes with being reborn there. Drama can also serve as a felicitous method (*shanqiao*). During the first several days of the New Year, students of the Foguangshan Monastic Academy perform several skits that they have written about Buddhist etiquette. Some of the topics covered are mainly of interest to clerics. In 1997, for instance, there were skits about the need for monastics to do their best to fulfill even the most unreasonable requests of guests (especially foreigners), to finish getting dressed before hurrying off to an appointment, always to bow before an image of a buddha, to use proper dining etiquette since eating is a form of cultivation (i.e., avoid slumping in the seat, glancing around, dipping a finger into the bowl, eating too fast, or giving away food to others), and to give proper respect to senior clerics. Two skits dealt with correct conduct on the part of laity. One emphasized showing respect to monastics (e.g., greet them with "Amituo Fo," and serve them tea from the right side); the second dealt with temple decorum (e.g., do not kneel down before any of the images; offer incense by lifting it to the forehead, then placing it in the urn; make sure that children behave while in a temple, but do not hit them or scold them severely).

Entertainment that carries explicit Buddhist themes and values is best, but any form of recreation that provides moral guidance or a healthy outlet for people's emotions and energies is permissible. Certain television shows are, therefore, deemed appropriate. Master Xingyun even appeared in a commercial touting a series from mainland China giving insight into traditional Chinese culture and describing the tribulations and victories of an upright official. Most of the programs on Foguang Television are not Buddhist in content. Of course, there are daily lectures given by senior Foguang venerables. The majority of the shows, however, are simply wholesome family entertainment: movies exemplifying virtuous behavior; educational shows about nature, science, or culture; and reruns of such American shows as "Life with Father" and "Leave It to Beaver." The station is also commercial free, an effort to shield children from the worst of consumer capitalism.

Entertainment need not necessarily be instructive to aid in cultivation. The various art forms, for example, are believed to have the potential to give people a positive means to express deep sentiments and emotions or to develop physical and/or social skills. Large-scale Foguang dharma activities will, therefore, often include dance performances. Usually, the program will be of traditional Chinese dance, but not always; the opening ceremony of the 1998 BLIA World Conference in Toronto began with a presentation by a multiracial experimental dance troupe. Such performances are regarded as celebrating human physical abilities and glorifying cultural advancement in such a way as to sublimate the emotions triggered by the six fields of the senses (*liu jing*; i.e., the data of the five sense faculties and of the mind). Although normally these senses act as the "gates" through which enters the "dust" that covers people's buddha nature, they are also the only access points through which the dharma can penetrate people's mental faculties and eradicate the three poisons (i.e., craving, anger, and ignorance). Master Xingyun emphasizes that, while seeking pleasure through gratifying the six sense fields causes suffering, if such pleasure is given appropriate outlet and gradually transmuted into dharma joy, it furnishes a starting point for the cessation of suffering.

The master considers sports to be yet another potential expedient means for properly channeling emotional and physical energies. He lists five lessons that Buddhist youths can, for example, learn from playing basketball — discipline, teamwork, patience, perseverance, and humility. Because it inculcates such social skills, basketball has been an important part of the shramanera curriculum. Master Xingyun relates that, when the Shramanera School was established in 1967, some of the students came from broken homes and, therefore, frequently misbehaved. Many teachers recommended that these troublemakers be expelled as they deflected attention from and, therefore, disrupted the progress of their better-behaved classmates. Instead of giving up on the boys, however, Master Xingyun taught them how to play basketball. The result? "They gradually learned how to follow rules and to function as a member of a team. Eventually these boys became excellent electricians and plumbers without any formal training at all" (Shi Xingyun 1994, vol. 3, entry for 22 January 1990).

Many Chinese Buddhists who share Master Xingyun's view that entertainment can act as an expedient means disagree with his methods; they feel that, by offering such attractions as the Welcoming Buddha and the Pure Land Cave and setting Buddhist lyrics to popular Taiwanese melodies, he is simply vulgarizing the dharma. Critics also doubt that his methods inculcate in people anything more than a superficial understanding of and appreciation for Buddhist teachings. The harshest animadversions, however, focus on the master's willingness to allow monastics to also participate in many of these forms of entertainment.

In his diary, Master Xingyun tells of the resistance that he encountered in his early years as a monk when he tried to involve other clerics in athletic activities. He writes:

> Many people know of my love for sports, especially basketball. As a child, I loved to swim. When I had to stop because I had renounced, it was very painful. While in Buddhist college I liked to play Ping-Pong, but the teach-

ers often would hide the balls so we couldn't play. Then I contacted my classmates about building a basketball court. The school thought that I wasn't keeping the rules, that I was attached to playing and to sports, so they wanted to kick me out.

After I arrived in Taiwan, I first taught for the Taiwan Buddhist Jiangxi Association. I encouraged the students to play basketball. They all were afraid and didn't dare to touch the ball. They thought that monastics didn't play ball, that it wasn't dignified enough. I was upset, thinking: "When I was a student, I liked to play sports, but the teachers would not let me. Now I am a teacher, encouraging the students to exercise, but they do not dare. Who is in the wrong?" Aren't Buddhist pilgrimage, wandering, worshiping as one climbs mountains, and walking meditation all exercise? . . . Why can't one change the form?

When I first opened Foguangshan, I had the students exercise, but they did not do well because they were not interested. I nonetheless built three basketball courts and eventually built a gym at Universal Gate High School. (Shi Xingyun 1994, vol. 3, entry for 22 January 1990)

Master Xingyun advocates exercise as part of monastic education, not only because it is a means to foster social skills, but also because, in his opinion, cultivation of the mind requires rigorous training of the body. Without physical health, a cleric (or, for that matter, anyone) will find it much more difficult to focus on spiritual cultivation. Furthermore, discipline of the body can be a gateway to control of the mind, for it requires patience, endurance, and diligence.

Foguang clerics are, furthermore, permitted to watch television and movies, as long as the content is wholesome, and especially if it is educational. Monastics are strongly discouraged from keeping a private television set (although a few do), but each temple provides a communal set, which will often be turned on for the news. At Foguang headquarters, movies are shown in the Devotees' Hall auditorium two or three Sunday evenings per month. The only residents not permitted to watch these films are students in the college, although those in the English-Language Buddhist Academy regularly watch English-language videos as a means to improve their listening comprehension.

There are, of course, limits to monastic involvement in entertainment. Venerables in the college, for example, may act in skits, but only as a narrator or in the role of a cleric. They may watch dance performances, but may not participate. Likewise, swimming continues to be out of bounds, both because it is expressly forbidden in the vinaya and because it would require wearing a swimsuit, which is inappropriate attire. Although monks and nuns may watch movies within the monastery, they may not do so in public theaters. Nor may they visit coffee shops. Exceptions to these last two rules are made only if a cleric is accompanying a guest of the monastery.[40]

Cultivation as Entertainment

Just as entertainment can act as an expedient means aiding people in cultivation, Buddhist practice can be a highly refined source of entertainment. Master Xingyun argues that dharma functions and lectures need not be dry, boring affairs. Cultivation is to be a source of joy (*yule*), not pain and suffering. According to the scholar Jiang Canteng, Foguangshan was the first monastery in Taiwan to hold large-scale, elaborate dharma functions. The ever more lavish ceremonies both attracted and required widespread support. The combination of posh proceedings and a diverse range of participants, says Jiang, has lent to Foguangshan's religious activities a "rather carefree, leisurely flavor of 'Xingyun's casino'" (Jiang 1997, 22). By this Jiang apparently means that even dharma functions at Foguangshan can have a carnival atmosphere. This is certainly true of the headquarters' Chinese New Year celebration, with all its parades, lights, and food stalls. In fairness to Foguangshan, events deriving directly from the Buddhist heritage instead of from Chinese folk custom have a more august atmosphere. The point to remember is that the categories "recreation" and "cultivation" overlap: in the Foguang view, fun can lead to spiritual advancement, and religious cultivation can be fun.

The blurring of lines between secular and sacred that allows recreation and cultivation to be deemed compatible also finds expression in the way in which Foguangshan has capitalized on the musical element permeating Buddhist chanting. With the creation of "Buddhist tunes" in the 1950s, the distinction between singing Buddhist songs (*changge*) and chanting scriptures (*songjing*) grew more hazy. The "lyrics" were now similar, using much of the same vocabulary; only the "melodies" differed significantly. Songs having been brought into the temple, the next logical move was taking chanting out into the streets. As the master says in one essay: "Humanistic Buddhism takes Buddhist music out of the temple to carry the magnificent reverberations of the dharma to every corner of society. In addition, by setting dharma words and gathas to beautiful melodies that can be sung, and by performing Buddhist stories through song and dance, we are able to employ music to spread the dharma and purify people's minds" (Shi Xingyun 1995a, 10:172). In this spirit, Foguang monastics perform concerts of Buddhist chanting in public halls. One such event held in 1994 in the Sun Yat-sen Memorial Hall in Taipei attracted over five thousand people to each of the three performances. In more recent years, clerics have taken the Foguang show on the road, one hundred monks and nuns touring twelve European cities the fall of 1999, and a similar number performing in New York City's Lincoln Center in January 2002.

The relation between aesthetic experience and religious cultivation has been of concern to Chinese Buddhists ever since the tradition of Buddhism first arrived in the Middle Kingdom some two thousand years ago. As indigenous art forms were adapted to express Buddhist themes, questions about the relation of aesthetic sensibility and spiritual cultivation inevitably arose. Chinese Buddhists have generally regarded participation in and appreciation for the "high arts," such as painting, poetry, and tea drinking, as a legitimate means for refining and expressing one's understanding of the dharma. Master Xingyun follows his predecessors in this regard. Where he differs from them is in his efforts to make such appreciation more widely accessible: Buddhist chanting has been brought out of the monastery and into the concert hall; Buddhist artwork may be seen in a variety of museums and galleries; a representation of the Western Pure Land has been given concrete form (literally).

Popularizing the arts has required economizing at points. This is most readily evident in the Pure Land Cave. The question thus becomes, Can recreation serve the same transformative purposes as the high arts? When tourists come to Foguangshan, can their entertainment transmute into religious pilgrimage? Can less refined outlets of the senses play the same role as highly subtle expressions? Although Master Xingyun obviously believes that they can, the cloistering of the order's headquarters, which essentially closed down Foguangshan's two best-known tourist attractions (the Welcoming Buddha and Pure Land Cave), indicates that his faith in this expedient means has waned.

CONCLUSION

Whether the issue is that of money, diet, relations between the sexes, or entertainment, the Foguang perspective on the role of precepts in guiding modern life requires that the master and his followers constantly balance the stability offered by tradition with the need for applicability and relevance in ever new circumstances. Because the precepts for laity are so broad in scope, maintaining such a balance is for them relatively easy. For monastics, it becomes a more precarious hermeneutical endeavor owing to the greater specificity of their hundreds of vows. On the one hand, the malleability of the vinaya and of custom is quite evident; it is precisely this that has allowed the tradition to adapt to each new cultural and historical circumstance, thereby creating the internal diversity within the sangha. On the other hand, this plasticity nonetheless displays certain tensile properties. Buddhist clerics share certain commonalities in their lifestyle that differentiate them from all others—both Buddhist laity as well as religious specialists of other traditions—and it is primarily the precepts that shape those distinctive qualities.

7 Institutionalizing Buddhism

FOGUANGSHAN AS ORGANIZATION

The creation of a large, popular religious institution requires both a charismatic figure whose personality and ideas can attract great numbers of people and someone who can coordinate activities, mobilize resources, and organize a core group of devotees. Foguangshan has grown so tremendously over the past three decades because Master Xingyun brings together these two qualities: along with his ability to establish with others a deep sense of personal connection, he also has a genius for conceiving and implementing large-scale enterprises. He knows how to garner people's loyalty, spark their idealism, and synchronize their talents and energies. Chinese Buddhism will prosper, the master learned from Ven. Taixu, only to the degree that its monastic and lay communities undergo institutionalization (*zhiduhua*).[1] In terms of his own organization, he realizes that, while Foguangshan may be the phenomenal manifestation of his own ideas, this manifestation can endure only if appropriate bureaucratic mechanisms are put into place. Master Xingyun is the cause (*yin*) from which Foguangshan has sprouted, to employ phraseology from Buddhist lexicon, but, for this seedling to flourish, favorable conditions (*shan yuan*) must persist, and one key condition is organizational framework.

The blueprint for Foguangshan as institution is found in its bylaws (*zhangcheng*), a series of regulations initially drafted in the 1970s and periodically amended as the organization has grown. The document has three main sections, first providing general rules, then giving more specific guidelines covering personnel and administration. Budgetary matters are also touched on, although in considerably less detail.

CATEGORIES, RESPONSIBILITIES, AND RIGHTS OF FOGUANG MEMBERS

The bylaws concerned with personnel are worded in terms of membership and deal with such issues as who may become a member, the types of membership, and the privileges and responsibilities that come with these various types. Not surprisingly, the two main categories of members are those distinguishing laity and monastics.

Lay Members *(xinzhong xintu huiyuan)*

Any law-abiding citizen who has taken the triple refuge may become a lay devotee of Foguangshan.[2] Such members fall into four subcategories: general devotee-member *(yiban xintu huiyuan)*; dharma-protector devotee-member *(hufa xintu huiyuan)*; benefactor *(gongdezhu huiyuan)*; and the Buddha's Light International Association (BLIA) member *(Foguangren huiyuan)*. The first of these categories refers to anyone who has taken the triple refuge at a Foguang temple. Dharma-protector devotee-members are those who have participated in one or more Foguang activities. Neither of these groups has any special privileges or obligations. Note that, in each of these categories, the term used is "devotee-member" *(xintu huiyuan)*. The establishment of "membership" is a very recent phenomenon in Chinese Buddhism, evidently a technique borrowed from Christian churches. The people who fall into these first two categories should be thought of more as "devotees" than as "members" in that they have no long-lasting formal relationship (economic or otherwise) with the organization.

A more official sense of mutual obligation occurs at the level of benefactor. Master Xingyun established this honorary designation in 1989 as a way publicly to thank those laypeople who had made a long-term commitment to the monastery and to encourage others to display similar dedication. Benefactors are organized into nine ranks depending on level of contribution (the ranks paralleling the nine classes of those reborn in the Western Pure Land). In theory, the contributions may vary widely in nature, anything from offering a significant amount of one's time or introducing many people to Foguangshan, to writing a favorable book about Buddhism. In practice, financial donations are the primary consideration. Those at the lowest rank donate approximately NT$10,000 (U.S.$333) annually, those at the highest rank, millions. Since 1997, Foguangshan has maintained a roster of just over ten thousand benefactors. Master Xingyun thanks these patrons at the annual benefactor's meeting. All who come receive a variety of small gifts, typically books and souvenirs, and attend a special gathering presided over by the master in which they hear reports by senior monastics on recent and upcoming Foguang activities. Another benefit for benefactors is the right to have their remains stored in appropriate alcoves in Longevity Funerary Complex.

Official membership as determined through paying set annual dues plays a role only in BLIA. This society was founded by Master Xingyun in 1991 as a means to formalize his relationship with lay devotees throughout Taiwan. At the request of followers who lived abroad, he expanded the association's scope to become international and moved its headquarters from Taipei to Los Angeles. BLIA had expanded by 1997 to include hundreds of thousands of members organized into 110 regional headquarters *(zonghui)* and chapters *(xiehui)* worldwide: 33 in Asia; 8 in the Pacific (Australia, New Zealand, and Papua New Guinea); 25 in North America; 5 in Central America; 7 in South America; 22 in Europe; and 10 in Africa.

BLIA has five primary levels: world headquarters; regional headquarters; chapter; subchapter; and organizational member. A regional headquarters must have under its jurisdiction at least two chapters. At present, the only such headquarters is that of Taiwan, despite the fact that there are sufficient chapters in several other countries (including the United States, Canada, and India) to create regional headquarters in them as well. Rules stipulate that chapters are to have at least one hundred members and can be divided into subchapters as the situation warrants. Unlike the categories of devotee-members and benefactors, BLIA constitutes a separate entity from Foguangshan, the latter being merely an organizational member within the association. Unofficially, of course, the two are inseparably linked, Foguangshan providing direction and a center of unity, BLIA giving structural coherence to a globally dispersed devotee base.

BLIA members must pay annual dues of NT$1,200 (U.S.$40) and pledge allegiance to the BLIA articles, which exhort them to show reverence to the three gems, spread Humanistic Buddhism, and act as beacons so that the light of Buddha's teachings will shine universally. In return, they receive a variety of privileges. When giving a birthday, wedding, or funeral, for instance, they can request help from Foguangshan, such as asking for the presence of a cleric to conduct a suitable dharma function. They can also apply to live in one of the dormitories for laity at Foguang headquarters (or at one of the branch temples) if they wish to acquire merit through volunteering full-time, or they can apply for charitable assistance if experiencing financial hardship. Finally, BLIA members are given preference in allotment of space in either Longevity Funerary Complex or the Hall of Rebirth.

BLIA is one of the approximately twenty Buddhist associations that have been founded in Taiwan since the passage of the 1989 Revised Law on the Organization of Civic Groups.[3] The two most influential of such groups have been BLIA and the Compassion Relief Foundation, known in Chinese as Ciji Gongde Hui. By the mid-1990s, Ciji Gongde Hui had blossomed into the island's largest and wealthiest Buddhist group, with a reported membership of over four million (although, as we shall see in chapter 9 below, these numbers are most likely inflated). BLIA, Ciji Gongde Hui, and the other associations were all formed as a means to better organize Taiwan's lay Buddhist population and to give it a greater leadership role. Master Xingyun has frequently said that he founded BLIA because, with the rapid growth of Buddhism's popularity both in the Republic of China (ROC) and worldwide, there is simply too much work to be done for monastics to shoulder all the responsibility themselves. Lay devotees therefore fill, not only the BLIA rosters, but most of its leadership positions as well. As of 1998, the organization's treasurer, five of its six vice-chairpeople, and twelve of the fifteen members on the board of directors were laypeople. That same year, Master Xingyun abdicated his position as president of the ROC regional chapter so that his most prominent lay devotee, Wu Boxiong (who had recently stepped down as chairperson of the Kuomintang party), could be elected to the post. Virtually all positions of authority on the local level (chapter president, vice-president, secretary, treasurer, etc.) are filled by laity, the only exception to this being the consultative post of "guiding cleric" *(fudao fashi).*

BLIA differs from Ciji Gongde Hui in two important respects. The first major difference is in focus and, therefore, in membership. As can be seen in the very names of the two groups, BLIA places greater emphasis on being a specifically Buddhist organization. BLIA bylaws explicitly state that the society has been formed to propagate Humanistic Buddhism so as to create a pure land in the human realm. Ciji Gongde Hui, on the other hand, focuses on doing works of compassion and, in fact, is incorporated under the legal rubric of a charitable rather than Buddhist group. As a result, this association has attracted more non-Buddhists (including both people of other faiths and those with no particular religious affiliation) as members than has Foguangshan.[4]

The second major difference between BLIA and Ciji Gongde Hui lies in the fact that clerics play an important leadership role at all levels of BLIA's institutional hierarchy, not just at the highest echelon. As would be expected, Master Xingyun and Ven. Zhengyan are each their organization's chairperson, and their senior disciples fill many of the organization's influential posts.[5] In the case of BLIA, Ven. Cihui is the association's liaison officer, and Vens. Cirong, Xinding, and Huili sit on the board of directors. At lower levels, venerables play a less official role, yet they are still omnipresent. Every chapter's guiding cleric plays a major part in shaping local activities. BLIA is not a lay organization but, rather, an association through which lay devotees can play a greater role in cooperation with, and usually under the supervision of, monastics.

Monastic Members *(sengzhong xintu huiyuan)*

The greater significance of clerics in BLIA than in Ciji Gongde Hui is not surprising given the relative numbers of disciples under Master Xingyun and Ven. Zhengyan, more than one thousand renouncing under the former and being stationed worldwide versus only several dozen under the latter, all of whom remain stationed at Tranquil Thoughts Hermitage (Jingsi Jingshe), the headquarters for Ciji Gongde Hui, located in Hualian, Taiwan. The large number of Foguang monastics, and the fact that they are dispersed around the world, has resulted in the development of a complicated hierarchical administrative system. By grouping his disciples into well-defined ranks with opportunities for promotion, Master Xingyun has sought to clarify lines of authority and to encourage continual self-improvement.

Foguangshan's organizational edifice is an elaboration of the system of generation and class that has long served to specify relationships among clerics who have renounced under the same master. There are three generations *(dai)* of Foguang monastics (see table 2). Master Xingyun, as the founder, is the first generation. All those who have been tonsured directly by him constitute the second generation. Shramaneras and shramanerikas, who fill the third echelon, have been tonsured by the most senior members of the second generation: currently Ven. Xinding for shramaneras and Ven. Cizhuang for shramanerikas (as of 1998, there were fifty-two shramaneras but no shramanerikas). Second-generation monastics refer to Master Xingyun as "Shifu." The young people of the third generation call the master "Shigong" and their second-generation predecessors "Shifu."

Each generation is identified by both "interior" *(neihao)* and "exterior" *(waihao)* names. Monks and nuns of the same generation share the same interior name, but the two genders have different exterior names. Master Xingyun, for example, has the interior and exterior names "Wu" and "Jin," although he hardly ever uses either. The second generation goes by the interior appellation "Xin." Monks have as their exterior name "Hui," and nuns will be called one of six names—"Yi," "Yong," "Man," "Jue," "Miao," or "Ru." The third generation has the interior name "Zong," with shramaneras also being called "Cheng" and shramanerikas "Dao."

In theory, the interior name is used only by other monastics within the same order who are of comparable or superior seniority. The exterior name is used by subordinate monastics and by laity. In practice, however, the interior names were utilized by everyone when Foguangshan was still quite small. Once the order grew in size, monastics began to be called by their exterior names. This change was made because, unlike the interior appellation, which invariably applies to all monks and nuns of the same generation, the exterior name can be changed from time to time,

TABLE 2
Foguangshan Monastic Generations (1998)

GENERATION	NUMBER OF MONKS	NUMBER OF NUNS	TOTAL
First	1	0	1
Second	135	1,117	1,252
Third	52	0	52
Total	188	1,117	1,305

a custom that in this case was employed to highlight relative status within the same generation. Hence, because the vast majority of Foguang monastics are nuns of the second tier, they are further distinguished by the six exterior names mentioned above (i.e., the six classes of "Yi," "Yong," "Man," "Jue," "Miao," and "Ru"), which loosely reflect their ages and the approximate length of time that they have been in the order. Nearly all monastics at Foguangshan are, therefore, known by their exterior names. A few of the most senior monks and nuns, however, such as the abbot Xinding, continue to be known by their interior names.

The application of names is fairly flexible, as can be seen by the shift from *neihao* to *waihao*. Some monastics may even be known by another name entirely. Master Xingyun, for instance, chose this name for himself on entering Taiwan, preferring an appellation derived from astronomy (his name means "Star Cloud") since the Kuomintang suspected many monastics from the Nanjing region of being Communist sympathizers. Freedom in adopting an alternative *waihao* is also evident in the identification of Foguangshan's five most senior nuns as "Ci." The original *waihao* of these doyennes was actually "Yi." "Ci" is the lay dharma name that they received from Master Xingyun on taking the triple refuge in the early 1960s. When they renounced, they were already so well-known by these names that Master Xingyun and others continued to refer to them as such. In doing so, the master emphasized their early association with him and the closeness of their relationship. Affectionate respect by Master Xingyun and other Foguang monastics for senior clerics is also displayed through referring to them by their personal name only, dropping the class appellation entirely. The Venerable Xinding, for instance, is frequently referred to as "Ding Heshang," or "Monk Ding." The Venerables Cizhuang, Cihui, and Cirong are known as "Zhuang Shifu," "Hui Shifu," and "Rong Shifu."

Just as the most senior nuns are known by their dharma name "Ci," many of the nuns who originally renounced under Master Xingyun as shramanerikas have chosen to retain either their original exterior or their original interior third-generation name rather than adopting their second-generation class name, as by right they could have on reaching age twenty. Twenty-seven bhikshunis have opted to indicate their early renunciation by keeping the name "Zong" or "Dao" (those with the name "Zong" having renounced as shramanerikas early on in Foguangshan's history, those with the name "Dao" more recently). Curiously, no bhikshus have kept the names "Zong" or "Cheng," indicating either that no shramaneras have continued as bhikshus or that all who have have changed to the name "Hui."

Except in the case of the nuns who retain their shramanerika name even after graduating to the rank of bhikshuni, clerics' current generation (and class) is readily known as it constitutes the second part of their trisyllabic name. It follows the surname "Shi," which places the monastics as scions of Shijiamouni Fo (Shakyamuni Buddha), and precedes the personal name, which distinguishes each from his or her brethren. A nun's full exterior name might, therefore, be something like "Shi Manhua" or "Shi Miaoqi," and a monk might be known as "Shi Huiyong." The interior names for each would be "Shi Xinhua," "Shi Xinqi," and "Shi Xinyong," respectively.

The Lamp Transmission Committee, in consultation with Master Xingyun, assigns each person his or her class name (*zihao*, also *shang*) and personal name (*xia*) at the time of tonsure. Most personal names are allocated randomly, although, in certain cases, Master Xingyun may provide a name that he considers especially suitable or one that has been requested by the person himself or herself. The person's generation and class are determined by taking into account his or her age, education level, and work experience. Also, where applicable, the person's previous contributions to Foguangshan or his or her years of tonsure under another master will be considered. For example, a twenty-year-old nun who has studied in the Foguangshan Monastic Academy for one year would be assigned to the most junior class of the time (as of 2002, that would be the class of "Ru"). Another nun tonsured at the same ceremony who is twenty-six years old and who has worked as an accountant for a trading firm for four years before joining the Foguangshan Monastic Academy would be placed in the second most junior class ("Miao"). Yet another nun in the ceremony, a thirty-five-year old former lay monastic who has lived at Foguangshan for fifteen years, would fall into the third category ("Jue"). For monks, young men still enrolled in the Foguangshan Monastic Academy are given the generation name "Cheng," while bhikshus with more experience receive the name "Hui." As can be seen from these examples, novices renouncing at the same tonsure ceremony will not all share the same generation or class name. Hence, of the thirty-eight nuns who renounced on 6 January 1998, eight were given the exterior name "Jue," five the name "Miao," and twenty-five the name "Ru." Of the ten monks at the ceremony, five were given the name "Hui" and the other five the name "Cheng."

The decision to institute a new class is not particularly systematic. The Lamp Transmission Committee and Master Xingyun apparently make a list of personal names that would suitably follow the class name. Once the end of that list approaches (leaving leeway for later additions), a new class is designated. Because the number of nuns has increased so rapidly over the past decade, four new classes have been designated in that brief span. The class name "Hui" for second-generation monks, conversely, has persisted for some three decades, reflecting the fact that considerably fewer men have tonsured under the master. Tables 3 and 4 provide more detailed information about each class of monastics at Foguangshan as of May 1997.[6]

Foguangshan's Monastic Classification Scheme in Historical Context

The Foguang method of determining generation and class names is typical for a Chinese Buddhist organization.[7] The framework within which this method has been devised, however, differs from the standard models found in mainland China up through the Republican period. To better understand just how Foguangshan's system compares with those of other Chinese Buddhist temples in recent history, we must briefly outline the traits that have characterized the chief types of monastic organization.

Temples in China have generally been divided into five categories. The vast

TABLE 3
Foguangshan Bhikshus and Shramaneras: Generations and Classes (1997)

GENERATION	CLASS	SPECIAL NAMES	INITIAL YEAR OF CLASS	NUMBER OF MONASTICS	AVERAGE AGE
Wu	Jin	Xing		1	71
Xin	Hui		1961	135	42.2
Zong	Cheng		1961	52	16.3

TABLE 4
Foguangshan Bhikshunis and Shramanerikas: Generations and Classes (1997)

GENERATION	CLASS	SPECIAL NAME	INITIAL YEAR OF CLASS	NUMBER OF MONASTICS	AVERAGE AGE
Xin	I		1961	67	45.8
		Ci		5	60.4
		Yong	1979	152	39.4
		Man	1986	161	36.6
		Jue	1989	273	32.8
		Miao	1992	332	30.1
		Ru	1996	61	29.5
Zong		Dao	1961	34	36.6

majority have fallen under the rubric "hereditary temple" (*zisun miao*). Holmes Welch estimates that, during the Republican period, China's landscape was dotted with approximately 100,000 such temples. The facilities themselves were the property of the monks who had been tonsured there. Any of the fully ordained monks in residence could take disciples, and all the monastics were regarded as a "family." There would typically be several generations of masters and disciples, all "heirs" (*zisun*, lit. "sons and grandsons") to the lineage. Those tonsured by the same master referred to him as their "teacher-father" (*shifu*) and to each other as "brothers" (*xiongdi*). They in turn became the "teacher-fathers" of their own disciples and the "teacher-uncles" of their tonsure brothers' disciples. Those with different tonsure fathers of the same generation were "cousins" to one another. Such establishments tended to be on the smaller side, with an average of five monks each, and, hence, were also called "small temples" (*xiao miao*), although some actually grew to include a considerable number of disciples and to have extensive landholdings. These temples usually maintained a fairly relaxed atmosphere, seldom having a code of bylaws, paying little attention to the vinaya, and maintaining no regular schedule of recitation or meditation.

The second category was that of "public monasteries" (*shifang conglin*). Welch believes that there were approximately three hundred such establishments during the Republican era, housing a total of twenty to twenty-five thousand bhikshus. These were regarded as the common property of the entire sangha, not of any particular tonsure family. Hence, the only person allowed to accept disciples at such establishments was the abbot, and he could not perform the tonsure ceremony on the grounds but had to do so at a nearby hereditary temple. On the other hand, it was only these centers of orthodoxy that could hold triple altar ordinations (although not all did). Laypeople could receive no training at public monasteries. In fact, they were not even supposed to spend a night there. Discipline and practice were in general more rigorous, with strict schedules, codified bylaws, and firm rules against taking private donations.

Larger public monasteries often opened "branch temples" (*fenyuan*) and "subtemples" (*xiayuan*). No novices could be tonsured or receive training at these posts. Branch temples typically served as housing for elderly monks no longer fit enough to endure the rigorous schedule of the main temple but without sufficient rank to enjoy a private apartment. Subtemples were located either in a large town, to serve as an office for the main temple, or along the road to the central monastery, to serve as rest stations for pilgrims if the route was long.

The final category of monastic organization has been that of "hereditary public monastery" (*zisun shifang conglin*), which includes those hybrid institutions that combined the characteristics of public and hereditary temples. Such monasteries might be large in size and have quarters to lodge visiting clerics, yet novices would also be tonsured on the premises, and control over the facility would remain within the resident tonsure family.

Foguangshan regards itself as a public monastery, and, for the most part, this self-perception is accurate, for the headquarters shares many of the qualities that have characterized such establishments. Foguang headquarters is home to a considerable number of monastics; in fact, with some 450 resident monks and nuns, it has a much greater population than did most public monasteries during the Republican period, which averaged sixty to eighty-five occupants.[8] The clerics are organized and regulated according to codified bylaws that, among other things, specifically forbid them from receiving their own disciples, opening their own temples, or collecting private donations. The master often speaks to the monastic community about the vinaya and how best to implement it under current circumstances. Foguang daily life follows a strict schedule with expectations that all will engage in various forms of practice. The college is open to all lay and monastic devotees, regardless of who their master is, a point emphasized by the first word of its name: *conglin*, that is, the same term used to designate public monasteries. Finally, as we have seen, Foguangshan has several times sponsored ordinations.

Foguangshan differs from public monasteries, however, in one important respect: all but a handful of its residents have been tonsured by the master. Hence, they use such familial language as "grandfather-teacher," "father-teacher," and "brothers." Not surprisingly, just as his own disciples fill the college and monastery, Master Xingyun's first two successors as abbot have also been tonsure disciples, a practice common in hereditary temples but strictly forbidden in public monasteries. Foguangshan should, therefore, be regarded as falling under the hybrid rubric "hereditary public monastery."

Lay Residents of Foguangshan

Foguangshan differs from public monasteries in another important respect: not only are laity permitted to spend one or more evenings on the premises (a practice that, although in name prohibited, had in fact been common at many of the better-known public monasteries), but there is also a contingent of laypeople who live and work at the headquarters and at larger branch temples on a long-term basis.

Lay residents at Foguang headquarters fall under three categories. First, there are those who live or work in the mountain's secular section, that is, the teachers, students, and senior citizens associated with Universal Gate High School and Preschool, the Great Mercy Children's Home, and the Hermitage. One could argue that the social-service section is not part of the monastery proper, but never before has a Chinese Buddhist organization kept such a large and diverse lay populace on the same property as its main temple. As mentioned earlier, this may change in the future, for Master Xingyun has voiced a desire to move all these facilities elsewhere, thereby reasserting Foguang headquarters as religious pilgrimage site.

Second, there are those devotees who have donated their time to serve the temple. Laity who are volunteering for a relatively short period, perhaps several weeks or months, stay in Pilgrim's Lodge. Women who plan to stay at least a year live in Miaohui Hall, one of the dormitories in the social-service section, while men are boarded in a small lodging just outside the monastery's back gate. Short-term volunteers typically help slice and dice the mounds of vegetables prepared each day for meals or tend to the mountain's extensive grounds. Longer-term lay residents will be posted in an office to work alongside the monastics.

Third, there are approximately three dozen women who have proved themselves to be among the master's most loyal followers. Some of these women have devoted themselves to aiding him in spreading the dharma since his days at Leiyin Temple in Jiayi and have lived at Foguang headquarters since the opening of its first dormitory in 1968. In order to provide formal recognition of their special status, in the late 1980s the master devised the special category of *shigu* for them, simultaneously creating the title of *jiaoshi* for any men making a similar long-term commitment to Foguangshan (although few have). *Shigu* and *jiaoshi* vow to remain celibate and unmarried so that they may wholeheartedly serve Foguangshan for the rest of their lives. They make this pledge during a tonsure ceremony for monastics, although their heads are not shaved. Assuming this status does not require taking any additional precepts beyond those that they have already accepted, typically the bodhisattva vows. These people have "left home" *(chujia)* without tonsuring *(titou)*; they are "disciples" *(tudi)* but not clerics *(fashi)*. For lack of a better term, I refer to such lay residents of the monastic community *(changzhu)* as "lay monastics." They too live in Foguangshan's secular section, sharing the Hermitage with retired nuns and aged female lay devotees.

Given the marginal status of *shigu*, one may wonder why women choose this route instead of taking full ordination. Lay monastics provide three explanations for their decision. In certain cases, the women state that they prefer the greater freedom afforded by this status. Still within the laity, it is more acceptable for them to keep private savings accounts and personal property provided by family members. As some *shigu* come from quite wealthy backgrounds, such financial security allows a considerable degree of independence. They state that this autonomy permits them to serve Foguangshan better than they could have had they fully renounced, for they can donate large sums for Foguang initiatives. Furthermore, as it is more seemly for laity to handle money, they are in a position to act as Foguangshan's accountants. Women also become *shigu* because they are not yet completely sure that they wish to renounce. To break a vow, especially one as sacred as leaving home, is viewed with great disapprobation. To avoid possibly exposing themselves to such censure should they change their minds, they assume the status of lay monastic for a trial period. There are others who become *shigu* simply because their family refuses to grant permission for their renunciation. As we have seen, such permission is absolutely necessary for the master to accept a disciple. Those women who are unable to obtain the necessary letter from their parents become lay monastics, a status requiring no family approval. In some cases, the family is not even aware that the person has taken this step, believing that she is simply volunteering for the organization.

The institution of a cadre of lay monastics is evidently a unique development, having no precedent in the history of Chinese Buddhism. Never before has a contingent of lay devotees been granted a formal status that allows them to live side by side with clerics. In creating this special category, Master Xingyun may have been guided by the tradition of "vegetarian nuns" (*zhaigu*) that has been found in Taiwan for well over a century. Because draconian imperial laws during the Qing dynasty prevented women from renouncing until age forty, there arose the phenomenon of groups of women living together in small vegetarian halls (*zhaitang*) but not tonsuring or taking any formal precepts (Jiang 1997, 49–56; Jones 1999, 14–24, 88–92). Such marginal communities have mostly faded away with the opportunity to take bhikshuni precepts, not to mention the rise of Yiguandao. At Foguangshan, however, a vestige of this tradition lives on.

RANKING

Creating a category of lay monastics is not the only innovation that Master Xingyun has made in his efforts to clarify and expand variations of status within the monastic community. In most Chinese Buddhist monasteries, whether hereditary, public, or a hybrid of the two, once a cleric has been assigned a generation name and class name, the designation typically remains fixed. Only in rare instances — for example, when a monastic has displayed outstanding talent and achievement — will he or she be reassigned to a higher class (this sign of superlative ability is not readily available for Foguang monks since nearly all have the same class: "Hui"). The more usual way of gauging a venerable's progress within the organization is through a unique system in which each is assigned a rank (*xulie*).[9]

Foguang clerics are ranked according to a hierarchy with five main categories: purifier *(jingshi)*; learner *(xueshi)*; cultivator *(xiushi)*; teacher *(kaishi)*; and master *(dashi)*. The first four of these are subdivided into grades: six grades within the ranks of purifier and learner and three grades within the ranks of cultivator and teacher. Most monastics enter the order in the midrange grades of the purifier rank. Shramaneras and young novices will be assigned to the lowest three grades. Students in the Foguangshan Monastic Academy are placed in one of the upper four grades of purifier. Older newcomers typically receive a ranking of the lowest grade of the learner category, although those who come to Foguangshan with particularly good credentials, perhaps a university degree or several years of work experience, will be assigned to a correspondingly higher rank.

A person's rank on entering the order is determined according to education level, seniority, work experience, and special skills. In determining entry rank, the Lamp Transmission Committee starts with education level as a foundation. Those who have graduated from elementary school, for instance, come in at the rank of purifier, grade 2; university graduates receive the rank of purifier, grade 6; and those with a doctoral degree enjoy a rank no lower than learner, grade 2. In addition to education level, years of practice are considered. By "seniority" *(nianzi)* is meant years of service to Foguangshan, especially while living on the mountain or in a branch temple as a volunteer worker or lay monastic. Every two years that a person has worked in such a capacity tally as one year of seniority. Similarly, every year in the Foguangshan Monastic Buddhist Academy counts as one year of seniority. For those who have tonsured under a cleric other than Master Xingyun, the number of years that they have been tonsured and ordained *(jiela)* are considered.

A person's work experience, special skills, and contributions to society also factor in, especially if they are of such a nature as to be beneficial to the monastery. Personality, knowledge, and character are considered as well. There is no set standard by which to gauge such achievements, so Master Xingyun will typically be called in by the Lamp Transmission Committee to determine the person's rank. For example, Ven. Huichan had already established himself as a well-known artist in mainland China before emigrating to Canada in 1989, so, when he entered the order in the fall of 1996, he was immediately assigned the rank of learner, grade 6, placing him above 97 percent of all monastics, despite the fact that he had had very limited training in Buddhist practice before renouncing.

Promotion

All monastics are evaluated annually to determine what, if any, promotion they should receive. Advancement is based on four factors: seniority *(nianzi)*; educational attainments (*xueye*); work ethic (*shiye*); and religious cultivation (*xiuye*). Seniority influences promotion as follows: purifiers are promoted one grade annually; learners are promoted one grade every other year; cultivators are promoted one grade every three to six years; and teachers are promoted one grade every five to ten years.

Everyone is, therefore, assured of gradually rising in rank simply by remaining a loyal member of the Foguang community. Master Xingyun is highly critical, however, of basing promotion on longevity alone, considering the practice a root cause for the poor leadership that plagues many monasteries. Individuals may, therefore, gain more rapid advancement in status through excelling in education, work, and/or cultivation. Educational attainments resulting in promotion include conducting research on Buddhist texts, showing progress in lecturing, publishing papers and essays, and continuing one's education, especially by gaining a graduate degree. Also important in determining rate of promotion is one's work ethic. The Lamp Transmission Committee considers attitude toward assigned tasks, noteworthy achievements or contributions to the monastic community, and the degree to which creative insight in dharma propagation has been displayed.

The final criterion playing a role in promotion is the cleric's religious cultivation. There are two basic points of evaluation. First is the degree to which the person participates in the five daily services (*wu tangke*): breakfast and lunch and the morning, afternoon, and evening sessions of recitation.[10] Second is the person's deportment and adherence to precepts. Beyond this, the monastic's virtuosity with dharma instruments is also considered. Hence, anyone who does not participate in the five daily services and has not mastered the use of dharma instruments may not be promoted beyond the rank of learner.

The process through which evaluation for promotion is conducted is as follows. Every year at the end of June, department chiefs (*danwei zhuguan*) utilize hundred-point scales to evaluate, respectively, the religious, educational, and work merit of each monastic and lay monastic under their charge. Outstanding achievement receives a grade of 90 or above, superior progress a grade of 80–89, average attainment a grade of 70–79, below average progress a grade of 60–69, and unacceptable achievement a grade below 60. The three grades are then averaged together, with religious merit accounting for 40 percent and educational merit and work merit each accounting for 30 percent of the total. The final numbers are converted to the Chinese equivalents of letter grades: "*you*" for outstanding; "*jia*" for excellent; "*yi*" for average; "*bing*" for satisfactory; and "*ding*" for unacceptable. Only 10 percent of the monastic community are honored with the highest rating, 30 percent receive a grade of "*jia*," 40 percent receive a grade of "*yi*," and 20 percent receive a grade of *"bing"*—all set percentages. There is no set percentage for the failing mark, which is used only in cases of extreme neglect of duty.

Once the department head has completed all the annual personnel evaluations for his or her department, they are sent to the Lamp Transmission Committee, which then provides to each monastic a copy of his or her evaluation, along with a self-evaluation form. The cleric fills in the self-evaluation, then has a conference with the department head. The personnel evaluation form, self-evaluation, and conference notes are all sent to the Lamp Transmission Committee's promotion commission. If, on reviewing the material, the commission finds a significant discrepancy between the reports given by the evaluator and the person evaluated, a meeting is held with the former, and perhaps the latter, to clarify the situation. The final evaluation is sent to the Lamp Transmission Committee, which forwards it to the Religious Affairs Committee (RAC), or Zongwu Weiyuan Hui, for final review.

The Foguang system of assigning rank and determining promotion is significantly different from that found in large monasteries of early-twentieth-century China. The terminology is completely different, and, more important, the Foguang process of promotion is much more elaborate. According to Holmes Welch (1967, 36–39), in mainland monasteries rank and promotion were supposed to reflect religious attainment through meditative experience but were, in practice, assigned according to the office that one held. The process of evaluation at Foguangshan is much more involved. Master Xingyun is proud of his order's innovative procedure, extolling it as an important mechanism for the institutionalization and modernization of the sangha.

With such an intricate system in place to determine promotion, one might assume that a monastic's rank has a major impact on his or her life. In truth, rank has little direct bearing on daily routine, at least on a material level. It does affect the amount of stipend received and the nature of one's housing, although differences are nominal, as we saw in chapter 6 above. Also, only those with a ranking of cultivator or higher may be nominated to serve on the RAC, and one must be of the rank learner, grade 3 or higher to vote in the RAC election. The sequence for queuing for dharma functions is supposed also to be in accordance with rank, although, in actual practice, people often let those who have renounced earlier go first, even if the rank of these predecessors is lower.

The most important implication of the ranking system is simply what it says about a person's standing in the organization. Every year the new list of rankings is published in the *Foguang Newsletter*, the internal periodical for clerics. The twenty- and thirty-year commemorative albums also listed the most recent rankings. Hence, all monastics, and even a good many lay devotees, can see the relative place of each cleric in the organization's hierarchy. Such public notice of status garners instant prestige for those who have risen rapidly and indicates who can be expected to be assigned tasks and posts of responsibility in the near future.

Because a person's rank is the public evaluation of his or her level of cultivation and contribution to the community, it is a source of frustration for those who feel that their abilities and services have not been adequately recognized. Dissatisfaction with the outcome of promotions inevitably comes up at monastic meetings held shortly after their disclosure. Discontent arises for two, related reasons. First, while educational achievements are fairly straightforward to record, work ethic and, especially, religious cultivation are less easily tracked. Much of the appraisal process is, therefore, quite subjective. Second, an individual is evaluated primarily on the basis of the report provided by his or her department head. If the two do not get along well, this will be reflected in the evaluation. To justify the system and pacify the dissatisfied, Master Xingyun reminds his wards that any large organization must have a means to select those who are to lead. That one has not been marked as among the elite should not become a source of resentment, which will only further impede cultivation. "Don't think 'I got cheated [*chikui le*],'" exhorted Master Xingyun at one meeting. "A monastic must remain calm, patient, respecting both his or her own and others' progress. A Foguang Buddhist should follow this guide: When your services are needed, provide them; when it is not yet your turn, be patient. Causes and conditions may simply not yet have coalesced for one's talents to be adequately displayed." Master Xingyun went on to note that, in several instances, those who had for many years progressed through the ranks only slowly suddenly attained a degree of enlightenment, leading to a correspondingly rapid jump up the ladder.

LEAVING THE ORDER

Many who are dissatisfied do not remain patient. Shortly after I arrived at Foguangshan, I inquired about two nuns whom I had met at Hsi Lai Temple four years previously. The first several times I asked about the pair, there was an uncomfortable pause and then either a quick change in subject or a vague mumbling to the effect of not knowing their whereabouts. Only several months into my research did I learn that both had returned to lay life (*huansu*). Reticence about those who drop out is not surprising, for the fact that some do not find that for which they are searching at Foguangshan reflects poorly both on the organization and on monasticism as a way of life. Let us now turn to consider the degree to which, and the reasons why, clerics leave Foguangshan.

Master Xingyun's order has seen its population increase steadily over its thirty-five-year history. The number of people renouncing lay life has reportedly grown over these years, especially throughout the 1980s and early 1990s, and many of Taiwan's new breed of young monks and nuns have selected Foguangshan as their home. The several dozen venerables who had renounced under Master Xingyun by 1970 saw their ranks swell to five hundred by 1985 and to nearly fifteen hundred by the year 2000. While the overall number of monastics at Foguangshan has skyrocketed, quite a few of those who have renounced have found either that the lifestyle is not all that they had expected or that their own criteria for a fulfilling life have changed. The question is, Just how many are unable to stick it out?

The great unwillingness of clerics to discuss this subject makes acquiring accurate statistics very difficult. Nonetheless, since Foguangshan included in both its 1988 and its 1997 commemorative albums (see Shi Xingyun 1988b, 1997a) a comprehensive roster of the order's monastic population, by comparing these one can determine who remained in the organization over that nine-year period and who slipped away (see table 5).[11]

Such an analysis shows that 274 of the 430 ranked monastics present at Fo-

TABLE 5
Comparison of Monastic Community Numbers, 1988 and 1997

	1988 Total	1996 Total[a]	Present in 1988 and 1996	New to Roster since 1988, Present in 1996	Present in 1988 but Not in 1996	% from 1988 Still Present
Yi	90	67	63	4	27	70
Ci	6	5	5	0	1	83
Xin	3	3	3	0	0	100
Yong	169	129	114	15	55	67
Man	65	127	48	79	17	74
Zong	14	7	7	0 (?)	7 (?)	50[b]
Dao	22	12	10	2	12 (?)	45[b]
Hui/Xin	49/2	105/1	19/1	86/0	30/(1)	39/(50)
Cheng	4	50	1 (now Hui)	49	3 (?)	25[b]
Other	6	3	3	0	3	50
Total	430	509	274	235	155	63

[a] Excluding ranks instituted after 1988.
[b] The statistics displayed here give only a rough indication of the dropout rate (see n. 10 of chapter 7).

guangshan in 1988 were still to be found on the roster there in 1997, a retention rate of 63 percent. As would be expected, those who were in the late 1980s already senior members of the organization were the most likely to remain through the subsequent nine years: five of the six nuns using the dharma name "Ci" continued to be active in the organization, as did all four of the surviving monastics using the interior name "Xin" (the fifth of this group, Ven. Xinping, passed away in 1995) and 70 percent of the nuns using the class name "Yi." Many of those who had entered the order at a very young age had, however, become dissatisfied and left: half the nuns who had joined as shramanerikas apparently disappeared from the Foguang ranks, as did three of the four shramaneras.[12] Regardless of seniority, the retention rate within a particular class was directly proportional to rank: those who in 1988 were high in the hierarchy relative to others in their class were more likely to persist as Foguang monastics.[13] That success in the organization encouraged continued allegiance to it is not surprising.

The most striking statistic to come out of a comparison of the two rosters is the much higher dropout rate among monks than among nuns. There were forty-nine bhikshus with the name "Hui" in 1988, but only nineteen, or 39 percent, of these persisted within the order (compared to a 67 percent retention rate for bhikshunis). Not only do significantly fewer men than women renounce at Foguangshan, but only a fraction of those men who do come actually stay for any length of time. Furthermore, unlike the case for nuns, for monks there is no correspondence between rank and likelihood of remaining in the organization: bhikshus high within the Foguang hierarchy have been even more likely to disappear than have those in the lower echelons.[14]

The fact that, within one nine-year period, there was an overall dropout rate of 37 percent indicates that only a few of the monastics who tonsure under Master Xingyun will spend the rest of their days under the Foguang aegis. The majority of those who come will sooner or later depart. In some cases, individuals receive permission to transfer to a non-Foguang monastery. Such former Foguang disciples usually maintain cordial relations with Master Xingyun, still regarding him as their teacher despite no longer being a part of his organization. Others register for an extended leave of absence but then never return (of the twenty-four clerics listed as being on leave in 1988, only two came back to remain until 1997). In the majority of cases, however, individuals simply disappear with no warning or formal notice (the Chinese term is *liudan*, lit., "to stray from one's place").[15] What becomes of such truants is rarely known. Some depart to join another order; others return to lay life. Once someone has made such a decision, he or she typically cuts off contact with Foguangshan entirely.

Reasons for leaving Foguangshan fall into two main categories: disillusionment with the monastic lifestyle and dissatisfaction with Foguangshan as an organization. Some simply discover that the career of a cleric is not all that they had thought it would be and, therefore, quietly return to lay society. One nun explained that many renounce with unrealistic expectations, believing that life in a monastery will be as ideal as it is depicted in stories to be. When they see that slipping arhat sandals on one's feet is no guarantee of progressing to rarefied levels of spiritual achievement and that those who don them often still suffer from impatience and anger, they become disenchanted. This disenchantment may then be compounded by a sense of isolation, for many monks and nuns apparently do not feel that they can admit to their peers that they are having pangs of self-doubt or disappointment, fearing that word will spread in the community about their low level of self-cultivation or lack of proper reverence for seniors.

Clerics told me that some people find the many precepts and the strict routine of monastic life too constraining. This sense of confinement can become accentuated for those punished for misbehavior. As noted in chapter 2 above, Master Xingyun has been known to scold disciples publicly and even to slap them for their disobedience. Some people are simply too proud to endure this type of censure. Yet others leave because they no longer wish to be celibate. Both the nuns whom I had known at Hsi Lai Temple left the order because of romantic involvements, one marrying a Euro-American man, the other moving in with a woman.

Finally, monastics return to lay life because it is socially acceptable to do so. When a Tibetan lama asked a Foguang nun if it was considered a disgrace in Taiwan for a monk to return to lay life, as it is in his own heritage, the nun told him that, no, people held no prejudice against those who did so. She later further explained to me that, because in Taiwan the social status of Buddhist monastics is low, the general public thinks that those who shed their robes have, in fact, bettered themselves. Monks feel the lack of prestige for their chosen profession even more than do nuns. Furthermore, they most likely feel great pressure to return to lay life during their two or three years of compulsory military service. At least, as Master Xingyun laments, very few return to the religious life afterward.

Not all who leave Foguangshan return to lay society. Many wish to join another order or to start their own. Those who depart Foguangshan to begin anew elsewhere do so for either philosophical or political reasons. By "philosophical reasons," I mean the decision that Humanistic Buddhism, at least as it is practiced at Foguangshan, does not allow for sufficient self-cultivation and that a temple with a more tranquil, "traditional" form of practice would be more congenial. By "political reasons," I mean the decision that the interpersonal maneuvering inevitably found within such a large bureaucracy is unwelcome, owing either to the competitiveness involved or to a lack of success rising through the ranks. Even some who have risen quite high in the hierarchy may depart in frustration. One bhikshu who had already reached the rank of cultivator, grade 3 and been made a member of the RAC left Foguangshan in bitterness in 1994, complaining that monks had no say in the organization, every department being dominated by nuns.

Because those who drop out to affiliate with another temple carry with them either an implicit or an explicit critique of Foguangshan, the Foguang leadership finds such cases to be especially embarrassing. To dissuade his disciples from making such a move, Master Xingyun quotes the saying: "I would rather sleep in a large monastery than practice in a small temple" (*ningyuan zai da miao shuijiao; bu zai xiaomiao bandao*). By "small temple" he does not merely mean a temple with few monastics in residence since even many Foguang clerics live under such circumstances. Rather, he is referring to small, independent monasteries. The master warns his disciples that, while such organizations may seem to promise more freedom and, hence, control over one's daily life, in fact their very laxity hinders any serious advancement in cultivation.

Reaction to Those Who Have Left

When a person leaves the order, those who remain loyal to it naturally claim that the fault lies in that person's own inadequacies rather than in any that may be found in either the order or the monastic way of life. In Buddhist terms, the person is said to lack sufficient merit to persist as a Foguang monastic—or as a monastic at all. The problem is commonly attributed either to insufficient strength to withstand the rigors of treading the bodhisattva path or to an inability to overcome a strong sense of self. Those who have returned to lay life, for instance, are regarded as lacking the will to suffer on behalf of others or to control the urges of greed or sexual desire. Those who have left Foguangshan so as to establish their own monasteries, conversely, are described as self-centered, unwilling to be a team player, and unable to follow the leadership of others. (The clerics so described would probably retort that there is too much politicking and infighting at Foguangshan for those with true religious talent to flourish.)

At one meeting with his disciples, Master Xingyun related how he goes through three stages of reaction on hearing that monastics have left the order. First, he feels great sorrow (*tongku*): people with whom he has established ties of affinity and who have wonderful potential have not followed through on an important vow. Later, he feels concern (*tongxin*): he fears that those who have left to go to a smaller temple will lack proper guidance and direction and that those who have returned to lay society will find that life disappointing and full of unanticipated difficulties. Ultimately, however, he experiences a sense of relief (*tongkuai*): only those with the proper mettle to be effective monastics will remain; that is, those who possess neither the character nor the background to be a cleric and could not, therefore, contribute as they should, possibly even giving the order a bad name, have been weeded out.

Relief is not the only reaction on hearing about those who have surreptitiously left the Foguang order, as the following story, related by the master in his diary, reveals:

> As more and more disciples have come to Foguangshan to cultivate themselves and offer their services, the expenses to cover medical care, education, and daily needs have increased drastically. I remember a period when the bills for dental care rose tremendously. One day, an accountant came in with a pile of bills, saying: "Master, an especially large number in the monastic community have required dental care. Having a toothache is not serious, but, once a tooth does ache, it is hard to bear. But, because the monastery is providing everyone with this service, our dental bill has become extremely high. It costs over NT$1,000 or even NT$10,000 to fill cavities or provide false teeth for a single person. The monastery cannot afford this."
>
> The accountant then continued: "Some of these people receive so much from the monastery, but they never repay anything or express any gratitude. Some of them even criticize us. Then, once their teeth have been fixed, they leave the order. In my opinion, it's a waste of money to be helping them in the first place."
>
> I replied: "These people may not use their mouths to say nice things, but I still feel that I must give them a mouthful of good teeth." (Shi Xingyun 1995a, 10:599)

In this anecdote, Master Xingyun suggests that he harbors no resentment toward those who leave yet also does nothing to dispel the sentiment that such people have exploited Foguangshan's goodwill. By taking undue advantage of the free education and other benefits provided by the order without having made sufficient contribution in return—and, in many cases, even criticizing the mountain after leaving—truants have "forgotten gratitude and turned their back on righteousness" (*wang'en beiyi*).

Those who leave Foguangshan without permission almost never return. Master Xingyun says that it is easy to enter Foguangshan, and easy to leave it, but very difficult to reenter. Several monastics told me of a nun who had left the organization, becoming the abbess of her own temple in Taipei. Eventually, she regretted her decision and asked the master for permission to return. He said that she could but that to do so she would have to do the same as he requires of all truants asking for a second chance: kneel before, not just him, but the entire monastic community and ask forgiveness for what she had done. The nun could not bring herself to do this, so she once again disappeared. Some others who left have returned. One nun apparently came back after leaving the order for six years. Another resurfaced in the spring of 1997 after a hiatus of one or two years. This latter repented in front of the Buddha and all in attendance during the first morning recitation session on her return, explaining why she had left and then offering incense to the Buddha.

That many of the approximately three thousand men and women who over the years have tonsured under Master Xingyun have failed to persist within his organization is not surprising given the rigors of monastic life and the requirements of such a large community.[16] The Foguang explanations for the dropout rate give us insight, not only into why clerics leave, but also into the type of personality it takes to stay.

The successful Foguang monastic tends to be achievement oriented and capable of adjusting to the politicking inevitable in a large institution. One nun who was chafing under the restrictions imposed by the bureaucratic hierarchy wondered aloud whether a young Master Xingyun would survive within his own organization or whether a Ven. Yinshun would be able to make the type of contributions that he has to the Chinese Buddhist community. Someone like Master Xingyun, she suggested, would soon need to break out from under his superiors' control, just as he had ventured to Jiayi in the 1950s to escape the bickering and infighting of Taipei's senior monks. A Ven. Yinshun would also most likely leave the organization, lest all his energy be sapped away in coordinating various activities for laity, leaving too little time for the quiet philosophical pondering that he has pursued with such wonderful results.

Foguangshan's size and institutional framework is, thus, both its strength and its weakness, providing the appropriate conditions for clerics of particular inclinations and personality to thrive, but proving unsuitable as a place of cultivation for others. Since bureaucratic structure plays such an important role in shaping monastic life and determining the nature of the relationship between venerables and laity, let us turn to a description of Foguangshan's institutional apparatus in more detail.

FOGUANGSHAN'S INSTITUTIONAL STRUCTURE

Electing the RAC and the Abbot

Once a person has reached the rank of cultivator, he or she is eligible to serve on the RAC, the nine-member board that formally sets policy for Foguangshan. Elections for the RAC are held once every six years.

One such election occurred on 15 May 1997 (the day before the cloistering of the mountain). On that morning, monastics of the rank learner, grade 3 and higher solemnly filled assigned seats in the Tathagata Hall auditorium to cast their votes. Master Xingyun, Ven. Cihui (who was overseeing the election), and Ven. Xinding were positioned on the stage. The twenty candidates who, along with Ven. Xinding, had been nominated by the current RAC sat in the front row. Clerics of rank learner, grades 1 and 2 sat in the back as observers. Master Xingyun opened the meeting by reviewing the rules for election; then Ven. Cihui instructed several monastics to distribute the ballots. Once all votes had been placed in the ballot boxes, they were counted and tabulated. This done, Ven. Cihui read off the top nine finishers—Vens. Xinding, Cirong, Huikai, Yikong, Huiri, Yihua, Yonggu, Manguang, and Huikuan. The names of the four clerics and one lay monastic who were to serve as alternates were also announced.

Master Xingyun said that he was very pleased with the results. Whereas only two monks had served on the outgoing RAC, four would serve on the incoming one, giving the bhikshus an equal voice. Four of the candidates were already serving (Vens. Xinding, Cirong, Huikai, and Yikong), while five would be on the committee for the first time, balancing continuity and fresh ideas. The master also noted that the incoming committee members were highly educated—three holding doctorates (Vens. Huikai, Yikong, and Yihua)—and that they were young, with an average age in the early forties. Finally, the master highly praised Vens. Cihui, Cizhuang, Cijia, and Huilong, the senior clerics who had sat on the outgoing RAC but would not be doing so on the next. These four, the master told the audience, had willingly stepped aside to give the next generation the opportunity to lead, thereby once again exemplifying for all the Foguang spirit.

With the election over, the committee's first task was to elect its chairperson, who would also serve as the abbot (*fangzhang*) of Foguang headquarters. This post was filled by the master from 1967 to 1985. On his retirement, Ven. Xinping, who had been one of Master Xingyun's earliest disciples, was elected as the mountain's second abbot. That the master voluntarily stepped down from his position so that another, younger cleric could take over the reins was immediately acclaimed by the organization as proof of his commitment to institutionalizing and democratizing Buddhist leadership. Foguang bylaws have since stipulated that no one can serve more than two terms as abbot. The Venerable Xinping was in the fourth year of his second term when he passed away of cancer in 1994. The final two years of his term were, therefore, filled by Ven. Xinding.

The 1997 election for abbot occurred during the annual benefactor's meeting, which took place several hours after the RAC election. The nine newly selected RAC members filed onto the auditorium stage, each putting his or her ballot into a box. The Venerable Cihui then took out the slips of paper and read them one at a time. To no one's surprise, Ven. Xinding was reelected, having received seven of the nine votes. Master Xingyun was not present. Once the outcome was known, Ven. Xinding went to present himself to the master, and the two men came back to the auditorium together. Master Xingyun sat behind a table on a small platform just in front of the image of Amitabha. The Venerable Xinding sat just in front of and below the master. The eight other members of the RAC returned to the stage to make a pledge to Foguangshan and Ven. Xinding, after which the abbot made some remarks, emphasizing: "Master Xingyun may no longer be the abbot, but he will always be our master, our teacher, our spiritual guide."

The ceremony at which Ven. Xinding was officially inaugurated as abbot was held the following morning. The master sat on the raised platform as he had the previous day. The Venerable Xinding stood facing him. To either side were forty VIPs, including vice-ministers from the Department of Interior and the Department of Foreign Affairs, the head of the Kaohsiung office of the American Institute in Taiwan (the de facto U.S. embassy), the director of the Spanish Chamber of Commerce (who several years previously had taken the triple refuge under Master Xingyun), the commissioner of Kaohsiung County, the Catholic bishop of Kaohsiung, several elderly monks from prominent temples elsewhere in Taiwan, the president of Foguang University, and Ven. Xinding's parents. The eight members of the RAC mounted the stage, bowed to Ven. Xinding, and renewed their pledge of loyalty to him and Foguangshan. As they left, Master Xingyun read the Linji dharma scroll *(fajuan)*, then gave Ven. Xinding a walking staff, scroll, and wooden sword (all of which in the Chan tradition symbolize authority).

The Venerable Xinding made no remarks during the ceremony. It was the master who gave a short talk to the gathering of monastics and benefactors, introducing the members of the RAC and informing all that one of the members, Ven. Huiri, had attained enlightenment *(kaiwu le)*. Master Xingyun's comments were followed by remarks made by ten of the VIPs. The representatives of the Department of the Interior and the Department of Foreign Affairs took the opportunity to present the master with the Grand Interior Medal and the Diplomacy Medal, the highest honors given to citizens by these ROC offices.

Although the ceremony served to inaugurate Ven. Xinding as abbot, the focus was not particularly on him. The fact that he did not make any comments, that two prestigious awards were presented to the master, and that it became public knowledge that another monk on the RAC had attained enlightenment all served to deflect attention elsewhere. The Venerable Xinding may be the formal head of the institution, and he may have received the dharma scroll from the master, but he has by no means become the organization's central figure. As he readily observed himself, Master Xingyun remains the master, teacher, and spiritual guide.

THE FOGUANG LEADERSHIP STRUCTURE IN HISTORICAL PERSPECTIVE

The separation of institutional leader and spiritual master has often occurred in Chinese monasticism. According to Holmes Welch (1967, 147), abbotship has not been a post particularly sought by senior clerics, for it requires attending to so many mundane affairs that it easily detracts from one's own religious cultivation. Prominent monks have, therefore, often declined to assume the responsibility involved in being the abbot or some other top temple official (or, once in such posts, retired as soon as possible). The language used at Foguangshan to explain why the most senior monastics step down from leadership positions is not that of increasing focus on personal practice (for that would sound selfish and contrary to the ideals of Humanistic Buddhism) but, rather, that of moving aside to bring the fresh perspective and greater energy of youth to the helm. Of more importance than this difference in rhetoric are the innovations that Foguangshan has introduced in the method for selecting administrative leaders and in its interpretation of the significance of the dharma scroll as a sign of authority.

The methods employed by Chinese monasteries when selecting official leadership were, in the early twentieth century, fairly consistent: a new administrative head of a temple would typically be chosen from among senior disciples by the current abbot in consultation with other temple leaders and with abbots at nearby temples (Welch 1967, 137). The process for selecting the abbot was more complicated for Chan public monasteries than it was for public monasteries of other schools because it often involved the handing down of a dharma scroll to indicate the transmission of teaching authority.

To see how this worked, we must consider for a moment the Chan understanding of dharma transmission. According to Chan accounts, the Buddha entrusted "the subtle dharma gate that does not rest on words or letters but is a special transmission outside the scriptures" to Kashyapa when the latter alone among all the arhats understood the deeper meaning when the Buddha silently raised a golden lotus blossom. The dharma is said to have continued to be transmitted from one Chan patriarch to the next, being brought to China by Bodhidharma in the early sixth century. Four generations later, Chan patriarch Daoxin transmitted the dharma to four disciples who had attained enlightenment. Doing so caused the lineage to branch out, which it did several times again subsequently. Hence, not only does each school of Chan have its own lineage, but multiple sublineages have also evolved. Master Xingyun has received transmission of the dharma (*shou fa*) as an eighty-fifth-generation disciple of the Buddha, a fifty-eighth-generation disciple of Bodhidharma, a forty-eighth-generation disciple within the Linji school, and a fifth-generation disciple of the Qixia subschool. He is also regarded as the first-generation lineage master of Foguangshan (Shi Xingyun 1988b, 524–525).

The practice of passing on a written attestation of transmission of the dharma evidently began some time within the last three centuries.[17] Such scrolls have acted as an imprimatur that their possessors have prerogative to teach. The retiring abbot would typically transmit the dharma and provide the dharma scroll to his designated successor as a seal of the transferal of authority. The relation between receiving dharma transmission and ascension to the post of abbot has varied, however. In Jiangsu Province, for instance, collective transmission has been the norm, with several masters jointly passing down the dharma to several disciples, who have then all served as abbot on a rotational basis. Receiving the dharma therefore has indicated both the right and the obligation to serve as abbot. Masters Xuyun (1840?–1959) and Taixu, however, strongly condemned any system that linked dharma transmission and abbotship, arguing that doing so led to a range of abuses by confounding institutional and spiritual authority.[18] In the public temples over which they presided, there was, therefore, no relation between the two, and any monk, whether or not he had received dharma transmission, could be selected to serve as abbot (the only restriction was that he could not have been tonsured by the retiring abbot).

Foguangshan differs from other public monasteries within a Chan lineage in its interpretation of the significance of dharma transmission, especially as this is related to ascension to abbotship. When in 1985 Master Xingyun transmitted the dharma scroll to Ven. Xinping, he simultaneously transmitted the dharma to thirty other clerics as well (twenty-five of whom were his tonsure disciples), although he did not provide them with scrolls (Shi Xingyun 1988b, 525). The Venerable Xinping therefore represented their collective authority.

Several points can be made about this arrangement. First, for the first time in Linji history, a master transmitted the dharma to nuns (twenty-three of the thirty recipients were bhikshunis). Second, the master transmitted the dharma to many more disciples than is typically done. In the past, no more than five disciples have been designated as dharma heirs. Master Xingyun's move both broadened access to this mark of authority and attenuated its significance. Third, there does not appear to be any formal connection at Foguangshan between dharma transmission and high positions of institutional authority, even the abbotship. Dharma transmission neither indicates the right nor the obligation to fill that post or even to serve on the RAC. In fact, at least two of the current members of that committee are not dharma heirs. Finally, the fact that Master Xingyun made a public announcement that a monastic other than the abbot had attained enlightenment, specifically pointing out that the abbot had not reached a comparable level of cultivation, indicates that, in the Foguang view, transmission of the dharma does not indicate enlightenment of the highest degree. (That this is the case can also be seen in the fact that Ven. Huiri had, in 1985, already become a Foguang dharma heir, as had Ven. Xinding and twenty-eight others.)

It will be interesting to see exactly how dharma transmission will occur in the future and what significance it will hold. Most likely, Foguangshan's third generation of dharma disciples will be designated through a collaborative effort of Master Xingyun's immediate successors still active in the organization and will formally receive transmission through the second-generation disciple serving as abbot at the time.

At this stage of Foguangshan's history, dharma transmission is not an import issue. It certainly was not in the 1997 elections. Much greater voice was given by the master to how democratic the election had been. "Buddhism is fundamentally democratic in spirit," said the master, "and voting in elections is a modern expression of democracy." By "democratic," Master Xingyun meant that the election had been conducted in an open and fair way, with each monastic of qualifying rank having an equal voice in determining the outcome. Without question, the monastery had taken great steps to ensure accountability and exactness in the balloting process. The votes themselves were secret, but they were tabulated and checked in such a way that everyone in attendance could observe the process.[19] Such a method certainly represents both a modernization and a systematization of the means for determining institutional governance. In the past, monastery leaders tended to be selected through informal consultation, and, in some cases, the post of abbot was even filled by lot (Welch 1967, 151–154).

The Foguang electoral system was not, however, quite so cut-and-dried as at first appears. The evening before the election, all clerics attended a preliminary meeting in which the rules were explained and the names of the twenty-one candidates revealed ("Religious Affairs Committee Election Preparatory Meeting" 1997). Master Xingyun took the opportunity to discuss the various candidates' credentials. The amount of time that he spent describing a person's accomplishments made it quite clear whom he especially wanted to see selected. His comments that he hoped that the new RAC would be filled with well-educated monastics and that there would be more monks on it than on the current committee also influenced the election's outcome. By the end of the evening, it was basically a foregone conclusion as to who would fill seven of the nine slots. The process therefore was democratic, yet guided. Master Xingyun may no longer be the abbot of Foguangshan, but his presence is continually felt, not just as a religious teacher, but also as an institutional force.

One reason the master may have felt the need to interject himself into the electoral process was to ensure that the Foguang community would live up to another value that has been associated with exemplary monastic life for a much longer time than has the ideal of democracy and that is in tension with the competitive spirit inherent in that modern notion, namely, harmony. As one pamphlet notes, "Foguangshan is based on the principles of law, respect, harmony, and the democratic spirit of Buddhism" (*Women de baogao* 1995, 44). Foguang monastics certainly do not campaign for themselves to be named to the RAC or as its chairperson. They leave that to Master Xingyun! They do not even play a role in being nominated; the RAC attends to that. On the other hand, those who are nominated would not dream of declining the honor, for to do so would be contrary to the Foguang bodhisattva spirit of service regardless of personal sacrifice.[20] Foguangshan's interpretation of "Buddhist democracy" is, therefore, one strongly influenced by the ideals of consultation, cooperation, and communal harmonization. One could say that the process is characterized as much or more by immanent charisma as it is by rationalization.

POLICY IMPLEMENTATION
The RAC is the organ that formally creates Foguangshan's policy. It currently functions, however, not so much to create policy as to implement the programs that have been devised by the master. The importance of the RAC has decreased with time. For the first eighteen years of its existence, when Master Xingyun served as its chairperson and filled it with his most senior disciples, the board did serve as the central agency for steering Foguangshan's course. Once the master retired from the RAC in 1989, it rubber-stamped decisions that the master made in consultation with key RAC members. With this latest election, only one of the master's most senior disciples, Ven. Cirong, has remained on the committee. As a result, while the RAC still has some input in formulating programs, for the most part its function has shifted to implementation.

The most important decisions are now made in the Founding Abbot's Chamber (Kaishan Liao), that is, by Master Xingyun, and by the Veterans Council (Zhanglao Yuan), which is essentially composed of the same elders who once served on the RAC—Vens. Cizhuang, Cihui, Cirong, Cijia, Xinding, Ciyi, and Huilong.[21] Officially, the council is under the jurisdiction of the RAC, which merely means that the RAC formally approves its membership. Beyond that, the RAC would not dare dictate policy to those on the Veterans Council. Policymaking at Foguangshan runs the following course: ideas formulated by Master Xingyun are first refined through informal collaboration with the Veterans Council and then ratified as official policy through the RAC, which then oversees implementation.

Once a policy has been made and ratified, it is the responsibility of the RAC to assign the task outlined therein to the appropriate department. Under RAC aegis are seventeen such agencies, which may be roughly divided into three categories: committees (*weiyuanhui*); councils (*yuan*); and foundations (*jijinhui*). There are four committees, three of which are designed to fine-tune particular policies or programs. Hence, the RAC Policy Development Committee drafts the proposals to be considered at the RAC's monthly meetings, the University Education Development Committee maps out the objectives of Foguangshan's two liberal arts institutions (Foguang University in Jiayi, Taiwan, and Hsi Lai University in Los Angeles), and the BLIA Development Committee coordinates large-scale BLIA events and devises strategies for creating new chapters. The fourth committee, known as the Lamp Transmission Committee (Chuandeng Hui), differs in function, for it handles all personnel issues of the monastic community, not only administering promotion, but also tending to any medical or personal problems that monastics may have and settling internal disputes or squabbles that may arise. This committee reports directly to the master rather than to the RAC so as to allow clerics safely to lodge complaints even against those high up in the hierarchy.

The actual implementation of policies is largely the responsibility of the various councils. The Domestic Supervisory Council and the Overseas Supervisory Council manage Foguangshan's network of temples. The Education Council runs the religious training programs, especially the monastic academies. Foguangshan's various publications, audiovisual materials, and CD-ROM projects are attended to by the Culture Council. In addition to these four councils, there are five other departments that also enact policy, although with a more focused scope. The Abbot's Chamber manages the affairs of the headquarters. The meditation hall is run by the Cultivation Center, which also organizes pilgrimages to Foguangshan. The International Buddhist Progress Society, which was formed in the late 1980s when Master Xingyun began to extend his interests and connections beyond Taiwan, both provides formal structure linking together those Foguang temples that are outside the ROC and acts as the headquarters' liaison with Buddhist organizations, political leaders, and cultural figures around the world. The Foguangshan Tripitaka Editing Committee has assumed the mammoth task of reissuing the Chinese Buddhist canon. Finally, Foguang Satellite Television runs the organization's noncommercial television station.

Finding funding for all this is largely the job of three foundations. The Foguangshan Culture and Education Foundation raises funds for Foguangshan's monastic academies, publications, ten art galleries, various summer camps, and the Foguangshan Tripitaka Editing Committee. The Foguangshan Pure Land Culture and Education Foundation accumulates and distributes funds for constructing new temples. Foguangshan's various philanthropic endeavors, including its medical clinic and vans, the annual winter relief campaign, and Great Mercy Children's Home, are all supported by the Foguangshan Compassion Foundation. In addition to these, another very important source of revenue is Foguangshan's contingent of benefactors; it is the task of the Benefactors' Headquarters to attract and sustain such long-term donors.

The specifics of how Foguangshan raises and allocates its money remain murky; temple leadership does not like to discuss such matters with outsiders. A rough sketch of Foguangshan's financial system follows. Before addressing this issue, however, I would like to first explain the organization of the domestic and international supervisory councils since these two are structurally the most complicated of Foguangshan's departments.

Foguangshan's Network of Temples

In a little over three decades, the Foguang network has expanded to include 152 facilities. Never before in the history of Chinese Buddhism has a monastic had as many temples and affiliated institutions under his direct supervision as does Master Xingyun.[22] Foguangshan can hardly be called a "Pan-China" organization since the country's political division makes the establishment of temples in the mainland impossible. The organization is, however, certainly Pan-Chinese in scope in that it caters to Buddhists throughout the Chinese diaspora. Within Taiwan, Foguangshan has fifty-seven temples, more than any other Buddhist organization, with branch temples or Pure Land Chan centers in every community of any size.[23] Even more remarkable than Foguangshan's system of temples within Taiwan is the fact that Master Xingyun has been able to extend this network to every corner of the globe. As of 2001, in addition to its centers in Taiwan, Foguangshan had ninety-five temples spread across six continents.

Foguang temples, whether in Taiwan or overseas, fall into nine categories, generally determined by size of the devotee base and the range of activities offered (see table 6):

1. Chief temples *(bieyuan)*: Foguangshan's grandest temples are typically found in metropolises and, therefore, usually require fifteen to twenty monastics to serve the large devotee clientele adequately.[24] Because of their considerable facilities and staff, these are the temples most likely to hold large-scale dharma functions and to sponsor a wide range of activities. Foguangshan has six such banner temples: the Taipei Vihara; Pumen Temple (Taipei); Puxian Temple (Kaohsiung); Hsi Lai Temple (Los Angeles); Linji Foguangshan (Tokyo); and Nan Tien Temple (Wollongong, Australia).
2. Branch temples *(fenyuan)* and viharas *(daochang)*: These are smaller than the chief temples but, like them, usually maintain standard Taiwanese temple architecture.
3. Pure Land Chan centers *(chanjing zhongxin)* and lecture halls *(jiangtang)*: The centers and halls tend to be smaller than temples and to have fewer staff. They are also apt to be more recent additions to the Foguang network. Many of the lecture halls date from between the years 1987 and 1991, and the majority of Pure Land Chan centers were completed only between 1992 and 1996. The change in nomenclature from "temple" to "lecture hall" and then "Pure Land Chan center" parallels a move away from the exterior architecture typical of Taiwanese Buddhist temples. Both the new names and the new look are part of an effort to identify Foguangshan with a broader range of services than have been provided by Buddhist temples in the past.
4. Propagation centers *(bujiao suo)* and Foguang gardens *(Foguang yuan)*: These are subsidiary to a chief or branch temple, providing facilities in another part of a city so that devotees do not always have to travel to the temple but, instead, can have the clerics on occasion come to them. All but one of these are found outside Taiwan.
5. Educational branches *(xueyuan)*: Temples that are located near an academic institution and that therefore focus on attracting college and university students to Buddhism go by the name "educational branch." Foguangshan has two such centers, one in Taizhong, the other in Yonghe.
6. Youth hostel *(qingnian huiguan)*: When a dwelling is purchased in the vicinity of a university to be used as both a meeting place and a short-term lodging facility for lay college students, it will be designated a

"youth hostel." No cleric lives on site, but one or more will visit regularly to give dharma talks and run other activities. Foguangshan has two youth hostels, both in the United States (in Oklahoma and Texas).
7. Educational hermitage *(xueshe)*: The dormitory for the monastics studying in the Chinese Buddhist Research Academy at Nanhua Management College is referred to as an "educational hermitage."
8. Hermitage *(jingshe)*: A building that provides housing for visiting monastic and lay devotees will be referred to as a "hermitage." Usually, it will be a house in the vicinity of a Foguang temple.
9. Retreat center *(yuan)*: Foguangshan has two retreat centers, the four-hundred-acre Deer Park in New York State and an equally impressive center at the foot of Mount Fuji in Japan (purchased in 2001).

These temples have become part of the Foguang system in a number of ways. Most often, a group begins by meeting in devotees' homes. Once the group accumulates the financial resources, it rents or purchases a space for its meetings, simul-

TABLE 6
Distribution of Foguangshan Temples (1997)

	TAIWAN	OVERSEAS	TOTAL
Headquarters	1	0	1
Chief branch temples	3	3	6
Branch temples/viharas	21	36	57
Pure Land meditation halls	17	21	38
Lecture halls	10	4	14
Dharma propagation centers	1	11	12
Foguang gardens	0	7	7
Education gardens	1	0	1
Youth hostels	0	2	2
Education hermitages	2	0	2
Hermitages	1	9	10
Retreat centers	0	1	1
Total	57	94	151

Source: Foguang tongxun, no. 424 (August 1997): 1–21.

taneously requesting that Foguangshan dispatch one or more monastics to oversee the facility and its activities. In some cases, a wealthy benefactor will donate land or a building. Other temples have been donated to Foguangshan by the abbot or the owner, usually after falling on hard times. Anguo Temple, for example, built in 1938 by Ven. Yingmiao, was given to Foguangshan in 1991 by its aging abbot, Ven. Mingding. Daxi Heping Chan Temple, a very large structure in a beautiful rural pocket of northwestern Taiwan, had been a Daoist establishment until 1994, when its abbot both renounced under Master Xingyun and simultaneously donated the facilities to Foguangshan (the former Daoist priest continues to serve at the temple, although he is not its abbot).

Any time an organization expands to include multiple subsidiaries, it becomes necessary to create mechanisms that will preserve unity and loyalty to the central authority. Master Xingyun has, therefore, instituted a variety of measures designed to ensure that lay devotees' allegiance is to him and to his organization as a whole rather than to the monastics stationed in their particular locality. First, only Master Xingyun is permitted to accept disciples. Other Foguang monastics may accept only lay devotees, and those on behalf of the most senior cleric in their generation (i.e., Ven. Cizhuang and Ven. Xinding). Second, Foguang monastics may not collect donations for their own, private projects, especially the building of a temple. Any fund-raising done is to be for the organization as a whole. Similarly, venerables are dissuaded from sinking too much of their own money into any particular Foguang project, especially if they play a role in its administration, since this may easily lead to a sense of proprietorship over that project (Shi Xingyun, n.d.-b, 17).[25] Monks and nuns are also discouraged from establishing particularly close relations with any lay devotees and should not ask for private favors. Finally, Foguangshan's bylaws stipulate that all monastics are to be transferred at least once every three years (although, in practice, some remain in a posting much longer). "Monastics should be like water," explained Master Xingyun to the parents of clerics during the annual Family Reunion Day (9 November 1996). "To stay still in one place too long is to stagnate. Freshness remains through movement. That is why Foguangshan's monastics are sent from temple to temple all over the world. Movement is part of the Foguang system."

Such movement is said, not only to preserve vitality, but also to cultivate a carefree lack of attachment *(bu zhizhuo)* and an existential understanding of impermanence. In addition to such idealistic motivations, there is, of course, also a more prosaic reason for keeping clerics on the move: by thus gradually rotating temple staff, the loyalty of devotees is guaranteed to remain focused on the temple as community, Foguang headquarters, and the master himself.[26] In all that they do, monastics should represent Foguangshan as a whole so that devotees are loyal to them as stewards of the order, not as individuals. Lay devotees are to regard all Foguangshan's clerics as their teachers but only Master Xingyun as their master.

It will be interesting to see what becomes of the Foguang network in the future. Temples that are part of the system either joined because of devotees' respect for Master Xingyun or as a means to deal with financial hardship. Most have joined only within the last fifteen years. Such a recent coalition could certainly disintegrate just as quickly if the master's eventual successor cannot maintain loyalty to the organization and, thereby, preserve an adequate flow of donations.

FOGUANGSHAN'S FINANCIAL STRUCTURE

ESTIMATING THE MONASTERY'S MONETARY WORTH

The property value of Foguangshan's worldwide network of temples is certainly in the hundreds of millions of U.S. dollars. Foguang literature states that Hsi Lai Temple near Los Angeles and Nan Tien Temple just south of Sydney each cost between U.S.$25 and U.S.$30 million to construct. The Taipei Vihara, Pumen Temple (Taipei), and Puxian Temple (Kaohsiung), all major centers located on choice urban real estate, are probably worth comparable amounts, as will be the temple in Houston once construction is completed in 2005. Foguang headquarters easily must have a value four or five times that of any of these. The rest of Foguangshan's temples, lecture halls, and Pure Land Chan centers are worth much less, mostly ranging somewhere from U.S.$100,000 to several million U.S. dollars. The total value of Foguangshan's property therefore probably surpasses, and may well exceed, U.S.$300 million.[27]

Property value is only one part of the equation, of course. The annual budgets for Foguangshan's various programs cumulatively reach millions of U.S. dollars. Some figures are provided in table 7 to give a rough indication of the organization's expenditures. *Washington Post* reporter Kevin Sullivan stated in a 1996 article that the "Foguangshan empire" was estimated to be worth more than U.S.$400 million. From the sketchy information that I have obtained, this figure seems reasonable, although perhaps a bit on the conservative side.

FOGUANGSHAN'S METHODS OF RAISING FUNDS

The great wealth amassed by Master Xingyun in such a short span of time has led his critics to contend that he is but a "commercial monk" (*jingying heshang*) who has transformed Buddhism into big business. A principal reason why this sobriquet has been attached to him is that he was one of Taiwan's first clerics (if not the very first) to develop his monastery as a large-scale recreational site. The Welcoming Buddha, the Museum of Buddhism, Pilgrim's Lodge, and various shops that sprouted up on the mountain in the 1970s drew millions of sightseers, many of whom bought souvenirs, ate in the vegetarian hall, and perhaps even stayed for one or more nights. Foguangshan therefore became known as a major tourist attraction on an island with few places for young people and families to go on holidays. As I noted in chapter 1 above, this source of revenue decreased by the late 1990s, and, with the cloistering of the mountain, the focus and terminology shifted from "tourism" to "pilgrimage."[28] If Foguangshan has been able to meet its goal of attracting one thousand participants to each of its weekend cultivation retreats and each of those participants provides at least the NT$1,000 donation expected, that would bring in an annual revenue of NT$52 million.

In addition to tourism and pilgrimage, Foguangshan employs numerous other methods for raising funds and acquiring assets. A fairly sizable income must derive

TABLE 7
Examples of Foguang Budgets

DEPARTMENT OR PROJECT	BUDGET
Awakening the World magazine	As of 1997, more than U.S.$50,000 each month for printing and free distribution
Foguang Medical Clinic	1995 budget over NT$6 million
Cloud and Water Mobile Unit Clinic	1995 budget approximately NT$10 million
Winter relief efforts	1995 budget NT$2.35 million
Emergency aid	1996 expenditures over NT$19 million; 1998 expenditures approximately NT$8 million
International Buddhist Progress Society	1995 budget U.S.$2.7 million
Foguang University	More than NT$1 billion being raised for endowment
Universal Gate High School	Annual budget in the tens of millions of New Taiwan dollars
Foguang Satellite Television	As of 1998 an annual budget of more than NT$350 million
BLIA	1999 budget U.S.$494,000
BLIA Emergency Relief Foundation	1998 assets U.S.$328,016

Note: BLIA = Buddha's Light International Association.

from the books, cassettes, videos, and CD-ROMs produced by Foguang Publishing House and sold both through Foguang temple gift shops and via mail order as advertised in the magazine *Universal Gate* and the newspaper *Merit Times*. So many of these articles are also given away as "gifts of affinity" (*jieyuanpin*), however, that the net income may not be as great as appears prima facie. Foguang temples also receive some revenue through renting meeting rooms and auditorium space, although not an appreciable amount. Monasteries periodically hold charity sales and fairs, where devotees contribute goods and services to be sold for the benefit of the temple or a particular project. A much more lucrative fund-raising method is the holding of art auctions. The pieces donated for these events are worth thousands, and sometimes millions, of New Taiwan dollars. At an auction held in 1994 to benefit Foguang University, 180 artworks ranging in price from NT$45,000 to NT$2,000,000 were put on the auctioneer's block. Most were in the range of NT$250,000–NT$500,000. Although the total amount raised was not made public, it must have been at least NT$50 million (*1994 Foguang University Art Auction Album* 1994).[29]

Foguangshan's most significant source of revenue is donations. For lay devotees, a chief means of attaining merit is by *dana*, generously giving whatever material resources may be needed by the sangha to spread the dharma. As do other Chinese Buddhist temples, all Foguang shrines have donation receptacles placed prominently in front of the main image or just inside the entryway. Most devotees will insert anywhere from NT$100 to NT$1,000, although some will apparently give as much as NT$10,000.

Two types of events are especially financially important: the initiation of a large-scale project, such as the construction of a new building, and the holding of dharma functions. Whenever a sizable structure is being built, devotees are canvassed for contributions. This tactic has a long history in Chinese Buddhism; strolling down the halls of a monastery, one will inevitably see the names of patrons engraved in the walls or under buddha images. Often, the donor's name is etched in that portion of the building for which he or she took financial responsibility, anything from a doorway to an entire wing. Master Xingyun has continued this technique, but with a new twist: rather than depending on a few wealthy donors, each of whom funds a significant section of the building project, the master has "democratized" the process, amassing smaller donations from a much wider range of devotees. Hence, the entire hallway surrounding Foguangshan's main auditorium (on the fifth floor of Tathagata Hall) is covered with thousands of names, each representing a contribution of at least NT$20,000. This strategy is employed, not just for construction projects, but for any undertaking ambitious enough to require significant monetary backing, for example, Foguang University and Foguang Television.

Master Xingyun says that he prefers this method so that no devotees are too heavily financially burdened. The scholar Jiang Canteng (1997, 22) offers another benefit of the master's modus operandi: by keeping a wide network of supporters, the master assures that none within the laity gain too much financial power within the organization, which could give them leverage and, thus, allow them to interfere in monastic affairs. Another strength of this strategy is that it aims higher than the particular project—in the sense that contributions to several campaigns may be solicited at one time. The effect is to attenuate individual patrons' influence even further. This is not to say that Foguangshan has no major donors; some benefactors give millions of New Taiwan dollars. These dollars are spread over multiple projects, however, and, given Foguangshan's total assets, the contributions of even the wealthiest followers come to but a small percentage of overall donations.

As already noted in chapter 4 above, Master Xingyun has instituted a system in which donors may make their contributions by installment (a strategy that he introduced in the 1970s and that has since been adopted by all Taiwan's large Buddhist organizations). An important component of the Foguang University endowment campaign, for instance, was the "One Million People Promoting Education" fund-raising drive, which was designed to bring together one million sponsors, each contributing NT$100 per month over a three-year period, thereby raising a total of NT$3.6 billion by the year 2000. Master Xingyun believes that allowing devotees to make small, frequent donations not only gives them the ability but also encourages the inclination to continue giving over the long run, thereby providing the monastic community with a more stable financial base.

Devotees supplement these ongoing contributions with larger, one-time donations made during important dharma functions. Days marking the birth, the enlightenment, and other important anniversaries of various buddhas and bodhisattvas are all occasions for attaining merit through monetary contribution. Lists of relatives or ancestors to whom the accumulated merit is to be transferred will cover one or more walls of the dharma function location. Differences in amount contributed, and, hence, the degree of merit acquired, will be reflected in the merit-transferal certificate's placement, wording, size, and coloring.

Land and sea dharma functions (*shuilu fahui*) prove extremely lucrative as many devotees are eager for this opportunity to be present at such an auspicious gathering of buddhas, bodhisattvas, dragon kings, and gods. Every shrine around Foguangshan will be utilized on such occasions, each designated as the site for reciting a certain sutra. Shorter sutras will be chanted multiple times, but some of the longer ones might take the entire five days of the dharma function to recite from beginning to end. Only the most important donors will have the privilege of joining the recitation at the inner altar (*neitan*), where the dharma function's supramundane visitors are said to focus their power. (Foguangshan's records indicate that, for a land and sea dharma function that was held in the spring of 1991, participants donated NT$50,000 for this privilege, with the choice positions being reserved for those who had contributed at least NT$100,000 [*Foguangshan wanfo santan luohan qi jiehui* 1992, vol. 1, chap. 2].) Such land and sea dharma functions used to occur every two to three years at Foguang headquarters and periodically at the chief branch temples. As the financial requirements of Foguang University and other projects have increased, however, these functions have taken place more often—annually at the headquarters and nearly as frequently in the other temples as well. Over one thousand devotees will usually participate, so the resulting revenue is considerable.

In addition to land and sea dharma functions, devotees are particularly likely to provide donations to sponsor a triple altar ordination. For Foguangshan's 1991 ordination, contributors donated anywhere from NT$1,000 to NT$100,000. As is typical of Chinese Buddhist monasteries, this ordination had been preceded by a land and sea dharma function, so the combined revenue must have been substantial. The ordination was three months long, however, so the expenses would also have been quite high. Nonetheless, in the end, it was certainly a money-generating activity.

Chinese New Year is another important time for receiving donations. For many years, thousands of people have visited Foguang headquarters to offer incense to the Buddha, sample vegetarian treats at the various stalls, and watch the daily parades (including floats with Buddhist themes, the Universal Gate High School marching band, the Great Mercy Children's Home drum corps, costumed preschool students, and a silent procession of novice monks from Foguangshan's Shramanera School). Many stay late into the night to view the over one million lights and several thousand lanterns festooned around the mountain. The glow of each of the tiny bulbs is said to represent the blessings of Buddha's light and, therefore, to shine forth hope for the coming twelve months. The name for the new year activities as a whole is, hence, the "lamp offering dharma function," and each evening people may offer their own small votive candle to the Buddha during a ceremony in the courtyard just before Great Heroes Hall. Because Foguangshan is so well-known for this program (which, accordingly, provides an important source of revenue), even after the cloistering of the mountain the gates have been reopened to the general public for the Chinese New Year, although the festivities now last only two weeks rather than a full month, as they had in the past. This period is also a busy time at all Foguang branch temples. None draw the numbers that the headquarters does, of course, but, at larger centers, thousands will stop by.

The lamp offering dharma function provides revenue in three ways. First, use of temple facilities is intensified, so more money than usual comes in to pay for lodging, board, and souvenirs. Second, each of the name tags hanging under the thousands of lanterns strung around Foguangshan represents a donation of at least NT$500 (and the fancier lanterns around the main shrine represent donations of NT$10,000 each). Third, devotees provide individual monastics with red envelopes, some of which contain a large wad of money. As is always the case when receiving such personal donations (see chapter 6 above), monks and nuns are expected to give at least half of funds so obtained to the monastery treasury.

Clerics also hand over all funds that they receive during alms processions. In yet another innovative twist to Buddhist practice, Master Xingyun periodically dispatches a hundred or more of his disciples to walk Taiwan's city streets seeking alms. Since the time of the Buddha, monastics have made daily rounds to fill their bowls with food offerings, a routine followed to this day in Thailand. In China, however, the custom did not take root, apparently clashing too directly with native sensibilities. Nonetheless, in recent centuries, some large public monasteries did introduce this means of gaining material support. The Chinese alms processions differed from those found in other Buddhist countries in two ways. First, the Chinese version was on a grander scale—anywhere from several dozen to over a hundred monastics winding down the streets. Second, offerings to the clerics were not food but cash.

Master Xingyun has appropriated this method, but on an even larger scale and on a much more regular basis. When he first instituted this fund-raising method in 1989, more than two hundred clerics of every rank participated, and the procession, a journey lasting weeks and covering nearly six hundred miles, made national news. In more recent years, the distances covered have been less ambitious, and usually only venerables in the Foguangshan Monastic Academy have participated, accompanied by their lay classmates, who manage traffic and clear out each cleric's alms bowl as it fills with coins and bills. The money so gathered all goes to the academy's budget. It is unclear how much is actually raised. According to one college administrator, the intake is not much more than the expenses involved in transporting and lodging the students during the trip. Such alms processions are, therefore, regarded as more important for their value as advertising than for whatever funds are raised.

Foguangshan also receives donations in conjunction with the various activities that it sponsors. Theoretically, such programs as the summer camps, retreats, and lectures are all free. That donations of at least a certain amount are expected, however, is made clear. Hence, the line between providing a donation and paying for a service is quite hazy. This is also the case for another very significant source of revenue: funeral services. The number of services conducted over the forty-nine-day mourning period and the number of clerics assigned to each service depend on the bereaved family's socioeconomic status. Devotees may request such mortuary services as care for the terminally ill, which includes round-the-clock recitation and, if necessary, assistance writing a will; preparation of the corpse (i.e., placement in the casket, writing the funerary tablet and the obituary); a farewell ceremony (*gaobie dianli*); the ceremony to dispose of the body (*anzang yishi*), either by burial or cremation; recitation services at the conclusion of one or more of the first seven weeks after death (*qiqi*, the "seven sevens,"); and services performed on death anniversary days (hundredth-day and annual observances) (Shi Xingyun 1995a, 7:245–332). Clerics remain reticent about the amount of money requested to perform these rites. The very size of the staff for the funerary complex at Foguang headquarters indicates its importance to the monastery: in 1998, seventeen monastics and four lay monastics were assigned to Longevity Funerary Complex, making it the largest department on the mountain.

The Longevity Funerary Complex staff also has as its responsibility the upkeep of the mountain's cemetery and columbarium, which between them have over fifty thousand niches for crematory urns (only two thousand of which are currently being used). On the top floor of the columbarium is the Hall of Rebirth, where temporary and permanent tablets honoring the deceased may be placed so that they may benefit from the instruction and merit generated by twice-daily recitations by clerics. I was unable to learn the size of donations expected in return for caring for tablets or storing remains in the headquarters' complex. A monastic at Daxi Heping Chan Temple (Taoyuan County) did tell me that the one-time cost for keeping an urn in the temple's columbarium is NT$19,000. Nearly all Foguang branch temples have at least a room, and in larger temples an entire building (often a pagoda), serving as a funerary facility with a mantle for tablets and anywhere from hundreds to thousands of niches for urns. In 1999, Hsi Lai Temple completed a pagoda with fifty thousand niches, making it the largest Buddhist columbarium in North America.

Foguangshan's Fund-Raising in Historical Perspective

The fact that conducting funerals and caring for tablets is a significant source of income for Foguangshan is not surprising, such services long having been a primary means of gaining revenue for Chinese Buddhist monasteries.[30] Sangha leadership—at least that of the twentieth century—has had an ambivalent attitude toward these practices, however. The criticisms have focused on two issues. First, Vens. Taixu, Yinguang, and others lamented that their brethren too often expended the majority of their energy in carrying out these rites, often for no other purpose than to make money. Such commercialization tainted Buddhism's reputation. Second, an overreliance on funerals as a means of monastic support results in Buddhism being too closely associated with death in the general public's mind. The Venerable Taixu gave this as a fundamental reason for the lack of interest in Buddhist teachings among the young and intellectuals, the former deeming the religion of concern only to the elderly, the latter associating it with superstition. Master Xingyun agrees with such criticisms, and has, therefore, called on clerics to place more emphasis on "liberating the living" (*du sheng*) than on "liberating the dead" (*du si*) (Shi Xingyun, n.d.-b, 7). No other activity can replace requiems as far as income potential is concerned, however, so neither Foguangshan nor any other Buddhist organization in Taiwan can totally forgo this activity.

The necessity of relying on funerals has been especially keenly felt because of the lack of another source of income that had been available to mainland monasteries: the renting of farmland. According to Holmes Welch (1967, 220–241), any monastery in a rural area of mainland China that had over two hundred monks probably had better than fifteen hundred acres of land, a portion of which the monastery used to grow its own food, but most of which it rented out to local farmers. Urban monasteries could similarly have major propertyholdings to lease for housing or businesses. This provided significant income, even allowing the richest temples to be financially independent of the laity and free from the need to perform rites for the dead. Taiwan's monasteries simply do not have comparable landholdings. As do many other monks, Master Xingyun felt himself fortunate when, in the 1950s, he was given a small temple to run. Nearly all the property that he has acquired subsequently he has utilized for his own organization's operations, not as a source of rental income.

Without land from which to make a livelihood, and unwilling to specialize in funerary services, Master Xingyun has focused his efforts on gaining revenue through donations and multimedia publications. Clerics on the mainland had actually already shifted toward these methods during the later Republican period. Holmes Welch (1967, 241–242) noted that land reform, combined with the Japanese and Communist infiltration of the countryside, imperiled Buddhist land ownership. He continued: "At the time that monastic Buddhism was losing its economic base, lay Buddhism was burgeoning. Increasing support from lay devotees in metropolitan areas became available just when there was the need to make up for the decline of landed income. This is one reason for the turning out of the sangha, the spread of public lectures, charitable activities, and associations of the sangha. As monks had to devote more time to outside activities, they had less time to give to religious cultivation for its own sake." Master Xingyun has, therefore, continued a trend already under way when he first renounced, but he has also brought such techniques to a height far beyond what his predecessors could have imagined.

These, then, are the primary means through which Foguangshan raises money to support its monastic community and to sponsor activities: tourism/pilgrimage; sale of religious paraphernalia, souvenirs, and publications; and procurement of donations through holding fund-raising drives, dharma functions, alms processions, activities for laity, and mortuary rites (see table 8). Some of these methods were already important during the Republican era (e.g., donations of land, funds raised through mortuary rites, and reliance on benefactors). Others that in the first half of the twentieth century were tried on a small scale Master Xingyun has expanded to become important sources of revenue (e.g., the sale of publications and souvenirs). Yet others are Foguang innovations (e.g., donations for activities designed especially for laity, regularly scheduled alms processions).

With the exception of the alms processions, even those fund-raising methods that were once Foguang innovations no longer differentiate Foguangshan markedly from other contemporary Chinese Buddhist organizations since monasteries have been quick to adopt from one another any strategy that has proved effective. What distinguishes Foguangshan is mainly the scale and breadth of its operations. Only the efforts of Ciji Gongde Hui and a select few other megaorganizations can compare with Foguangshan's multifaceted and ambitious fund-raising approach.

INSTITUTIONAL MECHANISMS FOR DISTRIBUTING FUNDS

The Foguangshan empire has been able to grow so quickly, not only because of the enormous amounts of money pouring in, but also because Master Xingyun has put into place a sophisticated mechanism for controlling the dispersal of those funds. As mentioned earlier, three foundations provide important structure for receiving and distributing Foguangshan's finances: the Foguangshan Culture and Education Foundation; the Foguangshan Pure Land Culture and Education Foundation; and the Foguangshan Compassion Foundation. Foguang Television and Foguang University each have a foundation as well. Every branch temple has its own, semi-independent budget. By "semi-independent," I mean that each temple has been expected to become financially self-sufficient within three to five years after being established. For those that have been unable to do so, the Foguangshan Pure Land

TABLE 8
Fund-Raising Activities: Republican Era Monasteries and Foguangshan

ACTIVITY	REPUBLICAN ERA MONASTERIES	FOGUANGSHAN
Lease of land	Major source of funds (especially for public monasteries)	Very minor
Lease of urban property	Major source of funds (especially for public monasteries)	Moderate
Lease of temple facilities	Not done	Minor
Cultivation of land	Very minor (largely symbolic)	Very minor (largely symbolic)
Funeral rites	Major (especially for hereditary temples)	Major (although role is downplayed)
Care of funerary tablets and storage of crematory urns	Major	Major (although role is downplayed)
Sale of publications	Beginning to become significant for public monasteries as land taken away	Major (multimedia)
Sale of religious paraphernalia and souvenirs	Not done	Moderate
Donations left in temple donation boxes	Moderate	Moderate
Fund-raising campaigns for construction projects	Major (typically relied on a few wealthy benefactors)	Major[a]
Donations of property to be used as temples	Major	Major
Donations during dharma functions	Moderate	Major
Pilgrimage/tourism (donations for lodging, food, etc.)	Major for pilgrimage centers, insignificant for most monasteries	Major
Alms procession	Rarely done	Moderate
Donations in conjunction with camps, retreats, etc.	Not done	Moderate
Reliance on benefactors for ongoing support	Major	Major[b]

[a] Three innovations by Master Xingyun: (1) method extended to fund other large-scale projects; (2) relies on thousands of devotees, each contributing a relatively small amount; (3) provides mechanism to pay by installment.
[b] Innovation by Master Xingyun: increase numbers of such benefactors and organize them into formal group with grades depending on level of contribution.

Culture and Education Foundation provides the necessary funds to supplement those accumulated from local devotees. In the case of especially large, expensive temples, such as Hsi Lai, Nan Tien, and Nanhua Temples, the amount of money contributed by the foundation for the initial construction and subsequent upkeep has run into the millions of U.S. dollars. Once a temple has gained firm financial footing, it has been expected to remit any surplus to the foundation to be used to build and support other temples. Under no condition, however, is a temple to give any money directly to another Foguang temple or any other organization; all such transactions must go through the headquarters. Branch temples must also provide monthly financial statements and gain approval from the RAC before making any large expenditure, such as the purchase of a building or even a computer.

CONCLUSION: RICH OR POOR?

Despite Foguangshan's obvious affluence, Master Xingyun takes every opportunity to object to characterizations of his organization as wealthy. In a 1992 entry in his journal, he observed that economists listed ten other Buddhist and Daoist temples in Taiwan as having greater assets than did Foguangshan.[31] In his opinion, people overestimate Foguangshan's prosperity because they mistake its ornate exterior for proof of full coffers within. While the facilities of the headquarters and branch temples may look fancy, the master contends, if one looks closely, it can be seen that the materials used are of relatively cheap quality. He also reminds people that much of the labor for construction and upkeep has been voluntary. Senior disciples proudly reminisce about the days in which they hauled supplies up Foguangshan's steep slopes and personally laid bricks or did other manual chores. Master Xingyun and Ven. Xinding both tell of carting up rocks to fill in the valley that once steeply separated the headquarters' two main ridges. "Foguangshan may look wealthy," the master has said on many occasions, "but we are actually quite poor."

It may sound strange to hear the head of an organization worth some U.S.$500 million claim financial hardship, but there is truth to the master's assessment. The physical facilities of Foguangshan are not very well built. Within a few years of construction, tiles begin to peel off, cement cracks, and roofs start to leak. More important, every dollar received is immediately spent. The organization's success over the past thirty years is partially due to a factor that, ironically, is also a source of risk for its future viability: Master Xingyun's willingness perpetually to push the economic envelope. As Jiang Canteng (1997, 22) observes, Master Xingyun "deeply understands the practice of constantly investing to expand the scope of activities, to not accumulate wealth, but rather constantly to invest it in Buddhist activities." In meetings with his disciples, Master Xingyun has frequently referred to his method as "accepting money with one hand and immediately giving it away with the other."

Master Xingyun's apparently carefree attitude toward money and his aggressive "investment" strategy encourage ever greater donations because of their very boldness and the long list of tangible accomplishments that can be cited. The master assumes that, if the ideas are both creative and timely, sufficient funding will follow, an assumption that gives his devotees the sense of being on the forefront of Buddhist practice, but one that also exposes his organization to continual financial pressure. One cleric informed me that Foguangshan's accounting department has run on the edge for years, constantly shifting assets from one account to another so that checks do not bounce, and often relying on bank loans to meet bills. Financial strain has increased over the past decade. Not only have the master's projects become ever more ambitious, but also, just as Foguangshan has needed more money, the number of Buddhist organizations in Taiwan has proliferated, thereby thinning devotee support, and the island's economy has slowed. Foguangshan's monetary situation is, therefore, by no means secure. Of course, it never has been, and, if in the future it ever is, that will signal that the founding spirit animating the organization and giving it its dynamism has faded away.

8 Perpetuating Traditional Modernism

PRESERVING CHINA'S HERITAGE

Foguang clerics pride themselves on introducing ever more ambitious innovations into Sino-Buddhism. Ironically, they also regard themselves as forming the strongest bulwark protecting China's heritage. This heritage has two interrelated aspects that are of particular value and are notably imperiled by the onslaught of modern popular culture: aesthetics and ethics.

China's Aesthetic Culture

Buddhist temples, the master observes (Shi Xingyun 1995a, 8:666), have long served as vital repositories for some of China's best art. The monasteries themselves are often architectural splendors, their layout and features calling to mind China's glorious Tang and Song dynasties. Today, in the wake of the destruction of so many historical landmarks in mainland China during the Cultural Revolution, and in the light of both the American hegemony in mass entertainment and the limited government support for the arts in the Republic of China (ROC), Buddhist temples play a more important role than ever in ensuring the continuation of China's culture. Master Xingyun is very proud of the nine museums and art galleries that have been opened by Foguangshan, each of which is filled with calligraphy, paintings, sculpture, and ceramics by some of the most famous Chinese artists of recent centuries.

Simply collecting and displaying works by famous masters of the past, however, is not sufficient. Preservation requires continued production by contemporary artists if the tradition is to remain vibrant. In this spirit, Foguangshan has provided financial support to several well-known artists, most notably Li Zijian and Shi Guoliang (who eventually renounced in 1996 and since then, as Ven. Huichan, has supplied the artwork for many of the covers of the Foguang magazine *Universal Gate*). Preservation through creative embodiment is even more evident in the performing arts, for example, the concerts of Buddhist recitation and of Dunhuang dance that are regularly organized by Foguangshan. On a simpler scale, the Water Drop Teahouses found in most large Foguang temples provide a casual setting where anyone can enact the art of serving and drinking tea. Here, Chan and art commingle, reminding one that, as the master says, "art must be connected with life.... Only when it is connected with daily living [*shenghuo*] does art have life [*shengming*]" (Shi Xingyun 1994, vol. 1, entry for 8 October 1989). Just as art finds its relevance in life, the master also asserts that, to reach its highest refinement, life must undergo "aestheticization" *(yiwenhua)*. The museums, galleries, concerts, and teahouses are said to be designed to remind people that art inherently pervades all aspects of life.

CHINA'S ETHICAL HERITAGE

When Master Xingyun speaks of preserving his country's culture, he means, not only its artistic tradition, but also the ethical teachings that have served as the bedrock of Chinese society. The distinction between aesthetic culture and ethical tradition remains hazy for the master. Appreciation of artistic phenomena sparks in humans their own form of beauty, that is, moral goodness. Master Xingyun's approach to cultivation is, therefore, in certain important respects quite Confucian in tone, his emphases on preserving culture and aestheticizing life themselves perpetuating core values found in such Scholarly classics as the *Analects* and the *Mencius*. The master is well aware of his reliance on Confucian teachings. He frequently quotes Confucius, the Cheng brothers, Zhuxi, and other famous Scholars and proudly declares that Foguang University is modeled after the multidisciplinary spirit exemplified by Confucian academies. The Confucian aspect of Master Xingyun's worldview is evident in other respects as well. We already noted in chapter 3 above that the trends toward secularization and laicization implied by Humanistic Buddhism, whereby the divisions between supramundane and mundane and between monastic and lay life are blurred, transform Buddhist practice so that it is fully compatible with the Confucian assumptions of immanent transcendence and embeddedness in one harmonious community. In chapter 6 above we saw that, in Foguang ethics, precepts function in a manner much closer in spirit to Confucian rites *(li)* than to a code of laws or injunctions. The master's views of wealth are often explained by his devotees in Confucian terms; as one nun put it, the master, like any sagely gentleman *(junzi)*, "cherishes wealth and obtains it according to the way" *(junzi ai cai; qu zhi you dao)*. Master Xingyun's attitude toward politics similarly reverberates with Confucian sensibilities. His notion that a religious leader should be concerned about politics but not interfere with them reminds one of the Mencian passage about the three sources of societal authority: age; government leadership; and virtue (Lau 1970, 87). As there are no longer any Confucian pundits whom officials may visit for moral guidance, it is incumbent on Buddhist masters to fulfill this service.

Master Xingyun's rendering of Buddhist teachings is, therefore, deeply imbued with Confucian undertones. His appreciation of music as a healthy outlet for emotions is very Mencian. In "A Blueprint of Humanistic Buddhism" (see Shi

Xingyun 1995a, 1:151–182), he even plays on the double meaning of the character *yue/le* as both "music" and "joy," just as is to be found in the *Mencius* (Lau 1970, 60–61). The virtues of shame, humility, and respect for those in positions of authority are also given prominence. Soon after one of his disciples received a graduate degree, Master Xingyun specifically advised her henceforth to follow Confucian values closely, especially that of remaining humble. The very fact that clerics are being sent to earn higher degrees and that everyone, monastic and lay, is encouraged to continually take courses and engage in self-study is based on the Confucian love for learning as a lifelong venture whose primary goal is deepening self-awareness and moral cultivation. The emphasis on the social implications of education also perpetuates a central theme of the Scholarly tradition. The Campaign of Compassion and Love described in chapter 5 above is predicated on the model found in the *Great Learning (Daxue)*, which bases social transformation, first, on the moral regeneration of the individual through the purification of the heart and, then, on the harmonization by those so regenerated of family and community relations.

There is one virtue closely associated with the Confucian tradition that many argue has always been and will always be threatened by Buddhist monasticism: filial piety. Let us now turn to the Foguang response to such a claim.

Monastic Filial Piety

Ever since Buddhist missionaries first arrived in the Middle Kingdom some two millennia ago, their tradition's monasticism has been attacked as antithetical to the Chinese core virtue of filial piety. Because they leave their homes, shave their heads, and vow to remain celibate, monks have been accused of failing in their responsibility to care for their parents and, worse yet, to produce sons to continue patrilineal descent. The rhetoric against nuns has been less severe, but, nonetheless, there has been the sentiment that they too have followed a track unnatural, unfilial, and dangerous to the rightful (i.e., patriarchal) social structure. Feelings regarding monasticism run deep to this day. Monastics admit that Chinese New Year is a difficult holiday for them, both because it would normally be a time to return home to reaffirm familial affection and because some who visit a Foguang temple to welcome in the New Year either unintentionally or sometimes even maliciously remind the clerics of their failure to fulfill this minimal act of filial respect.

The ongoing suspicion that Buddhist masters scheme to lure young people away from their parents was confirmed in the eyes of many when, in September 1996, Ven. Weijue tonsured 158 new disciples without their parents' consent. The novices in question had initially gone to Zhongtaishan to join a short-term retreat.

At the conclusion of the program, nearly all the participants renounced, without even returning home to talk over this decision with their families. Taiwan's news media was flooded with images of shocked, grieving parents flocking to Zhongtaishan in an effort to retrieve their sons and daughters. Families did take back home twenty-one of the novices, only to have some return to the temple. Later, seven of the newly tonsured novices officially disrobed during a ceremony presided over by Ven. Weijue. It remains unclear how many other novices subsequently returned to lay life. Editorials lambasted the pressure techniques used to "brainwash" the young people and voiced concern over the rising popularity among Taiwan's young people of entering monastic life ("Niuda jiaoma sheng zhong" 1996, 3).[1]

As Foguangshan had a tonsure ceremony a mere three weeks after the Zhongtaishan debacle, Master Xingyun found it necessary to state very clearly why Buddhist monasticism is not inimical to filial piety. His first move was to reassure the public about the fairness and openness of the process through which monasteries accept disciples. He did so, not only in word, but also in deed, by inviting the news media to witness the Foguang ceremony. As a result, reporters, photographers, and television news teams swarmed throughout Great Heroes Hall, each trying to capture the best angle from which to record the tonsuring of the 142 monks and nuns. The reporters also joined the novices, their families, and senior Foguang monastics at the ceremony's end for a carefully choreographed press conference in which the master defended monasticism. During this meeting, and on other occasions, Master Xingyun has utilized a variety of strategies to ease concerns.

First, Master Xingyun asserts that most Buddhist leaders do not want to force or trick people into becoming clerics. "Buddhism does not encourage everyone to renounce," the master assured one audience when a person brought up the Zhongtaishan incident. "Proper conditions must come together. Both monastic life and lay life are fine, so long as a person can practice" ("BLIA Youth Conference" 1997). At Foguangshan, continued the master, people certainly are not rushed into renouncing, and the monastery has even instituted measures to prevent people from making rash, impulsive decisions. Most notably, Foguangshan requires a one- or two-year stay in its college system before it will grant permission to undergo tonsure.[2]

Second, Master Xingyun confirms that Buddhist tradition requires a person to obtain his or her parents' approval before tonsuring. It is assumed that the person has been able to receive such permission because one or more siblings have agreed to provide primary care for the parents as they grow old. In one journal entry, Master Xingyun praises the virtue of a certain Xu Junxi who, by promising to "sacrifice herself to care for the family," had freed her two younger sisters to renounce at Foguangshan (Shi Xingyun 1994, vol. 3, entry for 1 February 1990). Such arrangements can be said to represent a division of labor, siblings who remain in lay society attending to the continuity of the family line and taking the lead in caring for the parents, and those who have renounced assuring a better rebirth for the parents by transferring to them the great store of merit that they acquire through monastic practice. Such a Buddhist family is, hence, the acme of Confucian filial piety. That this is regarded as being the case became especially evident when, during a meeting, the master made a special point to introduce an audience member who was a descendant of Confucius. The master highly praised the man for, not only permitting, but actively encouraging two of his daughters to renounce at Foguangshan.

This division of labor indicates that, far from preventing the observance of filial responsibilities, renouncing actually fulfills them in a more profound way than does merely staying at home to serve one's parents directly in this life. This is so even if there is no sibling to take care of the more mundane concerns.[3] Shortly after the Zhongtaishan incident, the following passage was printed on the back cover of the October 1996 issue of *Universal Gate*:

> There are three levels of filial piety:
>
> The lowest level is simply to repay one's parents' love by taking care of them.
>
> The next level is to cause them no dishonor.
>
> The highest level is to protect them from rebirth in any of the six modes of existence through one's faith and right understanding.

A brief commentary under the quote goes on to say: "Continuing the family line by having a son does not necessarily guarantee that the descendants will be any wiser than were their predecessors. Transmitting one's cultural heritage and spiritual enlightenment, on the other hand, ensures that the spirit of the ancients will live on."

Buddhist clerics have long used this line of reasoning to justify "leaving home." The Foguang version of this rationale does differ slightly, however, by shifting the focus from benefits in the hereafter to more tangible, immediate benefits that parents can reap from their monastic children. As one nun told me:

> Particularly if your parents have not yet studied Buddhism, even though you may have just started, you can still help them understand. You can

especially help them understand life and death. I discovered this when my father needed to undergo surgery. My sister, who has studied law at National Taiwan University, is usually very self-assured. When my father suddenly got very sick, however, she lost all composure and didn't know what to do. She was crying as my father was going in for the operation, but I felt very calm. As a Buddhist, I had considered all these issues before, so I knew exactly what to do. Just accompanying a person is not always enough. We have to know what to do to help his condition. Not only did I understand what was going on, but I knew precisely how to help my father.

When my father came home from the hospital, he said that for the first time he understood why I had renounced and that he supported my decision—he had not particularly supported it before. My father has always considered himself to be a Daoist. But, after the operation, he started to read Buddhist scriptures. To this day he recites "Amituo Fo" while he drives. We Buddhists are very filial.

Foguang clerics emphasize that they bring the expertise and the calmness of mind to help parents at the most critical moments. They may not be available to care for parents' everyday material needs, but, as Confucius said, such matters are but the most base expression of filial piety.[4] By guiding their parents to an appreciation of the dharma, monastics show the highest reverence possible.

Buddhist monks and nuns are regarded as unfilial, not only because they are believed to neglect their parents' daily needs, but also because, by entering a lifestyle that is difficult, grueling, and uncertain, they cause their parents unnecessary concern and anxiety. Master Xingyun specifically assured the families of his new disciples in the fall of 1996 that they need have no qualms in this regard. He would henceforth take full responsibility for their children's well-being, as he does for all his disciples. By renouncing under him, the clerics were now part of the Foguang family. As we saw in chapter 2 above, Master Xingyun and his disciples frequently use the language of family and parent-child kinship (as is typical at a monastery). The master is *shifu* or *shigong*. He provides his disciples with everything a parent would, as is readily evident from the stories relating the times that he has bought medicine, daily necessities, treats, and even extravagances such as nylon stockings or Ice Capades tickets. Such stories have two morals. First, they assure parents of clerics that they may rest easy about their children's well-being. Second, they remind Foguang venerables that, as Master Xingyun's dharma children, the focus of their filial piety has now shifted from their biological parents to him, their "teacher-father."

Joining the Foguang family does not require a cleric to break all ties with his or her birth family. Master Xingyun insists that, while other monasteries may force disciples to sever contact with their parents, this is not the case at Foguangshan. He points out that the mountain even has an annual "Family Reunion Day." These events are well attended. Parents are given bouquets, treated to lunch, led on tours of the headquarters, and invited to attend a meeting presided over by the master. The Family Reunion Day in November 1996 (i.e., less than three months after the Zhongtaishan scandal) attracted some two to three thousand family members. During the meeting at that reunion, the master organized a "family-relations committee" so that parents of monastics would have an official agency through which to voice any concerns that they might have. At Foguangshan, the master tells his disciples' parents: "Your son will always be your son. Your daughter will always be your daughter." Venerables are free to visit their parents as often as once per month and may take extended leave if their parents fall ill. Hence, becoming a monastic does not obstruct the fulfillment of any aspect of filial duty, including this-worldly care. For women, Master Xingyun argues that it actually increases their ability to do so. As he phrased it during the reunion meeting: "Your daughter will never become someone else's wife and join his family." In other words, a daughter could not provide descendants in any case, and, by renouncing, she frees herself to continue to care for her parents rather than having to exert her energies on in-laws.[5]

Instead of trying to cut off relations between clerics and their biological families, the master includes biological families as part of the Foguang extended family. In one story, he tells of treating Ven. Yikong's father to a bowl of peanut soup since stomach problems had made that delicacy one of the few dishes that the elderly man could enjoy. In closing the anecdote, Master Xingyun states: "In truth, not only do I require that all my disciples show filial respect to the parents of all Foguang disciples, but I too regard these people as though they were my own parents. For me, treating a disciple's parents as if they were my own is my way of thanking them for giving their children to me as monastics. I believe that this is Humanistic Buddhism's way of expressing filial piety" (Shi Xingyun 1995a, 10:627–628). Master Xingyun, as the center of this large clan, is both the parent (or grandparent) of all the monastics and the eldest, most filial son of his disciples' birth parents.[6] The more important lesson communicated by this anecdote, however, is that, by allowing a child to renounce, parents have not lost a son or daughter, they have gained an entire order of them!

This notion of the overlap of biological and dharma family gains particular prominence when multiple members of one family have renounced under the master. As we have seen, there have been more than two dozen instances in which two or more members of the same family have become Master Xingyun's disciples, in some cases a parent and one or more children all "leaving home" to join the Foguang order. Here, the Confucian celebration of family unity and the Buddhist ideal of leaving behind mundane attachments are felt to gain full harmonization.

Master Xingyun as Exemplar of Monastic Filial Piety
Senior venerables in the Foguang hierarchy play a very important role as symbolic representatives epitomizing what might be called "monastic filial piety," that is, the dual reverence shown by clerics to both their master and their parents. Pronounced effort is made so that the parents and siblings of senior monastics can attend the annual Family Reunion Day and any event of special importance. From 1989, when Master Xingyun saw his mother, Liliu Yuying, for the first time in over forty years, until 1996, when she passed away, the relationship between these two provided abundant material for the portrayal of exemplary monastic filial piety. Master Xingyun's journal over these years, especially during the first months after his mother's immigration from China to the United States and in the period just after her death, is replete with paradigmatic instances of ideal parent-monastic interactions and with the master's own reflections on the nature and role of filial piety among those who have renounced.

Time and again in his diary Master Xingyun speaks of the great debt of gratitude that he owes his mother. He depicts her as embodying the simple, earthy wisdom of a person who, although illiterate, has learned the deepest lessons that life has to offer. To her he is thankful for his early training in loyalty, filial piety, integrity, and righteousness. More than that, the master considers himself deeply indebted to his mother for all the suffering that she bore on his behalf. First, there was the pain that she endured simply in giving birth. Second, there was the sorrow that he caused her by renouncing, an act that required them to separate when he was only twelve. Master Xingyun tells in his biography of his mother's unwillingness to let him tonsure and of her tearful farewell after he insisted. The master would not see his mother again for ten years, when his teacher finally gave him permission to return home for a visit (Fu 1995, 22). Third, there was the fact that, by fleeing to Taiwan (owing to circumstances beyond his control), he added to his mother's grief both because she worried that much more about him, having no idea of his whereabouts, and because the Communist authorities regularly badgered her and her other children about the son who had run away with the Nationalists.[7] Ashamed of his inability to repay his mother, the master did not celebrate his birthday for the first thirty-seven years that he was in Taiwan. To his mother, says the master, that day was really a day of suffering. To salve his conscience, the master would rise especially early on his birthday and offer incense to the Buddha so that he could transfer the resulting merits to the well-being and longevity of his mother.

Once he had reestablished correspondence with his family in 1986, the master did his best to make up for lost time, immediately sending enough money for new lodgings to be built for his mother and for the homes of his sister and two brothers to be refurbished. When three years later he returned to Jiangdu, Jiangsu Province, for the first time in over four decades, his arms were laden with gifts and his sleeve pockets full of money. Still not satisfied, he arranged for his mother to emigrate to the United States so that she could live in one of the lodges bordering Hsi Lai Temple. The high point for the master in showing his mother that her sacrifices had not been in vain was in February 1990, when she journeyed to Foguang headquarters to join in the Chinese New Year celebrations. The master writes in great detail in his diary about the tour that he gave her of the mountain, describing the throngs of devotees that constantly surrounded her and her obvious pride in what her son had accomplished (Shi Xingyun 1994, vol. 3, entries for 16–28 February 1990). There is an irony in this homecoming event: rather than the master returning home to his mother, he brought her to what she described as a pure land on earth. This is the acme of the Humanistic Buddhist version of monastic filial piety.

In all the journal entries in which the master discusses his relationship with his mother, he describes his own psychological state as an intermingling of three emotions: excitement at being in her presence; concern for her welfare; and shame that he still was not doing enough for her. In his diary entry for 13 October 1989, for instance, the master wrote of his nervous anticipation while waiting for his mother's flight to California and his apprehension that she may have been nauseous during the trip (Shi Xingyun 1994, vol. 1). Shortly after her arrival, the master's mother slipped and broke a leg. Master Xingyun had already returned to Taiwan when the mishap occurred, so, although he telephoned his mother constantly to comfort her, he nonetheless felt ashamed to have sent her so far from home and then neglected personally to watch over her. "I have been so busy that I have not been able to be at my mother's side while she has been in America," wrote the master on 10 January 1990, "and I am deeply troubled about this" (Shi Xingyun 1994, vol. 3).

As portrayed in his diary and in the descriptions given by his devotees, the master was in every respect a model of monastic filial piety. His excitement, eagerness to please, and constant concern for his mother's welfare all position him as the perfect Confucian son. When considered carefully, even his apparent failures reveal a profound fulfillment of filial responsibility. For instance, the manner in which the master passed his birthdays so as to atone for straying so far from home both points to an inner sensitivity to filial duty and indicates the means by which monastics can utilize their own high level of self-cultivation to best benefit their parents. Once he was able to aid his mother more directly, the master still harbored a sense of shame in not doing enough for her, which, since he obviously had done everything possible, reveals another central virtue of any model son: the sense that one can never fully repay the debt to one's parents, no matter how attentive one is to their every wish and comfort. As a monastic, one comes closest to satisfying one's parents needs, not by personally attending to them, but, rather, by serving all sentient beings. The master's mother often made this point to her son, as his journal entries make clear. In one meeting with Foguang devotees, she is recorded as having announced: "Everyone has been so good to me. I don't have anything to give to you. I have only my son that I can give to everyone" (Shi Xingyun 1994, vol. 3, entry for 25 February 1990). Not just Master Xingyun but all clerics become their parents' "gifts" or "offerings" to Buddhism, thereby assuring their own vast store of merit.

How do the interactions between Master Xingyun and his mother as recorded in Foguang literature fit in with other Chinese Buddhist models of filial piety? In his book *Mothers and Sons in Chinese Buddhism* (1998), Alan Cole argues that four motifs have structured the Chinese Buddhist understanding of this virtue. First, in contrast to Confucian characterizations, the focus is not on the relationship between father and son but, rather, on that between mother and son. Second, the texts that have been foundational to the Chinese Buddhist conceptualization of filial piety have invariably served to nurture in sons a deep feeling of guilt and of indebtedness to their mothers. No son could possibly repay his mother for the pain that she underwent in childbirth or for the sacrifices that she made over the years of rearing him. Third, in tension with this almost oppressive sense of gratitude, the texts also foster suspicion regarding the mother's sexual and, therefore, sinful nature. The very fact that she became pregnant indicates that she had desires and engaged in actions worthy of infernal punishment. Finally, the Chinese Buddhist version of filial piety teaches that the best way to cancel one's debts and to expiate one's mother's transgressions is to patronize the Buddhist monastic institution since only it has the expertise to transfer sufficient merit to ameliorate the mother's doleful condition once she is in the underworld.

Comparing the model presented by Cole to the paradigm constructed around the relationship between Master Xingyun and his mother, we can see both continuity and differences. As in the scriptural accounts, the focus of Master Xingyun's filial piety is on his maternal rather than his paternal line. Of his father Master Xingyun has virtually no memory. The man apparently played very little role in his son's upbringing. Nothing is said of him in the master's biography except vague reference to his disappearance during the Nanjing Massacre of 1939 (after already having been away for two years). Master Xingyun had very little contact with anyone on the patrilineal side of his family. He tells in one journal entry of his mother talking about such relatives but of he himself having no memory of them. He had never met his father's parents since they had both died before he was born (Shi Xingyun 1994, vol. 3, entry for 26 January 1990). In contradistinction to this, Master Xingyun has very fond memories of his maternal grandmother, who, as a pious Buddhist, chanted and meditated daily and followed a vegetarian diet. She more than anyone influenced the master to renounce.

Given the lack of any emotional link to his father's side of the family, the shift in allegiance from patrilineal family to dharma family must not have been too traumatic for young Ven. Wuche (Master Xingyun's tonsure name). The Venerable Zhikai, the abbot of Qixiashan, did not merely symbolically take the place of Master Xingyun's father; evidently he filled an emotional void. The master reminisces fondly about his teacher's compassion, telling, for instance, how Ven. Zhikai once specially sent a bowl of salted vegetables to him when he was suffering through a bout of malaria. Even his teacher's strict discipline and the rigorous training that he imposed are topics of romantic glorification by the former student. When Master Xingyun returned to Qixiashan after a forty-six-year hiatus, he openly shed tears while prostrating to the stupa for Ven. Zhikai. In the years since, he has provided financial support to his teacher's family.

The personal and historical factors that dictated Master Xingyun's much stronger affective bond with the maternal than with the paternal family significantly deaccentuated the tension inherent between patrilineal and dharmic filial piety. The impulse to perpetuate a family line probably was not particularly strongly felt by the master since he had no sense of personal contact with that line. Master Xingyun did not forsake his ancestors so much as they abandoned him, a truth crystallized in the fact that it was not the master but his father who first left home and that, in fact, the master renounced only after his search for his father made it obvious that the latter would never return. Such circumstances have made it that much easier for the master to be viewed as a paragon of monastic filial piety.

The shifting of attention from patrilineal to matrilineal family accords with Cole's model. Furthermore, as we have seen, in writing about his mother the master emphasized both his indebtedness to her and his feelings of shame and guilt for having so long neglected her. In this respect, too, his personal experience parallels the paradigmatic mother-son relationships recorded in the apocryphal texts analyzed by Cole. Unlike these texts, however, in which the assumption of the mother's inherent lack of virtue was a key point, providing the justification for the absolute necessity of sponsoring rites of the dead on her behalf, Foguang literature has made no such unflattering portrayal of the master's mother. This is not surprising; it would certainly be seen as very inappropriate for her son or any of his devotees to voice such doubts about her character. With Master Xingyun and Liliu Yuying, we are not talking about mythical figures comparable to Maudgalyayana (Mulian) and his mother; rather, we are talking about two real people. Far from making any insinuations of inherent defilement, descriptions of Liliu Yuying celebrate her great virtue. Master Xingyun described her as a compassionate and skillful mediator who gained everyone's respect and whose simple lifestyle was exemplary. He also talked of how impressed his disciples were by her strength and courage when she broke her leg. An organization devoted to encouraging virtuous conduct even asked to interview her so that she could be included in its book *Biographies of Virtuous Mothers*, although in her humility she denied the request (Shi Xingyun 1994, vol. 3, entries for 19, 20 February 1990). Hence, the Foguang depiction of Madame Liliu has followed more closely the Confucian model of the virtuous mother than it has the Buddhist paradigm of "the sin of birth."[8]

Given the relative neglect by Foguang Buddhists of the final two motifs of Chinese Buddhist filial piety, why has so much been made by the master and his disciples of his gratitude toward and filial reverence for his mother? What function or functions has this served? Two answers seem most probable. First, such discourse has, in fact, continued to buttress the entire Chinese Buddhist model of filial piety. As this paradigm is not a conscious scheme but works on a more subtle plane, continued reference to the master's deep gratitude toward his mother would call to mind the entire model, even without any overt reference to its other elements. Filial gratitude and patronage of the Buddhist monastic institution even gained fairly direct association in Master Xingyun's biography, in which it is related that his maternal grandmother had told him that, since he was her only grandchild to have renounced, she expected him to attend to her funeral, which he promised to do. Because of subsequent political events, the master was unable to fulfill his pledge, a source of great remorse for him. The lesson here is that those who do not provide Buddhist services for their parents or grandparents will surely regret this lapse.

Second, Master Xingyun's relationship with his mother has served as a model of filial piety of a unique kind, that is, that of a cleric. His glowing descriptions of his relationship with his mother were primarily framed as a response to the ongoing charge that venerables are unfilial and, hence, suspect moral leaders. They served to reduce anxiety among monastics and their parents about their own relationship and reassured the general public about the suitability of monks and nuns as moral guides. As noted earlier in this chapter, Foguang literature stresses that, rather than marking the termination of filial piety, renunciation signifies a doubling of that virtue's scope so that, henceforth, it has as its object, not only the birth parents, but the dharma parent (i.e., the master) as well. Biological filial piety remains directed toward the mother. Loyalty to the father also persists but is subordinated to reverence to the teacher. Although, in the master's case, the focus on the relationship between cleric and mother has been a natural consequence of personal history, this relationship better serves to symbolize monastic filial piety than would the cleric-father dyad since incompatibility with the Confucian version of filial piety is there much more direct. Having proved himself to be a paragon of filial piety, the master has the authority to exhort all Chinese to be filial to both parents.

Perpetuating *Li* in Post-Confucian Society

The broad lines of Master Xingyun's interpretation of filial piety, as well as of his perspectives on politics, wealth, precepts, music, humility, and education, are not unique to him or even to Chinese Buddhists. Instances of similar attitudes and hermeneutics may be found in all Buddhist traditions—Indian, Sri Lankan, Thai, Tibetan, Japanese, etc. The presuppositions and specifics of argumentation in airing such views, however, do differ depending on the cultural and historical context. It is not surprising that the term "Humanistic Buddhism" was coined and has gained prominence among the Chinese Buddhist community, for such an emphasis on transforming this world here and now is quite natural for those who live in a society strongly shaped by Confucian values. The fact that Humanistic Buddhism is a modern form of "Confucianized Buddhism" merely indicates that contemporary masters are perpetuating a leitmotif that has always shaped the expression of Chinese Buddhist practice. With every step of the Buddhist conquest of China, the conqueror was itself Sinicized, with the result that, by the Tang dynasty, Confucian and Daoist sensibilities had infused Chinese Buddhist teachings.[9] Humanistic Buddhism merely utilizes some twentieth-century catchwords to rephrase this theme of mutual interpenetration. Hence, despite the rhetoric highlighting disjunction with tradition, the axiology of Humanistic Buddhism points as much to continuity as it does to reformation.

There is one important difference between the assimilation of Confucian values by Chinese clerics in the past and their current espousal by those promoting

Humanistic Buddhism. Master Xingyun and many of his devotees regard Buddhism in general, and Foguangshan in particular, as perhaps the most important vehicle for preserving Confucian values in what is generally regarded as a post-Confucian age. Ever since the May Fourth Movement of the 1920s, when "Confucius and Sons" (Kongjiadian) were pronounced dead, the Scholarly tradition periodically has suffered scathing attacks. Even in Taiwan, where Confucian symbols have been appropriated by the government as a means to legitimize itself as the paladin of traditional Chinese culture, the intricate ritual system that long gave substance to Confucian values has mostly disappeared, leaving a theoretical superstructure with little concrete base to exemplify its significance in life.[10]

Foguang Buddhists assert that their activities fill this void, insisting that their large-scale ceremonies are now the most visible enactments of *li*. During the inauguration of Ven. Xinding for his first full term as Foguangshan's abbot, for example, Gong Pengcheng (the president of Foguang University) observed: "Chinese Confucian culture is carried by Buddhism. Several years ago, mainland scholars participated in a conference on Confucianism sponsored by Foguangshan. There is no remnant of the tradition on the mainland, but on Taiwan, especially at Foguangshan, the Confucian notion of *li* persists. The magnificent ceremonies performed at Foguangshan carry profound significance and have a great impact on society. This is a wonderful contribution" ("Foguangshan Abbot Installation Ceremony" 1997). Prominent Foguang devotee Chen Lü'an has made similar observations, although not in quite so direct a fashion. In his preface to the *1994 Foguang University Art Auction Album* (1994), Chen laments that finely synchronized ritual, once the prerogative of imperial courts, is no longer to be found as part of any government affairs. He contrasts this with a land and sea dharma function that he had recently witnessed at Foguangshan, remarking especially on the imposing splendor of the setting and the regal enactment of the elaborate liturgy and sophisticated etiquette.

High ritual may not be nearly as evident in official ROC government activities as it once was in the imperial court, but, in compensation for this, any visit by a notable politician to Foguangshan becomes an opportunity for a very public display of orchestrated formality. When Vice President Lian Zhan and his wife visited Foguang headquarters during the Chinese New Year celebrations of 1998, for instance, every phase of the stay was carefully choreographed by the master, from the welcoming parade to the farewell send-off. Of special concern was the determination of where the guests were to sit and stand in relation to the master and Abbot Xinding during the main functions so that the status of the vice president would be recognized without giving the impression that either of the clerics was subordinating himself to the government official. To ensure symbolic balance between secular political leadership and religious authority, it was decided that the vice president and his wife would always be to one side, Master Xingyun and Ven. Xinding to the other, so that no one would occupy the central position.

The ritualization of Foguang relations with the ROC government as a means symbolically to affirm the religioethical basis of Taiwan society gained particular salience with the elaborate Buddha Tooth Welcoming Ceremony (Foya Sheli Gongying Qi'an Dianli). In the spring of 1998, shortly after the launching of the Campaign of Compassion and Love, a group of ten Tibetan rinpoches living in northern India expressed to Master Xingyun the desire to present him with one of the three buddha teeth still in existence since they did not have the resources to preserve and protect it adequately. The master readily agreed, so, in early April, the rinpoches flew from India to Bangkok, where they transferred the tooth to the master.

Millions of Thailand's Buddhist population took the opportunity to view the *sarira* during its brief stay in their country. For the flight to Taiwan, a China Airlines jet was specially chartered, and the master designated Wu Boxiang, president of the ROC regional headquarters of BLIA, as the head of the deputation accompanying the relic for the flight. Thousands greeted the treasure on its arrival at Chiang Kai-shek International Airport. At the head of the throng were several government officials, most notably Xiao Wanchang, Liu Songfan, and Xu Shuide, the chief ministers of the executive, legislative, and examination yuans, respectively. These VIPs joined the escort party for the drive to Taipei, a much quicker journey than usual since the highway had been specially cordoned off for the cavalcade, although devotees lined the route at many points. The next stop was the Chiang Kai-shek Memorial, where Chief Minister Xiao presided over the ceremony. Master Xingyun pronounced a prayer for peace; then the chief minister, along with ROC vice president Lian Zhan, represented the ten thousand in attendance in offering incense, flowers, candles, fruit, and rice to the relic. The two men led the gathering in a united pledge to purify society through promoting the "three goods": "speaking good words, keeping a good mind, and doing good deeds." Afterward, the tooth was sent to Foguangshan's Taipei Vihara for temporary exhibition until a permanent pagoda could be constructed.

The Buddha Tooth Welcoming Ceremony was a major event in Taiwan, given front-page news coverage for a week. It also had its detractors, however. Some (including mainland political authorities) questioned the tooth's authenticity. Others declared the entire episode no more than superstition, whether or not the tooth had actually been the Buddha's. Still others were uncomfortable with the participation of the high-ranking government officials in such a blatantly religious affair. Master Xingyun had a response for each of these criticisms. As to the relic's authenticity, he stated that the affidavit signed by the ten rinpoches that affirmed it to be a tooth of the Buddha was proof enough for him (for a monastic to fabricate a lie about something this important to the religion would be a grievous transgression of the precepts). Since the chances were remote of finding any solid evidence that would either confirm or repudiate the tooth's authenticity, ultimately it must remain within the realm of faith. And, as faith, it would be authentic rather than superstitious in nature so long as it planted in people a seed of purity. Because of the powerful symbolic import of the tooth, Master Xingyun argued that it could play a vital role in ameliorating Taiwan's social milieu. The political figures were present as links between the Buddhist community and general society.

The Buddha Tooth Welcoming Ceremony placed in particular relief the sociological aspect of all large-scale dharma functions and visits to temples by state officials. Such majestic public rituals symbolize communal harmony. They offer a metaphor for the unity of all dimensions of human existence, thereby serving as "an emphatic, intensified and sharply elaborated extension of everyday civilized intercourse" (Fingarette 1972, 11), a function formerly served by the great Confucian rites. In other words, these grand ceremonies remind people of the significance of *all* ritualized activity. Clerics often stress to devotees the very practical import of the many ritual acts that are learned during retreats. Eating meditation, bowing, all the details of Buddhist etiquette are praised for their ability to sanctify and aestheticize each aspect of life. Hence, Foguangshan serves as a vital carrier perpetuating Confucian values in contemporary Chinese society. For some, such as Gong Pengcheng, this function is consciously recognized and celebrated. For others, it plays out on a more subconscious level.

BUDDHIST PALADINS OF CONFUCIAN VALUES IN POSTMODERN CHINA?

One should not go too far in asserting the Confucian imprint on Master Xingyun's worldview. Over the centuries, Confucian temples and institutions developed a very particular cycle of rites and sacrifices as well as their own forms of "quiet sitting." Neither the master nor any of his disciples would dream of performing any such ceremonies or practices as part of their cultivation. It is not the specifics of Confucianism that are perpetuated at Foguangshan but, rather, the tradition's underlying spirit and ethos. There is irony in Foguangshan serving as protector of Confucian values. Although Master Xingyun and his devotees emphasize the harmonious interpenetration of the Chinese and Buddhist cultures, historically the foreign origins of Buddhism have caused many in the Middle Kingdom to regard it with a certain unease and ambivalence.

From the time missionaries from India first entered China in the first century, Confucian scholars warned that the foreign tradition's institutionalized monasticism posed a serious threat to family and civic loyalties. The discomfiture over Buddhism's cultural invasion did not lessen with time. In the eighth century, the Confucian Hanyu lambasted the religion as a "cult of barbarian peoples" that was corrupting China's high culture and violating its venerable customs. The Buddha, Hanyu continued, neither spoke Chinese nor understood the duties and affection that bind sovereign and subject, father and son. This ongoing cultural tension toward Buddhism's alien system of values periodically rose to feverish heights, catalyzing the emotional turbulence that fueled violent political outbursts. Anti-Buddhist campaigns led to the defrocking of thousands of monks and nuns and the destruction of innumerable temples in 446, 574, and 844, the last of these campaigns, according to some, signaling the decline of Buddhism as a dominant cultural and intellectual force in China. Another twelve hundred years of assimilation has not completely dispelled the tension between the Buddhist and the indigenous value systems. During the May Fourth Movement of the 1920s, the scholar Hu Shi blamed the otherworldliness of Buddhism for truncating the humane, rational culture prototypical of China, causing it to fall behind the West. Remedying this, he argued, would require China to liberate itself from the "Indianization" that had so perniciously adulterated Sinic culture (Hu 1937).

Foguangshan has inverted Hu Shi's logic, asserting that the best means for China to deal with the challenges of modernity is through mining and amalgamating the resources offered by the Confucian and Buddhist traditions. The strongest and most loyal ally that traditional, Confucian China now has is none other than Buddhism. In fact, some of the most visible protectors of Confucius's core ideals and spirit are the tonsured monastics who have "left home" and, to a degree, set themselves apart from the secular world. Although they may not follow specific Confucian practices, it is they who continue the rites of cosmic renewal, who provide the ethicoreligious symbolism legitimating the government as the country's moral leadership, and who best fulfill the highest requirements of filial piety.[11]

CULTURE, HOME, AND LAND

IN SEARCH OF THE HOMELAND

The fact that Foguangshan perpetuates certain cultural customs and values is not in itself remarkable since every social organ does so. Of greater note is the group's conscious promotion of itself as fulfilling this function. While certain traditions identified as relatively recent developments within Chinese Buddhism are rejected, "authentic" values of the heritage certainly are not and, in fact, are explicitly espoused. As we saw in chapter 3 above, modernism and traditionalism are regarded as mutually interpenetrating and complementary. The danger, in the Foguang view, occurs when one or the other of these polarities eclipses the other. Within Chinese Buddhism, overreliance on (a misunderstanding of) tradition has left the religion enervated. The problem of general Chinese society, on the other hand, is seen to be just the opposite: in the rush to modernize, people have drifted away from inherited values. This trend, as we observed earlier, is traced back to the May Fourth Movement of the 1920s, when Hu Shi, Chen Duxiu, and others called for their countrymen to overthrow the stultifying ritualism of "Confucius and Sons" and to rid themselves of the otherworldly escapism of Buddhism. The Communist Party stepped up this direct assault, especially in the 1950s and 1960s.

For those under the Nationalist regime of Taiwan, the steady corrosion of tradition is attributed, not to political campaigns, but to the ubiquity of Western, especially American, influence. This foreign presence has been welcome for the most part, if for no other reason than, without it, the ROC could not have withstood its Communist adversaries. Hence, the fundamentalist vituperations against the West that have erupted in many other places around the world have found little expression among Taiwan's religious groups. Despite the lack of a strong reaction against Westernization, there nonetheless has been a response to it utilizing indigenous resources. As Tu Wei-ming (1991b, 742–745) has observed, this "search for roots" bears a family resemblance to fundamentalism and proceeds from a critique of modernity. Taiwan's "mainland complex" (*dalu qingjie*), to employ the term that the island's media have made current to describe this pervasive heightened concern for asserting Chinese cultural continuity, derives from four factors: an underlying ambivalence about the tremendous American presence; discomfort with Taiwan's political status and future; recognition of the island's peripheral historical ties to China proper; and a sense of ever-increasing dissonance with contemporary mainland society.[12] Let us consider the latter two of these in more detail.

Taiwan is not the homeland for Han Chinese. It became a formal part of the Chinese Empire and began to be settled by appreciable numbers of Fujianese and Hakka farmers only in the latter half of the seventeenth century, after the Dutch and the Spanish had already established outposts along its coasts.[13] From 1895 to 1945, the island was claimed by the Japanese. Taiwan is, therefore, geographically and historically marginal. This fact is compounded by a sense of exile from the heartland. The political situation prevented most of those living outside the People's Republic of China (PRC) from even visiting until the 1980s. Since that time, sojourns to attend family reunions, to tour, or to conduct business have become increasingly common. Such contact has, however, proved bittersweet for the many who have been unprepared for the lack of resonance that they have felt with their Communist countrymen.

The Foguang nun mentioned in chapter 6 above, for example, who had traveled through mainland China for a year and a half while still a layperson remarked that she had found the experience deeply troubling, for, while she loved "China the place," she could not relate to "the mentality of the people." By "China the place," the young bhikshuni meant the physical sites, both of natural beauty and of historical significance, about which she had heard so much while growing up. The symbols of home are there. Yet present realities undercut these symbols, with the result that, as do many Chinese who have visited the PRC, this woman felt herself a stranger in her own land. Communist China is not home, for state socialism is believed to have left the populace bereft of any appreciation for its heritage, leading many on Taiwan to see themselves as more legitimate bearers of Chinese culture than are their relatives living in mainland China. On returning to Taiwan, the woman had come home, yet that home is in a marginal space whose oldest cultural landmarks are aboriginal, Dutch, and Portuguese. Hence, the sense of homeland has been bifurcated, home and land separated into two entities.[14]

Foguangshan's self-proclaimed role in protecting and perpetuating China's heritage is one manifestation of Taiwan's search for roots. In the case of the nun just mentioned, dynamics associated with the mainland complex played not a little role in her decision to renounce under Master Xingyun. As noted in chapter 6 above, shortly after returning to Taiwan from her journey the young woman came on a book by the master that so affected her that a steady stream of tears gushed down her face as she read it. "Not only the thoughts of the master moved me," related the nun, "but the fact that here was a man from mainland China who now had struck such a deep chord with people in Taiwan. Here was my bridge." The fact that Master Xingyun originally hails from the mainland has played a vital role in his popularity, for he embodies the transferal of Chinese culture from China proper to Taiwan and the outlying diaspora. Because the master plays such an important symbolic role in this dynamic, let us turn to consider in more detail the status of his efforts to plant Foguang temples in the PRC.

Returning Home to Spread the Dharma

In the spring of 1989, Master Xingyun traveled through mainland China for the first time in forty years. Over the course of the trip, billed as an occasion for "dharma preaching and family visiting" (*hongfa tanqin*), the master led a delegation of over two hundred monastic and lay devotees. From Shanghai to Dunhuang, Beijing to Chengdu, vast crowds pressed in to see Taiwan's famous master firsthand. Lu Keng, the publisher of the Hong Kong periodical the *People's Monthly* (*Baixing yuekan*), described scenes in which thousands would line streets, fill doorways, and climb trees to cheer the passing procession. According to Professor Charles Fu, another Foguang devotee who made the journey, the master's arrival in the mainland gave a timely boost to Buddhism and offered a "religious unification" (*zongjiao shang tongyi*) that could transcend the political enmity that continues to divide Taiwan and the PRC. By all accounts, the tour was a resounding success.[15]

For Master Xingyun personally, the trip was an extremely emotional experience, granting him the opportunity finally to reunite with his mother and to sweep the stupa of his teacher, Ven. Zhikai, thereby fulfilling the dual responsibilities of monastic filial piety. His return to his childhood home in Jiangdu allowed him to become reacquainted, not only with his octogenarian mother, but with his sister and two brothers as well. The time was spent in recalling their life together more than half a century before, with special prominence given to incidents that foretold the master's subsequent greatness as a Buddhist leader. Before leaving, Master Xingyun improved his family's housing and even worked out a monthly stipend for three elderly neighbors as remuneration for playing mah-jongg with his mother. Such arrangements were short-term, of course, for within a year he had made it possible for her to emigrate to the United States.

The master's return to his monastic family struck equally deep sentiments within him. The television producer Zhou Zhimin, who accompanied the Foguang entourage throughout the tour, later described the master's arrival at Qixiashan:

> Although the welcoming procession was overflowing and the drums and bells were resounding, Master's steps were heavy.... Master's eyes glistened with tears.... [H]e did not say a word, but only devoutly prostrated before the Buddha time after time, again and again. When during the welcoming ceremony Master was asked to give some remarks, he was so choked with tears that he could not utter a word. Only after ten minutes when the abbot again requested that Master speak, did he say, "I renounced at Qixiashan. I have already been away for forty-six years. Today, I have returned to my ancestral temple. When I see how well everything has been preserved, I know that all of you clerics guarded it with your lives. When Elder Zhikai was persecuted, it was you who saved him, and when he was in such pain that he no longer wanted to live, it was you who consoled him, protected

him.... I do not know how to thank you! (At this point, he again wept.) ... I consider myself to be very strong and brave, yet as I face my ancestral temple, a hundred emotions well up. (Fu 1995, 29)

Master Xingyun also visited Ven. Zhikai's hometown of Hai'an (in Jiangsu Province) during the trip, taking several opportunities to chant and offer incense before his teacher's tomb. Since then, the master has provided financial support for Ven. Zhikai's relatives.

Master Xingyun's trip seemed at first a harbinger of Foguang expansion into the mainland. His mother had even elicited from him a promise to build a temple in his hometown. Any such plans, however, were short-lived. Not three months after the master's journey, the Tiananmen Incident occurred, sparking throughout Taiwan calls to support the prodemocracy demonstrators. As leaders of the student movement fled to the United States and the ROC, Master Xingyun welcomed them to his temples. An economist surnamed Qian arrived at Hsi Lai Temple on 13 July, remaining there with his wife for several months until they could find permanent employment and housing. In August, Wu'er Kaixi, Yan Jiaqi, Wan Runnan, Ge Yang, and several other recent exiles also visited Hsi Lai, where they met with the master and, presumably, received financial assistance. After Master Xingyun returned to Taiwan in the fall, several more groups made the journey to Foguangshan.

The high point of Master Xingyun's involvement with prodemocracy political refugees came in May 1990, when he granted asylum to Xu Jiatun, head of the New China News Agency in Hong Kong (the de facto PRC political agency for the territory before its repatriation in 1997). Xu and the master had had dinner together the previous spring at the conclusion of the latter's trip to the mainland. Because Xu had voiced support for the students during the ill-fated democracy movement, he felt himself targeted for retaliation within the Communist Party and, therefore, left for the United States, where he quietly took up residence in the vicinity of Hsi Lai Temple. His whereabouts were unknown for several weeks until he, the master, and the journalist Lu Keng gave a joint news conference. Thus sponsoring Xu placed the master's involvement on an entirely new level, for Xu had been a fifty-year veteran of the Communist Party and its highest-ranking member to flee China in the aftermath of the prodemocracy protests. By providing him with refuge, the master publicly embarrassed PRC authorities, leading them to issue an order banning him from visiting the mainland again.

People have wondered why the master aided Xu, especially in such a public way, when he must have known that, in so doing, he was seriously jeopardizing any chances of establishing a Foguang presence on the mainland in the foreseeable future. The master's own explanation is that anyone in need of shelter is welcome at his temples; when the prodemocracy demonstrators called for help, his immediate instinct was to come to their aid, regardless of the cost to him or his organization. Others have not found this rationale satisfactory. The reasons for the master's decision to sponsor Xu remain unclear, although four factors may have played a role.

First, Master Xingyun has long touted Buddhism as a democratizing force. It was, therefore, very natural for him actively to demonstrate support for the movement and, after its collapse, for its exiles. In fact, it would have been quite strange if he had not, especially given the general political climate in Taiwan at the time. How better to display Buddhism's compatibility with progressive democratic ideals than to forge an alliance with those at the forefront of mainland China's democracy movement? Master Xingyun certainly must have been pleased when Wan Runnan gave a speech in which he drew a parallel between the statue of democracy in Tiananmen and the Welcoming Buddha at Foguangshan and then went on to observe that the prodemocracy movement and Buddhism share a spirit of democracy, peace, and rationality. Even more gratifying must have been the occasions when several members of the Student Independence Association and the economist Qian took refuge and when Wu'er Kaixi toyed with the idea of renouncing at Foguangshan (Shi Xingyun 1994, vol. 3, entries for 3, 4, 13, 27 January 1990).

Second, despite the glowing appraisals of his tour of mainland China, it may be that Master Xingyun felt the same culture shock that has jolted other residents of Taiwan on reentering the mainland. Perhaps he too found it difficult to relate to the mentality of the people. Furthermore, he may have come to realize that the country's political authorities were not yet ready to allow a prominent Buddhist monk in Taiwan, especially one with well-known ties with government officials, to gain a foothold in the PRC. In other words, Master Xingyun may have felt that there was little to be sacrificed in the mainland and much to be gained at home and on the international scene by publicly aligning himself with the prodemocracy exiles.

Third, the master also may have given asylum to Xu partially as a response to those who had criticized him for having visited with many government officials, including some quite high in the Communist Party, during his mainland travels. According to Fu Zhiying's biography of the master, he "shook hands and dined with every governor and mayor in every province and city he toured" (1995, 230). In Beijing, he entered the People's Hall to discuss the status of religion in the country with such leaders as Li Xiannian and the Central Committee chairman Yang

Shanggun. These meetings did not cause a stir in Taiwan until after the Tiananmen Incident. In September 1989, an article in *New News (Xin xinwen)* contended that Master Xingyun had flaunted his organization's wealth, inappropriately given money to the governments of Jiangdu and Hai'an, and had overstepped his bounds when he met with Communist Party leaders (see "Da heshang dang mishi" 1989). By helping Xu, the master sent a clear message that he had no special affinity with the mainland's Communist regime (Shi Xingyun 1994, vol. 1, entries for 13, 20 September 1989).

  The final factor that may have buttressed Master Xingyun's decision to help Xu in the manner that he did was the fact that the dalai lama had received the Nobel Peace Prize in October 1989. Master Xingyun's affiliation with the democracy movement exiles, especially Xu, may have been part of a bid to be nominated for this prestigious award himself. In fact, through the early 1990s, Foguang devotees repeatedly proclaimed that the master richly deserved such recognition.

  Master Xingyun would not agree with any of the latter three explanations given, especially the last. He and Xu had established a link of affinity in Hong Kong. As a friend, how could he not help Xu in his time of need? Such reasoning is persuasive, given the importance of noble relational sentiment *(you qing you yi)* in shaping the master's modus operandi. Regardless of his motives in 1990, one thing was certain ten years later: with the Xu affair having faded into history, Master Xingyun very much wanted to return to mainland China again. The order prohibiting him from entering the country was officially annulled by Jiang Zeming in 1993. Unofficially, the ban remained in place. Master Xingyun therefore had been extremely careful not to say or do anything that would jeopardize the possibility of making another trip. This is why he kept his distance from the dalai lama (e.g., when the latter visited Foguangshan during his tour of Taiwan in 1997, Master Xingyun neglected to return from abroad to welcome him). Finally, in the year 2000, the master was able to make the trip to the mainland again, although this second time he did so with much less fanfare.

  Master Xingyun recognizes that his identity, Foguangshan's identity, is intimately connected with the mainland. The past few years, sustaining that sense of connection has been difficult. Foguangshan did sponsor an ambitious project through most of the 1990s that utilized the talents of Beijing and Nanjing University scholars to create a 132-volume set of vernacularized Buddhist texts. More recently, the organization has opened a teahouse in Beijing and a small outpost in Nanjing (thereby keeping the master's promise to his mother). Such projects, however, clearly do not in any way approach the scale that the master would like. In wistful tones, he occasionally even speaks of the possibility that one day Foguang headquarters could move to the mainland. Such a dream represents the hope to collapse the separation between home and land. Until that is possible—if it ever is—to voice this ideal serves to strengthen the role of the master and Foguangshan in establishing miniature homelands throughout Taiwan and around the world.

9 Globalizing Chinese Culture, Localizing Buddhist Teachings

Master Xingyun first went abroad in 1963, when he joined a contingent of bhikshus sent to India, Thailand, Malaysia, Singapore, the Philippines, Japan, and Hong Kong on a government-sponsored initiative to bolster support for the Republic of China (ROC). The beginnings of Foguangshan's globalization are, however, to be traced to a more recent trip: the master's visit to the United States in 1976, at which point he recognized the great potential for serving the rapidly expanding Chinese American population. Twelve years later, Master Xingyun opened the doors of the largest Buddhist temple in the Western Hemisphere. He chose to call it "Hsi Lai," meaning "Coming to the West." This is a play on words, for Chinese Buddhists have long referred to Buddhism as having come from the West, that is, from India.

CHINESE BUDDHIST PIONEERS

One year after the founding of Hsi Lai, the theme of bringing the dharma to the West gained even greater salience when Tang Degang, a historian then at New York University, gave a lecture at the Foguangshan Buddhist Youth Academic Conference entitled "From Master Huishen to Master Xingyun." In his lecture, Tang stated that, during the North-South dynasties (420–589 C.E.), Ven. Huishen, a monk of Indian origin but living in China, sailed to America to spread the dharma. The cleric returned to the Middle Kingdom some forty years later, presenting to the Liang emperor many gifts from the distant land, which he called "Fusang." Tang cited three pieces of evidence to support his thesis. First, he quoted passages from the *Twenty-five Histories* (*Ershiwu shi*) that relate Ven. Huishen's descriptions of his voyage and of the peoples, flora, and fauna that he observed in the land that he had made his home for so long. Second, Tang noted that there are many ancient "stone anchors" (*shi mao*) in America with craftsmanship so Chinese in style that they must have derived from China and been brought over by the monk. Finally, Tang asserted that there are still people in Acapulco who are Buddhists, having received the tradition from their ancestors who had learned of the dharma from the Indian-Chinese missionary. The Venerable Huishen's early "discovery" (*faxian*) of America, a full millennium before Columbus arrived, was of such historical importance to Buddhists, Chinese, and all Americans, stated Tang, that he recommended that Hsi Lai Temple build a "Master Huishen Memorial Hall" (Shi Xingyun 1994, vol. 3, entry for 2 January 1990).

Tang Degang was not, in fact, the first scholar to hypothesize about an early Buddhist arrival in America. This theory had been raised and debated within the European academic community during the eighteenth and nineteenth centuries. More recently, a Professor Wei Zhuxian of Taiwan National University devoted virtually his entire career to cataloging archaeological, anthropological, and historical evidence for pre-Columbian contacts between Chinese and American peoples. In Wei's opinion, Huishen represents a relatively late interaction since, one thousand years earlier, Confucius had already made references to the North American hummingbird (Chandler 1998a, 14–16).

Whether "Fusang" was, in fact, a Chinese name for the Americas will probably never be known definitively. Most of the evidence that Tang and his predecessors cited to substantiate their claims is tentative at best. To scrutinize the soundness of the data offered, however, is to miss the point. For the Foguang community, the theory's importance lies, not in the degree to which its historical validity can been demonstrated, but, rather, in its potential for creating a new mythology, that is, an expressive history that helps establish the group's sense of purpose. The power of the Huishen legend arises from three elements: the portrayal of him as carrier of Chinese culture; the conviction that he successfully planted the seed of the dharma on American shores; and the transnational profile that he is given. I shall return to each of these components as I discuss Foguangshan's missionary work, not only in America, but around the world. Before doing so, I must contextualize the Foguang efforts by briefly describing the history of Chinese Buddhism as it has spread into the United States, Australia, Africa, and Europe.

Even if the land of Fusang mentioned by Ven. Huishen was not America, immigrants from China were, nonetheless, the first Asians to import Buddhist statuary and devotional practices to the United States. Those who did so were not monastics but laymen drawn to California by the lure of gold. The first ship of Chinese arrived in 1849, one year after the precious metal had been discovered at John Sutter's sawmill. By the 1880s, the early Chinese population had peaked at slightly over 100,000. Not surprisingly, as the community grew, it set aside places of worship.

The first Chinese religious establishments to be constructed in the continental United States were the Tin Hou Temple, devoted to the Daoist Goddess of Heaven, and Kong Chow Temple, whose central figure was Guangong, a folk deity of martial prowess and commercial prosperity. Both were built in San Francisco around 1853 (Wells 1962, 19–28). By 1875, the number of temples in that city had grown to at least eight, and, by the turn of the century, there were hundreds of "joss houses," as Chinese shrines were called, throughout the western United States. One cannot characterize such structures as strictly Buddhist, however, since, in most cases, a variety of Chinese Daoist, folk, and Buddhist figures received shelter and homage together. The vast majority of these dwellings were abandoned shortly after they were completed. With the passage of anti-Chinese legislation, starting with the Chinese Exclusion Act of 1882, the number of Chinese in the United States steadily declined, the various temples in the Chinatowns received ever fewer devotees, and, one by one, they were abandoned.

The history of Chinese Buddhism in Australia is remarkably similar to that of Chinese Buddhism in the United States.[1] At the same time that Chinese men from the Canton region were embarking for California, some of their relatives and neighbors were on their way to the gold mines of Victoria and South Australia. Here, too, joss houses proliferated. Buddha images do not appear to have been included in these shrines, but, alongside statues of such deities as Guangong and Caishen, one could find likenesses of Guanyin and Maitreya. As in the United States, these structures soon disappeared, and subsequent nativist backlash resulted in legislation that virtually halted all immigration from China until the early 1970s.

The lure of gold also played an important, but fleeting, role in the history of Chinese immigration to Africa. Nearly sixty-four thousand Chinese men were imported into present-day South Africa from 1904 to 1907 to work in the fifty-five mines that had sprouted up along the gold reef just south of Johannesburg. Unlike in the United States and Australia, where significant numbers of the men ended up staying on to form Chinatowns, in South Africa virtually all the Chinese workers were immediately repatriated on the expiration of their three-year contracts. Once the mine laborers had left, a mere 1,905 Chinese remained in the country, nearly all of whom had arrived during the second half of the eighteenth century.[2] Elsewhere in Africa, only such places as Lourenço Marques and Beira along the coast of Portuguese East Africa (present-day Mozambique) and Bulawayo, Umtali, and Salisbury in Rhodesia (now Zimbabwe) became home to small groups of Chinese traders, shopkeepers, and farmers. Several thousand Chinese lived on the nearby islands of Madagascar and Mauritius (Snow 1988, 42).

These immigrants brought with them the same Chinese folk religion as did their contemporaries who had ventured to America and Australia. Hence, one finds reference to two attempts in the 1890s to obtain land in Johannesburg for the erection of a Chinese temple, mention of the construction of a Guandi Temple in Kimberly around the same time, reports of the completion of a pagoda in 1903 in Mozambique, and a description of "an extremely picturesque little Jos house" as well as of "priests" on Saint Helena (Yap and Man 1996, 87–88). As for the laborers who toiled in the gold mines, the majority of those who followed religious practices identified themselves as Buddhists. All traces of such worship soon disappeared, with the exception of the Guandi Temple in Kimberly, which remained standing for several decades and whose altars may still be found in the headquarters of that city's Chinese association.

The introduction of Chinese Buddhism into Europe can be said to have preceded, yet also to have lagged behind, its arrival on other continents. Marco Polo and his fellow adventurers, Christian missionaries such as Matteo Ricci, and a small fraternity of academic scholars incrementally gave European elites knowledge of Chinese Buddhist doctrine and practice (albeit a knowledge usually biased by ethnocentric assumptions). By the late eighteenth century, such Sinologists as Abel Remusat, J. H. Klapoth, and Stanislas Julien had made available translations of some of Chinese Buddhism's most important sutras and historical documents (deJong 1987). Hence, while in the western United States, southern Australia, and eastern Africa there were devotees who worshiped Buddhist images (along with various deities) but who displayed little interest in the philosophical nuances of the tradition's teachings, in Europe, which lacked economic incentives for Chinese immigration, Sino-Buddhist doctrine was present, yet devotees were nowhere to be found. Chinese communities of any appreciable size emerged in Europe only in the latter half of the twentieth century.

The initial spread of Sino-Buddhist practice and teachings outside Asia was a haphazard, undirected phenomenon carried out by Chinese laity, on the one hand, and European scholars, on the other. Noticeably absent from the enterprise were monastics. This is not too surprising since, through the centuries, Chinese clerics rarely left the Middle Kingdom even for other Asian destinations. The Venerables Xuanzhao and Xuanzang and the other intrepid adventurers who during the Tang dynasty ventured to India are a notable exception. These men, however, journeyed in search of sutras, not to spread Buddhism. Only in the twentieth century did finances and incentives provide the proper conditions for the sangha to extend its range of activity around the globe. The first Chinese cleric to travel through Europe and the United States was Master Taixu, who spent nine months visiting universities and Chinese associations in France, England, Germany, and the United States in 1928-1929. He did not, however, make a concerted effort to establish a long-term institutional base in any of the nations that he visited. The impetus to gain a footing among overseas Chinese communities came with the founding of the People's Republic of China in 1949 and the subsequent waves of antireligious campaigns there over the next two decades. Finding there to be insufficient resources in Hong Kong and Taiwan to support the surge of monastics seeking asylum, a handful decided to continue on to one of the Chinese enclaves dispersed around the world.

The first Chinese monk to settle in the United States was Ven. Xuanhua, who landed in California in 1959. A steady stream of clerics trickled into America in the twenty years following the Immigration Act of 1965, with the result that, by the time Foguangshan consecrated Hsi Lai Temple, there were several dozen monks and nuns already living in small temples in various Chinatowns around the country.

One finds a comparable history in Australia. In fact, Ven. Xuanhua appears to have been the first resident Chinese monastic on that continent as well, having relocated there in 1961. He found it even more difficult to establish a base Down Under than in the United States, however, so he soon returned to California. No Chinese monk or nun is known to have followed Ven. Xuanhua's tracks to Australia until the 1970s, when abolition of racial quotas in immigration laws made it much easier to settle there. By the close of the 1980s, there were one or two dozen clerics serving the overseas Chinese communities of Sydney, Brisbane, Melbourne, and Perth (Croucher 1989, 68–69).

Chinese monastic migration to the United States and Australia was paralleled by similar movements throughout the world, with small numbers of monks and nuns establishing themselves in Europe and South America. Foguang venerables were the first ever to take up residence in South Africa, founding seven centers there in the early 1990s. The only region of the globe evidently without any Chinese sangha at the advent of the twenty-first century is the Middle East.

THE PERIMETERS OF FOGUANGSHAN'S GLOBALIZATION

With the exception of Ven. Xuanhua, who eventually founded a total of six monasteries in the United States and Canada (including the 237-acre City of Ten Thousand Buddhas in Talmage, California), none of the Chinese clerics who journeyed outside Asia attempted to serve more than one local community. Even Ven. Xuanhua's accomplishment pales in comparison to Master Xingyun's success in planting so many centers over such a broad geographic range. In less than a decade, Foguangshan went from having virtually no overseas branches to embracing nearly one hundred. By 1997, the headquarters oversaw ninety-five temples, Pure Land Chan centers, and lecture halls in a total of twenty-nine countries (excluding the ROC): 27 in Asia (8 in Japan, 7 in the Philippines, 7 in Malaysia, 1 in Thailand, 2 in Hong Kong, 1 in Singapore, and 1 in South Korea); 13 in Australia and the Pacific Islands (10 in Australia, 2 in New Zealand, and 1 in New Guinea); 19 in Europe (3 in the United Kingdom, 1 in Sweden, 1 in the Netherlands, 3 in Germany,

1 in Belgium, 2 in France, 1 in Switzerland, 2 in Spain, 2 in Italy, 1 in Hungary, 1 in Portugal, and 1 in the Czech Republic); 7 in Africa (7 in South Africa); 5 in South and Central America (1 in Costa Rica, 2 in Brazil, 1 in Paraguay, and 1 in Argentina); and 24 in North America (19 in the United States and 5 in Canada). Master Xingyun has decided to hold off on constructing any new centers, so the number of Foguang temples will probably remain steady for the foreseeable future. The one exception to this was the purchase in 2001 of a beautiful tract of land at the base of Mount Fuji in Japan, bringing the total of Foguang overseas centers to ninety-six.

This network is supplemented by the Buddha's Light International Association (BLIA), which by 1997 had grown to include 111 regional chapters (*zonghui*) and local chapters (*xiehui*) spread over fifty-five countries worldwide: 33 in Asia (2 in the ROC, 2 in Japan, 1 in Hong Kong, 1 in Macao, 1 in Brunei, 2 in Malaysia, 1 in Singapore, 1 in Thailand, 2 in Indonesia, 10 in India, 1 in the Philippines, 2 in South Korea, 1 in Cambodia, 1 in Vietnam, 1 in Myanmar, 1 in Nepal, 1 in Bangladesh, 1 in Bhutan, and 1 in Sri Lanka); 8 in Australian and the Pacific Islands (6 in Australia and 2 in New Zealand); 25 in North America (18 in the United States, 6 in Canada, and 1 in the Bahamas); 5 in Central America (1 in Costa Rica, 1 in Mexico, 1 in El Salvador, 1 in the Dominican Republic, and 1 in Panama); 7 in South America (1 in Brazil, 1 in Argentina, 1 in Paraguay, 1 in Chile, 1 in Uruguay, 1 in Guatemala, and 1 in Belize); 22 in Europe (3 in the United Kingdom, 1 in France, 1 in Switzerland, 2 in Germany, 1 in Belgium, 1 in Denmark, 1 in Norway, 2 in the Netherlands, 1 in Spain, 1 in Hungary, 1 in Yugoslavia, 1 in Italy, 2 in Sweden, 1 in Portugal, 1 in Austria, and 2 in Russia); and 11 in Africa (9 in South Africa, 1 in Congo, and 1 in Tanzania).

Foguang temples may be found virtually anywhere a relatively large expatriate population from the ROC has coalesced. The reach of BLIA is still farther, extending to areas with even small communities of emigrants from Taiwan. It is very difficult to determine exactly how many devotees frequent the temples or join BLIA chapters since specific statistics are not made public. Foguang clerics have unofficially claimed BLIA's worldwide membership to be anywhere from one to three million. I doubt that the roster of active members has ever reached even the more modest of the two estimates, although the total number of people who participate in BLIA events in a given year probably achieves, and very well may exceed, the three million mark.

The question is, How many people are members of BLIA, how many of these live in Taiwan, and how many live abroad? Given that approximately five million people in the ROC frequent a Buddhist temple, that Foguangshan is only one of several large Buddhist organizations, and that many of Taiwan's Buddhists do not join any of these groups, I would estimate that perhaps 400,000–600,000 people, or 8–12 percent of the island's Buddhists, currently align themselves with Foguangshan as active members of BLIA. The lower estimate corresponds to the number of *Awakening the World* magazines that were distributed each month from 1997 to 1999.

Since Foguangshan has only fifty-seven temples in Taiwan but ninety-six centers overseas, it would appear at first glance that the majority of members and devotees live outside the ROC and, therefore, that the total number could well exceed one million. On closer inspection, however, it becomes clear that this is not the case. The extent to which Foguangshan has thus far carried its banner of Humanistic Buddhism beyond the shores of Taiwan can be roughly determined by analyzing personnel distribution and temple fund-raising strategies. Some of Foguangshan's overseas branch temples, such as Hsi Lai, Nan Tien, and Nanhua Temples, are multimillion-dollar structures that have become prominent landmarks and tourist attractions. Most other outposts are of much more modest scale, occupying former homes, warehouses, schools, and churches. Since, typically, these outposts rely on a small and dispersed Chinese population, there is neither the need nor the financial resources to support ornate halls or large staffs. Hence, although international temples greatly outnumber domestic ones, they account for less than one-quarter of full-time worker assignments. Of Foguangshan's 1,096 monastic, lay monastic, and lay devotees who as of August 1997 worked full-time for the organization, 434 worked at Foguang headquarters, 423 were stationed in a temple in Taiwan, and 239 were assigned abroad.[3] Overseas centers had an average of 2.4 workers, compared to an average of 6.2 for the temples in Taiwan, a finding that supports the conclusion that the devotee base is much lower elsewhere in the world than it is in the ROC.

The smaller number of devotees per monastery creates a significant financial strain. Several lay followers active in the fund-raising efforts of overseas Foguang temples confided to me that their branch would not be able to meet its bills if it were not for the generous contributions made by key donors who periodically visited from Taiwan. One nun revealed that as much as 80 percent of the funds raised at Hsi Lai derives from either people who visit from Taiwan or people who, while having a second home in the Los Angeles area, still spend most of their time in the ROC (although other monastics claimed a much lower percentage). Given these statistics and comments, I doubt that any overseas BLIA chapter, even the one in Los Angeles affiliated with Hsi Lai Temple, has a roster of over a few thousand or that those chapters with no temple nearby are able to maintain a membership larger than several dozen people. BLIA therefore probably has approximately fifty to sixty thousand members whose primary residence is outside Taiwan.

Although the picture I provide of the extent of Foguangshan's global operations is not nearly so grand as that given by Foguang devotees, one still has to be impressed by what the order has done in so brief a time, particularly when one keeps in mind that such global outreach is unprecedented in the history of Sino-Buddhism. The only Chinese Buddhist organization with a comparable global network is Ciji Gongde Hui, which as of 2001 included seventy-eight offices in twenty-seven countries (excluding Taiwan): 38 offices in the United States; 5 in Malaysia; 5 in Australia; 6 in South Africa; 2 in Canada; and 1 in each of Argentina, Austria, Brazil, Brunei, the Dominican Republic, France, Germany, Great Britain, Hong Kong, Indonesia, Japan, Jordan, Lesotho, Mexico, the Netherlands, New Zealand, Paraguay, the Philippines, Singapore, Spain, Thailand, and Turkey (*Tzu Chi Quarterly* 8, no. 3 [fall 2001]: 97). There is one significant difference between Foguangshan's and Ciji Gongde Hui's strategies for international outreach: the latter opens overseas offices, not temples. In other words, no monastics have been stationed abroad. The "offices" are typically homes or businesses where small groups of members meet to discuss Buddhism and raise money for the headquarters' worldwide humanitarian efforts. This is not to imply that Ciji offices are any less active than are Foguang temples. Overseas Ciji members undertake a wide range of programs and raise considerable sums of money, not only for the initiatives of the headquarters, but for local philanthropic endeavors as well.[4] Nonetheless, the lack of overseas temples and monastics has resulted in Ciji offices having a generally lower profile outside the immediate Chinese community than do the Foguang outposts. The organizational structure of Ciji Gongde Hui more closely approximates that of the lay Buddhist group Soka Gakkai, although neither of the Chinese organizations comes anywhere close to their Japanese counterpart in scale.

Not only does Foguangshan's international network of temples exceed that of other Chinese Buddhist institutions, but it is also one of the most extensive of any Buddhist organization. Thich Nhat Hanh's Order of Interbeing has a semiformal arrangement of affiliates that, by 1998, included a handful of temples and approximately three hundred "lay sanghas." The vast majority of Thich Nhat Hanh's disciples, however, remain in Plum Village, the order's headquarters in France. The only other international Buddhist organization in which clerics play an important leadership role is Sangharakshita's Western Buddhist Order (WBO) (and, of course, the affiliated Friends of the Western Buddhist Order [FWBO]), which in 1998 incorporated fifty-five city centers and fifteen retreat centers, mostly in Great Britain (where the order was founded), but also in Australia, New Zealand,

Malaysia, Sri Lanka, India, Nepal, and North and South America. Sangharakshita has been particularly active in India, where his efforts to carry on Ambedkar's work among *dalits* is estimated to have brought several tens of thousands into FWBO's fold.

Foguangshan therefore probably has more temples and clerics around the world than any other Buddhist organization. The global profile of its lay devotee base is also among the most impressive. Having given an indication of the extent of Foguangshan's internationalization campaign, I will now turn to consider more closely its nature. To do so, I will focus on its three main objectives: the creation for the Chinese diaspora of a bridge back to the cultural motherland; the fostering of ecumenical ties among Buddhists of all lineages and ethnicities; and the forging of mechanisms with which to reach out to non-Buddhists. I begin my discussion at the same place that Master Xingyun chose to launch his organization's globalization: Hsi Lai Temple in the United States.

BY LEAVING HOME ONE GAINS A MYRIAD HOMES

When Master Xingyun first visited the United States in 1976 to enjoy the bicentennial celebrations, he was immediately impressed by the can-do attitude of Americans and optimistic about the possibility of spreading the dharma there. Within a year, he sent a team of monastics to find a suitable location for a temple. The scouting group was discouraged at first; the exorbitant California real estate market seemed beyond the organization's reach. When the clerics eventually found a church for sale at a reasonable price, Master Xingyun instructed them to purchase it. He found the idea of transforming a Christian property into a Buddhist temple especially appealing since Protestant and Catholic organizations have often acquired temple lands in Taiwan to build churches.

The former church building essentially served as a preparatory site from which to plan a much more ambitious temple. In 1978, fourteen acres were purchased in Hacienda Heights and plans drawn for a large monastery, including an eight-story statue of Amitabha Buddha. Gaining approval from the city government to build the complex, however, proved much more difficult than anticipated. Local residents feared that the presence of a Buddhist "cult" into their midst would endanger their children and send real estate values plummeting. Finally, after six public hearings and over one hundred negotiation sessions, permission was granted to build the temple, although on a smaller scale than originally envisioned and without an outdoor statue of Amitabha. The cornerstone was laid for the structure in January 1986. Just under three years later, Master Xingyun made the journey from Taiwan to conduct the consecration rite. According to one account, bright lights were seen coming from the back of the main hall during the ceremony, and "auspicious clouds gathered around the temple forming into the shape of Guanyin riding on a dragon" (Shi Xingyun 1988c, ii).

Since the opening of Hsi Lai, Foguangshan has established branch temples in New York City, San Francisco, San Diego, Las Vegas, Austin, Houston, and Mangilao (in the U.S. protectorate Guam). Pure Land Chan halls can be found in Phoenix, Kissimmee (Florida), Boston, Honolulu, Kansas City, and Piscataway (New Jersey). There are also lecture halls in Dallas and Denver, youth hostels in Edmond (Oklahoma) and Arlington (Texas), and a four-hundred-acre retreat center in southern New York State. Altogether, more than sixty clerics are stationed in the country, accounting for one-quarter of Foguangshan's overseas personnel. None of the other Foguang establishments in the United States can rival Hsi Lai Temple in size or magnificence, although all are quite pretty inside and the exteriors of the Austin and Mangilao temples prominently display Chinese architectural features.[5] The rest of the temples, halls, and hostels are in office buildings, former houses or stores, or, in the case of the New York Vihara, a four-story abandoned warehouse. Other than small signs identifying the organization, little differentiates these structures from their neighbors.

Hsi Lai Temple, Hsi Fang Temple of San Diego, and Three Buddhas Hall in Boston have English-language programs designed to introduce Buddhist teachings to non-Chinese. At the rest of the establishments, virtually all activities are conducted in Mandarin or Taiwanese. Many who frequent branch temples do so not so much as devoted Buddhists as expatriates seeking the familiar tastes, sounds, and sights of their mother country. Weekly services, retreats, and large-scale dharma functions are religious and social events. The Chinese-language schools run at many of the temples are a major drawing card. Parents regard these schools, as well as the Boy Scout troops and other Foguang children's programs, as effective means to steep their children in the ethical values and cultural legacy of what otherwise would be a far-removed heritage. The perception that Foguangshan is a vital carrier of traditional Chinese culture has, therefore, played an especially important role in attracting new devotees. To better understand how Foguangshan fulfills its cultural function, let us think more broadly about the role of religion in the immigrant experience.

In his penetrating analysis of trends within the Protestant, Catholic, and Jewish communities in the United States over the course of the first half of the twentieth century, Will Herberg (1960) noted that the first three generations of new Americans differed in their attitudes toward their inherited religion. The immigrant generation gained strength from its imported religious beliefs and practices since these maintained "something of the old life," thereby providing continuity and order in what was otherwise a confusing new land. The second generation typically saw the vestiges of the old country as a source of confusion and disadvantage. "To them," Herberg observed, "religion, along with the language of the home, seemed to be part and parcel of the immigrant baggage of foreignness they were so eager to abandon. To the dismay of the parents, and to the distaste of better acculturated Americans, many of the second generation tended to draw away from the religion of their fathers and from religion altogether" (19). The third generation, fully assimilated into the American way of life, and, therefore, much more secure than the second, recognized that, while the language and many of the customs of the first generation could not be perpetuated on these shores, not only could the religion of one's forebears be maintained, but also an important element of American identity was precisely the preservation of one's religious legacy. For this and later generations, then, according to Herberg, religion "has become the differentiating element and the context of self-identification and social location" (21).

Herberg did not regard his model as accurately depicting the experience of Buddhist Chinese and Japanese immigrants. He thought this tradition simply too alien, so alien, in fact, that the Americanization of East Asian immigrants required "dropping the non-American faith and becoming a Catholic or Protestant, usually the latter" (1960, 44 n. 26). Perhaps making such an exception seemed accurate in the 1950s; half a century later, it appears that the general thrust of the three-generation model works as well for Buddhists as for Protestants, Catholics, and Jews. The shift in nomenclature and practice within the Japanese-American Jodo Shinshu community is a case in point. From 1899 to 1942, this organization was known as the Buddhist Mission to North America. Hoping to demonstrate its full loyalty to the U.S. government and fidelity to the American way of life, with the Second World War the community changed its name to the Buddhist Church of America (BCA), added pews and an organ to its places of worship, and adopted Christian-style hymns and responsive readings as part of its services. As members in recent years have more openly recognized that being Buddhist and American is not antithetical, a growing number of BCA chapters, such as Senshin Buddhist Temple (Los Angeles) and Midwest Buddhist Temple (Chicago), have returned to the more traditional terminology and service.

The late-twentieth-century Chinese Buddhist experience as exemplified by Foguangshan introduces a different set of variables into the equation. Foguang devotees in the United States have not necessarily brought Buddhist beliefs and practices as part of their "cultural baggage." An informal survey suggests that at least a significant minority, and probably a majority, had negligible knowledge of Buddhist teachings before reaching these shores. In other words, these first-generation immigrants are returning to Buddhism, much as third-generation practitioners have in other communities. The parents of these Chinese had already psychologically distanced themselves from much of their heritage in the intellectually and politically iconoclastic movements of the past seventy-five years, with the result that, even in Taiwan, mainland China, and Hong Kong, there is widespread questioning of cultural identity. For those from Taiwan, such discomfiture has been accentuated by their island's geographic, historical, and political marginality, leading, as we have seen, to a "search for roots" and a "mainland complex." This uncertainty is even more likely to reach a point of crisis on emigration. It then becomes imperative to find a means to return to one's heritage, at least to selective aspects of that heritage. First-generation Chinese Americans who become Foguang Buddhists are not maintaining a directly inherited identity so much as reconstructing one.

These comments about the cultural function of Foguang outposts in America apply, mutatis mutandis, to the organization's branches around the world. It is safe to say that over 99 percent of BLIA members are ethnically Chinese. Foguangshan's worldwide forays therefore represent the globalization of a national tradition. In other words, the Foguang network is geographically international but remains almost completely associated with one cultural group and highly focused on that group's concerns with the notion of homeland. Chinese tradition has historically been grounded in one particular setting: the Middle Kingdom. As the number of Chinese living elsewhere in the world, even outside Asia, has multiplied dramatically over the last half century, organizations such as Foguangshan have served a very important function in maintaining for their members a sense of Chinese identity.

Clerics serve as important symbols for this reconstructed sense of home. Master Xingyun likes to quote the phrase: "By leaving home, one gains a myriad homes." In the past, this saying was taken primarily as alluding to the fact that all bhikshus had the right to take up temporary lodging in any public monastery. So long as the monk had a certificate of ordination and pledged to abide by the monastery's rules, he could not be turned away. He was homeless, yet he benefited from countless abodes throughout the country. For Foguang venerables, their own organization provides the myriad homes. These clerics, in turn, act as the channels through which Chinese culture is continually transmitted to the laity. Just as, by leaving their biological relatives, monks and nuns join a larger monastic family, Foguang devotees who have strayed far from the Chinese homeland have, by joining the BLIA, actually become part of a family that extends around the world. Each

Foguang temple, as a center of Chinese culture, is home. It is not only a miniature pure land but also a microcosmic, archetypal homeland. Mainland China may be situated physically where the Middle Kingdom once was, but the periphery is now where that kingdom's cultural legacy thrives. The geographic center has become marginal, the margins transformed into cultural centers. In fact, there are more than a few within the Chinese diaspora who believe that it is from these multiple centers that China's heritage can one day be reintroduced to the physical core.

UNITING GLOBAL BUDDHISM
Master Xingyun very much recognizes that his overseas temples and BLIA chapters serve as cultural bridges back to China. For this very reason, he often emphasizes that these outposts are not meant merely to be overseas Chinese associations with a Buddhist veneer. Foguang temples are to be centers of Chinese Buddhism, with the emphasis on "Buddhism." Just as the bringing of Chinese culture was an incidental feature of Ven. Huishen's venture to Fusang, so is it said to be a secondary aspect of Master Xingyun's vow to globalize Buddhism. The master's internationalization campaign therefore strives to affirm Buddhist identity, regardless of specific lineage or ethnicity. The master encourages his fellow Buddhists to think of themselves, not so much as Chinese, Japanese, Tibetan, Thai, British, etc., or even as within the Mahayana, Theravada, or Vajrayana streams, but simply as Buddhists, all sharing a single tradition based on the teachings of Shakyamuni. Three methods have been employed to carry out this ecumenical objective: participation in Buddhist associations; promotion of BLIA as an organization for all Buddhists; and the sponsoring of an annual intrafaith conference for clerics.

Foguangshan regularly dispatches monastics to attend ecumenical conferences, most notably those sponsored by the World Federation of Buddhists (WFB). Since the WFB's founding in 1950, it has largely remained under the control of Thai monks. Representatives from a variety of organizations throughout Asia have continued to participate in its conferences, but interest has waned with time and political infighting. As part of the efforts to revive the association and counter allegations that it is a thinly veiled attempt to impose the Thai understanding of Buddhism on others, in 1997 WFB officials asked Master Xingyun if he would become the honorary president of the organization. The master accepted this title but has not been particularly active in the federation since, although he did arrange for the 1998 WFB annual conference to be held at Nan Tien Temple.

One reason that Master Xingyun has had little interest in pushing the agenda of the WFB is that he has envisioned his own BLIA as the means through which to bring together all Buddhists. Indicative of that organization's ambitious scope have been the locations of the annual world meetings—Los Angeles, Taipei, Vancouver, Sydney, Paris, Hong Kong, and Toronto. The master envisions BLIA as becoming a fully international Buddhist society, not only spanning the globe geographically, but also representing Buddhists of all ethnicities and traditions. In 1995, one of the association's three vice-chairpeople and two of its seven directors were non-Chinese of South Asian Buddhist traditions. To date, however, efforts to attract Buddhists other than the master's own devotees (virtually all of whom, as we have seen, are Chinese) have had negligible success. Of the 111 BLIA chapters located outside Taiwan as of 1997, 26 were listed as conducting their meetings in a language other than Chinese.[6] At first glance, this is an impressive number. None of these chapters, however, has very many members, typically around one or two dozen people. In some cases, economic considerations have played a prominent role in motivating the leader of a non-Chinese Buddhist organization to form an alliance with BLIA. The Foguang leadership now appears to be reassessing BLIA's mission and lowering its ambitious goals. In 1999, for the first time since the association's inauguration, no worldwide meeting was convened. The effort to attract a wide ethnic membership has certainly declined: only one of the society's six vice-chairpeople at the turn of the century was non-Chinese (Ven. Anuruddha of Sri Lanka), and all fifteen directors were Chinese. Symbolic of the organization's "return home" was the site for the 2000 meeting: Foguang headquarters.

Concurrent with the BLIA campaign to bring non-Chinese Buddhists into the Foguang fold, venues have also been sought through which to foster ecumenical cooperation among ordained sangha. Since 1993, Foguangshan has sponsored an annual International Buddhist Monastic Conference at which clerics of lineages and traditions from around the world have been invited to participate, with Foguangshan footing the entire bill. The conference has attracted some well-known Buddhist leaders, such as Ven. Dr. Dhammananda (the chief prelate of Malaysia) and Ven. Henepola Gunaratana (the chief *sanghnayaka* of North America), both of whom participated in the 1998 conference in Toronto, but the vast majority of the attendees run smaller, less affluent organizations. There are certainly economic ties involved; most of the participants find an opportunity to visit privately with Master Xingyun to request funding for their own projects. For Foguangshan, the opportunity to sponsor such an event, and, thereby, assert itself as the vanguard of international, ecumenical Humanistic Buddhism, is satisfaction enough. This symbolic element comes to the fore during the annual BLIA World Conference (which takes place just before or after the International Monastic Conference), when the clerics as VIP guests proceed into the venue immediately after Master Xingyun.

Although monetary and symbolic motives play a significant role in the staging of the conferences, it would be a mistake to discount these gatherings as merely superficial productions. Very constructive interactions occur there. During the 6–9 May 1997 meeting, for instance, the official theme of how to create institutional mechanisms for implementing Humanistic Buddhism soon played itself out, to be replaced by much more lively discussions of the need for elevating the status of women renunciants in most Buddhist countries. By the concluding session, participants had drafted and signed a letter urging Master Xingyun and Foguangshan to sponsor an international ordination to reintroduce the bhikshuni order into Theravadin and Tibetan traditions. The Bodhgaya ordination, previously only one of many potential Foguang projects, was held the following spring.

10 Globalizing and Localizing: Three Case Studies

Master Xingyun would like for Buddhists to work more closely together because he believes that such solidarity will strengthen the tradition's place vis-à-vis other religions. This brings us to yet another prong of Foguangshan's globalization program: promoting interfaith communication. All religious leaders who share a humanistic perspective must, in the master's view, ensure that their traditions will work harmoniously together while respecting each other's differences. Foguangshan is, therefore, a visible participant in interfaith conferences. Larger branch temples make a point of inviting representatives of local religious groups as VIPs for special events. In February 1997, Master Xingyun met with Pope John Paul II, the two men using the opportunity to set the groundwork for joint educational projects and exchanges. Little came of the specific proposals raised, but the very fact that the master had an audience with the pope further legitimated his status as an important religious leader on the world stage and attested to his commitment to interfaith cooperation.

Master Xingyun's globalization program is in many ways a response to the history of Christian missionary activity in China. As he told students during a class at Hsi Lai University: "Catholics and Protestants have built churches all around the world, so why can't Foguangshan? I hope everyone will vow to spread Buddhism throughout the world and will aspire to read a myriad books and travel a myriad miles, to understand the world's literature, religions, and people, and to become an international disseminator of Buddhism" (Shi Xingyun 1994, vol. 1, entry for 24 August 1989). For the tradition to be international, the seed of the dharma must be planted in every country, and not just among emigrants from Buddhist lands, but among the general populace. This is the missionary component of globalization. The master and his disciples are still struggling with how best to accomplish this goal.

Through the first dozen years of Foguangshan's worldwide expansion, three primary methods of outreach have been employed: creating links of affinity; sparking people's curiosity; and localizing Buddhist teachings and practice. I will consider each in turn. First, I will focus on Vice President Al Gore's controversial visit to Hsi Lai Temple for a fund-raiser. Then, I will analyze the self-understanding of Euro-Australians who participate in Nan Tien Temple events. Finally, I will consider the Foguang campaign to nurture a non-Chinese monastic corps, especially the efforts in this regard at Nanhua Temple in Bronkhorstspruit, South Africa.

PLACING PALMS TOGETHER AND THE AMERICAN SPIRIT

When Vice President Al Gore arrived at Hsi Lai Temple on 29 April 1996, he was greeted at the main gate by Master Xingyun and other senior Foguang monastics.[1] The master led his guest past the local high school's 150-piece marching band to the temple's main shrine to pay respect to the Buddha. The two men next proceeded to the dining room, filled with about one hundred guests around twelve tables. After the exchange of small gifts, the vice president spoke briefly to the gathering. His remarks did not deal with American politics directly. Instead, he praised the Buddhist practice of greeting others by joining one's palms. "The placing of palms together is very much in the American spirit," he said. "To bring together, one, two, three, four, so so many, is simply wonderful. It is an act of cooperation, union, mutual respect, and harmony."[2] After the *Wall Street Journal* reported that this Hsi Lai banquet netted $140,000 for the Democratic National Committee (DNC) and that a significant proportion of this amount was donated by Foguang monastic and lay members (see Kuntz 1996, A1), journalists and others not only questioned the event's legality but also tried to puzzle out why a Chinese Buddhist organization would be delving so deeply into American presidential politics. In this section, I endeavor to dispel some of the mystery enshrouding the event by analyzing the possible motivations that may have impelled Master Xingyun and his devotees to invite Gore to their Hacienda Heights temple and to donate funds to the DNC. In order to set the scene, let me begin by providing some historical context.

"COME EAT VEGETARIAN FOOD WITH US . . . I'LL TREAT"

Al Gore first met Master Xingyun in January 1989 during a three-day excursion to Taiwan. The trip, sponsored by Foguangshan, was organized by Maria Hsia, who, along with John Huang, would eventually play a leading role in putting together the Hsi Lai fund-raiser. It included meetings with Taiwanese and U.S. officials and a visit to Foguang headquarters. Reflecting back on the event ("BLIA Youth Conference" 1997), Master Xingyun recalls casually remarking to Gore, then still a senator: "Hey, you could be president." Gore replied: "Do I look presidential?" "Very much so, very much." It was from this meeting, states Master Xingyun, that he and the future vice president established a relationship.

When Gore and Master Xingyun met, the present Hsi Lai Temple had only just opened its doors and was struggling to gain acceptance among its American neighbors. Doing so would prove a long, arduous task. The following summer, for instance, Hsi Lai staff were initially very pleased when the local Chinese Chamber of Commerce invited them to provide a float for the town's Fourth of July parade. Unfortunately, it turned out to be a terrible experience, for their float was booed and heckled much of the way. For many years following that debacle, the Hsi Lai community maintained a low public profile while quietly contributing to service projects (such as donating Thanksgiving and Christmas food baskets to needy families) and launching various public relations initiatives. The traffic congestion that occurred during large festivals proved to be a source of tension with immediate neighbors, so the temple made a concerted effort to include them in the celebrations. Since at Chinese New Year thousands of pilgrims would visit the temple, several days beforehand a special banquet would be held for the neighborhood. From 1993, five hundred people have attended the feast each year.[3]

As another means to establish Hsi Lai Temple as a fully accepted member of the community, Master Xingyun and the temple's various abbots consistently sought to secure ties of affinity with local and national political leaders. California secretary of state March Fong Eu was invited to view the Hacienda Heights property just as construction got under way. Evidently, it was she who arranged for Master Xingyun to perform purifying services to start the December 1988 session of the California legislature. Foguang literature proudly states that this is the first time that a Buddhist monastic has performed this rite on government premises in the United States. (Master Xingyun later conducted such services in New York City and Chicago as well.) That same year, the mayors of Austin and Houston, Texas, honored Master Xingyun as a friendship ambassador. Letters of congratulations have been sent to the temple by numerous Californian politicians, including Governor Pete Wilson, Senator Alan Cranston, and Los Angeles mayor Tom Bradley. Visiting Hsi Lai have been such political figures as California Senate president David Roberti, U.S. congressman Mel Levine, and U.S. congressman Matthew G. Martinez (Shi Xingyun 1994, vol. 1, entries for 1, 7 July 1989, and vol. 3, entries for 7, 20 January 1990).

From its inception, Hsi Lai Temple maintained at least nominal links with the White House. President Reagan both wired a telegram and dispatched a representative to the temple in honor of its opening in 1988. President George H. W. Bush invited Master Xingyun to his inauguration, and, when the Buddha's Light International Association (BLIA) was founded in 1992 in Los Angeles, he sent a letter, praising the group for its compassionate tenets and devotion to relieving the suffering of all beings.[4]

Such contacts with the Oval Office increased and became more direct with the Clinton administration. In September 1993, three Foguang monastics attended a vice-presidential fund-raiser (organized by Maria Hsia) in Santa Monica, California, donating a total of $15,000 to the DNC. An additional $5,000 was given to the party at a 1995 event attended by both Clinton and Gore, and $25,000 was contributed in February 1996 when Ven. Cirong, the abbess of Hsi Lai, led a team of Foguang members to meet President Clinton at a DNC fund-raiser at the Hay Adams Hotel in Washington, D.C. (Akers 1997, A1). One month later, John Huang arranged for Master Xingyun to make a ten-minute "courtesy call" on Vice President Gore at the White House. It was during this meeting that Master Xingyun invited Gore to visit Hsi Lai Temple (Weisskopf and Sun 1996, A1, A20, A21).

At first, the vice president was merely going to stop by the temple for a brief tour. "When Vice President Gore was coming to Los Angeles," recalled Master Xingyun during a meeting of Foguang youths, "he was going to go somewhere else for a fund-raising dinner. When he called, I said, 'Don't go there; come eat vegetarian food with us.' . . . Al Gore declined the invitation, saying that the other place was already set up for the event and that it was unlikely that he could come to Hsi Lai Temple for lunch. . . . I said, 'No problem, you come here to eat. I can prepare twenty tables. I'll treat'" ("BLIA Youth Conference" 1997). In the end, Gore did not have to choose between the two venues. The other luncheon, a fund-raiser sponsored by the Asian Pacific American Leadership Council, did not attract the anticipated number of donors, so John Huang decided to combine the two events.

Those who investigated the 29 April banquet wondered whether it was viewed by those who attended it as a fund-raiser. Al Gore steadfastly asserted that he considered the event to be "community outreach," although one also "finance-related" and designed for "donor maintenance" (Tumulty 1997). Master Xingyun characterized it as an opportunity to reaffirm his link of affinity with the vice president. Many of the other participants, however, came with checks in hand. All those contacted by the Asian Pacific American Leadership Council knew from the outset that money was being collected. Foguang devotees who attended had similarly been told that they could contribute funds to the DNC. The combined donations came, however, only to approximately $85,000, far below the $200,000 that John Huang had predicted would be raised. To increase the take, the day following the banquet, Huang had Maria Hsia contact Ven. Manhe (the Foguang monastic in charge of coordinating the event) to press the temple to raise more money. The Venerable Manhe forwarded this request to Master Xingyun, who readily agreed, personally providing $5,000. The Venerable Manhe then bid the temple treasurer, Ven. Yiju, to round up fifteen devotees—eleven monastics and four lay monastic followers—to contribute as well, thereby raising a total of $55,000.

On discovering that the Hsi Lai banquet had served as a fund-raiser for the DNC, the *Wall Street Journal* reporter Paul Kuntz (1996, A1) questioned the event's legality on three fronts. First, by law no political fund-raising can occur at a tax-exempt religious organization. Second, it appeared that not all the contributors were U.S. citizens: Master Xingyun certainly was not, having only a green card, and there were doubts about others as well. Third, the ultimate source of some of the money was unclear. Kuntz wondered how Buddhist monks and nuns living on $40 monthly stipends could come up with $5,000 contributions.

Kuntz was right to raise doubts about the event's legality. Any fund-raising on the premises of a tax-exempt religious organization clearly contradicts federal election statutes. The permissibility of those with permanent residency status donating funds to a political party proves to be more problematic. It appears that, under the laws of the time, such contributions were permissible, although there was soon a push to rewrite this aspect of campaign-finance legislation.

The third legal question, that concerning the unknown source of the funds supplied by the monastics, became the focal point of investigations undertaken by the U.S. Justice Department, the Senate's Governmental Affairs Committee (GAC), and the House Reform and Oversight Committee. An audit of temple bank records revealed that Master Xingyun and all the other clerics and lay monastics who had contributed funds to the DNC on 30 April were reimbursed that same day by the International Buddhist Progress Society (the incorporated name of Hsi Lai Temple). When Vens. Manhe and Yiju (along with a third nun, Ven. Manya) were called to testify before the GAC on 4 September 1997, Ven. Yiju not only testified that she had reimbursed all fifteen Foguang disciples but also admitted to having subsequently doctored some of the checks to make it appear that they had come from the individuals' personal *futian* accounts rather than from the temple's general fund. Both she and Ven. Manhe, however, steadfastly asserted that all the moneys reimbursed had been raised here in the United States through devotee donations and bookstore sales. None had come from the Taiwan headquarters.[5]

For all the scrutiny by government and news agencies, the Hsi Lai banquet proved to hold little long-term significance for either American politics or the status of Foguangshan in the United States. The Justice Department chose not to indict the temple or any of the monastics for criminal wrongdoing. Only BLIA member Maria Hsia was taken to court, where she was convicted on five felony counts of conspiracy to defraud the U.S. government. Hsi Lai Temple eventually had to pay a civil penalty of $120,000 to the Federal Election Commission. Not surprisingly, morale was low in the Hsi Lai community during the two years of news stories and investigations, and certain of the temple's neighbors renewed their concerns about the "cult" in their midst, but even these local repercussions have faded with time. Despite the short-term notoriety suffered by his own organization, Master Xingyun, ever the optimist, believes that the controversy itself may have served the positive function of dispelling misconceptions and introducing a wide range of Americans, especially those in the media and political circles, to Buddhist teachings. He may be right. The general assumption that Buddhist monastics take a "vow of poverty," for instance, was gradually dispelled, at least in some quarters. Although many news agencies continued to mention this supposed vow even through the GAC hearings, others, such as the *Washington Post* (Sun and Mintz 1997, A1), eventually corrected themselves on this point. For Master Xingyun, even such minor and fleeting glimpses into the Buddhist world may be all that is necessary to plant the seed of the dharma so that it can fully sprout forth in the future.

This rosy spin on the controversy's outcome leads us to a consideration of the underlying question that baffled many Americans about the entire event: What were these Chinese Buddhists with only a tenuous formal tie to the United States hoping to gain by feting the vice president at a banquet and donating large sums of money to the DNC? To answer this quandary, I now turn to consider Foguangshan's possible motivations.

"I Am Also American, I Have Residency Status"

Several politicians and journalists speculated that Master Xingyun and his followers were acting as clandestine agents for Taiwan's government or its business interests. The fact that the master has long had a close relationship with political and corporate leaders of the Republic of China (ROC) added fuel to such suspicions. Furthermore, ROC government officials invariably stop by Hsi Lai Temple when passing through Los Angeles.[6] While it is possible that Master Xingyun was surreptitiously acting on behalf of Taiwan's power elite when he invited Al Gore, it nonetheless remains highly improbable that he was directly given funds by them in an attempt to influence the U.S. government. Neither journalists nor investigators for the House, Senate, or Justice Department found any evidence that funds were transferred from Taiwan into Hsi Lai coffers. On the other hand, the master himself has characterized the temple as at least an unofficial liaison for Taiwan. When in 1986 Liu Daren, then head of the Los Angeles office of the Taipei Cultural and Economic Office, visited Master Xingyun at the Hsi Lai construction site, the master jested: "I would like to congratulate you on having added a new work unit *[danwei]* in Los Angeles." Liu looked puzzled, so the master added, "Hsi Lai Temple!" (Wu 1994, 51). Such a comment, even when offered as a joke, coupled with the fact that in February 1997 the master accepted a position on the ROC cabinet's Overseas Chinese Affairs Commission, indicates that, although he most likely was not acting as a direct agent for the government, he certainly had its relationship with the overseas Chinese community and the general American public in mind.

Another possible motive behind the largesse of Master Xingyun and his followers was to benefit their own organization, Foguangshan. Whether in the United States, Europe, or Australia, creating ties of affinity with local and national political leaders can help ease bureaucratic red tape for branch temples.[7] Even more important, such ties with the political elite provide prestige, both in the country of the temple and back in Taiwan. The symbolic import of having one's photograph taken with government officials should not be underestimated. What could better legitimize Foguang Buddhism and signify its compatibility with American values than a photograph of the abbess of Hsi Lai Temple with President Clinton and an American flag in the background or of Vice President Gore offering a bouquet of flowers to an image of the Buddha? Back in Taiwan, what could better display the global importance of Foguangshan than an album filled with pictures of Master Xingyun, not only with the dalai lama and the pope, but with Vice President Gore, President Diosdado Macapagal of the Philippines, and His Excellency Sir Clarence Seignoret of the Commonwealth of Dominica as well?[8]

Contributing funds to the DNC would amplify this symbolic importance. Taiwan's citizens are well aware of the enormous amount of money and resources that the United States sank into the ROC economy in the 1950s and 1960s. For the DNC to request donations from one of the island's leading religious figures gives concrete evidence that the two societies are no longer patron and client but peers. Those living in Taiwan take great pride in the fact that they now dispense charity worldwide rather than receive it. Certainly such dynamics have been at work when Foguangshan and Ciji Gongde Hui have run social-service programs in the Philippines, Bangladesh, India, Nepal, South Africa, and the United States. The satisfaction of being able to give money to others and the prestige that accompanies such generosity are reward enough. No future restitution or favors are necessary or expected.

Master Xingyun would not agree with either of the motives proposed above. He chafes at any mention of influence peddling. He also strongly denies that he and his followers acted to gain benefit or prestige for themselves. Instead, he has proffered three explanations for sponsoring the banquet and leading his disciples in providing a donation to the DNC.

First, he insists that his motivation was expressing his deep gratitude to the United States. The master often emphasizes gratitude (*gan'en*) as an essential virtue for those engaged in Buddhist cultivation. Such gratitude must be pure, however, neither sycophantic in nature nor driven by any ulterior aim. During an interview with GAC investigators in June 1997, he explained: "I must play the role of elder to you since you are all young. Thirty or forty years ago President Truman ordered a fleet to protect Taiwan. The living standard was very low at the time. The United States usually asked Catholics and Protestants to give relief food. I told myself that, when Buddhism has the ability, I want to repay the United States. No matter what it may be, I want to help. Many disciples see me take the lead, so they emulate" (Government Affairs Committee 1997). In fact, this sense of gratitude has generally led Master Xingyun to favor the Republicans over the Democrats, for it has been the former who have pushed harder over the years to maintain military aid for Taiwan. His donation to the DNC, therefore, he explained as being an expression of his sincere appreciation for all that the American political system represents and all that it has done for his country.

Second, Master Xingyun has also said that he was acting on behalf of the Asian American community. If he was trying to "peddle influence," he was doing so, he insists, to benefit, not the government of Taiwan, but, rather, the Chinese American community. After Ven. Cirong attended a DNC fund-raiser at the Century Hotel in Los Angeles in July 1996, an article in a Foguang publication praised President Clinton for being "the first U.S. president to pay particular attention to Asian Americans" (IBPS *Quarterly*, winter 1993, 8). The article went on to state that, under Clinton, 197 Asian Americans had already been appointed to top government posts and a bill allowing one million Asians to immigrate to the United States had recently been ratified. Master Xingyun and his followers hoped to express their gratitude to the administration and to encourage the continuation of such policies. The people who had the most to gain through the Hsi Lai banquet were, admittedly, Chinese, but they were also Americans.

Of course, if this second explanation is to be given credence, it must be determined when a person of Chinese heritage can also claim to be an American. Master Xingyun assumes that any Chinese who spends time in the United States is more or less American. And this makes the master himself an American. As he told me in one interview: "The United States should not consider us to be aliens. I am also American; I have residency status. I always try to encourage Chinese Americans to assimilate into American society. It is not right to go to America but try to still live like a Chinese or Japanese. When you are in America, be American. When you come to Foguangshan, be a part of Foguangshan. When you are in a family, be a member of that family. When you are in a country, be a part of that nation" (Chandler 1997a).[9]

The perimeters of the Chinese American community are, therefore, murky.

The general American public tends to consider citizenship as a minimum requirement for identifying oneself as American. That this is the case became quite evident when, even after it became general knowledge that permanent residents have the right to donate funds to political parties, news reports continued to emphasize that the donations to the DNC by Foguang members were suspect because most of these people were not citizens. Legally, the debate centered on whether residents can still make such donations if they spend most of their time in their country of origin rather than in the United States. Culturally, the issue was one of identity: When do people truly have the right to wave the American flag? To what degree can people be Americans culturally even if they are not Americans legally? Do American ideals transcend territorial and juridical boundaries?

For Chinese, especially diaspora Chinese, cultural factors are much more important than territorial or political considerations in constituting identity. Because these factors are so fluid, a person can participate in multiple cultures simultaneously. Such openness to multiple allegiances is, as Homi K. Bhabha (1994, 4, 185) phrases it, fertile ground for cultural hybridity. Hence, Master Xingyun finds no incompatibility in claiming himself to be both thoroughly Chinese and fully American. For him, cultural identity depends on actualization of ideals, not on legal status. Globalization has created a new form of nomadic existence, one in which growing numbers of people spend appreciable amounts of time in two or more countries, thereby greatly relativizing the significance of citizenship. The flow of labor, capital, and information is now so fluid that the function of national boundaries has been greatly attenuated. The Foguang banquet for Gore, and, in fact, all the political-donations controversies of the 1996 electoral cycle, was an inevitable outgrowth of globalization's assault on each and every nation's sovereignty.

Third, in sponsoring the banquet and subsequently donating funds to the DNC, Master Xingyun repeatedly asserted, his overriding motivation was reaffirming his tie of affinity with the vice president. I described in chapter 2 above how *"jieyuan"* refers to planting the seed of the dharma in people's consciousness so that it may bear fruit in the future. I also noted that creating such a relationship with government leaders is especially meritorious since it makes it that much more likely that the seed will enjoy nurturing circumstances. This background clarifies Master Xingyun's motives for fostering a tie with Vice President Gore. The seed of the dharma has only recently been planted in the United States. No fruit may emerge in the immediate future, but the master is confident that, in due time, it will develop. Gore and others who now come to Hsi Lai Temple to garner political or financial support will eventually realize more noble intentions for visiting, and, because of the prestige that such leaders hold in American society, their favorable impression of Buddhism will affect a great number of others as well.

Master Xingyun's reliance on such a trickle-down method to promote Buddhism in the United States is quite evident in a statement (a portion of which has already been quoted in chapter 4 above) that he made to a group of American scholars two months before Hsi Lai Temple's official opening. In line with the conference's topic of "Religion and Society in the Tang and Song Dynasties," the master remarked that, in the early centuries of the common era, Buddhism had been able to assimilate into Chinese society quickly because it gained the support of that country's officials and scholars. He went on to add: "Mahayana Buddhism and American society are very compatible. Buddhism is different from other religions in its lack of exclusivity, its magnanimity, and its affinity with nature. Whether or not Americans can recover the golden era of Tang and Song dynasty Buddhism will depend on people's efforts. If those of high status and power support it, it will develop even faster" (Shi Xingyun 1994, vol. 1, entry for 14 October 1989).

As the number of American politicians visiting Hsi Lai Temple mounted, Master Xingyun told his disciples: "For us Buddhists to come to America and be able to receive positive acceptance by the U.S. government is our greatest vow and hope!" (Shi Xingyun 1994, vol. 3, entry for 23 January 1990). The master's observation that "Mahayana Buddhism and American society are very compatible" is a cornerstone assumption of his strategy for promoting Buddhism in the country and explains why he feels so confident that many Americans will soon follow Buddhist teachings. In his opinion: "Although America is not a Buddhist country, Americans have the character and spirit of Humanistic Buddhism and the Mahayana bodhisattva path."[10] In fact, he believes that America already displays many of the features of a pure land, by which he means that, compared to other nations of the world, its material prosperity, political system, and core values especially lend themselves to spiritual cultivation. Americans may not realize it, but they are already treading the Mahayana bodhisattva path.

The belief that America can be a pure land rests on the assumption that the bodhisattva path is related to, yet distinct from, institutionalized Mahayana Buddhism. This assumption has three implications. First, there are those outside the Mahayana Buddhist tradition who tread this path. The dharma that serves as the foundation for Buddhist teachings in fact permeates the entire universe. People are all potential Buddhists, all having buddha nature. Most, however, simply do not recognize this truth. Americans and others who unwittingly follow Buddhist dictates are, to adapt Karl Rahner's phrase, "anonymous Buddhists."[11] Second, not all those who self-identify as Mahayana Buddhists actually follow the path. Just as

Master Xingyun and other leading Foguang figures often refer to the compatibility of American values with the bodhisattva path, they also decry what they see as a straying away from bodhisattva ideals and practices by Chinese Buddhists since the Song dynasty. Finally, while not all Buddhists actualize the dharma as well as do some non-Buddhists, it is only through consciously recognizing the dharma as such that one can maximize one's potential. At a certain point, one must tap into the conceptual and pragmatic resources provided by the Buddhist tradition to continue treading the bodhisattva path. The Buddhist tradition acts as a map. One may tread the path without such a map, but it is quite easy to go astray without proper guidance.

As a non-Buddhist pure land, America is especially fertile ground for planting the seed of the dharma. The nation's principles already correspond with Mahayana ideals, so efforts must now concentrate on making its citizens favorably predisposed to the Buddhist message so that they will recognize the resonance of the value systems. Once this is accomplished, Americans will quite naturally adopt Buddhism since it provides a means for more deeply understanding and refining core American values. America has a dream, a dream as yet incompletely realized, but one that can be fulfilled through Buddhist practice. Adopting the Buddhist conceptual framework and techniques will make Americans more American. The true American is the Buddhist American. Because Americans already unwittingly follow the Mahayana path, they are more "Buddhist" than many putative Buddhists, yet a Buddhist far along the bodhisattva path is more "American" than any American.

On Being Chinese, American, and Buddhist

Did Master Xingyun invite Al Gore to Hsi Lai Temple to aid Taiwan business and political interests, to benefit his own organization, to help the Chinese American community, to express his gratitude to the United States, or to enhance American's potential as a place for Buddhist practice? Only he knows the answer for sure. All five motives may very well have played a role. Given that he is a Buddhist master, however, it makes sense that his primary goal in engaging in international politics has been Buddhist in nature.

This brings us back to Tang Degang's "From Master Huishen to Master Xingyun" (see chapter 9 above). Attributing the discovery of America to an Asian Buddhist rather than to a European Christian inverts the rhetoric of forebear and newcomer, thereby radically transforming the notions of national heritage and identity. Most Euro-Americans will continue to draw strength from their own myths. For Foguang Buddhists in America, however, to regard the United States as

Fusang is to place themselves within an ancient and noble missionary adventure. Master Xingyun, who was quite taken with Dr. Tang's work, noted in his diary: "Regretfully, after Master Huishen, no one else went to spread the dharma in America. Only today with Foguangshan's establishment of Hsi Lai Temple have Americans again regarded the dharma as important. Therefore, 'The New Discovery of Master Huishen' has allowed Hsi Lai Temple to gain that much more significance for the times" (Shi Xingyun 1994, vol. 3, entry for 2 January 1990).

As the title of Tang's paper asserts, Master Xingyun is the Huishen of the twentieth and twenty-first centuries, although he is not so much "discovering" a new land as "recovering" an ancient heritage. In other words, he and his disciples do not regard themselves to be asking Americans to adopt a foreign religion; they are helping them realign themselves with their true history and actualize their deepest ideals, thereby speeding them along the bodhisattva path and transforming their society into a full pure land.[12]

FAIR DINKUM BUDDHISM

Up until now, I have analyzed Foguangshan's globalization mainly in terms of its interplay with cultural identity issues within the Chinese American community. This focal point evolved quite naturally since, as we have seen, Foguangshan's earliest and most sustained overseas effort has been in North America and the vast majority of its devotees are ethnically Chinese. Nonetheless, the organization has expended considerable energy to plant branch temples elsewhere around the globe as well and to spread its message beyond the Chinese diaspora. I now turn to look more closely at two issues. First, I will continue the discussion of cultural identity but invert it, analyzing the interpretations given by non-Chinese Foguang devotees of the significance of their participation in a Chinese Buddhist organization. Second, I will consider what other methods in addition to *jieyuan* Master Xingyun and his devotees have employed to further their missionary goals among non-Chinese. Since this discussion will begin with a case study of Foguang activities in Australia, it will be helpful to set the scene by describing the group's network of temples on that continent.

FOGUANGSHAN DOWN UNDER

Foguangshan has established ten outposts in Australia. The flagship temple, which goes by the name of "Nan Tien" or "Southern Heaven," is located an hour's drive south of Sydney in the industrial city of Wollongong. By the time that it was completed in 1996, the complex had cost some A$50 million (approximately U.S.$30 million) to build. Facilities include a main shrine capable of accommodating eight hundred people, a 330-seat auditorium, a 190-seat lecture hall (with simultaneous translation capability), a large refectory, a museum, a meditation hall, and a library. Just beyond a pond to the right of the temple is the hundred-room Pilgrim's Lodge. To the left, a seven-story pagoda serves as a columbarium. The fifty-five acres on which the compound is located are perched aside a gentle slope. Nan Tien Temple owns only twenty-nine of these acres; the other twenty-six were leased to the monastery by the Wollongong city government for a century at A$1 per year, with the understanding that the temple would see to the plot's reforestation with native tropical vegetation. Nan Tien looks down over the main highway linking Sydney to coastal New South Wales. Just the other side of the hill behind the pagoda, one catches a glimpse of the massive steel works of BHP Steel, its tall smokestacks constantly spewing forth white clouds. After the sun sets, the gaily lit outline of both the temple and its pagoda are clearly visible for miles from the sharp escarpment rising just the other side of the Wollongong Valley.

BHP Steel played an important role in bringing Foguangshan to Wollongong. The president of the company had attended a conference in 1989 that had been sponsored by the China Steel Corporation (CSC) and that had taken place at Foguang headquarters (the president of CSC was a devotee of Master Xingyun's). Hearing that this wealthy Buddhist group was in the midst of founding a multimillion-dollar temple in the United States, the BHP president immediately recognized the potential boost in tourism that such a temple could spark in his hometown. The Wollongong City Council agreed and offered to supplement the twenty-nine acres to be donated by BHP for the project by leasing an additional twenty-six acres. Construction took over three years, and the final product was certainly impressive.

Nan Tien Temple is regarded by Foguangshan as its frontier post for introducing the dharma to the general Australian public. In fact, the closest enclave of Chinese immigrants is sixty miles to the north in Sydney.[13] Unlike at Foguangshan's other overseas centers, at Nan Tien the vast majority of visitors milling around the grounds are not East Asians. The temple is a favorite among school and senior citizen groups, who take tours, sample the vegetarian buffet, and perhaps spend a night in Pilgrim's Lodge. These groups are shown around the monastery, not by a cleric, but, rather, by one of the volunteers of the Wollongong BLIA's Euro-Australian subchapter. Nan Tien provides more English-language activities than do other Foguang temples. At least two meditation classes meet each week. Also offered are sutra study, vegetarian cooking, and *taijiquan*. English-speaking devotees are kept apprised of such activities and other news through a monthly newsletter. Owing to its very visible and striking architecture and its various outreach programs, Nan Tien unquestionably has a higher profile among non-Chinese locals than do other overseas Foguang centers, its public stature rivaled only by Hsi Lai Temple in the United States.

Chung Tien ("Central Heaven") Temple, Foguangshan's second largest monastery in Australia, has a much different feel and mission than does Nan Tien. Rather than overlooking a highway and factories, Chung Tien is nestled within a densely forested wildlife refuge just outside Brisbane. Koalas are frequently spotted slowly lumbering in the upper reaches of the eucalyptus trees surrounding the temple, and kangaroos visit the front entryway each evening to sample whatever flowers might be sprouting in the garden. The temple compound is much smaller than that of Nan Tien, although there are plans to expand significantly if the proper permits can be obtained (which has proved difficult because the temple is located in a nature sanctuary). Almost no Euro-Australians ever pass through Chung Tien's front gate. The Chinese devotee base, however, is considerable and quite vibrant, for there is a flourishing "Little Taiwan" in a nearby suburb. Every day at least a few devotees come to the temple, and the weekend Chinese-language school, dharma service, and vegetarian lunch consistently draw dozens of families. The ambience of Chung Tien is, therefore, much less that of a tourist attraction and more that of a community center for Chinese from Taiwan.

Foguangshan's other two branch temples in Australia are relatively small. Most of the devotees who frequent Melbourne Foguangshan or Foguangshan's Western Australia Vihara (located in Perth) come from Hong Kong or Southeast Asia. A majority speak Cantonese rather than Mandarin or Taiwanese. These communities are not as affluent as those supporting the Nan Tien and Chung Tien Temples. The monasteries themselves are simpler, with few external markings indicating that they are Chinese Buddhist establishments.[14] The common bond bringing together the devotees is also more tenuous, being based on a shared Chinese heritage rather than on linguistic compatibility or recent geographic proximity. Ironically, although "Foguangshan" appears in the names of both these temples, the connection with the headquarters and Master Xingyun is not so strongly felt. Devotees seem primarily to think of themselves as coming to a Chinese Buddhist temple; that it happened to have been founded by Foguangshan of Taiwan is not so important.

Promoting the Dharma in Heavenly Australia

It is no mere coincidence that Master Xingyun included the term *"tian"* (heaven) in the names of Foguangshan's two largest temples in Australia. His first morning on the continent in 1989, he awoke to the chirping of birds and the gentle fragrance of flowers. "The air was fresh, and from the room I could see the clouds and watch the sea," he noted in his diary. He continued: "The surroundings are incomparable. Australia is truly a paradise *[letu]* on earth" (Shi Xingyun 1994, vol. 1, entry for 9 September 1989).

The master and his disciples rave about the country's natural beauty and spacious, ideal living conditions, invariably referring to it as either a "paradise" or, more often, a "heaven" on earth. This is very much meant as a compliment, yet there is also a subtle critique in this characterization. Buddhists often say that, while existence is much more pleasurable in one of the heavens than it is on earth, the very lack of suffering renders such realms less suitable for self-cultivation, for there is little incentive spurring on devas to improve themselves or their lot. Foguang clerics tend to feel the same way about Australia: it is so peaceful and clean that its denizens have become complacent. One nun explained: "Because conditions are so good, people have little drive to seek an even better state. Unlike Taiwan or the United States, people are content with the status quo, so there is little drive to create even better conditions. That is why Australians have not contributed much to the advancement of technology or science. The work ethic is very laid back, with little drive to push oneself. This may, in fact, be bad for their spiritual advancement as well."

The small band of Euro-Australians who have joined the English-speaking subchapter of the Wollongong BLIA hardly see their country's pristine landscape and comfortable lifestyle as detrimental to promoting Buddhism. In fact, they regard Australia as the perfect setting in which to expunge the various customs and superstitions that have appended themselves to the tradition over the centuries in Asia. Because Buddhism has arrived on the continent only very recently, Australian practitioners see themselves as being in a better position to practice the dharma in its purest, unadulterated form than even the missionaries who have brought over the teachings. As several of Nan Tien's Euro-Australians phrased it to me, they are the ones best placed to practice "fair dinkum Buddhism," "fair dinkum" being the Australian English colloquial term meaning "genuine" or "the real thing." In other words, fair dinkum Buddhism is "true Buddhism," which, when pressed further, the Euro-Australian Foguang Buddhists described as being the Buddha's teachings shorn of ritual and pageantry.

The self-understanding of these Euro-Australian Buddhists introduces an interesting twist into the model currently employed by academics to describe the evolution of Buddhism in Western countries. This model, first formulated by Charles Prebish in the 1970s to characterize the emerging Buddhist tradition in the United States, identifies two parallel types of Buddhism: "ethnic Buddhism," or that practiced by immigrant groups, and "elite Buddhism," or that practiced by converts, who generally have been drawn from the upper socioeconomic classes. Scholars have generally followed Prebish in postulating that, while ethnic forms of Buddhism serve to preserve immigrant cultural identity and, therefore, tend toward conservatism, elite Buddhism concerns itself more with the transformation of society, thereby serving as a catalyst for change (see Prebish 1979, 51).

In this model, the Chinese devotees of Nan Tien, Chung Tien, Melbourne Foguangshan, and Foguangshan's Western Australia Vihara all practice ethnic Buddhism. Euro-Australian Foguang Buddhists are practitioners of elite Buddhism who nonetheless have joined an ethnic Buddhist community. Such devotees do see themselves as a catalyst for change. The focus of their attention, however, is not general society, as Prebish would predict, so much as the Buddhist tradition. In other words, for these devotees, the arrival of Buddhism in Australia is regarded as an opportunity to purge it of cultural accretions and superstitions, thereby returning the teachings to their "authentic" core form. No longer in China, yet not indigenous to Australia, the tradition is viewed as neither Chinese nor Australian but, rather, pure and simple Buddhism.

Of course, the opposite is really the case; what is being practiced at Nan Tien Temple is Chinese Australian Buddhism. Ironically, even the phrase "fair dinkum Buddhism" points to this hybrid status. The term "fair dinkum" evidently derives from Australia's nineteenth-century gold rush, which, as we have seen, attracted thousands of men from South China and led to the founding of Australia's earliest Chinatowns. The phrase combines the English word "fair" with the Cantonese term for gold nugget and, hence, originally meant "true gold" as opposed to fool's gold. Fair dinkum Buddhism is authentic Buddhism, not in the sense of being abstracted from all cultural context, but, rather, as a genuine expression of the coming together and harmonization of the Chinese, Australian, and Buddhist traditions.

The ambiguous status of Euro-Australian Foguang devotees as simultaneously members of both "ethnic" Buddhism and "elite" Buddhism underscores the limitations of differentiating religious groups on the basis of ethnicity. Instead of understanding the term "Chinese" as referring to ethnic identity, it may, in fact, be more fruitful to think of it as a cultural designation, hence parallel to the category "Australian." In other words, a person need not necessarily be ethnically Chinese to be a Chinese Australian Buddhist; the vast majority of those participating in the meditation classes at Nan Tien Temple certainly are not. Such individuals practice the Buddhist teachings as they have developed in and been mediated through Chinese culture. To the degree that Chinese elements come to the fore in the manner in which a person experiences the Buddhist teachings, that individual becomes, not only Buddhist, but Chinese as well, regardless of his or her ethnic background. The assumption of Chinese identity even finds explicit symbolic expression through the donning of traditional Chinese garb during dharma functions and the adoption of a Chinese dharma name on taking the triple refuge.

Other scholars have also called for an expanded definition of cultural China. Tu Wei-ming argues for a conceptualization incorporating three overlapping symbolic universes. First, there are the societies in which ethnic Chinese constitute a majority—China, Taiwan, Hong Kong, and Singapore. Second, there is the Chinese diaspora—those Chinese communities scattered throughout the world from Sydney to Paris. Finally, there are the individuals who seek to comprehend China intellectually and to bring this understanding to their own communities. This latter category includes teachers, scholars, journalists, industrialists, and writers of a variety of linguistic backgrounds. Ironically, states Tu, "for the last four decades the international discourse on cultural China has unquestionably been shaped by the third symbolic universe more than by the first two combined" (1991a, 13).

Although Tu does not explicitly state that such individuals need not be ethnically Chinese, his model strongly implies that participation in the Chinese cultural universe, both as receptor and as contributor, extends far beyond, not only geopolitical, but also ethnic definitions of the Sinic world. Tu wishes to emphasize the effect that individuals who fall into the third category have on Chinese society. My emphasis is on the profound influence that the Chinese worldview can have on those who sympathetically delve into its value system. Thus, employing "Chinese" primarily as a cultural rather than an ethnic designation serves to give nuance to the discussion of self-identity. So long as the analysis of the dynamics between Chinese and Australian (or American, or French, etc.) identities remains couched in ethnic terms, it perpetuates the assumption that the issue is mainly sociological in nature. In fact, however, the tensions and interplay between Chinese and Australian identities are as much psychological as sociological. The "culture war" occurs, not only between groups, but within each individual.

Just as the designations "Chinese" and "Australian" refer to cultural symbolic systems, so does the term "Buddhist." The issue before us, then, when considering the dynamics of self-understanding for those who practice a Chinese form of Buddhism in Australia is one essentially concerned with the tensions and transformations that occur with the internalization of three cultural complexes whose practices and values at points conflict. The Australian preoccupation with rugged individualism, for example, clashes with the Chinese emphasis on filial piety and reverence for authority. Similarly, many of the Christian elements that underlie the assumptions shaping mainstream Australian values differ radically from the Buddhist worldview: the notions of sin and an eternal soul, for instance, versus those of *duhkha (ku)* and *sunyata (kong)*.[15] The felt need to unearth fair dinkum Buddhism derives from a desire to assert a sense of stability and personal authenticity that will transcend the sociological and psychological tensions that inevitably accompany the meeting of multiple cultural systems, in this case the Chinese, Australian, and Buddhist worldviews.

LOCALIZING THE DHARMA

Two Methods for Spreading the Dharma

When a news reporter from Wollongong asked Ven. Xinding how Foguangshan planned to spread Buddhism among non-Chinese Australians, he replied: "People will increasingly come simply through human curiosity. Seeing the beautiful temple, they will be drawn to see what goes on inside" (Duffy 1987). As this statement indicates, clerics believe that the very splendor of Buddhism, and the impressive, unique way in which it is propagated by Foguangshan, will naturally draw people's interest. This mode of operation assumes that, as all people share buddha nature, those who have proper roots will spontaneously seek out the dharma once they have had even the slightest exposure to it. Hence, there is no need to proselytize aggressively. Buddhists can rely instead on simply sparking people's curiosity so that they will ask about the dharma on their own initiative. Such a tactic calls, not only for creating impressive structures and organizing large-scale events to attract attention, but also for accentuating the uniqueness of both Buddhism and Chinese culture.

In dialectical tension with the method of celebrating difference to spark curiosity is the recognition that too strong a sense of foreignness can repel people and incite prejudice. Foguang devotees from Malaysia and the Philippines report that they must keep a low profile to avoid harassment. In Indonesia, where relations with the majority Javanese Muslim population are quite fragile, and where it is reportedly illegal to import literature written in Chinese, devotees have had to smuggle in Foguang material. There are also significant challenges in promoting Buddhism in Africa. There, people look askance at the black robes and tonsured heads of clerics since the color black is associated with evil magical power and a person will usually shave his or her head only after the death of a parent or some other close relative. Buddhist monastics are, therefore, vulnerable to suspicions and often the target of countermagic.

There have been hurdles in promoting the dharma in the United States as well. It took nearly a decade punctuated by six volatile town meetings before permission was granted for the construction of Hsi Lai Temple. Only after several years of carefully cultivating good relations with neighbors and local religious leaders did the accusations that the Hsi Lai community was a cult die down, unfortunately to be raised again with the DNC political-donations controversy.

To lessen tensions with the mainstream society in each country in which Foguangshan establishes a temple, and to smooth the transition for those attracted to the dharma, Master Xingyun has called for the "localization" (*bentuhua*) of Buddhism. By this, he means that centuries-old customs can be replaced by other customs more appropriate to the region in question. The essential teachings remain the same; only culture-specific practices vary. The difficulty in applying this method lies in determining just where core truth ends and custom begins. In fact, the debate over the degree to which to localize touches every aspect of temple life: Should dharma functions be altered in any way? What language should be used in conducting various activities? What kind of food should be served? What music is appropriate?

Master Xingyun believes that the people most competent to resolve these issues are natives of the non-Buddhist countries in question who have gone through intensive training in a Foguang academy, preferably on the campus at the headquarters. The ideal is to find such individuals who aspire to renounce. The Foguangshan Monastic Buddhist Academy has a special department to tend to the education of such candidates. As they are for all monastic academy students, tuition, room, and board are provided free of charge. For those who come from an underprivileged background, airfare to Foguangshan is also taken care of.

To date, however, Foguangshan has managed to keep few such clerics within the organization. Many leave within a few months of matriculating in the college; others make it through the period of training but disappear soon after. Non-Chinese monastics typically voice two frustrations: either they find it too difficult to acclimate to Chinese customs and values, or they feel that their Chinese brethren do not take them seriously. One French nun who had lived in the Foguang temple outside Paris for a year and who was preparing to return there after having completed an additional year's training at the headquarters, explained:

> I think it has been a challenge for me, but also for the people here. Because, when I arrived [at the headquarters], I could feel that the people were very afraid to receive a French nun. Because they didn't know how to deal with me. They didn't know, and I didn't know how to deal with them. So, in the beginning, we tried our best to understand together. It was

difficult, but, fortunately, some nuns took care of me. They spoke English, so it was easier for me. In the beginning, every detail in the daily life was very strange. Just like to use the Taiwanese toilet—you know I used it in the wrong way! Also, for example, the way for me, here, to walk, to sit, and to talk. Everything was very different. In the beginning, some of the nuns asked me to follow the Chinese way for everything. But I think that maybe I am lucky because I said, not directly "no," but I just tried to explain to them: "OK, I am a nun, and I belong to Foguangshan, but it is just like if you want to ask the cat to become a dog and a dog to become a cat. It is just ridiculous. It is impossible. You can ask a cat to become a good cat, but that's all." So I tried to tell them: "OK, I will try to learn about Foguang rules and about Foguang Buddhism if I can do it, but don't ask me to think like you, to walk like you, because it is not possible. This is not natural for me." So I think they understood very well. (Chandler 1996b)

The nun who made these comments did not return to Paris as planned. Instead, she went to India and was not heard from again. Her case is typical. Of the approximately one dozen Europeans and Americans who have tonsured under Master Xingyun, only two may still be found in the Foguang order. The arrangement to bring young men and women from Ladakh, India, to Foguangshan to be groomed as monastics has also suffered a high dropout rate, with many of the students requesting to be repatriated within two or three months of arriving in Taiwan.

An African Pure Land and an African Sangha

Foguangshan's most sustained effort to localize Buddhism through developing a native sangha has occurred in Africa, where the order has opened the continent's largest Buddhist monastery and only seminary. Nanhua Temple sits on a broad field overlooking Bronkhorstspruit, a middle-sized township not far from Pretoria. "Nanhua" has a double significance, meaning both "Southern Flower" and "South Africa–China."

The story of the temple's founding is similar to that of Nan Tien Temple's in that, in both cases, it was the local government that approached Foguangshan with the idea of building a facility. The Bronkhorstspruit government officials were even more ambitious than their Wollongong counterparts were, for they hoped, not only to spur tourism, but also to establish an entire Chinese community that could galvanize industry in the region. To do so, they offered to grant Foguangshan a plot of land gratis if, in exchange, the master would help them attract 550 investors willing to relocate to the town. By purchasing one of the small lots in the compact "Platteland Chinatown" for a sum of R 750,000 (approximately U.S.$125,000), investors would be assured that their families would receive permanent residency on the completion of their fourth year in the country. This was to be a deal to everyone's advantage: the immigrants would enjoy the cleaner environment, open space, and cheaper living costs than could be found in Taiwan, the local economy would benefit from the influx of wealth and managerial talent, and the Foguang branch temple would have a ready-made devotee base.

Master Xingyun saw this project as a perfect opportunity to establish a Foguang Humanistic Pure Land. He has never described Africa itself as either a pure land or a heaven. Instead, he has referred to its pristine simplicity (*danchun*) and raw potential. Nanhua Temple is by no means regarded as a choice assignment by clerics. Monks and nuns especially fear the violence of South African society.[16] Yet it is this very combination of natural beauty and widespread suffering that, when brought together with technological know-how and Chinese Buddhist culture, can transcend a mere heaven to create a this-worldly pure land.

In 1992, construction on the ambitious project began. First to be completed was the Devotees' Center, a sprawling two-story hexagonal structure whose central courtyard is surrounded by a reception area, gift shop, library, museum, dining hall, and offices. On the second floor are a teahouse and sixty-seven guest rooms. The town equipped the future community with the necessary infrastructure. Streets with such names as "Fo Kuang," "Pu Men," "Tz'u Pei," and "Nanhua" were paved in overlapping semicircles jutting out from the Devotees' Center (thereby both forming the shape of a lotus and providing protection against drive-by shootings). Plumbing and electrical facilities were installed. Ornate Chinese gates identified each of the four entrances. All was set for the country's newest Chinatown to emerge.

These preparations were finished in 1994, just as the Mandela government came to power. With new political leaders also came shifts in policies, including a decision that ROC investors wishing to settle in Bronkhorstspruit would have to pay, not R 750,000, but double that amount. The Taiwanese entrepreneurs repudiated this amendment, arguing that the new government had an obligation to honor the contract that had already been agreed on. The matter remained in the courts through 1999, at which point the Republic of South Africa severed its official ties with the ROC, essentially terminating the court proceedings and, therefore, any hope that a Little Taipei would emerge on the Transvaal plains.

With the exception of a few homes (all sporting Taiwanese architecture), the expanse around Nanhua Devotees' Center remains vacant. Dozens of lights each evening shed an eerie glow on the deserted lanes encircling the complex. There is only one building currently under construction: Nanhua Temple's U.S.$26 million Great Heroes Hall.[17] This hall, due to be completed in the year 2004, is vivid testimony to Foguangshan's determination to follow through with its side of the deal even as all other parties have forsaken the project.

In the absence of a local Chinese community to support the temple, the Foguang leadership has found itself scurrying to raise the millions of dollars necessary to finish construction, maintain the premises, and support the monastic and student communities. The Venerable Huili, the monk in charge of Foguangshan's African operations, returned to Taiwan over one hundred times from 1992 to 1997 in his quest to nurture long-term commitments from patrons. Both he and Harold Lemke, an American lay devotee who has played a major role in running the temple's seminary, recognize that the Nanhua complex will not always be able to rely on the generosity of donors in the ROC.[18] The temple has, therefore, returned to a fund-raising method practiced by Buddhist sanghas in China up through the Republican era: the renting out of farmland. Nanhua has purchased four large parcels of land and created a joint venture with a farmer from Taiwan to raise maize, soy, and wheat. For now the produce is being sold on the open market, but the intention is also to set up factories to turn out baked goods and other vegetarian fare. The Nanhua leadership believes that, eventually, 60 percent of the temple's budget can be taken care of through these enterprises.

Great Heroes Hall is not being built for the benefit of local devotees—there simply are not any present—but so that triple altar ordinations can take place on African soil. Now that political circumstances have rendered impossible the creation in the near future of a Foguang pure land, the focus of activity at Nanhua Temple has shifted so that it has developed into Foguangshan's premiere station for undertaking the localization of Buddhism through the establishment of an indigenous sangha. The temple took its first steps toward realizing this goal in 1994, when it opened the doors to its seminary. By the turn of the millennium, the organization had provided full scholarships allowing some two hundred students, not only from South Africa, but also from Congo, Tanzania, Malawi, and Madagascar to register for classes.

The young men who have come to the seminary have known almost nothing about Buddhism when they arrived. Most had applied after reading the newspaper advertisements promising an education with free lodging, food, and transportation, not to mention access to a weight room and training in martial arts. The students have soon realized, however, that these perquisites come at a price: once having taken the shramanera vows, which all do on entering the program, they must abstain from alcohol and contact with women. In fact, the students rarely even leave the seminary compound, going into town only once a week to help care for children with AIDS at a Catholic orphanage.

The neophyte Buddhists encounter other challenges as well. Having grown up in different regions, tribal animosities run high. For the first several months, fights and threats of violence occur regularly. To deflate such tensions, the seminary tries to make dormitory assignments ensuring that no more than two of the six residents in each room share a tribal or linguistic heritage, although this is often difficult to accomplish. Along with learning to get along with ethnic rivals, the Africans must acclimate themselves to Chinese Buddhist culture. As novices, they tonsure and wear gray monastic robes. Their days, filled with classes in the Chinese language, East Asian culture, and Buddhist teachings, begin and end with chanting and meditation. All meals are vegetarian, to be eaten in silence.

Not surprisingly, the rate of attrition is extremely high, especially the first few months. Only half a dozen students have made it all the way through the program's full three years, and even these six, who spent their third year at Foguang headquarters in preparation for taking full ordination in Bodhgaya, eventually returned to lay life.[19] Fewer than one-quarter of the sixty-three young men who matriculated in 1998 persisted even one year, and only four stayed for the entire second year. Smitten by such a high dropout rate, the seminary raised its entrance standards, requiring candidates to pass a written and oral examination testing their basic knowledge of Buddhism (based on four books supplied to them by Nanhua), and limiting admission to twenty students. This tactic bore fruit, for twelve of the twenty who joined the program in 1999 persisted throughout their freshman year.

While the seminary students who have stuck it out have had to make major adjustments, Foguangshan has also shown a sincere effort to respect indigenous culture and to ease the shramaneras' transition to monastic life. The novices wear gray work robes rather than the usual black cassocks to avoid association with evil magical power. The rules requiring silence in dormitories and prohibiting singing and dancing, all strictly enforced at other seminaries, do not apply; music is simply too integral to African culture to deny frequent outlets. There is also no insistence that the students don their robes during summer break. This both avoids problems with family (many of the young men come from devoted Christian or Muslim households) and makes it less likely that the reputation of Buddhism will be stained if any of the young men break one of the shramanera vows.

Despite the inability thus far firmly to establish Africa's first band of monks, both Ven. Huili and Master Xingyun are moderately satisfied with the progress to this point. Several of the young men, despite having returned to lay life, have remained in contact with Nanhua. One in Tanzania has opened an orphanage, which Foguangshan plans to support. Several others have stayed on in Bronkhorstspruit to help keep the temple grounds. Yet others have used their Chinese-language skills to find employment in trading firms. The Foguang leadership keeps a long-term perspective on missionary work. Those who renounce briefly as shramaneras in this life will return in their next existence to take the full vows. The Venerable Huili has, therefore, pledged to spend, not only the rest of this life, but his next four incarnations as well spreading the dharma in Africa.

Along with such determination is also a degree of frustration and a rethinking of method. By age twenty, when most of the men come to the seminary, habits are already deeply ingrained and, therefore, difficult to rechannel. Any hope of a deep commitment to the Buddhist way of life requires contact at an earlier age. Nanhua is, therefore, turning much of its energies to founding an orphanage. The first eight boys, all of ages seven or eight, were admitted in the early months of 2000. For now they are housed in a small building just across from Devotees' Center. Eventually, the expectation is to build a facility sufficient to house six hundred wards. Two populations of orphans will live side by side. Along with the children will be the other group that is being left behind by Africa's AIDS epidemic: the elderly. The young will, thereby, benefit from two sources of wisdom: the elderly passing on to them the best of African culture and Foguang clerics teaching life skills and Buddhist values.

THE LIMITS AND DANGERS OF LOCALIZATION

Accompanying the frustration with the inability of most non-Chinese (whether African, Australian, American, or European) to acclimate to Foguang monastic life is the fear that Chinese clerics and lay monastics who are posted abroad may acculturate too much, losing sight of Chinese and Buddhist values. There is some justification for this concern, for several clerics who have been stationed abroad for a long period confided that, if they were to be sent back to fill a post at the headquarters or a temple in Taiwan, they would find it very difficult to reacclimate. As one nun observed, she had come to feel much more comfortable in her adopted country than she did during her periodic returns to Taiwan. Another nun had a more sober view, revealing that she felt herself to be neither a part of her present environment nor at home in Taiwan.

Young monastics are regarded as being especially vulnerable to outside influences. It is for this reason that the English-language program of the Division of International Studies remains at Foguang headquarters rather than being moved to an English-speaking country. Foguang bylaws stipulate that a person must have renounced for at least five years before being eligible to be stationed abroad. Until a cleric has reached a certain level of cultivation, it is feared that curiosity for the novel may lead him or her astray. Nuns will be warned by Master Xingyun to keep their distance from foreign men. When a particularly beautiful and vivacious bhikshuni was on her way to be stationed in London, the master instructed her not to talk with any man during her entire stay. On another occasion, as he saw off a young lay monastic about to go to America, he told her that she was a rose but then asked whether she had yet grown thorns to protect herself. Just as concern over monastics losing their sense of identity has reasonable cause, the unease over the potential for romantic entanglement is also warranted; both the nuns whom I had met at Hsi Lai Temple in 1992 who ultimately returned to lay life did so because of amorous affairs.

The debate over the extent and ways in which Chinese Buddhist practice is to be localized affects laity even more than it does clerics, especially those devotees who are either non-Chinese or ethnic Chinese who have grown up outside China. Non-Chinese attracted to Foguang temples generally fall into two groups: Sinophiles, many of whom wish to take on a full Chinese persona, and those primarily interested in Buddhist teachings. The former are fascinated by Chinese customs, ritual, and language and, therefore, typically prefer to interact with the Chinese devotees rather than with any other non-Chinese who may also have become part of the community. The latter have only passing interest in things Chinese and, as we saw in the discussion of fair dinkum Buddhism, may even wish to strip the Buddhist teachings of what they see as Chinese cultural accretions.

The localization debate is arguably most keenly felt by second- and third-generation overseas Chinese. During the 1997 BLIA Youth Conference, a student from Malaysia said that he and others at his temple had held some activities not considered traditionally Buddhist and that, as a result, they had been reprimanded by the resident monastics. He felt that the criticism was unjustified and asserted that there had to be more openness to adapting to the lifestyle of young overseas Chinese. A woman disagreed, responding: "As Buddhists, we must maintain a strong line between right and wrong. Just because others do it doesn't mean that we should do it. We have to have a different standard."

This interchange brings up two issues. First, although the young man from Malaysia did not specify the types of activities that he and his friends had held, one can assume that they were much more influenced by global pop culture than they were by the country's dominant Islamic lifestyle. This underscores the complexity of today's world, in which multiple cultural worldviews, both religious and secular, converge in nearly every society. Second, the young woman's response reminds us that, because custom is so tightly bound up with notions of morality, any change in practice is often regarded as vitiating ethical standards.

The real issue however, is not so much one of morality as one of identity. I noted earlier in this chapter that the first prong of the Foguang globalization program is to act as a bridge back to the Chinese cultural homeland. The organization's capacity to serve as a vehicle to preserve Chinese identity is directly undermined by any effort to localize practice or to harmonize it with global pop culture. These three aspects of globalization are, therefore, in constant tension with one another. For Foguangshan to be able to claim itself as an international operation transcending all ethnic and cultural boundaries, it must extend itself beyond its core Chinese base. To the degree that it does so, however, it risks ostracizing its most important source of devotees and, hence, financial support.

Thus far, the vast majority of Foguang overseas temples have opted to continue to accentuate their Chinese heritage, making a few symbolic gestures toward accommodating local and global custom. Temples might provide a spoon and fork rather than chopsticks in the refectory, for instance, or clerics may shake hands with lay visitors. For the most part, however, life in the temple is essentially the same as it would be if it were located in Taiwan. In fact, non-Chinese who come to visit are frequently referred to as "foreigners" *(laowai)*.

These difficulties experienced by Foguang devotees in negotiating cultural boundaries point to the limitations of any language of global citizenry that implies a negation or transcendence of local ties. Exposure to the globalization of market and media forces and the setting adrift of imagined communities from their territorial anchorage interact either to multiply cultural allegiances or, as is often the case, to trigger retrenchment, that is, a reaffirmation of the primacy of one particular imagined community. Chinese Foguang devotees have mostly opted for this latter tactic as they have searched for stability in an increasingly fluid world system. Despite the predominance of this strategy, they nonetheless recognize that the global conditions of postmodernity call for an approach that better accords with the inevitable hybridity of contemporary life. I will conclude this book by exploring the Foguang Buddhist paradigm for global citizenry, a paradigm that empowers devotees, not only to come to terms with the global scope of humankind's cultural hybridity, but even to harness the dynamism of these conditions to further self-cultivation.

Conclusion: Global Homelessness

HOMELESSNESS

In the introduction to this book I quoted Heidegger's comment: "Homelessness is coming to be the destiny of the world" (Heidegger [1947] 1977, 219). Others have employed similar language to describe the modern human condition. In his book of essays treating the exploration of Australia, Paul Carter observes: "We are almost all migrants; and even if we have tried to stay at home, the conditions of life have changed so utterly in this century that we find ourselves strangers in our own house" (1992, 7-8). The anthropologist Iain Chambers echoes Carter:

> To be a stranger in a strange land, to be lost (in Italian *spaesato*—"without a country"), is perhaps a condition typical of contemporary life. To the forcibly induced migrations of slaves, peasants, the poor and the ex-colonial world that make up so many of the hidden histories of modernity, we can also add the increasing nomadism of modern thought. Now that the old house of criticism, historiography and intellectual certitude is in ruins, we all find ourselves on the road. Faced with a loss of roots, and the subsequent weakening in the grammar of "authenticity," we move into a vaster landscape. Our sense of belonging, our language and the myths we carry in us remain, but no longer as "origins" or signs of "authenticity" capable of guaranteeing the sense of our lives. They now linger on as traces, voices, memories and murmurs that are mixed in with other histories, episodes, encounters.
>
> This memory of primary loss [of home], persistently inscribed in the uncertain becoming of the outward journey, has made of exile a suggestive symbol of our times. Indeed, a significant tendency in present-day critical thought, confronted with the shrinkage of the European rationale that once claimed to speak for all and everything, is to adopt metaphors of movement, migration, maps, travel and sometimes a seemingly facile tourism. (Chambers 1994, 18-19, 2-3)

Such metaphors retain both positive and negative connotations. In some instances, the instability and insecurity accompanying movement and the meeting of cultures come to the fore. In *The Homeless Mind*, Peter Berger, Brigitte Berger, and Hansfried Kellner make the sobering observation that, with the breakdown of integrated, coherent life worlds through the pluralization of social structure, "*modern man has suffered from a deepening condition of homelessness.*" Later, the authors elaborate:

> The pluralistic structures of modern society have made the life of more and more individuals migratory, ever-changing, mobile. . . . Not only are an increasing number of individuals in a modern society uprooted from their original social milieu, but, in addition, no succeeding milieu succeeds in becoming truly "home" either. It is important to understand . . . that this external mobility has correlates on the level of consciousness. A world in which everything is in constant motion is a world in which certainties of any kind are hard to come by. Social mobility has its correlate in cognitive and normative mobility. What is truth in one context of the individual's social life may be error in another. What was considered right at one stage of the individual's social career becomes wrong in the next. Once more, the anomic threat of these constellations is very powerful indeed. (Berger, Berger, and Kellner 1973, 82, 184)

The homelessness of modern life has had an especially devastating effect on religion, according to Berger, Berger, and Kellner, for the pluralization of religious worldviews has thrown into doubt the plausibility of any of them, thereby secularizing both society and individual consciousness. In so doing, it has served critically to undermine those definitions of reality that previously made the finitude, fragility, and mortality of the human condition easier to bear.

The mobility of modern life that has spawned homelessness also has its positive aspects, note Berger, Berger, and Kellner, for geographic and social migrancy has contributed greatly to people's freedom and autonomy. Both Carter and Chambers, as well as Edward Said, have tapped into the transformative dynamism characteristic of movement to develop it as a powerful symbol for postmodern existence. Said points out that, because both migrancy and exile involve a "discontinuous state of being," they provide "a potent, even enriching, motif of modern culture": "The exile knows that in a secular and contingent world, homes are always provisional. Borders and barriers which enclose us within the safety of familiar territory can also become prisons, and are often defended beyond reason or necessity. Exiles cross borders, break barriers of thought and experience" (Said 1990, 365). Chambers asserts that migrancy provides a more effective symbol for modern existence than does mere travel since it "involves a movement in which neither the points of departure nor those of arrival are immutable or certain. It calls for a dwelling in language, in histories, in identities that are constantly subject to mutation. Always in transit, the promise of a homecoming—completing the story, domesticating the detour—becomes an impossibility. History gives way to histories, as the West gives way to the world" (Chambers 1994, 5).

Stuart Hall makes the same observation: "Migration is a one way trip. There is no 'home' to go back to" (Hall 1987, 44). Carter very much agrees with such characterizations, describing "the authentic migrant perspective" as being based on "an intuition that the opposition between here and there is itself a cultural construction, a consequence of thinking in terms of fixed entities and defining them oppositionally. It might begin by regarding movement, not as an awkward interval between fixed points of departure and arrival, but as a mode of being in the world. The question would be, then, not how to arrive, but how to move, how to identity convergent and divergent movements; and the challenge would be how to notate such events, how to give them a historical and social value" (Carter 1992, 101).

Master Xingyun would find nothing surprising in such observations. He would probably even aver that the Buddha had recognized these same truths and that clerics have put them into practice for the last twenty-five hundred years. Since he retired as abbot of Foguangshan in 1985, the master has been said to "wander the four seas like a cloud." This is the ideal lifestyle of all Buddhist venerables, who, as one sutra phrases it, on leaving home become "free everywhere, at odds with none, and well content with this or that" (Conze 1979, 79). The constant movement and simple life represented by forgoing any fixed abode embody the Buddha's teaching of impermanence and his ideals of detachment and equanimity. Shakyamuni and his disciples traveled daily in search of alms, taking refuge each evening in a convenient grove on the outskirts of some town. Only during the monsoon season did they stop their peregrinations to wait out the rains. Even in China, where monasticism has been the norm, clerics through the centuries have hoped to "travel the four quarters" (*canfang*) as symbolized by the country's four Buddhist pilgrimage mountains. To have an ordination certificate whose borders were embossed with the seals of China's most renowned monasteries was a source of pride, especially if one had prostrated every three steps over the course of the journey. Homelessness is not an undesirable state to be avoided or overcome. It is a religious ideal.[1]

Until recently, only clerics enjoyed the benefits to self-cultivation afforded by long-term homelessness, and they enacted this lifestyle within the borders of the Middle Kingdom. With the development of international migration and increased global mobility, all Chinese who have left the homeland partake of the itinerant life. For expatriate laity, homelessness does not entail foregoing a family, but it does involve separation from relatives, friends, and Chinese society. Even those who have remained within Taiwan are homeless, both because of their political separation from the mainland and because of the Westernizing and homogenizing effects of globalization.

Buddhist monks and nuns serve as symbolic guides revealing to lay devotees that homelessness is not at all debilitating or anomic but, in fact, the best condition for spiritual growth. Foguang clerics, shifting posts of duty every three years, are the paragons of global citizenry. For them, the badge of honor is not an ordination certificate filled with the seals of temples but a passport covered with the entry visas of various nations. One reason that the Huishen myth appeals to Foguang devotees is its transnational flavor. After all, Ven. Huishen was not Chinese but, rather, an Indian monk who merely lived in China before moving on to spend the majority of his life in America. The designations "Indian," "Chinese," and "American" were fleeting and secondary. First and foremost Ven. Huishen was a Buddhist.

Master Xingyun similarly lacks strong association with a particular place. He often notes that people in Taiwan refer to him as "that monk from the mainland." When he visited the People's Republic, however, and during his travels abroad, people have called him "that monk from Taiwan." Master Xingyun is, like Venerable Huishen, a monk without a home. This is, in the master's view, not a negative, but a positive, for it allows him personally to symbolize the ability of Buddhism to transcend all such nationalistic designations. As he once said to me in an interview: "I don't feel that you are Americans. I also don't feel that I am Chinese. We are all global. We are all the same. . . . If we could join together with one another with no regard to nationality or race, it would be wonderful. So [the] global character [of Foguangshan] doesn't simply mean building temples in various places; we want to spread peace, equality, forbearance, friendship, respect, tolerance, everywhere to everyone" (Chandler 1996a). Although Master Xingyun may say, "We are all global," his call to deaccentuate national identity serves to shift a person's primary loyalty to the vehicle that allows such deemphasis to occur, that is, to Buddhism. We are all global in that we all have buddha nature. This recognition occurs in tandem with the fading away of national and other local allegiances.

Such rhetoric points to what may be a growing trend in postmodernity, one in which the primary referent for identity increasingly reverts from national back to religious symbols and myths. It is more than happenstance that secularization occurred during the same period as the rise of nations. Religion and nationhood are in tension with one another as contending sources of primary allegiance and identity. The attenuation of national sovereignty brought about by global capitalism has left a vacuum, one easily filled by religious traditions since their worldviews incorporate the language of both particularity and universality. Postmodernity may, therefore, spur people once again to align themselves more fully with reconstructed elements of traditions that have been more or less under siege during modern times. In other words, while modernity may have been inimical to religion, as Berger, Berger, and Kellner aver, postmodernity may prove more congenial to such worldviews. It may prove so because, despite the continued and even accelerated pluralization of religious life worlds, within each are resources that give spiritual significance to this very plurality.

From the Foguang perspective, modern globalization is by no means antithetical to traditional Buddhist ideals or practices. Each realizes the other since, through globalization, people come to realize the truth of the Mahayana Buddhist doctrines of impermanence and universal interdependence. Master Xingyun and his devotees firmly believe that the Buddha, the dharma, and the sangha are not relics of the past but harbingers of postmodernity, actualizing the spiritual potential of economic, political, and cultural globalization.

GLOBAL IDENTITY

"I am a global person." This seems like a simple enough statement. Yet the significance of such self-identification can be determined only through carefully unraveling the skein of concepts and symbols within which it is entangled. A methodological issue that has permeated this book has been a concern for attending to the subtlety of language. What does a particular person or group mean when speaking of "modernization" and "globalization," "democracy" and "equality"? A common vocabulary does not necessarily entail a unified conceptualization of experience. When we forget that, important distinctions can be glossed over and communication compromised.

I have paid especial attention to the discourse of national and religious identity as it has been transformed through processes of globalization. Who is Chinese, who is American, and who is Buddhist? Scholars should handle with great care any group's lexicon of self-identification. For example, when the term "Mahayana" is used by Chinese Buddhists, it almost invariably carries normative and even polemical implications. If scholars wish to adopt such terminology for their own use, they should pay strict attention that the polemical penumbra is not unwittingly imported as well. The concepts "Mahayana," "Theravada," "Humanistic Buddhism," and "engaged Buddhism" are, in my opinion, of greatest value to scholars, not as heuristic categories, but as opportunities to better comprehend the self-understanding of those individuals and groups who employ them.[2]

Every statement of self-identification is embedded in a rich personal and communal history. Consider once again the statement, "I am a global person." For Master Xingyun, to be global means first and foremost to be actively carrying out the Mahayana vow of universal liberation. He sees himself as doing so through harmonizing the best of Buddhism and modernity. The master is a modernist precisely because he believes that certain techniques and values that have evolved in contemporary society hold profound import for human fulfillment. In fact, in his opinion, ultimate liberation is no longer possible without tapping the potential of these relatively new methods, norms, and ideals. Nonetheless, he remains a religious modernist in that he considers the secular modern worldview in and of itself insufficient for actualizing universal salvation. Humankind's highest goal requires the supramundane wisdom of the dharma.

Just as the master has secularized the sacred, sacralized the secular, modernized the traditional, and traditionalized the modern, he has also globalized the local and localized the global. He has globalized the local through an aggressive campaign to internationalize the Foguang organization and expand its devotee base beyond the Chinese community. As he has done so, he has localized the global, that is, developed yet one more particular rendition of the concept "global." If there are multiple modernities, then there are most certainly also multiple globalities. What Master Xingyun as Buddhist master means by "I am a global person" is, ironically, quite distinctive.

Appendix: Chronological Table: Master Xingyun and Foguangshan

YEAR	EVENT
1927	Master Xingyun is born in Jiangdu, Jiangsu Province, on the twenty-second day of the seventh lunar month, the third of four children.
1931	Master Xingyun becomes a vegetarian, influenced by his maternal grandmother.
1937	Master Xingyun's father goes on business trip to Nanjing, never returns.
1939	Master Xingyun goes with his mother in search of his father, midway to Nanjing vows to renounce, takes tonsure under Master Zhikai at Nanjing's Qixiashan, given outer and inner dharma names "Wuche" and "Jinjue."
1941	Master Xingyun receives full ordination at Qixiashan.
1945	Master Xingyun studies at Jiaoshan Buddhist Academy. Attends a class on personnel training taught by Master Taixu, and reads his works extensively.
1947	Master Xingyun becomes principal of White Pagoda Elementary School. Briefly detained by both Nationalists and Communists, each attempting to gain intelligence about the other.
1949	Master Xingyun follows Nationalist army to Taiwan as part of medical relief team of clerics. Arrested by Kuomintang (KMT), along with many other clerics, on suspicion of vagrancy, banditry, and espionage. Incarcerated for twenty-three days. Spends next few years living in various temples in the Taipei area.
1950s	After receiving reports that Master Xingyun is in radio contact with mainland China and is disseminating pro-Communist literature, the police follow him for one year.
1954	Master Xingyun becomes abbot of Leiyin Temple in Yilan, a small city in northeastern Taiwan. According to Foguang literature, the master soon becomes the first monk in Taiwan to use a slide projector with dharma talks and also organizes the island's first Buddhist choir.
1957	Master Xingyun founds *Awakening the World (Jueshi)*.
1963	Master Xingyun goes to India, Thailand, Malaysia, Singapore, the Philippines, Japan, and Hong Kong on a government-sponsored initiative to bolster support for the Republic of China (ROC).
1964	Shoushan Buddhist Academy established in the city of Kaohsiung.

YEAR	EVENT
1967	Master Xingyun purchases more than thirty hectares in Dashu Township, Kaohsiung County, as the site for the construction of a Buddhist college and monastery. Shoushan Buddhist Academy moves to Foguangshan, changing its name to Eastern Buddhist Academy. Two years later, twenty students graduate.
1969	Police search Foguangshan after hearing rumors that two hundred rifles are being stored there. Master Xingyun sends several nuns to Japan to pursue advanced degrees. Between the years 1969 to 2000, approximately two dozen Foguang clerics attend colleges and universities in Japan, Korea, India, the United States, England, France, and Brazil.
1970	Opening ceremony for the Great Mercy Children's Home at Foguang headquarters, established by Master Xingyun and Xu Huaisheng, the manager of Jiaotong Bank.
1971	Great Compassion Hall is built and the image of Guanyin consecrated, marking the completion of Foguangshan's first temple. Interior Minister Xu Qingzhong comes to Foguangshan to take part in the ribbon-cutting ceremony, said to have been witnessed by thousands of people. The Guanyin Release Pond and the Maitreya image are consecrated at the same time.
1972	Prime Minister Li Guangyao of Singapore and his wife visit Foguangshan.
1973	Jiang Jingguo, premier of the executive yuan, visits Foguangshan for the first time. He will visit it three more times over the next five years. Foguangshan Monastic Buddhist Academy, publicized as being the island's first Buddhist institute of higher learning, is founded.
1975	The Welcoming Buddha is consecrated on the eastern slope of Foguangshan. At 120 feet high, it is publicized as being the tallest buddha statue in Southeast Asia. The KMT allows Master Xingyun to give a lecture on Buddhism in the National Arts Hall. This is the first time that the government bestows such a privilege on a cleric.
1976	The Foguang Health Clinic, which provides medical services for the Foguang and local communities, is founded. Master Xingyun journeys to the United States for the first time, immediately recognizing the possibility of opening temples to cater to the needs of the rapidly expanding Chinese American community.
1977	Universal Gate High School founded at Foguangshan.

YEAR	EVENT
1978	Jiang Jingguo visits Foguangshan the day after winning his election campaign to succeed his father as president of the ROC. Master Xingyun establishes the Foguangshan Tripitaka Editing Committee. Master Xingyun receives an honorary doctorate in philosophy from the University of Oriental Studies (Los Angeles).
1979	The KMT permits Master Xingyun to televise dharma talks. "Sweet Dew," as the program is called, is the first such Buddhist show permitted on the airwaves. The program receives an award from the government's Education Department and Information Bureau. The first volume of the four-volume set *Lectures by Master Xingyun* (*Xingyun Dashi jiangyan ji*) is published by Foguang Publishing House. *Universal Gate (Pumen)* magazine is founded.
1980s	The Foguang clerics Vens. Cirong, Huilong, Yirong, Shaojue, and Yongsheng on separate occasions receive awards for meritorious work from the Ministry of the Interior.
1980	Master Xingyun serves as the president of the Chinese Cultural University's Research Institute of Indian Studies, the first such institute to receive government accreditation. The ROC government bestows on Master Xingyun a "Contribution to the Dramatic Arts Award." Master Xingyun teaches a course on Buddhist philosophy at Tung Hai University.
1981	Pure Land Cave is opened at Foguangshan. The completion of Great Heroes Hall coincides with Foguangshan's fifteenth anniversary. Approximately 100,000 people are reported to have participated in the festivities.
1983	The Museum of Buddhism opens at Foguangshan. Longevity Funerary Complex, Foguangshan's mortuary facility, is completed. The Foguangshan Tripitaka Editing Committee publishes its first work, a punctuated version of the Agamas.
1984	Pumen Temple in Kaohsiung opens the first of Foguangshan's "urban colleges."
1985	Master Xingyun retires as abbot of Foguangshan. Master Xingyun becomes first monastic to receive an award for meritorious service from the Education Department of the ROC government.

YEAR	EVENT
1986	Foguangshan invites dozens of scholars and four tantric dharma masters for a symposium on "The Integration of Sutric and Tantric Buddhism and the Development of World Culture."
Master Xingyun reestablishes contact with his family through mail and intermediaries.
1987	The government awards Foguangshan a "Golden Bell Award for Contributions to Society" in recognition of the television show "Xingyun's Chan Talk."
Chen Yueying, magistrate of Kaohsiung County, honors Foguangshan with a "Compassionate Service Award" and a "Cultural Promotion Award."
1988	Master Xingyun gives dharma talks to and confers the triple refuge among soldiers stationed on Jinmen Island. Over the next several years he will perform such services at various army bases and military academies and will meet with several of the ROC's most senior generals.
Master Xingyun joins the KMT's Central Advisory Committee.
The audiovisual center is established at Foguang headquarters.
The *Foguang Encyclopedia [of Buddhism] (Foguang da cidian)* is published.
Master Xingyun conducts opening ceremony for Hsi Lai Temple (Hacienda Heights, Calif.), Foguangshan's first overseas branch temple. From this time, the master increasingly regards himself as a "global person."
A month-long ordination ceremony is held at Hsi Lai Temple, with three hundred novices taking their vows. Foguangshan now has a monastic corps of over six hundred.
1989	Master Xingyun returns to mainland China for first time since 1949. He is reunited with mother and siblings, visits Qixiashan and stupa of Master Zhikai.
Master Xingyun presides over the board of directors of the ROC Mongolian-Tibetan Cultural Center Foundation.
Foguangshan brings fifty scholars from Taiwan, Mainland China, Hong Kong, Japan, Korea, Italy, and the United States to the headquarters to present papers at the conference "Investigations in the *Sixth Patriarch's Platform Sutra*."
System of Foguang benefactors established.
1990	Hsi Lai University in California is accredited as a religious seminary.
The Foguangshan Culture and Education Foundation holds its first Buddhism examination. More than 200,000 people are reported to have taken the test, publicized as being the first of its kind.
Master Xingyun begins giving annual dharma lectures at Hunghom Coliseum, Hong Kong. Each year, more than sixty thousand people attend.
Foguangshan sponsors a symposium on "Modern Buddhism." Forty scholars from Taiwan, Japan, Korea, Hong Kong, mainland China, Canada, and the United States present papers.
Master Xingyun arranges for his mother to emigrate to the United States.

YEAR	EVENT
1991	Devotees' Hall is constructed at Foguangshan.

The Buddha's Light International Association (BLIA) is founded during a meeting at the Sun Yat-sen Memorial Hall. President Li Denghui sends a telegram of congratulations. Director of the Executive Yuan Hao Bocun, Minister of National Defense Chen Lü'an, former Minister of the Interior Xu Shuide, as well as the KMT officials Jiu Jianhuang, Wu Boxiong, Xiao Dianzan, and Zhong Rongji all attend.

The television program "Xingyun's Dharma Words" is honored by the Department of the Interior's Information Bureau for outstanding contribution to society. Foguangshan will receive this award the next two years as well.

Nearly five hundred initiates from a variety of Buddhist organizations in Taiwan and East Asia take the triple altar ordination at Foguangshan in a session that takes over ten weeks to complete.

Master Xingyun slips and falls, breaking his leg.

The Foguang monastic corps reaches nearly one thousand. |
| 1992 | President Li Denghui and Provincial Governor Song Zhuyou (the secretary-general of the Central Committee of the KMT) visit Foguangshan. President Li will visit on two more occasions over the next eight years.

BLIA and the Foguangshan Culture and Education Foundation are simultaneously honored by the Education Department for "outstanding educational undertakings." Both awards are presented by President Li Denghui. |
| 1993 | The second BLIA World Conference takes place at the Chiang Kai-shek Stadium in Taoyuan. Guests of honor at the opening ceremony include President Li Denghui; Chen Lü'an, minister of the control yuan; Lin Yanggang, president of the judicial yuan; Wu Boxiong, minister of the interior; and Huang Guanhui, chairman of the Mainland Affairs Council.

The ROC Education Department grants Foguangshan permission to establish Foguang University.

Master Xingyun initiates the "New Life Movement through Purifying the Human Heart."

BLIA establishes its system of lay lecturers and teachers.

The Foguangshan Meditation College is established.

Queen Srimala Institute admits its first class of students. Each year approximately twenty young women travel around the world to conduct Buddhist studies at various Foguang branch temples.

Foguangshan's fifty-one-volume edition of the Chan canon is completed by the Foguangshan Tripitaka Editing Committee. |

YEAR	EVENT
1995	Master Xingyun undergoes triple bypass heart surgery.

Tathagata Hall at Foguangshan is completed.

The Foguangshan Culture and Education Foundation establishes the Foguang Art Gallery in Taipei. This is publicized as being the first art gallery in Taiwan specializing in Buddhist works. Smaller art galleries are established at Hsi Lai Temple (the United States), Nan Tien and Chung Tien Temples (Australia), the Paris Branch Temple, Dongchan Temple (Malaysia), and the branch temples in Tainan and Pingdong (Taiwan).

With the approval of the ROC Education Department, and cosponsored by two large newspapers, the Foguang Buddhism examination is administered to more than 800,000 students at two thousand elementary and middle schools and 300,000 adults. The test is also translated into fourteen languages.

The ten-volume *Anthology of Buddhism (Fojiao congshu)* is completed and distributed to monastics, lay preachers, and benefactors.

Foguangshan assumes responsibility for Nanhua Management College in Jiayi.

1996 Master Xingyun's mother passes away.

Foguangshan invites seventy scholars to a four-day conference on "Religious Faith and Modern Society." Among participants are professors flown in from the United States, England, Japan, Korea, Belgium, mainland China, and Hong Kong.

Master Xingyun lectures to eighty thousand people at the Shah Alam Stadium, Port Kelang, Malaysia.

Foguangshan commissions one hundred scholars from mainland China to write a vernacular version of the Chinese Buddhist tripitaka.

Foguangshan's Religious Affairs Committee publishes a CD-ROM version of its *Foguang Encyclopedia [of Buddhism]*.

More than ten thousand people participate in the inauguration of Nanhua Management College of Foguang University.

Several dozen scholars and representatives of religions from Japan, Korea, Hong Kong, Indonesia, Malaysia, Thailand, the Philippines, Russia, and Taiwan participate in the "International Symposium of Religion and Higher Education in Asia," held at Foguangshan.

Jueshi reaches its peak distribution, with 400,000 copies of each issue printed.

Master Xingyun proposes a plan for government involvement in the regulation of religion in the "Symposium on Religion and Social Trends," sponsored by the executive yuan.

Three hundred Foguang novices take full monastic vows in a month-long ordination at the headquarters. The Foguang monastic corps reaches nearly 1,350, leveling off at this number over the subsequent years.

YEAR	EVENT
1997	Foguang headquarters is closed to tourists.
Representatives of the Department of the Interior and of the Department of Foreign Affairs present the master with the Grand Interior Medal and the Diplomacy Medal, the highest honors given to citizens by these ROC offices.
Master Xingyun meets with Pope John Paul II at the Vatican.
Eighty thousand people attend the opening rally at the Sun Yat-sen Memorial Hall in Taipei to kick off the Campaign of Compassion and Love.
1998	Completion of Cloud Residing Hall at Foguang headquarters.
One hundred fifty novices from Buddhist traditions around the world take full vows in a nine-day ordination ceremony at Bodhgaya, India.
1999	Master Xingyun is one of five individuals given a "National Public Service Award." The honor is presented by the minister of the executive yuan.
Li Denghui visits Foguangshan for the third time.
Hsi Lai University holds the first of its annual international conferences on Humanistic Buddhism. Scholars from the United States and Europe participate.
2000	Master Xingyun returns to mainland China for a second time.
Inaugural issue of Foguangshan's daily newspaper, *Merit Times* (Chinese title: *Renjian fu bao*), appears. *Awakening the World* is discontinued.
Three hundred novices, including seventy women from Sri Lanka, take full ordination in a month-long ordination ceremony at the headquarters.
2001	During a visit to the United States, Master Xingyun conducts a purification ceremony at the site of the World Trade Towers terrorist attack.

Notes

Introduction
1. Wallerstein (1990) distinguishes two usages of the term "culture." It can refer either to the sense of the traits, behaviors, values, and beliefs characterizing a particular group or to the "higher" arts within a particular group, as opposed to popular, everyday practice. The first of these usages Wallerstein finds heuristically unhelpful. The second he believes to function alongside racism and sexism as a justification of inequities of the world system.

2. In the companion volumes *The Practice of Chinese Buddhism* (1967) and *The Buddhist Revival in China* (1968), Welch spoke of Sino-Buddhism in the past tense. This is partially due to the fact that he was recording temple life in mainland China as remembered by elderly monks whom he interviewed in Hong Kong. Beyond that, however, there is also a sense in his attention to detail that, given the antipathy toward the religion displayed at the time by Mao Zedong's Communist Party, Chinese Buddhism was a moribund phenomenon. Welch evidently agreed with Arthur Wright's assessment that people were then witnessing "the last twilight of Chinese Buddhism as an organized religion" (Wright 1959, 122).

3. Recent dissertations include Tien (1995), on the life and thought of Ven. Yinshun; Shi Jienshen (1997), on monastic education in Taiwan; Ting (1997), on the health-care approach of Ciji Gongde Hui; Laliberté (1999), on the role played by the Buddhist Association of the Republic of China, Foguangshan, and Ciji Gongde Hui in the democratization of ROC politics; Chern (2000), on Buddhist nuns in Taiwan; Li (2000), on women and Buddhism in Taiwan; Qin (2000), on a convent on Emei Shan, Sichuan Province; Huang (2001), on Ciji Gongde Hui; and Hurley (2001), on Ven. Yinshun's hermeneutics. Recent English-language articles include Lu (1998), on gender issues in Ciji Gongde Hui, and Laliberté (1998), on political involvement in Ciji Gongde Hui.

1 A Mountain Monastery in an Urban Society
1. Master Xingyun saw his mother for the first time in over fifty years in 1989 during his visit to mainland China. Months later, he attained a visa for her to emigrate to the United States. She spent her final five years at Hsi Lai Temple (Foguangshan's large branch monastery just outside Los Angeles), although she did travel somewhat, even making a short visit to Foguangshan in 1990.

2. Ironically, it was Vice President Chen Cheng who had issued the detention order. Chen Cheng never became a Foguang devotee. It was after his grown sons took refuge under Master Xingyun that they decided to transfer the remains of their parents from Taishan to Foguangshan (Fu 1995, 183).

3. For descriptions of miraculous events taking place at Foguangshan, including several concerning the Welcoming Buddha and Maitreya statues, see Shi Yikong (1994).

4. Foguangshan uses the categories *zongjiao* (religious) and *shehui* to distinguish the general intent of its undertakings, especially its education system. *Shehui*, the term that I am rendering as "social service" and "secular," literally means "society" or "social." I have chosen "social service" and "secular" to indicate that the programs on this part of the mountain are philanthropic in nature and carry less overt religious significance.

5. Lay monastics (*jiaoshi* for men, *shigu* for women) have not taken monastic vows but have pledged to remain celibate and to devote their lives to helping Foguangshan propagate Buddhism.

6. For a description of several orphanages run by Buddhists during the Republican era, see Welch (1968, 122–126). Of the thirty-nine monks interviewed by Welch, six had been orphans (Welch 1967, 259–269).

7. The Venerable Huichan had already become famous in mainland China for his depictions of Tibetan life before he emigrated to Canada in 1989 and, subsequently, renounced under Master Xingyun in 1996.

8. The relationship between Master Xingyun, Chen Lü'an, and Chen Yonghe came to light only after the latter, the Four Seas Gang leader, was gunned down by a rival. The news media included in its initial reports of this event the fact that Master Xingyun had recently put Chen Yonghe into contact with Chen Lü'an, although this turned out to have nothing to do with the assassination. Master Xingyun then made matters worse by announcing, not only that he had made the introduction, but also that, because Chen Yonghe was a Foguang devotee, his ashes would be inurned in Foguangshan's Longevity Funerary Complex.

9. The concept "Humanistic Buddhism" is discussed at length later in this book, beginning in chapter 3.

10. Maitreya is the bodhisattva who will next attain the full enlightenment of buddhahood. The pure land over which he presides is the inner chamber of Tushita Heaven. This is the closest of all pure lands, being located within the realm of desire, as is our own Saha world. Nonetheless, by human standards, it is immensely far away. At the entrance to Foguangshan, Maitreya's relative proximity was formerly accentuated by keeping his image at ground level. Since the mountain's cloistering, the emphasis has subtly shifted to remind all of even his separation from the mundane world.

11. When first laying down this rule, Master Xingyun ordered that the gate be locked, thereby more completely separating the religious and the secular areas. He eventually rescinded this part of the arrangement when the volunteer lay workers complained that, every time they wanted to go up the mountain for work or meals, they had to walk all the way around the driveway on the far side of Nonduality Gate, a much greater distance.

12. Especially influential in establishing a scholarly conceptualization of the sacred and the profane have been Durkheim (1957), Otto (1923), and Eliade (1959).

13. Because of the pejorative penumbra shadowing the word "profane," it is often difficult to use this term rather than "secular." It is for this reason that earlier in this chapter I re-

ferred to Foguangshan's "secular section." The more proper nomenclature according to my analysis is the "profane section." Such wording, however, simply sounds too coarse to use.

2   Master Xingyun: Foguang Patriarch

1. The master ranks his abilities to *guangjie shanyuan* and to be magnanimous toward those whose ideas differ from his own as the two character traits that have, more than any others, led to his success (Shi Xingyun 1994, vol. 3, entry for 16 February 1990). When I commented to several Foguang nuns about Master Xingyun being in charge of even daily affairs of Foguang temples and about his ability to engender loyalty to himself, they warned that these things should not be overemphasized. In China, they observed, a master is first and foremost a teacher, certainly garnering great respect, but neither eliciting the intense personal loyalty from nor exerting the degree of control over disciples that lamas in Tibet or Zen masters in Japan do.

2. In *You qing you yi* (Shi Xingyun 1997d, 275), the master notes that, in 1994, during his world tour, he gave U.S.$100 to every lay or monastic disciple who was studying in a college. Since there were hundreds of disciples attending different schools, thousands of dollars quickly disappeared from his pockets.

3. *Jieyuan* has definite missionary intent. Unlike Christian evangelism or Muslim *da'wa*, however, *jieyuan* is less direct in its method. To use Buddhist terminology, one could say that, while evangelism and *da'wa* strive to plant the causal seed of their faith, *jieyuan* is geared to creating nurturing conditions in anticipation of introducing the seed itself (or to aiding in the development of the seed already present). *Jieyuan* also differs from the other concepts in its distinct emphasis on deepening interpersonal relationships.

4. A full list of lectures given by Master Xingyun over the years 1988–1996 is provided in Shi Xingyun (1997a, 569–589).

5. Li Juehe was the father of Ven. Cizhuang, one of Master Xingyun's most senior nuns (it was she who for well over a decade took responsibility for finding property and overseeing the construction of Foguang temples outside Taiwan). The scholar Jiang Canteng (1997, 19–21) observes that Li's considerable translation ability gave Master Xingyun a distinct advantage over all the other monks who had come to Taiwan from the mainland, for it allowed him to leave Taipei and gain a pan-island following.

6. Two important examples of this are Shi Xingyun (1995, vol. 10), designed primarily for monastics, and Shi Xingyun (1997d), available to all devotees.

7. To create these journal entries, a monastic scribe would carefully record the master's various activities and conversations throughout each day. A first draft of the diary would be written from these notes, to be checked over and emended by the master. Although first published in *Universal Gate*, the diary was later incorporated into a twenty-volume set of books. This comment about wishing to convey his inner feelings and his mind and nature is made by the master in the preface found in all twenty volumes (see, e.g., Shi Xingyun 1994, 1:6).

8. One monastic told me that, when the master proposed creating free, week-long summer camps for young adults, a disciple voiced doubts, citing the significant financial drain that this would cause. In response, Master Xingyun walked over and slapped the person across the face.

9. Max Weber defines "charisma" as "a certain quality of an individual personality by virtue of which he is considered extraordinary and treated as endowed with supernatural, superhuman, or at least specifically exceptional powers or qualities. These are such as are not accessible to the ordinary person, but are regarded as of divine origin or as exemplary, and on the basis of them the individual concerned is treated as a leader" (Weber 1968, 241).

3 Foguang Humanistic Buddhism

1. I have capitalized the word "Humanistic" in the term "Humanistic Buddhism" because that is how it appears in most Foguang translations of "Renjian Fojiao." However, since the literature of what is termed "engaged Buddhism"—discussed in chapter 4—does not capitalize the word "engaged," I have again followed the general usage, despite the apparent inconsistency. The Chinese Buddhists have generally capitalized the phrase "Humanistic Buddhism" in their translations because they wish to emphasize that Renjian Fojiao is a new form of Buddhist practice. Those who have used the language of "engaged Buddhism" evidently do not want to make such a strong claim.

2. Master Taixu also employed the term "Renjian Fojiao" on occasion but found that "Rensheng Fojiao" better indicated the focus of his concerns. There are many subtle philosophical distinctions between Rensheng Fojiao and Renjian Fojiao as these were developed by Taixu and Yinshun. Because these differences have not been of great concern to Master Xingyun, who has given more emphasis to the practical implications of carrying out such Humanistic Buddhism, I have not discussed them. Jiang Canteng (2001a, 66–98) provides an excellent analysis of the shift from Rensheng Fojiao to Renjian Fojiao.

3. In the spring of 1999, Ven. Huiri, the director of Foguangshan's meditation hall, went into a year-long solitary retreat. Other Foguang monastics expressed the desire that they too could set aside such a long period to focus on their own cultivation. On the other hand, they indicated that to do so would be contrary to the spirit of Humanistic Buddhism. It was permissible for Ven. Huiri only because, as the director of the meditation hall, it was his specialty.

4. This debate concerning adherence to vinaya has not arisen merely with the advent of Humanistic Buddhism. It has existed as long as the monastic community itself. Holmes Welch (1967, 128) notes: "In general, observance of the rules [at Chinese monasteries] was in inverse proportion to contact with the populace. . . . Strict observance of the spirit as well as the letter of the rules could most often be found at monasteries that had their own landed income and hence did not depend on mortuary rites; that were not an object of pilgrimage and did not welcome lay people to dine or spend the night; that were so large that the only alternative to strictness was total disorder."

5. Although Master Taixu periodically made reference to establishing a pure land in the human realm, it was Ven. Yinshun who first explored the connotations of this concept in

detail. Master Taixu's thoughts on the subject may be found in his lectures "On Establishing a Pure Land on Earth" ("Jianshe renjian jingtu lun") (Shi Taixu 1953, 14, sec. 47, essay 5:426–429) and "How to Establish a Humanistic Buddhism" ("Zenyang lai jianshe Renjian Fojiao") (Shi Taixu 1953, 14, sec. 47, essay 6:431–456) and are discussed in Pittman (2001, 221–229). For a discussion of *renjian jingtu*, see Shi Yinshun (1992, 1993).

6. As the fourth of the six heavens in the realm of desire, Tushita is within the Trailokya (the triple world as misperceived through ignorance), and, therefore, its denizens remain in the cycle of rebirth. Only those in the heaven's inner department, Santusita, are drawing close to full liberation, which they will attain after being reborn in our Saha world one last time when Maitreya is reborn there as the next buddha. This particular aspect of Tushita is, hence, regarded as a lower-level pure land (those born in one of the other pure lands are said to remain in that pure land indefinitely, never dying, until attaining ultimate liberation; hence, the person enjoys "one-life completion"). The comfort and serenity experienced in other heavens, however, are regarded as impeding practice. Hence, although descriptions of heavens (*tian*) and pure lands (*jingtu*) share certain characteristics of an ideal existence, the two types of realms generally have significantly different implications for liberation.

Although some Chinese Buddhists have asserted that the Christian heaven is actually a pure land, Master Xingyun and most other Pure Land practitioners disagree. Following Ven. Yinshun, the master notes that the Christian heaven has three faults that distinguish it from the various Buddhist pure lands: the perpetuation of a kind of class difference since "God is God and the people of heaven can never become God"; Christians mistakenly believe that heaven is the final goal, not merely the ideal place to continue cultivating oneself so as to attain enlightenment; and, as with Tushita Heaven, residents are still within the cycle of rebirth and, thus, must retrogress to this world before gaining salvation. Master Xingyun therefore states that the term "heaven" (*tian*) is a totally appropriate term to use in order to identify the ideal realm that serves as a goal of Christian practice. In fact, he states, it is quite similar in many respects to Trayastrimsas Heaven, the second of the heavens in the realm of desire (Shi Xingyun 1979, 60–61).

7. Master Xingyun describes the attributes and deficiencies of the various pure lands in many places (e.g., Shi Xingyun 1979, 51–72; Shi Xingyun 1995a, 1:579–610). The master's observation that fully sincere recitation is too difficult for most to achieve may seem odd at first since Pure Land teachers feel that one of the practice's selling points is that it is the "easy method," compared to the "difficult method" of meditation. The method itself may be easy, but, as many practitioners have related, actualizing it with full concentration and sincerity is beyond the capability of most people's wayward minds.

8. It is not Master Xingyun but Ven. Huiri, the director of Foguangshan's meditation hall, who has coined the phrase "Foguang Chan." According to Ven. Huiri, the Foguang form of practice differs from others in its strong insistence on bringing realization to all daily activities. Teachers of other meditation halls do not see this as a distinction between the Foguang style and their own, as most other Chan adepts also emphasize this point.

9. Various aspects of the Chinese Pure Land tradition are treated in Cleary (1994); Corless

(1987); Foard, Solomon, and Payne (1996); Pas (1987, 1995); Shi Xingyun (1995a, 85–176); Thien Tam (1991, 1992a, 1992b); and Welter (1992).

10. The three-period doctrine was originally developed in India and introduced into China in the mid-sixth century. Although there is some variance in the length assigned to each of the three periods, one common chronology indicates that the first era lasted five hundred years, that the second extended over a millennium, and that the current, final era will continue for myriad years. Since at the time that this doctrine was brought to their country the Chinese dated Shakyamuni as having lived in the tenth century B.C.E., they believed that the last dharma age was just under way, an assertion confirmed in their minds by the suppression of Buddhism by Emperor Wu of the Northern Zhou dynasty in 574 C.E.

11. The Venerable Tanluan was the first Chinese master to write a systematic treatise on the methods for attaining rebirth in the Western Pure Land. According to tradition, he dropped his search for longevity through Daoist techniques and adopted the practice of *nianfo* after the monk Bodhiruci told him of Sukhavati and taught him the tenets of Pure Land doctrine.

12. The characterization of the Pure Land tradition as a "school" with a lineage of "patriarchs" can be misleading since, in the Pure Land tradition, there is no notion of any kind of mind-to-mind transmission from teacher to disciple, as there is, e.g., in Chan. The creation of a Pure Land patriarchal lineage appears to have first occurred in the Song dynasty through the works of the Tiantai monks Zongxiao (d. 1214) and Zhipan (1258–1269) in an effort to put the Pure Land tradition on a par with the Chan, Tiantai, and Vinaya traditions as a distinct school. The lists devised by these two have been modified over time, with the result that, by the beginning of the twenty-first century, there are now said to be thirteen such patriarchs, the most recent being Ven. Yinguang.

13. The *Sutra [of the Buddha] of Immeasurable Life (Wuliangshou jing)*, also known as the *Larger Sutra [of the Buddha] of Immeasurable Life (Da wuliangshou jing)*, is one of the "triple sutras," the three major texts of the Pure Land school. The other two are the *Amitabha Sutra (Amituo jing)*, also known as the *Smaller Sutra [of the Buddha] of Immeasurable Life (Xiao wuliangshou jing)*, and the *Sutra on the Contemplation [of the Buddha] of Immeasurable Life (Guan wuliangshou jing; Amitayur-buddhanusmrti)*.

14. During his thirty years in Chang'an, Ven. Shandao wrote at least five works in nine volumes, the most famous of which is the *Commentary to the Sutra on Concentration (Guanjing si)*. He is said to have made and distributed thousands of copies of the *Sukhavativyuha Sutra* and painted some three hundred paintings of the Western Pure Land. Shandao became especially influential on Japanese Pure Land Buddhists, who have considered him an incarnation of Amitabha.

15. Like Ven. Tanluan, Ven. Shandao wrote that there are five main activities that can lead to rebirth in the Western Paradise. Two of his five differ from those of his predecessor, however. Both men included praising the name of, contemplating, and worshiping Amitabha Buddha. Instead of advocating the practices of vowing resolutely to be reborn in Sukhavati and "turning toward" others, however, Ven. Shandao listed singing praises and making

offerings to Amitabha. Thus, although still considered secondary to invoking Amitabha, the various forms of worship come to the fore. The Venerable Shandao's interest in such activity is also indicated by the fact that he wrote three liturgies and that it was he who established "Amituo Fo" as the standard pronunciation for group chanting.

16. The Venerable Zhiyi is the first patriarch of the Tiantai school. His teachings may be summarized by the phrase "the five periods and the eight teachings," the periods and teachings by which he organized the tangle of Buddhist doctrines into one coherent system. For him, the teachings of the final period of the Buddha's life (and, thus, the most profound manifestation of the doctrines) are to be found in the *Lotus Sutra*. The Tiantai school typically places Pure Land practice in the third period, that of elementary Mahayana.

17. The Venerable Yanshou is credited with having been the first person to discuss in depth the compatibility of Pure Land and Chan practice. The Venerable Zhuhong, arguably the most influential monk of Ming dynasty China, is known for having used the chant "Amituo Fo" as the basis for a Pure Land–style *gong'an*. According to Ven. Zhuhong, in order to become fully mindful of Amitabha, one must not only continually repeat the buddha's name but also ceaselessly ask oneself who it is who is invoking Amitabha (Yu 1981, 57–63). This Pure Land–style *gong'an*, "Who is invoking Amitabha?" is standard practice at Foguangshan.

18. The Venerable Yinguang was the abbot of Lingyanshan (just outside Suzhou) in the 1920s and 1930s. Under his guidance, Lingyanshan went from a small, unknown establishment housing a couple dozen monks to one of China's largest monasteries devoted to Pure Land practice. His influence has spread mostly through the publication of his voluminous letters, all of which are collected in Shi Yinguang (1991).

19. Both the *Sutra [of the Buddha] of Immeasurable Life* and the *Amitabha Sutra* provide descriptions of the Sukhavati Pure Land. The first (and longer) of the two, however, goes into more detail and also includes a section that tells the circumstances under which Amitabha, as the bodhisattva Dharmakara, made the forty-eight vows that resulted in the creation of Sukhavati. The description of the pure land given by Master Xingyun comes directly from secs. 15–20 of this sutra (see Mueller 1894).

20. For a variety of examples of how this strategy has been employed by Pure Land, Tiantai, and Huayan Buddhists, see Li (n.d., 297–313).

21. William James distinguishes two basic forms of religious attitude. Those with a "healthy-minded" approach emphasize the goodness of this world and great potential for happiness in human life. Others are almost overpowered by the evil and suffering inherent in existence. Their view is that of a "sick soul" (see James [1902] 1936, 77–162).

22. I would like to thank Carsten Krause for calling this remark to my attention. It should be noted that Ven. Yinshun's hermeneutical moves caused much stronger censure among those within the Pure Land school (see Jones 1999, 124–133).

23. Statistics for 1990 concerning the triple refuge and frequenting Buddhist temples were gathered from records kept at the Buddhist Association of the Republic of China (see

Chandler 1998c). All statistics for 1992 provided by the ROC Department of the Interior, Bureau of Religion, Taipei (see Chandler 1998d). In 1990, Taiwan had a population of 20,156,587. By 1992, the population had increased to slightly over 20,330,000.

24. Yiguandao has enjoyed an even greater rise in popularity than has Buddhism. It has metamorphosed from a small, illegal "cult" relying on active yet surreptitious evangelizing to a legally recognized religion (as of 1986) claiming over one million members.

25. The ban prohibiting the use of Taiwanese on radio and television programs was lifted with the ending of martial law. Subsequently, the great antiquity of the Minnan dialect (i.e., Taiwanese) was celebrated. For instance, people remarked on the fact that the original cadence and flavor of many ancient Chinese poems are better retained when the poems are read in Taiwanese rather than in Mandarin.

26. Whether urbanization leads to an increase in religious activity and affiliation is debatable. Harvey Cox (1965), e.g., saw such trends in the 1960s as promoting secularization. Taiwan's urbanization can, at any rate, be said to have influenced the mode of religious activity by contributing to an increased tendency specifically to identify oneself as an adherent of a particular religion.

27. It is possible that there is some overlap in membership between the two organizations. This is doubtful, however, since they are in competition with one another. Also, not all Ciji Gongde Hui members are Buddhists. Nonetheless, the vast majority are. Foguang membership statistics are analyzed in chapter 7 below.

28. The actual figures are 4,858,500 for 1992 and 4,863,000 for 1997, an increase of a mere 0.09 percent over a period when the population as a whole had increased by 6.7 percent, from 20,330,000 to 21,696,500. No statistics were offered for people who had taken the triple refuge as of 1997. Statistics obtained from ROC Department of the Interior, Bureau of Religion, Taipei.

29. Clerics from many Buddhist temples noted this drop in donations, although I could locate no hard statistics to verify it.

30. Such religious modernists should be distinguished from secular modernists, who have held that modernization requires the shedding of all traditional cultural forms, including religion.

31. I prefer the term "traditionalist" over the term "fundamentalist" since the latter has become so charged with (largely negative) political connotations. Were I to employ the designation "fundamentalist," I would do so to identity those traditionalists who are in extremely high tension with modern values and who employ confrontational, and at times even violent, means to advance their agenda.

32. For the evolution of the term "modernism" in Western Christianity, see Ahlstrom (1972, 839) and Hutchison (1968, 88–97). John Esposito (1991, 196–200) identifies four orientations toward change within twentieth-century Islam: secularist (those who wished to restrict religion to private life); conservative (those who accepted inherited tradition intact);

neotraditionalist (those who claimed a right to return to Islam's revealed sources to cleanse Islamic law of those un-Islamic practices that had been incorporated over the years); and neomodernist (those who, like the neotraditionalists, claimed to be cleansing Islam of un-Islamic practices but, in their call for "Islamic modernization," simultaneously advocated acceptance of certain Western ideas.

33. Walpole Rahula (1974) articulates a remarkably similar model for the retreat of the sangha in Sri Lanka into isolated forest practice and its subsequent, recent return to political and social engagement, thereby reactivating the type of dynamic involvement found in the early community. For Rahula, the cause of the decline of engagement was to be traced to the activities of European colonists and their Christian missionary allies starting in the sixteenth century.

34. Master Xingyun notes that, when he first purchased an automobile back in the 1960s, it caused consternation among many Buddhists: "Thirty years ago, when there were still few private automobiles in Taiwan, I decided to buy a van to make it easier to spread the dharma. At that time, people in Taiwan were still conservative, and many held prejudices about what monks could do, and those monks who wore a watch, used a fountain pen, or rode a bicycle were criticized. So, when I brought up the idea of buying a vehicle, many devotees were quite disconcerted and questioned the plan. I kept to my plan nonetheless" (Shi Xingyun 1995a, 10:597).

35. Foguang sleeping facilities for visiting lay devotees are more lavish than those found elsewhere in Taiwan. Most rooms are equipped with standard beds for double occupancy. Lay volunteers and visitors to Ciji Gongde Hui's Tranquil Thoughts Hermitage share large dormitories with very broad bunks on which many people lay down bedrolls. At Zhongtaishan, most visitors share simple dormitory rooms with bunks and quilts. Neither Zhongtaishan nor Tranquil Thoughts Hermitage has air conditioners in these sleeping quarters.

36. The Venerable Yinshun quotes Master Taixu as saying that Chinese Buddhists "talk about the Mahayana teachings, but practice the Hinayana" *(shuo dasheng jiao, xiu xiaosheng xing)* (Shi Yinshun 1993, 45).

37. *Ci (metta)* is the Buddhist virtue of spreading joy to others. *Bei (karuna)* refers to alleviating suffering. Of course, the distinction between the two is not so cut-and-dried since the concepts are intimately interrelated.

38. As I pointed out earlier in this chapter, one should speak, not of the "secularization" of Buddhist practice, but of its "profanization" since the intent and goals are still very much religious. Such a neologism as "profanization," however, is simply too clumsy to use effectively.

39. "Immanent transcendence" is Tu Wei-ming's (1989, 93–122) terminology.

4 Humanistic Buddhism in Practice

1. For an explanation of why I have capitalized "Humanistic Buddhism" but not "engaged Buddhism," see n. 1 of chapter 3 above.

2. Kenneth Kraft (1992, 18) traced the English phrase's origin to Thich Nhat Hanh, basing his claim on the fact that the earliest reference to "engaged Buddhism" that he could find was in the title of a book apparently authored by that monk in 1963, although no other scholar has been able to track down the actual book or even find other references to it. Christopher Queen (1996b, 34 n. 6) notes that the French term *"engagé,"* meaning politically involved, had long before then been common among activist intellectuals in French Indochina. The Vietnamese term of which "engaged Buddhism" is a translation is *nhap gian phat giao*. According to Patricia Hunt-Perry and Lyn Fine (2000, 36), the 1930s reforms in China by Master Taixu inspired a similar movement in Vietnam. It is, therefore, quite likely that the Vietnamese Buddhist phrase is a direct translation of "Rensheng Fojiao."

3. Social activism and political activism inevitably entail one another, of course, as any change in social relations has political implications, just as political innovations invariably alter a society's structure. It is, nonetheless, heuristically helpful to distinguish between the two as they indicate differences in focal point and strategy of action.

4. For a discussion of how other Buddhist leaders have approached human rights, see Keown, Prebish, and Husted (1998).

5. There are lay women in the Buddhist traditions of Sri Lanka, Thailand, Myanmar, and Tibet who follow a monastic lifestyle, some practicing on their own, others on the premises of temples overseen by bhikshus, still others in independent communities with like-minded women. The *dasa sil matavo* of Sri Lanka, the *mai ji* of Thailand, and the *thila-shin* of Myanmar all take eight or ten vows. The *chola* of Tibet accept thirty-six vows. In each case, the women shave their heads and don special robes similar to those that could be worn by bhikshunis. These women do not receive the 348 bhikshuni vows, however. Foguang monastics and others who call for the reestablishment of full ordination argue that only this will accord women in these traditions the standing to teach the dharma as equals with the monks. For a discussion of the status of female renunciants in various Buddhist traditions, see Barnes (1996, 259–294).

6. In remarks made at the "International Conference of Outstanding Buddhist Women" (1996), Master Xingyun advised his audience that women should find employment while still young wives so that they would not be overly dependent on their husbands.

7. In this respect, Master Xingyun's attitude closely resembles that of Andrew Carnegie, William Lawrence, and other late-nineteenth-century Christian advocates of "the gospel of wealth." Carnegie's essay "Wealth" and Lawrence's lecture "The Relation of Wealth to Morals" may be found in Kennedy (1949, 1–8, 68–76).

8. At the beginning of his discussion of Buddhism, Weber noted that his remarks were aimed at the "mystical illuminative concentration of authentic ancient Buddhism," not at the "completely altered manifestations Buddhism assumed in Tibetan, Chinese, and Japanese popular religions." He went on to say, however, that, even after the tradition was assimilated into the Middle Kingdom, where it entered into "diverse combinations with Chinese Taoism," it continued to point beyond this world (Weber [1968] 1978, 627–629).

9. "[The] Confucian ethic, of course, had no idea of salvation. The Confucian had no desire to be 'saved' either from the migration of souls or from punishment in the beyond. Both ideas were unknown to Confucianism. The Confucian wished neither for salvation from life, which was affirmed, nor salvation from the social world, which was accepted as given. He thought of prudently mastering the opportunities of this world through self-control" (Weber 1951, 156).

10. This is a summary of a list given in Tu (1992).

11. Discussions of the post-Confucian hypothesis may also be found in Redding (1990), Hamilton and Biggart (1988), Tu (1988), Zhang (1999), Tamney and Chiang (2002), and C. K. Yang (1967). The theory is referred to as the "post-Confucian hypothesis" because the Confucian tradition itself no longer has any appreciable institutional framework to support it. Confucian values are, therefore, said to persist on a more informal, even subconscious level. Because of the lack of direct empirical evidence to prove a connection between Confucian values and economic success, the theory remains just that, a theory or hypothesis. Ezra F. Vogel (1991, 83–112) has given a succinct description of the importance of Confucian values in the rise of industrial East Asia, not only indicating the significance of such cultural dynamics, but also placing those dynamics in the context of a variety of other situational factors that have also played an important role. For more on the post-Confucian hypothesis, see chapter 8 below.

12. Baumann does not specifically say this, but, in several places, he does imply it. At one point, e.g., he notes: "Buddhist ethics originated in an Asiatic agricultural society. But how is it interpreted by contemporary Western Buddhists in modern, industrial societies? In the West, does the popular image of the 'withdrawn Buddhist' also apply, a Buddhist who supposedly does not take any direct action in the world so as not to get involved with suffering?" Elsewhere, he contrasts the FWBO's emphasis on right livelihood and social criticism with what he sees as the relative disinterest in these subjects evinced in the traditional texts and contemporary institutions of Asian Buddhism (see Baumann 2000, 372, 374 [quotation], 385).

13. Notice that, in this discussion, Master Xingyun has immediately shifted from the specifically Buddhist term *renru* to the more general concepts of *rennai* and *ren*.

14. Although I was unable to find the Chinese original for this text, I found other passages in the unpublished manuscript by the same anonymous translator to be quite accurate and, thus, have used his or her rendering.

15. In the lecture, the master states that the *Samyuktagama Sutra* advises laypeople to use one part of their money for food, two parts for business, and one part for savings. The *Maharatnakuta Sutra*, he continues, tells us that King Prasenajit divided the royal budget into three parts: one-third was used for the encouragement of religion, another third was devoted to helping the poor and disaster relief, and the last third was spent on national investments. The final canonical reference offered by the master as a Buddhist model for financial planning was a passage in the *Parinirvana Sutra* stating that whatever wealth is left over after attending to one's immediate needs should be divided into four parts: one part for taking

care of one's parents and immediate family; one part for helping other dependents, such as employees; one part to be given to friends and relatives; and one part to be donated to the monastic community (see Shi Xingyun 1995a, 10:220–222).

16. A survey of newspaper accounts of Chen Lü'an's itinerary during his months of campaigning shows him to have been a regular visitor at Buddhist temples. This was especially so during an eighteen-day pilgrimage (2 February–10 March 1996) that took him through much of Taiwan. According to Chen, the point of such stopovers was simply to attain religious merit through worship; they were not intended to garner votes (see Zhou Yilun in *Lianhe bao*, 5 March 1996, 1). Chen's speeches and news conferences were replete with references to such Buddhist virtues as compassion, generosity, and equanimity. See, e.g., the several articles in *Zhongguo shibao*, 7 October 1995, 4.

17. This information was given to me by a member of the staff of the American Institute in Taiwan (AIT). In the wake of the political-donations debacle involving Foguangshan and the Democratic National Committee (see chapter 10 below), the AIT was researching the political involvement of religious organizations in Taiwan. Political scientists in various universities had told this AIT official that, thus far, Yiguandao had been the only religious group at all successful in creating a voting bloc.

18. The 1996 series of scandals was covered in such newspaper reports as "Cult Leader Admits to Money Swindling" (1996), "Cult Leaders to be Questioned" (1996), Low (1996), "Miao Tien Denies Fraud" (1996), "Miracle Cult's Taipei Headquarters Raided" (1996), "More Accusations against Miao Tien" (1996), "PRC Devotees Donated NT$1.36 Million" (1996), "Renowned Temple Accused of Fraud" (1996), "Suspects Say They Too Were Conned" (1996), "Taipei Buddhist Master Allegedly Cheated Followers" (1996), "Tien Fo Believers Attempt to Stop Shrine Demolition" (1996), and those of Liang Yuli (*Zhongyang ribao*, 9 November 1996, 1) and Li Jianrong and Zhang Qikai (*Zhongguo shibao*, 9 November 1996, 1).

19. The Venerable Fotudeng (d. 348) used displays of magic to gain the ear of Shi Le (Later Zhao dynasty), who relied on him as imperial adviser for over two decades. He is, hence, widely regarded as the person who initiated the practice of clerical participation in affairs of state (Shi Zhuyun 1991, 1–11). The Venerable Huiyuan (334–416?) strongly asserted the independence of the sangha from imperial control, successfully persuading the Jin dynasty ruler Huan Xuan that monks should be left to administer their own affairs (Ch'en 1964, 76–80).

20. Early in his career, Master Taixu advocated quite radical changes in China's political and social structure and was more apt than is Master Xingyun to employ the language of "revolution." Later, however, the upheaval and violence that China experienced led him to lay greater emphasis on gradual transformation through individual improvement (Pittman 2001, 154, 183–184). Speaking on 7 December 1999 during the session "Buddhist-Christian Theological Encounter and Global Problems" of the Parliament of the World's Religions, held that year in Capetown, Sulak Sivaraksha observed that the Asian Buddhist community in general has emphasized personal transformation through education and self-cultivation rather than engagement in social reform. In his opinion, such an approach is severely limit-

5 Cultivating Talent through Education

1. As we shall see in chapter 6 below, novices undergo tonsure but take no vows. Becoming a shramanerika (ordained novice nun) or shramanera (ordained novice monk) necessitates taking ten vows.

2. One nun informed me that, because Buddhist colleges are not accredited as full-fledged universities by the government of the Republic of China, graduates of these schools are not permitted to take the examinations for admittance to graduate programs in Taiwan. Universities in other countries, such as the United States and Japan, typically do recognize these colleges as legitimate institutes of higher education.

3. The translation process was impressive. Authors' first drafts were typed, then proofread by two readers. After the corrected drafts were retyped, another two proofreaders went through them. After these drafts were retyped, they were checked by yet another two proofreaders, this time for readability as well as accuracy. These corrected versions were then sent back to the authors for their final approval. Then the texts were typeset so that, in the last reading, the layout could be finalized. Only then was the volume printed.

4. For four decades up until the year 2000, the magazine *Awakening the World (Jueshi)*, which was distributed free of charge, served as the organization's mouthpiece to lay devotees. Its circulation peaked at 400,000 in 1997, but the print run was cut back a year later when donations ceased to cover the high costs of production. Publication ceased entirely in 2000, when the magazine was replaced by the *Merit Times*, Foguangshan's daily newspaper. Each issue of *Awakening the World* featured the text of a recent dharma talk by the master, news of Foguang events and projects, profiles of model devotees, and brief essays on Buddhist topics by clerics and students of the Buddhist colleges.

5. According students of Foguang University whom I queried, the college as a secular educational institute has thus far at least maintained a high degree of administrative independence from its Buddhist sponsor. The connection with Foguangshan is, nonetheless, quite evident. After all, over twenty nuns are stationed at the Chinese Buddhist Research Academy, which is located on the Nanhua campus (making this one of Foguangshan's largest branch institutes). A pilgrimage path has been built on the campus' edge leading up to the Foguang Hermitage, in which the research academy is housed. Each weekend, large groups of devotees pilgrimage up the path and worship in the buddha hall in the Hermitage. Not only does hosting such groups function as an important fund-raiser for the university, but doing so has also established it as an important pilgrimage site among Foguangshan's northern branch temples.

6. Gong has previously run the Chinese Academy of Daoism (Zhonghua Daojiao Xueyuan). Just before taking his present assignment, he served as the head of the Culture and Education Bureau of the ROC executive yuan's Mainland Affairs Committee (Xingzhengyuan Dalu Weiyuanhui Wen-jiaochu).

7. Gong Pengcheng is one of the few "homegrown" academic leaders, having received his Ph.D. from Taiwan Normal University. Gong mentioned both religious and cultural pride as motivating forces when speaking at the Nanhua Management College, stating: "Chinese should be ashamed on two accounts. First, although China has long had a very advanced education system, in the last few centuries it has lagged behind the West; second, unlike Christian missionaries, Buddhists have heretofore not established first-rate universities. Nanhua Management College will be an important step in rectifying both of these sources of embarrassment" ("Nanhua Management College Grand Opening Ceremony" 1996).

8. The mayor of Taoyuan was killed execution style in his house along with seven friends and colleagues in the fall of 1996. Early the next year, one of the few women members of the ROC legislature was raped and murdered in Kaohsiung. Also in early 1997, the daughter of the popular television personality Bai Pingping was abducted, raped, tortured, and murdered. Bai Pingping walked beside Master Xingyun in the parade leading to the rally at the Sun Yat-sen Memorial that inaugurated the Campaign of Compassion and Love.

6 Cultivating Faith through Discipline

1. In practice, only the master or one of his senior disciples conducts the triple refuge ceremony. Virtually all Chinese Buddhist organizations provide such certificates to those who have taken refuge. Holmes Welch (1967, 359) observes that this documentation became increasingly popular during the Republican period (1911–1949), perhaps as a countermeasure to the baptismal certificates handed out by the Christian missionaries.

2. While the master does not totally neglect miraculous stories about the Buddha, he does tend to gloss over them. When speaking of Buddhism's rationality, the master also focuses on Shakyamuni Buddha, leaving aside the questionable historical status of bodhisattvas and other buddhas.

3. Typically, such retreats occur over a long weekend. Participants rise at 4:00 A.M. each of the five mornings. They not only take part in the purification, repentance, precept, and (for those taking the bodhisattva vows) scarification ceremonies but also attend rehearsals to ensure that each rite goes smoothly, listen to sessions of storytelling about Buddhist history, and sit through lectures on such topics as "Buddhist deportment" and "how to be a Foguang lay devotee."

4. My discussion of the five precepts and the bodhisattva precepts is principally based on two essays: Shi Xingyun (1998b, 320–330) and Shi Xingyun (1995a, 1:17–19).

5. Curiously, in Shi Xingyun (1998b, 328–329), the master cites the Confucian adage from the *Analects* "Having seen it alive, one cannot bear to see it die; having heard its cries, one cannot bear to eat its flesh. Hence, the gentleman keeps his distance from the kitchen." This passage does not, in fact, advocate vegetarianism, merely that one avoid the uncomfortable position of having to see or hear one's meal while it is still alive.

6. This is similar to the logic employed by Saint Paul when he encouraged members of the fledgling Christian community of Rome to maintain a vegetarian diet if that would attract

others to the church. Although Paul did not consider the partaking of meat to be a sin and, in fact, considered vegetarianism to be a sign of weakness in faith, for Rome's other Christians to continue eating meat could undermine the church's efforts—since some in the community thought it an important religious practice—and, in that respect, would be a sin after all (see Rom. 14:1-23).

7. Foguang literature explains that, according to the Agama, "broad beds are those with legs higher than one foot six inches or that are over four feet wide or over eight feet long." The revised version of the "Main Vinaya for the Ten Precepts" stipulates that "a bed is considered high if, when sitting on it, the person's feet do not touch the ground. A bed is considered wide if its width allows a person to roll over. A bed is called broad if it is both high and wide." The intent of the precept is to avoid luxury and indolence, allowing one's focus and energy to remain concentrated (Shi Xingyun 1995a, 1:25).

8. Information on the short-term monastic precepts program was gathered through participating in such a retreat at Nan Tien Temple, Wollongong, Australia, 27 September–2 October 1997. The Venerable Xinding flew in from Taiwan to preside over the 150 people who took part. Approximately four-fifths of the participants were ethnic Chinese. One-third of the participants had Mandarin as their first language, one-third Cantonese, and one-third English. (To accommodate the three languages, headsets were provided with separate channels for simultaneous translation into English and Cantonese.) Women constituted two-thirds of the group. Fifteen of the participants dropped out during the week, citing physical problems (especially the exacerbation of back problems from all the bowing) or an inability to adjust to the lifestyle.

9. A parent must generally be widowed before he or she can renounce, for, even if both husband and wife aspire to "leave home," making them go through divorce proceedings so that they can do so grates against the notion of family harmony. There are cases in which Master Xingyun has agreed to tonsure a man who has gone through a divorce, but on the condition that his former wife has fully supported his decision to renounce and, therefore, willingly agreed to the separation. The artist Ven. Huichan apparently received a very amicable divorce from his wife, who voiced complete support for his aspiration even though they had two young children at the time (Chandler 1997b). The Venerable Huida, my next-door neighbor in the senior citizen's home, also received an amicable divorce so that he could renounce. Unlike Ven. Huichan, Ven. Huida waited until he had already retired from work and his son had grown up. Even after he had been ordained, his wife visited him at least once per month, although he would invariably grimace when she introduced herself as his former wife. His son too came to Foguangshan regularly.

10. No monk told me that an adverseness to fatherhood initiated his decision to leave family life. For a man to say so would simply be too unfilial since it is the responsibility of sons to continue the family line. Hence, while some may have renounced in order to escape such family obligations, none would admit so openly.

11. C. K. Yang (1967, 330) also found that a main function of renunciation was to provide a "refuge for disillusioned individuals." He goes on to say: "Thus, many a thwarted statesman, a frustrated scholar, a bankrupt merchant, a jilted lover, a person who had failed to with-

stand the onslaught from life ... would suddenly waken to the futility of the struggle and flee into 'the door of emptiness,' the traditional phrase for conversion to Buddhist priesthood."

12. Most of my sources were nuns. It was therefore especially unlikely that any would mention to me, a male researcher, that they had renounced because they had been disappointed in love.

13. Most Chinese Buddhist communities do not require the taking of any precepts as part of tonsure. A few, such as Zhongtaishan, however, follow the Theravada custom of giving the shramanera vows at that time, considering this the more authentic procedure.

14. BAROC officials informed me that, even after independent ordinations were legalized in 1989, very few Buddhist organizations have opted to sponsor them. Most do not consider themselves to have the authority to do so. Performing an ordination ceremony improperly will bring about serious karmic retribution, so most dare not make the attempt. Only the largest organizations, such as Foguangshan, Zhongtaishan, and Lingyanshan, have the financial resources and consider themselves to have the necessary authority to carry on the tradition. BAROC continues to sponsor at least one ordination per year, varying the site each time.

15. It should be noted that the latter lists only four primary vows.

16. The number of scars varies from place to place, although it is always a multiple of three. At Baohuashan, the most important ordination center in mainland China during the Republican era, those who took the bhikshu ordination received twelve scars, people taking the laymen's vows received nine, and novices received three (Welch 1967, 298). Charles Jones (1997, 135) notes that the standardization of the placement of the scars on the left forearm for lay devotees is recent, having occurred on Taiwan since 1949.

17. All data about the 1991 ordination have been gathered from *Foguangshan wanfo santan luohan qi jiehui* (1992, vol. 1, chap. 2).

18. That is, the *Daily Requisites of the Vinaya (Pini riyong jieya)*, which is an adapted version of the eleventh chapter of the *Avatamsaka Sutra (Huayan jing)*.

19. According to the vinaya, a person must be at least twenty years old to take full ordination. Those younger than that may take the shramanera/shramanerika but not the bhikshu/bhikshuni vows. Foguangshan permits people to tonsure before age twenty but, with the exception of the young boys at the Shramanera School, rarely has them take even the shramanera/shramanerika precepts. Some other temples on the island, however, do follow this practice for both young monks and young nuns.

20. The 441 preceptees who were still present at the beginning of May included 108 shramaneras and 333 shramanerikas. Forty-eight of the 108 men (44 percent) were named Hui and 208 of the 333 women (62 percent) Man or Jue, indicating that they were tonsured by Master Xingyun (the assigning of generation names is discussed in chapter 7 below).

21. The Euro-American male developed heart problems but was later allowed to receive the precepts in a private ceremony without going through the long rituals.

22. All information about the Bodhgaya event has been taken from *Bodhgaya International Full Ordination* (1998).

23. Some more conservative monastics would argue that Foguangshan broke the precepts by providing me with a copy of the pratimoksha since one of the precepts expressly forbids the reciting of the monastic rules with a layperson. The key term of the vow is "recite," for many monasteries now consider it permissible to share the text of the *Pratimoksha Sutra* with scholars so long as they are not invited to the bimonthly *posadha* ceremony. Hence, numerous scholars have conducted research on the vinaya.

24. The letter of the precept forbidding eating after noon is kept by referring to the evening meal, not as *wanzhai*, "dinner," but, rather, as *yaoshi*, "medicine intake." Monastics are said, not to be eating, but to be ingesting medicine to maintain the body. As early as the Tang dynasty, Buddhist monasteries were engaged in such business activities as running mills, oil presses, hostels, and pawnshops and served as landlords for huge estates (Ch'en 1964, 261–271).

25. The *gurudharma* were the eight rules that the Buddha required his foster mother Mahaprajapati to accept before he allowed her to become the first woman to join the monastic order. An account of this episode and a listing of the *gurudharma* may be found in Horner (1963, 352–358).

26. Master Xingyun relates several instances in which the Buddha amended minor precepts that he had laid down earlier so as to provide reasonable convenience to his disciples. He tells, e.g., of the Buddha increasing the number of cassocks that could be used by arhats from one to two during the rainy season, doing so specifically after Upali (who was particularly known for adhering to the precepts) had declined to travel to arbitrate a dispute in a remote monastery because the long travel during the monsoon season would have meant soaked clothes. Similarly, Master Xingyun relates a story in which a downcast disciple explains to the Buddha that he had received a wonderful alms bowl that he wished to present to Ananda but that, since the latter would be away for six days, he could not do so without breaking the precept forbidding any arhat from keeping more than one alms bowl at a time. Shakyamuni immediately amended the precept, saying that disciples could keep a second bowl for up to one week. As can be seen, each of these stories emphasizes the Buddha's own flexibility in utilizing the precepts as general guidelines (see Shi Xingyun 1983, 316–317).

27. Chinese monasteries with a more conservative reading of the vinaya have allowed clerics to handle temple money but not keep any personal funds. At such temples, monastics relinquish all money and possessions to the sangha in exchange for having all their life needs met by the monastery, a practice called *"andan."* The monks and nuns of Zhongtaishan follow this practice, as do most clerics in Malaysia. Lay devotees may also establish such a relationship with a monastery. Neither venerables nor lay monastics at Foguangshan do so, all keeping personal accounts in the monastery banking system, but residents of the Hermitage (Foguangshan's retirement home) do, donating virtually all their money to Foguangshan in exchange for having their housing and daily needs met until death and the right to have their cremated remains stored in Longevity Funerary Complex (Chandler 1998b).

28. As Master Xingyun told as *Washington Post* reporter (see Sullivan 1996, A22), one television station in Taiwan had recently offered him about NT$880,000 (approximately U.S.$30,000) to tape twenty hours of speeches. "That makes my hourly rate about NT$44,000 [U.S.$1,500]," the master observed, continuing: "For twenty consecutive years I have made such speeches on local television. You can imagine what a handsome income I have. I am able to generate more income than does this monastery itself. But I have never calculated my net worth. I don't know how much I have, and everything I have, I give."

29. Master Xingyun is probably Foguangshan's most generous donor, consistently contributing millions of New Taiwan dollars. This gives him great flexibility in controlling the distribution of funds within the organization. When other monastics donate large sums of money for a relatively small project, such as the construction of a branch temple, this may cause problems. Disciples are not to build their own establishments, according to Foguang rules. In other words, they cannot personally seek out donations from devotees. Since they can, however, contribute their own money to a Foguang initiative, problems can arise when a particular cleric has contributed a large percentage of the funds used to build a temple, for he or she will naturally feel a great sense of personal connection to that center. In one instance, devotees at a Foguang branch temple were unhappy with the resident nun and wanted her replaced. Because she had provided so much of the money used to found it, however, neither the devotees nor other monastics felt comfortable transferring her elsewhere.

30. The paucity of personal belongings owned by monastics became very evident to me through two small occurrences. In the first, a nun mentioned that she was on her way to the dormitory to change rooms since another, more senior nun recalled to the headquarters from elsewhere required the room that she was presently in. When she returned a half hour later on completing her task, the nun quipped that she was horrified how long it had taken and wondered how she could have amassed so much. The lack of possessions also became apparent when I saw clerics as they were moving to new temples. Often, two suitcases sufficed to transport their belongings.

31. The physical manifestation of this transcendence of gender (i.e., the shaved heads of nuns as well as monks and the identical robes) is occasionally a source of bemused embarrassment for nuns who are stationed in countries without a heritage of tonsured female monastics. In more than one instance, a Foguang bhikshuni has had to resist the well-intentioned insistence that she go to a men's rather than a women's lavatory.

32. In the late 1990s, Buddhist rosary beads came into vogue around the world, although most who wore them had little or no knowledge of their Buddhist origin or import.

33. Before Master Xingyun retired in 1986, he too lived in Lamp Transmission Hall along with all the other monks. Since then, he has taken up lodging just next door in the two-story house that Ven. Xinping had built for him.

34. By "lower echelons," I mean the rank "learner, grade 1." Clerics with ranks ranging from "learner, grade 2" to "learner, grade 5" have their own rooms. Those who have reached the

level "cultivator" or "teacher" are provided with private bathrooms. The Foguang ranking system is discussed in chapter 7 below. At branch temples, generally all monastics are provided with private rooms, regardless of rank. In the few centers where both monks and nuns are present (e.g., Hsi Lai and Nanhua), strict segregation is enforced, with bhikshus and bhikshunis being housed in different buildings as far apart as possible. Any *shigu* present will be housed together with nuns.

35. There has been only one exception to the rule forbidding air-conditioning: a bhikshuni from the United States who found southern Taiwan's subtropical climate unbearable. Rather than sleeping on mattresses, clerics use thick quilts or bamboo mats as cushions.

36. One bhikshu who has practiced in Sri Lanka for over twenty years told me that, while monks there publicly comply with the prohibition against eating after noon, many eat evening snacks in the privacy of their own lodgings. Some clerics of the Theravada tradition openly join Foguang monastics in the medicine meal.

37. In explaining why they follow a vegetarian diet while monastics of South and Southeast Asia and Tibet do not, Chinese usually say that the Buddha had allowed monks to eat meat and fish so long as they had no reason to believe that it had been killed specifically for them. Since Chinese clerics do not beg for alms and for a long time have supplied a least a portion of their food themselves, it has been impossible to argue that any meat that they eat has not been prepared expressly for them.

38. Yiguandao—by detractors snidely dubbed "Chidandao," "The Way of Eating Eggs"—appears to have played an important role in changing the attitude among Chinese vegetarians about consuming eggs. This folk religion, claiming an islandwide membership of over a million, strongly encourages people to maintain a strict vegetarian diet, with the qualification that eating eggs does not contravene such a diet. Buddhists have benefited from the many vegetarian restaurants opened by Yiguandao devotees and see the reasonableness of the argument for eating eggs, yet they remain uneasy about fully embracing a dietary change initiated by a folk tradition otherwise viewed as unsophisticated and superstitious.

39. Several monasteries mentioned that such an article had been written, but none had actually seen it themselves, and I could not track it down. Whether or not such a story had reached the press, the rumor that it had made Foguangshan's monks and nuns especially careful never to be alone with one another.

40. When my family and I visited branch temples, resident monastics were always very enthusiastic about taking us out to see the local sights, thereby taking advantage of such exceptions. In one instance, some clerics took us to see a huge entertainment complex that included a five-star hotel, thirty restaurants, and a casino. We did not enter the casino area, but we did stay to view the pyrotechnic display and laser show. The clerics who took us were both regarded as having achieved a very high level of cultivation. As I watched them stroll through the ornate surroundings, they reminded me of the depictions of Vimalakirti remaining unmoved while visiting gambling dens.

7 Institutionalizing Buddhism

1. Through enacting such institutionalization, Master Xingyun sees himself as yet once again successfully putting into practice one of the core desiderata that Ven. Taixu had outlined as imperative for the revitalization of Chinese Buddhism but had not been able to realize himself. Master Xingyun makes no claim to having actualized the ambitious national network envisioned by Taixu; rather, he sees himself as having implemented on a more modest (and realistic) scale the underlying logic of Taixu's theoretical framework. For a description of Taixu's elaborate plans as to organize all Chinese monasticism, see Pittman (2001, 229-236).

2. Foguang bylaws phrase this in the negative, stating: "The following people may not become members of Foguangshan: those who do not honor the three gems and who do not believe in Buddhist teachings; those who have broken important national policies; those convicted of a crime who have not yet served their full time of punishment or whose civil rights have not yet been reinstated." Unless otherwise noted, information on Foguang membership, including the quotation given in this note, is drawn from Shi Xingyun (1998b, 82-84).

3. For general background about each of the Buddhist associations that have formed in the ROC since 1989, see *Shijie Fojiao tongxun lu* (1998).

4. This is the perception, at least, among members of both BLIA and Ciji Gongde Hui. Most likely this is true, although I was unable to locate any information regarding the extent of non-Buddhist membership in Ciji Gongde Hui.

5. Julia Huang, who wrote her dissertation (Huang 2001) and has penned several articles (see, e.g., Huang and Weller 1998) about Ciji Gongde Hui, informed me that, as of 1999, two nuns headed the personnel and information-technology departments of the Ciji Foundation (which focuses on institutional development) and several other bhikshunis played key roles in the accounting and publicity offices of Ciji Gongde Hui.

6. These figures are based on an analysis of the roster of Foguang clerics given in Shi Xingyun (1997a, 115).

7. There are some differences in detail. The order of Foguang interior names from one generation to the next, e.g., apparently does not follow a Linji gatha, as would be expected from the master's lineage. Instead, he has determined them himself. To compare the Foguang material with that from other monasteries, see Welch (1967, 279-281). The following information concerning types of monastic organization in Republican China is taken from Welch (1967, 3-4, 129-140).

8. I arrived at this figure by dividing the numbers twenty thousand and twenty-five thousand (the high and low estimates given by Welch for monks living in public monasteries) by three hundred (the number of public monasteries that he estimated [see Welch 1967, 4]). The 450 clerics at Foguang headquarters include approximately 350 with work assignments and 100 who are studying alongside their lay classmates in the Foguangshan Monastic Academy.

9. Information on rank and promotion is taken from Shi Xingyun (1998b, 109–111, 126–127).

10. The term *wu tangke* has been passed down through tradition; in fact, the afternoon session of recitation is not observed at Foguangshan or most other Chinese Buddhist temples.

11. The statistics displayed in table 5 give only a rough indication of the dropout rate. They do not, e.g., reveal possible variations in the rate by seniority; i.e., it cannot be determined whether there is a higher dropout rate among those who have just recently renounced than among those who renounced a decade ago. The statistics also do not reveal whether people are more likely to drop out at certain ages than at others. Nonetheless, they do provide insight into the general trend.

12. The evidence for shramaneras and shramanerikas is not necessarily conclusive since those novices who changed to second-generation names on turning twenty will have "disappeared" from the roster, their new names, not their old, having been recorded. Since, however, most were already in the middle ranks of the Foguang hierarchy in 1988 and must, therefore, already have taken bhikshu/bhikshuni ordination, this is probably not the case.

13. For example, among the bhikshunis with the interior name "Yong," fifteen of the nineteen of the rank learner, grade 2 or 3 (79 percent), forty-one of the fifty-seven of the rank learner, grade 1 (72 percent), thirty-one of the forty-six of the rank purifier, grade 6 (67 percent), and twenty-five of the thirty-six of the rank purifier, grade 5 (69 percent)—but only three of the seven of the rank purifier, grades 1–4 (43 percent)—remained at Foguangshan a decade later.

Among bhikshunis with the interior name "Yi," fifteen of the sixteen with the rank cultivator (93 percent), twenty of the twenty-five with the rank learner, grade 3 (86 percent), and twenty-four of the twenty-nine of the rank learner, grade 2 (83 percent)—but only three of the ten of the ranks learner, grade 1, or purifier, grade 5 or 6 (30 percent)—remained a decade later.

Similar figures are found for bhikshunis of other interior names.

14. Only four of the eleven bhikshus of the rank learner, grade 3 or 4 (36 percent) in 1987 and three of the twelve of the rank learner, grade 1 (25 percent)—but ten of the twenty-one of the rank purifier, grades 4–6 (48 percent) (two of whom, however, were on extended leave)—were still present in 1996.

15. Such people are automatically placed on extended leave so that, if they have second thoughts fairly soon after slipping away, they can return. Of the 1,305 members of the monastic community as of 1997, 99 clerics (7 percent) were on leave. Foguang statistics on the number of clerics in the organization always include those on leave, although the majority of these will never return.

16. Foguangshan does not disclose the exact number of clerics who have tonsured under Master Xingyun since this would make the attrition rate that much more evident.

17. The following information about dharma scrolls and the various systems of dharma transmission has been gleaned from Welch (1967, 156–176).

18. Master Xuyun was one of the preeminent Chan masters of the late-Qing and the Republican eras. He traveled widely, having visited the holy places of Tibet, India, Sri Lanka, and Myanmar in 1889, and having several times spread the dharma in Malaysia, Taiwan, and Thailand (where the king took the triple refuge under him) during the opening decades of the twentieth century. From Nanhua Temple, Liurong Temple, and Yunmen Temple, the three monasteries of which he was abbot, Xuyun not only enjoyed renown as a Chan master but also exerted considerable political influence, more than once resolving disputes between high officials. The master exemplified and espoused a more traditional form of Buddhism and remained uneasy with the Humanistic reformation advocated by Taixu.

19. Each monastic was given a slip of paper on which were printed the names of the twenty-one candidates. He or she could vote for up to, but no more than, nine candidates. Once completed, ballots were placed in one of five boxes positioned around the room. After everyone had finished voting, the results were tabulated. For each box there was a blackboard on which the names of the candidates were written (along with several spaces for write-ins). One person read out the names of the nine voted for on each ballot as another watched to make sure the reading was accurate. Another person recorded the vote on the board, again with someone watching for accuracy, and yet another person took the ballot once the information was transferred. After all the votes were recorded on the boards, the total for each person was computed for that station. When all the stations had completed their work, the totals were written on a master board on the stage so that the grand total could be determined.

20. As we have seen, there is one exception to this: those who have already long served and, therefore, step aside with the noble intention of giving the younger generation a chance to lead. The Venerables Cijia and Huilong were both among the twenty-one nominees in the 1997 elections, but they specifically told people not to vote for them so that younger clerics could take over the organization's stewardship.

21. When I told one nun that, after I had received permission to live at Foguangshan to conduct research on the organization, at the last minute this permission was rescinded, she replied that, most likely, someone on the Veterans Council had voiced reservations. Whether or not this was the case, the nun's reaction indicates the importance of this group in the Foguang decisionmaking process.

22. In the past, there have certainly been masters as influential as Master Xingyun, but their influence has been exerted through their teachings, not through their institution building. Chinese monasteries have followed an administrative system more in line with the Congregational style than with either the Presbyterian or the Catholic models. Hence, one speaks of "schools" of Chinese Buddhist thought and practice rather than of "denominations" of temples. Where masters have kept many disciples within an organizational structure, they have tended to do so through constructing and continually expanding one huge monastery. Limitations in communication and transportation, among other factors, kept branch temples in separate locations to a minimum. Direct ties with the local economy also appear to have fostered a sense of temple autonomy.

23. Ciji Gongde Hui has more chapters than does Foguangshan's BLIA. At the moment, however, I am discussing numbers of temples. Ciji Gongde Hui is almost entirely a lay organization. The only monastic order that comes close to Foguangshan's number of temples is Zhongtaishan, which, as of the year 2000, had approximately fifty meditation centers, mostly in the northern part of the island.

24. The number of monastics who reside at Pumen Temple and Hsi Lai Temple is actually much larger. Pumen Temple shares the same high-rise building with Foguang Publishing, Foguang Television, and the ROC headquarters of BLIA; altogether, the temple and these organizations utilize the services of more than fifty clerics. Hsi Lai houses twenty-three of its own staff (not including several lay monastics) plus another eight on the staffs of BLIA, Hsi Lai School, and the International Translation Center.

25. As we have seen with Daxi Heping Chan Temple, this guideline is not strictly followed. In another case, a nun who apparently donated a large portion of the construction funds for a temple in the United States has served as its abbess.

26. Jiang Canteng (1997, 23) notes that Master Xingyun may have modeled this system of rotation after Chiang Kai-shek's tactic of constantly transferring military leaders so that they would not gain too much authority or too many connections in a particular area.

27. These are my own estimates. Foguang clerics simply do not like to divulge such information. Hu Zongfeng, a reporter for *Caijing* magazine and the *Lianhe Daily*, estimated in 1992 that the land on which Foguang headquarters is perched was worth some NT$15,000,000,000 (approximately U.S.$500 million) (Shi Xingyun 1994, vol. 17, entry for 6 May 1993). This figure seems greatly exaggerated; nevertheless, it indicates just how wealthy Foguangshan must be in landholdings alone. Master Xingyun noted in his diary that it cost approximately U.S.$400,000 to build Lianhua Temple, a fairly modest structure in Las Vegas (Shi Xingyun 1994, vol. 3, entry for 30 January 1990). Other than this amount and the costs for Hsi Lai and Nan Tien Temples, I could find no references to temple construction costs.

28. Tourism may no longer be a significant source of revenue at Foguang headquarters, but it still plays an important role in the budget of some of Foguangshan's larger temples overseas, most notably Hsi Lai Temple in the United States and Nan Tien Temple in Australia. Both have a constant stream of visitors, and their vegetarian buffets draw steady business. Nonetheless, since the requested donation for the food is only $5 per person, the income could amount to only a small percentage of each temple's overall budget.

29. Master Xingyun tells a story about the auctioning of a piece of his own calligraphy during this event. Bids for the work had gone up to NT$200,000 when a young boy raised his hand and yelled out "NT$100." After a moment of surprised silence filled the room, the master looked at the boy and said: "I won't sell this for NT$200,000, but I will sell it for NT$100 to my little friend here." Of course, the boy burst into a broad smile, and everyone in the room applauded (Shi Xingyun 1995a, 10:620).

30. Much of the following information on Chinese Buddhist techniques for raising funds comes from Shi Xingyun (1998a). To supplement this, information has also been gleaned from Welch (1967, 207–241).

31. The master stated that there were ten Buddhist organizations reported to be wealthier than Foguangshan, but he only listed eight: Ciji Gongde Hui; Longshan Temple; Xingtian Temple; Zhinan Temple; Mazu Temple; Nongchan Temple; Nanzi Temple; and Kunshen Temple. He did not provide the source for this information, simply saying that he learned this from people who had considered religion from the angle of wealth (Shi Xingyun 1994, vol. 17, entry for 6 May 1993).

8 Perpetuating Traditional Modernism

1. The Venerable Jianshao, one of Zhongtaishan's senior monks, told me in a private interview that Master Weijue was not overly aggressive in pushing the women to renounce; all who tonsure under him are simply disciples from past lives who are returning to continue their cultivation.

2. As we have seen in chapter 5 above, this is generally the case, but not always. In the past, one semester was often deemed sufficient time, and, in certain cases (such as that of Ven. Huichan), those who are older have renounced without having spent any time in the college or volunteering on the mountain. These are exceptions, however, and the recent trend at Foguangshan has been to extend the prenovitiate trial period. It is interesting to note that the procedure followed at Zhongtaishan is first to renounce and only then to join the college.

3. Such reasoning continues to be especially stressed at Zhongtaishan and other monasteries where direct contact with families is more discouraged than it is at Foguangshan.

4. When once asked about filial piety, Confucius is recorded as responding: "Nowadays for a man to be filial means no more than that he is able to provide his parents with food. Even hounds and horses are, in some way, provided with food. If a man shows no reverence, where is the difference?" (Lau 1979, 64 [bk. 2, sec. 7]).

5. While the master certainly paints the Foguang system in glowing colors, his depiction is more than mere propaganda. Many of the monastics whom I came to know maintained close relationships with their parents, calling and visiting them regularly.

6. The analogy of family is extended to include all lay devotees as well, although the focus is definitely on the monastic "nuclear family." At one point, Master Xingyun literally became the adoptive father of orphans in the children's home to comply with ROC law that all children had to be entered in a family register to indicate who would take legal responsibility for them. At Ciji Gongde Hui, which has a much smaller contingent of clerics, references to all lay devotees as constituting one large "family" and as "returning home" (*huijia*) to the headquarters in Hualian is much more pronounced.

7. After the master was reunited with his mother, she told him that, when questioned about his whereabouts by the Communists, she would respond: "A mother always hopes that her

child will stay nearby to fulfill his filial duties, but I have no idea where he is" (Shi Xingyun 1994, vol. 3, entry for 21 February 1990).

8. Of course, this does not mean that such will always remain the case. It is entirely possible that, in the future, the glorification of Master Xingyun as exemplary monastic filial son will give rise to stories of him entering the underworld to assuage the condition of his mother and all other beings there.

9. Kenneth Ch'en makes this point in *Buddhism in China* (1964), his answer to E. Zurcher's *The Buddhist Conquest of China* (1959).

10. For a detailed description of Confucianism in twentieth-century Taiwan, see Wang and Li (1999, esp. pt. 2).

11. It should be noted that, while most Foguang monastics who have read this section on the relation between Foguang and Confucian values have agreed with my analysis, others have been almost affronted by it and strongly assert that Humanistic Buddhism is not Confucian at all but pure Buddhism. They also note that filial piety has been an important virtue in all Chinese traditions, not just Confucianism. (Furthermore, they have taken especially strong umbrage to Cole's analysis, deeming it hurtful to Buddhism.) Such clerics evidently believe that I am arguing that Foguangshan is primarily Confucian in its worldview and practices. My intent, however, is simply to show how indigenous Chinese values continue to shape the way in which Buddhism is practiced in that culture. Because both filial piety (*xiao*) and ritual decorum (*li*) are most strongly identified by the majority of Chinese with the Confucian tradition, I have chosen the adjective "Confucian" to describe this aspect of Sino-Buddhism.

12. Wang (1999) discusses the institutional tensions experienced in Taiwan in the 1980s and 1990s as the island confronted its political uncertainty and the challenges of globalization. Li (1996) places these issues in historical perspective. Weller (1999, 2000) indicates how capitalism, globalization, and the lack of statehood have influenced religion in Taiwan.

13. The Dutch planted trading posts along the southwest coast of Ilha Formosa (Beautiful Island) from 1624 to 1662. Their population on the island peaked at twenty-eight hundred, of whom twenty-two hundred were soldiers. The Spanish had settlements in the north from 1626 to 1642 (Wang 1980, 36). Before this time, only a smattering of Chinese came to the island to fish or conduct trade, with virtually none establishing permanent homes there with their families. Chinese began to settle and farm Taiwan's eastern coastal region under the protection of the Dutch and Spanish forts. Significant numbers, however, began to arrive only when Zheng Chenggong established his renegade anti-Qing regime there in 1661. The island became part of the Chinese imperial state for the first time two decades latter when a Qing fleet forced the Zheng leadership to abdicate power (Wills 1999, 84–103).

14. Michael Stainton (1999) has shown that, over the decades, there has been considerable scholarly debate over the degree to which Taiwan should be considered a long-standing part of the historical cultural Chinese homeland and that this debate has closely reflected evolutions in the island's political status. The discussion has often been couched in terms

of the origins of Taiwan's aboriginal population. During the first half of the twentieth century, Japanese scholars developed the thesis that the island's aborigines were Austronesian peoples who had arrived in several waves of migration from the south (mostly from the Philippines) and, hence, had no historical connection with China. Since "repatriation" in 1945, both ROC and PRC anthropologists have argued for a northern origin, i.e., from coastal China, thereby linking the island's population to the motherland right from the beginning. Increasingly popular on Taiwan since the 1990s has been the assertion that, while the aborigines originally came from the present-day China landmass, they did so long before there was any China to speak of and that any link is, therefore, extremely tentative at best. Furthermore, the Austronesian languages are said to have originated on Taiwan, eventually spreading elsewhere, e.g., the Philippines. Taiwan as an independent center is, therefore, emphasized. The point for our purposes is that the notion of Taiwan as part of the Chinese homeland has always had an ambivalent status.

15. The description of Master Xingyun's trip to mainland China is taken from Fu (1995, 14–17, 28–30, 232–235).

9 Globalizing Chinese Culture, Localizing Buddhist Teachings

1. Information on Chinese Buddhism in Australia comes from Croucher (1989, 1–3). Croucher even states that assertions have been made about Buddhist and Chinese explorers reaching Australia long before had any European. He notes that, in his *Aboriginal Men of High Degree* (1978), A. P. Elkin cited evidence for early exposure to Buddhist culture and claimed that certain aboriginal rock paintings depict the Buddha. Croucher then went on to say that it was highly likely that Zheng He's huge armada landed somewhere in Australia sometime between 1405 and 1433.

2. The primary reason for the workers' forcible return to China was not nativist fear over the competition that they posed to white labor (although that played a role as well) but moral outrage by British citizens against their own government for assisting mine owners in instituting what was little more than a modern form of slavery. Unless otherwise noted, all information on the history of Chinese religious life in South Africa comes from Yap and Man (1996).

3. These numbers are based on an analysis of the worker assignments listed in *Foguang Newsletter (Foguang tongxun)* (Foguangshan's Religious Affairs Committee), no. 424 (15 August 1997): 1–21. By "full-time workers," I mean those clerics and lay monastics who have already graduated from the Foguangshan Monastic Buddhist Academy and are not on some form of leave. An additional 110 monks and nuns were studying in one of Foguangshan's seminaries. Approximately one hundred monastics were apparently on extended leaves of absence.

4. Janet McLellan (2000, 294) records that the Vancouver Ciji office facilitated a donation of $6.2 million to a local hospital to open the Tzu Chi Institute for Complementary and Alternative Medicine (McLellan did not indicate whether that amount was in Canadian or U.S. dollars).

5. The temple being constructed in Houston is a multimillion-dollar project that may even surpass His Lai Temple in splendor.

6. These twenty-six were one of the two chapters in Russia, one of the two in Sweden, one of the two in Korea, one of the three in the United Kingdom, one of the six in Australia, one of the eight in South Africa, all ten in India, and the chapters in Yugoslavia, Sri Lanka, Nepal, Myanmar, Bhutan, Bangladesh, Bhutan, Vietnam, Congo, and Tanzania.

10 Globalizing and Localizing: Three Case Studies

1. Vice President Al Gore's visit to Hsi Lai Temple is treated in more detail in Chandler (1998j).

2. This is a translation of Master Xingyun's Chinese version of Vice President Gore's remarks (Shi Xingyun 1997c, vol. 38, entry for 29 April 1996).

3. Master Xingyun notes in his diary that, over the first two days of the Chinese New Year celebration of 1990, "15,000 cars passed through the temple gates, we used 11,200 Styrofoam cups for tea, more than 7,600 ate in the dining room, $37,846 was collected in red envelopes, and 516 volunteers worked in the kitchen and directed traffic (not including temple staff)" (Shi Xingyun 1994, vol. 1, entry for 28 January 1990).

4. According to Master Xingyun's diary, when it turned out that he would not be able to attend President Bush's inauguration, there was talk of arranging for him to go to the White House at another point to meet him. The master then goes on to say that the newly elected president had an interest in coming to Hsi Lai to visit. One can only wonder from this whether Bush's coffers were enriched with Hsi Lai contributions (see Shi Xingyun 1994, vol. 1, entry for 19 October 1989).

5. Nevertheless, most likely a good portion of the funds donated came from Taiwan indirectly. As we saw in chapter 9 above, it may be that as much as 80 percent of Hsi Lai funding is provided by devotees whose primary residence is in the ROC.

6. Among the host of ROC officials who have visited Hsi Lai are Xu Liulang, mayor of Xinzhuang City; Chen Xifan, head of ROC North American Department of Commerce; He Fengshan, the former ambassador to Egypt; and General Wang Dongyuan, the former ambassador to Korea.

7. To give one small example, Master Xingyun notes in his journal that, to change the name of a registered school in the United States, one must apply through the state, often a tedious task. He then goes on to say that, when he mentioned to California secretary of state March Fong Eu that he planned to change the name of the university associated with Hsi Lai Temple from "Pacific University" to "Hsi Lai University," she took care of the matter the very next day (Shi Xingyun 1994, vol. 1, entry for 17 September 1989).

8. One could say that the Hsi Lai affair was primarily about images. The very same photographs displayed with pride at the Foguang headquarters in Taiwan were repeatedly utilized by Republicans and conservative commentators to embarrass Gore. During the GAC panel hearings, committee Republicans gleefully displayed on easels and television screens six-

teen huge color photograph enlargements of the vice president's visit to the temple. Gore was shown clasping his palms together, offering flowers to the Buddha, and surrounded by two hundred tonsured, saffron-robed monastics. This series of photographs succinctly encapsulated the fear that underlay the entire political-donations scandal: a foreign people of radically different values was attempting to infiltrate our government. The Hsi Lai affair continued to be employed as a symbol of American anxiety about China long after the controversy itself had subsided. As concern was raised in 1999 about the PRC having compromised the security of U.S. nuclear missile technology, a cartoon appeared on 10 March on the Internet in which four robed Chinese are seen carrying out scrolled plans and a missile through a security gate. They assure the befuddled guard: "Not spies ... we come from Mister Gore's Buddhist temple."

9. Once while my family was having dinner with Master Xingyun, the master asked my five-year-old son, Evan, whether he was American or Taiwanese. When Evan answered that he was American, the master replied, "No, you are Taiwanese because you are living in Taiwan. I am the American because soon I'll leave to stay in America for a time" (Chandler 1998b).

10. After making this observation, the master then went on to paint for his audience a very idealistic picture of how Americans exhibit the six paramitas in their daily lives (see Shi Xingyun 1995a, 10:76–78). His description of American patience and diligence may be found in chapter 4 above.

11. The Catholic theologian Karl Rahner spoke of "anonymous Christians" (1966, 131–132).

12. The fact that Huishen is said to have landed in what is now Mexico rather than in the United States does not seem to affect the myth's symbolic import.

13. Chinese Foguang devotees from Sydney typically come to Nan Tien Temple once per month for a large-scale dharma function or a retreat. For weekly activities, they go to the lecture hall or one of the two Foguang gardens that have been opened in the Sydney area.

14. The look of Melbourne Foguangshan is quite utilitarian. The facility had been a Catholic elementary school before it was purchased by Foguangshan in 1994. The surrounding town of Yarraville is a Greek and Italian community, although a sizable Vietnamese enclave is just down the road. Many of the temple's neighbors think that the temple is a Vietnamese social club. Melbourne Foguangshan's devotees are Chinese who emigrated to Australia from Vietnam and, hence, live in the Vietnamese neighborhood or are Cantonese speakers who commute as much as an hour to the temple from the Little Hong Kong section of a suburb on the opposite side of Melbourne. The temple's building was purchased, not because it was convenient for the devotees, but because it was considerably cheaper than what could be found closer to the Chinese community. Many of the weekly activities take place at the Foguang garden on the edge of Melbourne's Chinatown.

15. In chapter 7 above, I noted Foguang Buddhist strategies to deaccentuate long-standing

incompatibilities found between Chinese and Buddhist values, i.e., tensions surrounding notions of filial piety and national loyalty.

16. There is justification for such concerns. One nun was mugged on a street in broad daylight. A monk who was filling up his car at a gas station was forced at gunpoint by three men to drive to an isolated sugarcane field, where they forced him to strip off his outer robes and then left in his car. According to Nanhua monastics, the fact that the men did not kill the dharma brother (as usually is the case in such hijacking) is testament to the protective power of Guanyin, whose name the unfortunate monk had continually recited throughout his ordeal.

17. This cost, mentioned by several devotees and given in Chen (1999), seems exaggerated. It may be that the cost of the entire complex, including the main shrine, community center, and seminary, comes to that amount. In any event, Nanhua Temple is a considerable undertaking.

18. Lemke not only acts as translator (few of the ten clerics stationed at Nanhua speak English) but also has taken responsibility for having the seminary accredited. Lemke spent much of his childhood in Taiwan. He was already in South Africa doing AIDS work when he became involved with Foguangshan. It was through his influence that seminary students all take a monthly workshop about AIDS so that they can become AIDS-education workers.

19. At least one of these young men, Ven. Huijin, did not do so willingly. Once his visa to remain in Taiwan ran out in the early part of 1999, he had to return to Congo for its renewal. Because of the civil war raging there, he apparently could never receive government permission to leave the country. He has not been heard of since, and former teachers fear that he may have become a victim of the country's escalating violence.

Conclusion: Global Homelessness

1. The difference in attitude between the Buddhist and the Jewish traditions toward homelessness is striking. For the former, it describes an individual's quest for liberation through renunciation. For the latter, it is a communal state intimately associated with exile. Having several times been exiled from home, the Jewish people see their enforced wanderings as anything but desirable. As Arnold M. Eisen has observed: "Homelessness is origin, not destination. It, not home, is the estate Israel leaves behind. . . . Israel's exemplification of a universal human condition (homelessness) and its articulation of a universal human longing (home) do not end with the Exodus from Egypt. Genesis is more than a prologue to the drama: it is the first statement of all the acts to come. Not-yet-home remains the condition of Israel and the human species" (Eisen 1986, 17–18).

2. Others have also noted the problem with thinking of Mahayana and Theravada in terms of geography or schools. Paul Williams (1989, 197–198) observes that, according to the *Bodhipathapradipa* and other texts, the distinction between ordinary worldly beings, arhats, and bodhisattvas rests on their aspirations: "One corollary of this . . . is that the distinction between Mahayana and non-Mahayana is not as such one of schools, traditions, Vinaya, robes, or philosophy. It is one of motivation, the reason for following the religious path. As such, there could in theory be a Mahayanist, one with the highest motivation of complete

Buddhahood for the sake of all sentient beings, following the Theravada tradition. This fits with what we know of the historical origins of the Mahayana, embedded firmly within the non-Mahayana traditions. One can speak of a particular philosophy, say the Sarvastivada or Sautrantika systems, as non-Mahayana philosophy, and the Madhyamaka and Cittamatra as Mahayana philosophies, but one cannot say for certain of a particular person whether he or she is a Mahayanist or not without knowing whether that person has developed the Mahayana motivation. There are said to be many who hold to Mahayana philosophies, and also carry out Mahayana rituals, who are not genuine followers of the Mahayana. Their real aspiration may be their own liberation, or even worldly goals such as fame of money."

Walpola Rahula (1978, 76–77) provides examples of people in Theravada lands whose aspiration to save all beings certainly would equal the bodhisattva ideal in compassion.

Glossary of Chinese Buddhist Terms and Names

Amituo Fo 阿彌陀佛
anzang yishi 安葬遺屍

bai fo 拜佛
baibai 拜拜
Baizhang Dashi 百丈大師
Baohuashan 寶華山
bei 悲
Beilian Jing 悲蓮經
Beitian Yuan 悲田院
benti zixing 本體自行
bentuhua 本土化
Biancang Chu 編藏處
bieyuan 別院
Bini Riyong Jieya 批尼日用劫要
biqiu 比丘
biqiuni 比丘尼
bu xin 不信
bu zhizhuo 不執著
Bu'er Men 不二門
bujiao suo 佈教所
Buoluotimucha Jing 波羅題木叉經
busa 布薩
bushi 布施

Caishen 財神
canfang 參方
chan 禪
chanding 禪定
chang ji guang tu 常寂光土
changge 唱歌
changshan 長衫
changzhu 常住
chanjing zhongxin 禪淨中心
Chaoshan Huiguan 朝山會館
Chen Cheng 陳誠
Chen Lü'an 陳履安
Cheng 乘
chikui le 吃虧了

chiming 持名
chuandeng 傳燈
Chuandeng Hui 傳燈會
Chuandeng Lou 傳燈樓
chujia 出家
chujiazhong 出家眾
chushijian fa 出世間法
ci 慈
Ci Bu 祠部
Cibei Aixin Huodong 慈悲愛心活動
Cihui Fashi 慈惠法師
Ciji Gongde Hui 慈濟功德會
Cirong Fashi 慈容法師
Cizhuang Fashi 慈莊法師
conglin xueyuan 叢林學院

da wangyu 大妄語
Da Bao Ji Jing 大寶積經
Dabei Dian 大悲殿
Daci Yuyouyuan 大慈育幼院
dai 代
dalu qingjie 大陸情結
danchun 單純
danwei 單位
danwei zhuguan 單位主管
dao 道
dao 稻
daochang 道場
Daochuo Fashi 道綽法師
daoye 道業
daoye shehui 道業社會
Dasheng 大乘
dashi 大師
Daxiong Baodian 大雄寶殿
Daxue Jiaoyu Choujian Weiyuan Hui
    大學教育籌建委員會
dejie heshang 得戒和尚
Dishui Fang 滴水坊
Dizang Dian 地藏殿

dizi 弟子
Dongfang Fojiao Xueyuan 東方佛教學院
dongzhong Chan 動中禪
du sheng 度生
du si 度死
duangua 短褂
dushi Foxueyuan 都市佛學院

Ershiwu Shi 二十五史

fa 法
fa xiongdi 法兄弟
Fagushan 法鼓山
fajie 法界
fajuan 法卷
falü 法律
faming 法名
fan jie 犯戒
fangbian 方便
fangbian wangyu 方便妄語
fangbian youyu tu 方便有餘土
fangzhang 方丈
fangzhang shi 方丈室
fannao 煩惱
fansheng tongzhu tu 凡聖同住土
Fanwang Jing 梵網經
fashen 法身
fashi 法師
faxian 發現
fayan 法眼
fayu 法語
fenyuan 分院
fo 佛
Fo Shuo Chujia Gongde Jing 佛說出家功德經
Foguang Da Cidian 佛光大詞典
Foguang Jingtu Wenjiao Jijinhui 佛光淨土文教基金會
Foguang Weishi Diantai 佛光衛視電臺
Foguang yuan 佛光緣
Foguangren huiyuan 佛光人會員
Foguangshan 佛光山
Foguangshan Cibei Jijinhui 佛光山慈悲基金會
Foguangshan Conglin Fojiao Xueyuan 佛光山叢林佛教學院
Foguangshan Conglin Xueyuan 佛光山叢林學院
Foguangshan Wenjiao Jijinhui 佛光山文教基金會
Fojiao congshu 佛教叢書
fotu 佛土
Fotudeng Fashi 佛圖燈法師
foxing 佛性
foxueyuan 佛學院
fu 福
fu 父
fudao Fashi 輔導法師
Fusang 扶桑
futian 福田
fuxing 復興

gan'en 感恩
ganshe 干涉
ganying 感應
gaobie dianli 告別典禮
Gong Pengcheng 龔鵬程
gong'an 公案
gongde 功德
gongdezhu huiyuan 功德主會員
gongdezhu Zonghui 功德主總會
gongping 公平
gongye 公業
gongzheng 公正
guan 觀
Guan Wuliangshou Fo Jing 觀無量壽佛經
guanfang 官方
guangjie shanyuan 廣結善緣
Guanshiyin 觀世音
guanxi 關係
Guanyin 觀音
Guanyin Beizhou 觀音悲咒
guiyi 皈依
guiyi dizi 皈依弟子
guo 果
Guoji Foguang Hui 國際佛光會
Guoji Foguang Hui Tuizhan Weiyuan Hui 國際佛光會推展會員會
Guoji Fojiao Cujin Hui 國際佛教促進會
Guoji Xuebu 國際學部
guojihua 國際化

guojiren　國際人
Guonei Dujian Yuan　國內都監院
guotang　過堂

haiqing　海青
Haiwai Dujian Yu　海外都監院
helixin　合理性
hongbao　紅包
hongfa tanqin　弘法探親
Hsi Lai Ssu　西來寺
Hualian Dian　華蓮殿
huansu　還俗
huashen　化身
Huayan Jing　華嚴經
Huazang Shijie　華藏世界
hufa xintu huiyuan　護法信徒會員
Hui　慧
Huichan Fashi　慧禪法師
huijia　回家
Huikai Fashi　慧開法師
Huiri Fashi　慧日法師
Huishen Fashi　慧深法師
huitu　穢土
huixiang　回向
Huiyuan Fashi　慧原法師
huohua　火化

jiari xiudao hui　假日修道會
jiasha　袈沙
jiangtang　講堂
jiaoshi　教師
Jiaoshou Buoluotimucha　教授波羅題木叉
jiaoshou heshang　教授和尚
jiaoyou　郊遊
jiaoyu yuan　教育院
jie　戒
jie　誡
jieba　戒疤
jiejia xiuzhen　借假修真
jiela　戒臘
jiemo heshang　羯磨和尚
jieti　戒體
jietuo　解脫
jiexin　結心
jieyuan　結緣
jieyuanpin　結緣品

Jile Jingtu　極樂淨土
Jin Fo Lou　金佛樓
Jingang Jing　金剛經
jingcai　淨財
jingjin　精進
jingshe　靜舍
jingshen　精神
jingshen zhidao　精神指導
jingshi　淨士
Jingsi Jingshe　靜思靜舍
jingtu　淨土
Jingtu Tongku　淨土筒窟
jingying heshang　經營和尚
jinjin jijiao　斤斤計較
jizhongzui　極重罪
ju　局
Jue　覺
juedui de gongping　絕對的公平
Jueshi　覺世
junquan shidai　君權時代
junzi　君子

kai jie　開戒
Kaishan Liao　開山寮
kaishi　開示
kaishi　開士
kaiwu le　開悟了
ke　課
kong　空
koucheng nianfo　口稱念佛
ku　苦

laoshi　老師
laowai　老外
le　樂
letu　樂土
li　理
li　禮
Li Chengbao　李成保
Liliu Yuying　李劉玉英
Lingyanshan　靈岩山
Linjim　臨濟
liu boluomi　六波羅密
liu jing　六境
liudan　溜單
loujintong　漏盡通

Lu Keng　陸鏗
luohan　羅漢

Man　滿
mang　忙
manye　滿業
Mazhu Yuan　麻竹園
mentu　門徒
Miao　秒
Mile Fo　彌勒佛
minquan　民權
minquan shidai　民權時代
minzhu zhuyi　民主主義
mixin　迷信
mofa shi　末法時
Mulian　目連

nan dao　難道
Nan Hua Ssu　南華寺
Nan Tien Ssu　南天寺
neihang　內行
neihao　內號
neitan　內檀
nianfo　念佛
nianmen　念門
nianzi　年資
Niepan Jing　涅槃經
nüquan　女權

panyuan　攀緣
paoxiang　跑香
pingdeng　平等
Pumen　普門
Pumen Zhongxue　普門中學
pusa jie　菩薩戒
Puxian Dian　普賢殿

qi　氣
qili qiji　契理契機
qinggouzui　輕垢罪
qingnian huiguan　青年會館
qiqi　七
Qixiashan　棲霞山

raoyiyouqing jie　饒有情戒
ren　忍

ren　仁
Renjian Fojiao　人間佛教
Renjian Fu Bao　人間福報
renjian jingtu　人間淨土
renlun　人倫
renmin zhuyi　人民主義
rennai　忍耐
renru　忍辱
rensheng　人乘
Rensheng Fojiao　人生佛教
Renwang Hufa　仁王護法
Riwen Foxueyuan　日文佛學院
Ru　如
Rulai Dian　如來殿
Rulaizang　如來藏

san du　三毒
sanmo(di)　三蓱(地)
seng shi seng jue　僧事僧決
sengzhong xintu huiyuan　僧眾信徒會員
shami　沙彌
shamini　沙彌尼
shan gen　善根
shan yuan　善緣
Shandao Fashi　善導法師
shang　上
shanqiao　善巧
shehui　社會
shelü yijie　攝律儀戒
sheng　聖
shenghua　聖化
shenghuo　生活
shengming　生命
shengquan shidai　聖權時代
shengwensheng　聖聞乘
Shengyan Fashi　聖嚴法師
shenquan shidai　神權時代
shentong　神通
shenzutong　神足通
sheshan fajie　攝善法戒
shi　實
shi　事
Shi　釋
shi mao　石錨
shibao wu zhangǒai tu　實報無障礙土
shifang conglin　十方叢林

Glossary • 349

shifu 師父
shigong 師公
shigu 師姑
Shijiamouni Fo 釋迦牟尼佛
shijian fa 世間法
shiye 事業
shiyong 實用
shou fa 受法
shou jie 受戒
shuli gan 疏離感
shuilu fahui 水陸法會
shuo buoluotimucha 說波羅題木叉
si 司
si 寺
si shefa 四攝法
si wuliang xin 四無量心
si xu jinqian 私蓄金錢
si zhi chanye 私置產業
songjing 誦經
sujia 俗家
sumingtong 宿命通

ta li 他力
Taixu Fashi 太虛法師
tan chi 貪吃
tanjiangshi 檀講師
tanjiaoshi 檀教師
Tanluan Fashi 曇鸞法師
Tanxin Lou 檀信樓
taxintong 他心通
tian 天
tianertong 天耳通
tianmo 天魔
tiansheng 天乘
Tiantai 天台
tianyantong 天眼通
titou 剃頭
tongku 痛苦
tongkuai 痛快
tongxin 通心
tongxing 童行
tudi 徒弟
tudi ming 徒弟名
tuzang 土葬

waidao 外道

waihang 外行
waihao 外號
Waiji Xuesheng Yanxiuban 外籍學生研修班
waijiao 外教
wang'en beiyi 忘恩背義
Wangsheng Tang 望生堂
wanzhai 晚齋
weide buoluotimucha 威德波羅題木叉
Weijue Fashi 惟覺法師
Weimoqi Suoshuo Jing 維摩詰所說經
weinuo 維那
wen 問
wen zheng bu ganshe 問政不干涉
Wenhua Yuan 文化院
Wenshu Dian 文殊殿
woju 臥具
Wu Boxiong 吳伯雄
Wu Jin 悟今
wu tangke 五堂課
wuwei 無為

xia 下
xiandaihua 現代化
xiang 相
xiangfa shi 像法時
xiao 孝
xiao guo 小鍋
xiao miao 小廟
xiao wangyu 小妄語
xiao yinku 小銀庫
xiaosheng 小乘
xiayuan 下院
xiejian 邪見
xiejiao 邪教
xiexin 邪信
Xilai Si 西來寺
xin 信
Xin Jing 心經
Xinding Fashi 心定法師
xing 行
xing 性
xingjie 性戒
Xingyun Dashi 星雲大師
Xinping Fashi 心平法師
xintuzhong 信徒眾

xinxing zongjiao 新興宗教
xinzhong xintu huiyuan 信眾信徒會員
xiongdi 兄弟
xiqi 習氣
xiuchi zhongxin 修持中心
xiushi 修士
xiuxing 修行
xiuye 修業
Xu Jiatun 許家屯
Xuanhua Fashi 宣化法師
xue 學
xuechu 學處
xueshe 學舍
xueshi 學士
xueye 學業
xueyuan 學苑
xueyuan 學院
xulie 序列
Xunshan Zhike 巡山知客

yang 陽
Yanshou Fashi 延壽法師
Yaoshi Fo 藥師佛
yaoshi 藥石
yeli 業力
Yi 依
yi 義
yi dao 易道
yiban xintu huiyuan 一般信徒會員
yibao 依報
Yiguandao 一貫道
Yikong Fashi 依空法師
yin 因
yin 陰
Yinguang Fashi 印光法師
yinguo 因果
Yingwen Foxueyuan 英文佛學院
Yinshun Fashi 印順法師
yinyang 陰陽
yinye 引業
yiqing 疑情
yiru 一如
yiwenhua 藝文化
Yong 永
yongyou jinqian 擁有金錢
you 有

you qing you yi 有情有義
Yu Fo Lou 玉佛樓
yuan 緣
yuan 願
yuan 苑
yuanjuesheng 緣覺乘
Yuanman Ting 圓滿庭
Yuanman Zizai 圓滿自在
yue 樂
Yujia Shidi Lun 瑜伽師地論
yule 娛樂
Yunju Lou 雲居樓
Yuyenü Jing 玉耶女經

Za Ahan Jing 雜阿含經
zaijiazhong 在家眾
zhaigu 齋姑
zhaitang 齋堂
zhangcheng 章程
Zhanglao Yuan 張老院
Zhanlan Guan 展覽館
zhejie 遮戒
zheng 正
zhengfa shi 正法時
zhengming 正命
zhengxin 正信
Zhengyan Fashi 證嚴法師
zhengzhi heshang 政治和尚
zhenzheng de gongping 真正的公平
zhi 智
zhiduhua 制度化
Zhikai Fashi 志開法師
Zhipan Fashi 志磐法師
Zhixu Fashi 智旭法師
Zhiyi Fashi 智顗法師
zhizhuo 執著
Zhong Tien Ssu 中天寺
Zhongguo Fojiao Jingdian Baozang
   中國佛教經典寶藏
Zhongguo Fojiao Xueyuan 中國佛教學院
Zhongtaishan 中台山
Zhuhong Fashi 袾宏法師
Zhuanxiu Xuebu 專修學部
zi 字
zi li 自力
zi lü 自律

zihao 字號
zisun 子孫
zisun miao 子孫廟
zisun shifang conglin 子孫十方叢林
ziyou 自由
zizai 自在

Zong 宗
zongjiao 宗教
zongjiao zhanzheng 宗教戰爭
Zongwu Weiyuan Hui 總務委員會
Zongxiao Fashi 宗曉法師
zongzhbng 宗長

References

Ahir, D. C. 1983. *Dr. Ambedkar on Buddhism*. Bombay: Siddharth.
Ahlstrom, Sydney E. 1972. *A Religious History of the American People*. New Haven, Conn.: Yale University Press.
Akers, Mary Ann. 1997. "More Events, Funds Linked to Hsi Lai Temple." *Washington Times*, 14 September, A1, A20.
Ambedkar, Bhimrao Ramji. 1959. *The Buddha and His Dhamma*. Nagpur: Buddha Bhoomi.
"American Institute in Taiwan Tour of Foguangshan." 1998. Foguangshan, 26 May.
Barnes, Nancy J. 1996. "Buddhist Women and the Nuns' Order in Asia." In *Engaged Buddhism: Buddhist Liberation Movements in Asia*, ed. Christopher S. Queen and Sallie B. King, 259-294. Albany: State University of New York Press.
Baumann, Martin. 2000. "Work as Dharma Practice: Right Livelihood Cooperatives of the FWBO." In *Engaged Buddhism in the West*, ed. Christopher S. Queen, 372-396. Boston: Wisdom.
Berger, Peter. 1969. *Elements of a Sociological Theory of Religion*. New York: Doubleday.
———. 1997. "Four Faces of Global Culture." *National Interest*, no. 49:23-29.
Berger, Peter, Brigitte Berger, and Hansfried Kellner. 1973. *The Homeless Mind: Modernization and Consciousness*. New York: Random House.
Berthrong, John H., and Evelyn Nagai Berthrong. 2000. *Confucianism: A Short Introduction*. Oxford: Oneworld.
Beyer, Peter. 1994. *Religion and Globalization*. Thousand Oaks, Calif.: Sage.
Bhabha, Homi K. 1994. *The Location of Culture*. New York: Routledge.
Bodhgaya International Full Ordination, 1998, Commemorative Magazine. 1998. Kaohsiung: Foguang.
"Bodhgaya Ordination Preparatory Meeting." 1998. Foguangshan, 25 January.
"Buddha's Light International Association [BLIA] Board of Directors Meeting." 1997. Foguangshan, 9-11 May.
"Buddha's Light International Association [BLIA] World Conference." 1998. Toronto, 1-4 October.
"Buddha's Light International Association [BLIA] Youth Conference." 1997. Foguangshan, 1-3 January.
"Buddha's Light International Association [BLIA] Youth Conference." 1998. Foguangshan, 1-3 January.
Carter, Paul. 1992. *Living in a New Country: History, Travelling, and Language*. London: Faber & Faber.
Chambers, Iain. 1994. *Migrancy, Culture, Identity*. London: Routledge.
Chandler, Stuart. 1996a. "Interview with Master Xingyun." Foguangshan, 27 December.
———. 1996b. "Interview with Ven. Miaochi." Foguangshan, 14 November.

———. 1997a. "Interview with Master Xingyun." Foguangshan, 27 December.
———. 1997b. "Interview with Ven. Huichan." Foguangshan, 2 January.
———. 1997c. "Interview with Ven. Xinding." Foguangshan, 19 February.
———. 1997d. "Interview with Ven. Yikong." Foguangshan, 18 January.
———. 1998a. "Chinese Buddhism in America: Identity and Practice." In *The Faces of American Buddhism*, ed. Charles Prebish and Kenneth Tanaka, 14–30. Berkeley and Los Angeles: University of California Press.
———. 1998b. "Interview with Master Xingyun." Foguangshan, 13 May.
———. 1998c. "Interview with Officers of Buddhist Association of the Republic of China." Taipei, 12 June.
———. 1998d. "Interview with Officers of Bureau of Religion, Republic of China Government." Taipei, 12 June.
———. 1998e. "Interview with Ven. Cirong." Foguangshan, 11 January.
———. 1998f. "Interview with Ven. Huijin." Foguangshan, 26 January.
———. 1998g. "Interview with Ven. Huikai." Foguangshan, 11 January.
———. 1998h. "Interview with Ven. Jianhu." Chungtaishan, 11 June.
———. 1998i. "Interview with Ven. Jianshao." Chungtaishan, 11 June.
———. 1998j. "Placing Palms Together: Religious and Cultural Dimensions of the Hsi Lai Temple Political Donations Controversy." In *American Buddhism: Methods and Findings in Recent Scholarship*, ed. Christopher Queen and Duncan Williams, 36–56. Surrey: Curzon.
Chappell, David. 1977. "Chinese Buddhist Interpretations of the Pure Lands." In *Buddhist and Taoist Studies I* (Asian Studies at Hawai'i 18), ed. Michael Saso and David W. Chappell, 20–49. Honolulu: University Press of Hawai'i.
Chen Dechuan. 1999. "Fayuan maigu Feizhou, yuan wu ci zhuan shi wei heiren sengjia: Huili Fashi" [Vowing to bury his bones in Africa and to spend five lifetimes creating a black sangha: Ven. Huili]. *Huaqiao Xinwen Bao* [Overseas Chinese news] (Pretoria), 23 October, 1.
Ch'en Hua. 1992. *In Search of the Dharma: Memoirs of a Modern Chinese Buddhist Pilgrim*. Translated by Denis C. Mair. Albany: State University of New York Press.
Ch'en, Kenneth. 1964. *Buddhism in China*. Princeton, N.J.: Princeton University Press.
Chern Meei-Hwa. 2000. "Encountering Modernity: Buddhist Nuns in Post-War Taiwan." Ph.D. diss., Temple University.
Cleary, Chris, trans. 1994. *Pure Land, Pure Mind: The Buddhism of Masters Chu-hung and Tsung-pen*. New York: Sutra Translation Committee of the United States and Canada.
Cole, Alan. 1998. *Mothers and Sons in Chinese Buddhism*. Stanford, Calif.: Stanford University Press.
Conze Edward, ed. and trans. 1979. *Buddhist Scriptures*. New York: Penguin.
Corless, Roger J. 1987. "T'an-luan: Taoist Sage and Buddhist Bodhisattva." In *Buddhist and Taoist Practice in Medieval Chinese Society* (Buddhist and Taoist Studies II: Asian Studies at Hawai'i, no. 24), ed. David W. Chappell, 36–45. Honolulu: University of Hawai'i Press.
Cox, Harvey. 1965. *The Secular City*. New York: Collier.

Croucher, Paul. 1989. *A History of Buddhism in Australia, 1848–1988*. Kensington: New South Wales University Press.
"Cult Leader Admits to Money Swindling, Says Pics Were Just a Trick." 1996. *China Post,* 14 October, 1, 20.
"Cult Leaders to Be Questioned." 1996. *China Post,* 23 October, 1–16.
"Da heshang dang mishi, kua liang an guan liang jie" [Master acts as secret envoy, interjects self into cross-strait affairs]. 1989. *Xin Xinwen* [New news], 13 September, 1.
deJong, Jan Willem. 1987. *A Brief History of Buddhist Studies in Europe and America*. Delhi: Sri Satguru.
Duffy, Jodie. 1997. "Interview with Ven. Xinding." Prime Television, Berkeley, Australia. Interview conducted at Foguangshan, 2 April.
Dumoulin, Heinrich. 1988. *Zen Buddhism: A History*. Vol. 1, *India and China*. New York: Macmillan.
Durkheim, Emile. 1957. *The Elementary Forms of the Religious Life*. Translated by Joseph Ward Swain. London: Allen & Unwin.
Eisen, Arnold M. 1986. *Galut: Modern Jewish Reflection on Homelessness and Homecoming*. Bloomington: Indiana University Press.
Eisenstadt, S. N. 2000. "Multiple Modernities." *Daedalus* 129, no. 1 (winter): 1–29.
Eliade, Mircea. 1959. *The Sacred and the Profane: The Nature of Religion*. New York: Harcourt Brace Jovanovich.
Elkin, A. P. 1978. *Aboriginal Men of High Degree: Initiation and Sorcery in the World's Oldest Tradition*. 2d ed. St. Lucia: Queensland University Press.
Eppsteiner, Fred, ed. 1988. *The Path of Compassion: Writings on Socially Engaged Buddhism*. Berkeley and Los Angeles: Parallax.
Esposito, John L. 1991. *Islam: The Straight Path*. New York: Oxford University Press.
"Family Reunion Day." 1996. Foguangshan, 8–9 November 1996.
Fingarette, Herbert. 1972. *Confucius—the Secular as Sacred*. New York: Harper & Row.
Foard, James, Michael Solomon, and Richard K. Payne, eds. 1996. *The Pure Land Tradition: History and Development*. Berkeley and Los Angeles: University of California Press.
"Foguang Headquarters Community Meeting." 1996. Foguangshan, 21 November.
"Foguang Headquarters Community Meeting." 1997. Foguangshan, 30 April.
"Foguang Headquarters Community Meeting." 1998a. Foguangshan, 10 February.
"Foguang Headquarters Community Meeting." 1998b. Foguangshan, 15 April.
"Foguang Headquarters Department Chiefs Meeting." 1997. Foguangshan, 15–16 April.
"Foguangshan Abbot Installation Ceremony." 1997. Foguangshan, 16 May.
"Foguangshan Benefactors Meeting." 1997. Foguangshan, 15 May.
"Foguangshan Benefactors Meeting." 1998. Foguangshan, 15–16 May.
"Foguangshan Pan-Taiwan Staff Meeting." 1997. Foguangshan, 28 January.
"Foguangshan sanshi nian dashi ji" [Major events in Foguangshan's thirty-year history]. 1997. Kaohsiung: Foguang.
"Foguangshan shijie Foxue huikao chengrenzi tiku" [Foguangshan world Buddhist general examination, adult division]. 1996. Kaohsiung: Foguang.

"Foguangshan shijie Foxue huikao manhua tiku" [Foguangshan world Buddhism general examination, cartoon version]. 1996. Kaohsiung: Foguang.
"Foguangshan Temple Administration Management Conference." 1998. Foguangshan, 22-24 April.
"Foguangshan Tonsure Ceremony." 1996. Foguangshan, 27 September.
"Foguangshan Tonsure Ceremony." 1998. Foguangshan, 6 January.
Foguangshan Tripitaka Editing Committee. 1984. *Zhong ahan* [Agama collection]. 4 vols. *Foguang Zhongguo Fojiao jingdian baozang* [Foguang Chinese Buddhist canon (punctuated edition)]. Kaohsiung: Foguang.
———. 1995. *Chan zang* [Chan canon]. 51 vols. *Foguang Zhongguo Fojiao jingdian baozang* [Foguang Chinese Buddhist canon (punctuated edition)]. Kaohsiung: Foguang.
Foguangshan Wanfo Santan Luohan Qi Jiehui: Yinli jiangxi hui ziliao; jiaowu kecheng shuoming [The 1991 Foguangshan Myriad Buddhas Triple Platform Lohan Period Precept Assembly: Material for the instructional period; explanation of instructional material]. 1992. 4 vols. Kaohsiung: Foguang.
Friedman, Jonathan. 1994. *Cultural Identity and Global Process*. Thousand Oaks, Calif.: Sage.
Fu Zhiying. 1995. *Chuandeng: Xingyun Dashi zhuan* [Passing down the light: The biography of Master Xingyun]. Taipei: Tianxia wenhua chubanshe.
Gong Pengcheng. 1996. "Foguang Daxue de linian yu shijian" [The ideals of Foguang University and their implementation]. *Foguang xuekan* [Foguang academic journal] (Jiayi: Foguang University Press) 1, no. 1 (November): 1–23.
Government Affairs Committee. U.S. Senate. 1997. "Special Investigative Team Interview with Master Xingyun." Foguangshan, 17 June.
"Group's Leader Claimed to Have Exotic Powers," 1996. *China Post*, 14 October, 30.
"Guai kelian de" [Strange and pitiful]. 1995. *Lianhe bao*, 25 August, Opinions and Editorial section, 10.
Gyatso, Tenzin (Dalai Lama XIV). 1990. *Freedom in Exile: The Autobiography of the Dalai Lama*. New York: Harper Collins.
Hadden, Jeffrey K., and Anson Shupe. 1989. *Secularization and Fundamentalism Reconsidered*. Vol. 3. New York: Paragon.
Hall, Stuart. 1987. "Minimal Selves." In *Identity, the Real Me: Post-Modernism and the Question of Identity* (ICA Documents 6), ed. L. Appignanesi. London: ICA.
Hamilton, Gary, and N. W. Biggart. 1988. "Market, Culture, and Authority: A Comparative Analysis of Management and Organization in the Far East." *American Journal of Sociology* 94, suppl:S95–S120.
Hay, Stephen, ed. 1988. *Sources of Indian Tradition*. Vol. 2. New York: Columbia University Press.
Hefner, Robert W. 1998. "Multiple Modernities: Christianity, Islam, and Hinduism in a Globalizing Age." *Annual Review of Anthropology* 27:83–104.
Heidegger, Martin. [1947] 1977. "Letter on Humanism." In *Basic Writings*, trans. Frank A. Capuzzi and J. Glenn Gray, ed. David Farrell Krell, 193–242. New York: Harper & Row.
Herberg, Will. 1960. *Protestant, Catholic, Jew: An Essay in American Religious Sociology*. Garden City, N.Y.: Doubleday.

Horner, I. B. 1963. *The Book of the Discipline (Vinaya-Pitaka), Volume V (Cullavagga)*. London: Luzac.
Hu Shih. 1937. "The Indianization of China." In *Independence, Convergence, and Borrowing in Institutions, Thought, and Art*. Cambridge, Mass.: Harvard University Press.
Hu Zengfeng. 1996. "Chen Yonghe ceng qing yi xuanzongtong shi" [Chen Yonghe was invited to help in presidential elections]. *Lianhe Bao*, 19 January, sec. 1.
Huang, Chien-yu Julia. 2001. "Recapturing Charisma: Emotion and Rationalization in a Globalizing Buddhist Movement from Taiwan." Ph.D. diss., Boston University.
Huang, Chien-yu Julia, and Robert P. Weller. 1998. "Merit and Mothering: Women and Social Welfare in Taiwanese Buddhism," *Journal of Asian Studies* 57:379-396.
Hunt-Perry, Patricia, and Lyn Fine. 2000. "All Buddhism Is Engaged: Thich Nhat Hanh and the Order of Interbeing." In *Engaged Buddhism in the West*, ed. Christopher S. Queen, 35-66. Boston: Wisdom.
Hurley, Scott. 2001. "Master Yinshun's Hermeneutics: A Study of His *Tathāgatagarbha* Theory." Ph.D. diss., University of Arizona, Tucson.
Hutchison, William R., ed. 1968. *American Protestant Thought in the Liberal Era*. New York: University Press of America.
"International Buddhist Monastic Conference." 1997. Foguangshan, 6-9 May.
"International Buddhist Monastic Conference." 1998. Toronto, 28-30 September.
"International Conference of Outstanding Buddhist Women." 1996. Foguangshan, 25-28 October.
"International Symposium of Religion and Higher Education in Asia." 1996. Foguangshan, 1-3 November.
Iqbal, Muhammad. 1964. *Thoughts and Reflections of Iqbal*. Edited by S. A. Vahid. Lahore: Sh. Muhammad Ashraf.
———. 1968. *The Reconstruction of Religious Thought in Islam*. Rev. ed. Lahore: Sh. Muhammad Ashraf.
James, William. [1902] 1936. *The Varieties of Religious Experience: A Study in Human Nature*. New York: Modern Library.
Jiang Canteng. 1989. *Renjian Jingtu de zhuixun—Zhongguo jinshi Fojiao si xiang yanjiu* [Pursuing a pure land on earth—a study of contemporary Chinese Buddhist thought]. Taipei: Daoxiang.
———. 1996. *Taiwan Fochiao bainian shi zhi yanjiu, 1895-1995* [Research into one hundred years of Buddhism in Taiwan, 1895-1995]. Taipei: Nantian Shuju.
———. 1997. *Taiwan dangdai Fojiao* [Modern Buddhism in Taiwan]. Taipei: Nantian Shuju.
———. 2001a. *Dangdai Taiwan Renjian Fojiao sixiang jia* [Thinkers in modern Taiwan's Humanistic Buddhism]. Taibei: Xinwen feng.
———. 2001b. *Ri ju shi qi Taiwan Fojiao wenhua fazhan shi* [A history of the development of Buddhist culture in Taiwan]. Taipei: Nantian Shuju.
Jiang Zhongming. 1995. "Xingyun Fashi: Li Zongtong yinggai hen huanxi jiaobang" [Ven. Xingyun: President Li should be very happy to pass on the baton], *Lianhe bao*, 20 August, Opinions and Editorials section, 10.
Jones, Charles Brewer. 1997. "Stages in the Religious Life of Lay Buddhists in Taiwan." *Journal of the International Association of Buddhist Studies* 20, no. 2:113-139.

―――. 1999. *Buddhism in Taiwan: Religion and the State, 1660–1990*. Honolulu: University of Hawai'i Press.
Kearney, M. 1995. "The Local and the Global: The Anthropology of Globalization and Transnationalism." *Annual Review of Anthropology* 24:547–565.
Kennedy, Gail, ed. 1949. *Democracy and the Gospel of Wealth*. Boston: D. C. Heath.
Keown, Damien V., Charles S. Prebish, and Wayne R. Husted, eds. 1998. *Buddhism and Human Rights*. Richmond, Surrey: Curzon.
King, Sallie B. 1996. "Conclusion: Buddhist Social Activism." In *Engaged Buddhism: Buddhist Liberation Movements in Asia*, ed. Christopher S. Queen and Sallie B. King, 401–436. Albany: State University of New York Press.
Kotler, Arnold. 1997. *Engaged Buddhist Reader*. Berkeley, Calif.: Parallax.
Kuntz, Paul. 1996. "Instant Karma: Cash Gets to Democrats via Buddhist Temple." *Wall Street Journal*, 17 October, A1.
Laliberté, André. 1998. "Tzu Chi and the Buddhist Revival in Taiwan: Rise of a New Conservatism?" *China Perspectives* 19 (September/October): 44–50.
―――. 1999. "The Politics of Buddhist Organizations in Taiwan, 1989–1997." Ph.D. diss., University of British Columbia.
"Lamp Offering Dharma Function." 1997. Foguangshan, 6 February–5 March.
"Land and Sea Dharma Function." 1996. Foguangshan, 14–20 December.
Lau, D. C., trans. 1970. *Mencius*. New York: Penguin.
―――, trans. 1979. *Confucius: The Analects*. New York: Penguin.
Li Dingzan. 1996. "Zongjiao yu zhimin: Taiwan Fojiao de bianqian yu zhuanxing, 1895–1995" [Religion and colonial discourse: The historical transformation of Buddhism in Taiwan, 1895–1995]. *Bulletin of the Institute of Ethnology, Academia Sinica* 81:19–52.
Li Shijie. N.d. "Jingtu de fenlei" [Classification of pure lands]. In *Jingtu sixiang lunji* [Papers on Pure Land thought]. Taipei: Dasheng Wenhua Chubanshe.
Li, Yu-chen. 2000. "Crafting Women's Religious Experience in a Patrilineal Society: Taiwanese Buddhist Nuns in Action (1945–1999)." Ph.D. diss., Cornell University.
Low, Stephen. 1996. "Lien Vows Crackdown on Religious Swindlers." *China Post*, 9 November, 1, 16.
Lu, Hwei-Syin. 1998. "Gender and Buddhism in Contemporary Taiwan—a Case Study of Tzu Chi Foundation." *Proceedings of the National Science Council, Part C: Humanities and Social Sciences* 8, no. 4:539–550.
Marty, Martin E., and R. Scott Appleby, eds. 1991. *Fundamentalisms Observed*. Chicago: University of Chicago Press.
―――, eds. 1993a. *Fundamentalisms and Society*. Chicago: University of Chicago Press.
―――, eds. 1993b. *Fundamentalisms and the State*. Chicago: University of Chicago Press.
―――, eds. 1995. *Fundamentalisms Comprehended*. Chicago: University of Chicago Press.
McLellan, Janet. 2000. "Social Action among Toronto's Asian Buddhists." In *Engaged Buddhism in the West*, ed. Christopher S. Queen, 280–303. Boston: Wisdom.
"Meeting of Foguang Abbots and Department Chiefs, Taiwan Branch Temples." 1997a. Foguangshan, 17–19 May.
"Meeting of Foguang Abbots and Department Chiefs, Taiwan Branch Temples." 1997b. Foguangshan, 20–21 June.

"Meeting of Foguang Monastics Assigned to Taiwan Branch Temples." 1997. Foguangshan, 27–29 January.
Metraux, Daniel A. 1994. *The Soka Gakkai Revolution*. New York: University Press of America.
"Miao Tien Denies Fraud: Zen Master Blames Smear Campaign." 1996. *China Post*, 24 October, 1.
"Miracle Cult's Taipei Headquarters Raided." 1996. *China Post*, 12 October, 1, 19.
"More Accusations against Miao Tien; New Probe Starts." 1996. *China Post*, 21 October, 1, 20.
Mueller, Max, trans. 1894. *Sukhavati-vyuha*. Sacred Books of the East 49. Oxford: Clarendon.
"Nanhua Management College Grand Opening Ceremony." 1996. Nanhua Management College, 29 September.
1994 Foguang University Art Auction Album. 1994. Kaohsiung: Foguang.
"Niuda jiaoma sheng zhong, Zhongtai Chan Si qi ren huansu" [In the midst of scuffling and shouting, seven people return to lay life at Zhong Tai Chan Temple]. 1996. *Zhongyang Ribao*, 30 September, 3.
Otto, Rudulf. 1923. *The Idea of the Holy: An Inquiry into the Non-Rational Factor in the Idea of the Divine and Its Relation to the Rational*. Translated by John W. Harvey. London: Oxford University Press.
Pas, Julien. 1987. "Dimensions in the Life and Thought of Shan-tao (613–681)." In *Buddhist and Taoist Practice in Medieval Chinese Society* (Buddhist and Taoist Studies II: Asian Studies at Hawai'i no. 24), ed. David W. Chappell. Honolulu: University of Hawai'i Press.
———. 1995. *Visions of Sukhavati: Shan-tao's Commentary on the Kuan Wu-liang Shou-fo Ching*. Albany: State University of New York Press.
Pittman, Don Alvin. 2001. *Toward a Modern Chinese Buddhism: Taixu's Reforms*. Honolulu: University of Hawai'i Press.
"PRC Devotees Donated NT$1.36 Million." 1996. *China Post*, 18 October, 16.
Prebish, Charles. 1979. *American Buddhism*. North Scituate, Mass.: Duxbury.
Qin, Wen-jie. 2000. "The Buddhist Revival in Post-Mao China: Women Reconstruct Buddhism on Mt. Emei." Ph.D. diss., Harvard University.
Queen, Christopher S. 1996a. "Dr. Ambedkar and the Hermeneutics of Buddhist Liberation." In *Engaged Buddhism: Buddhist Liberation Movements in Asia*, ed. Christopher S. Queen and Sallie B. King, 45–72. Albany: State University of New York Press.
———. 1996b. "Introduction: The Shapes and Sources of Engaged Buddhism." In *Engaged Buddhism: Buddhist Liberation Movements in Asia*, ed. Christopher S. Queen and Sallie B. King, 1–44. Albany: State University of New York Press.
Rahner, Karl. 1966. *Theological Investigations*. Vol. 5. New York: Seabury.
Rahula, Walpola. 1974. *The Heritage of the Bhikkhus: A Short History of the Bhikkhu in Educational, Cultural, Social, and Political Life*. New York: Grove.
———. 1978. *Zen and the Taming of the Bull*. London: Gordon Fraser.
Redding, S. Gordon. 1990. *The Spirit of Chinese Capitalism*. Berlin: de Gruyter.

"Religious Affairs Committee Election Preparatory Meeting." 1997. Foguangshan, 14 May.
"Religious Affairs Committee Elections." 1997. Foguangshan, 15 May.
"Renjian jingtu yu xiandai shehui: Di san jian Zhonghua Kuoji Foxue huiyi shilu" [Humanistic pure land and contemporary society: Record of third Zhonghua International Conference on Buddhism]. 1998. Taibei: Fagu wenhua shihye.
"Renowned Temple Accused of Fraud." 1996. *China Post*, 8 November, 19.
Robertson, Roland. 1978. *Meaning and Change: Explorations in the Cultural Sociology of Modern Societies.* Oxford: Blackwell.
———. 1992. *Globalization: Social Theory and Global Culture.* Thousand Oaks, Calif.: Sage.
Robertson, Roland, and William R. Garrette. 1991. *Religion and Global Order.* St. Paul: Paragon.
Said, Edward. 1990. "Reflections on Exile." In *Out There: Marginalization and Contemporary Cultures,* ed. Russell Ferguson, Martha Gever, Trin T. Minh-ha, and Cornel West, 357–365. Cambridge, Mass.: MIT Press.
"Sanbao dianli" [Triple refuge ceremony]. N.d. Kaohsiung: Foguang.
Santikaro Bhikkhu. 1996. "Buddhadasa Bhikkhu: Life and Society through the Natural Eyes of Voidness." In *Engaged Buddhism: Buddhist Liberation Movements in Asia,* ed. Christopher S. Queen and Sallie B. King, 147–194. Albany: State University of New York Press.
Shi Jianshen. 1997. "How Religious Professionals Learn: An Exploration on Learning by Buddhist Professionals in Taiwan." Ph.D. diss., University of Wisconsin.
Shi Jianzheng. 1989. *Yinguang Dashi de shengping yu sixiang* [The life and thought of Master Yinguang]. Taipei: Dongchu.
Shi Juezhao, ed. 1997. "Shui ban zhang chuang de ren" [Sleeping on half a bed]. *Jueshi* [Awakening the world] 1368 (20 January): 46–47.
Shi Taixu. 1953. *Taixu Dashi quanshu* [Compete works of Master Taixu]. Hong Kong.
Shi Xinding. N.d. "Busa yu *Buoluotimucha jing* de fazhan" [The evolution of the *posadha* ceremony and the *Pratimoksha Sutra*]. Kaohsiung: Foguang.
Shi Xingyun. 1979. *Xingyun Dashi jiangyan ji* [Lectures by Master Xingyun]. Vol. 1. Kaohsiung: Foguang.
———. 1983. *Xingyun Dashi jiangyan ji.* Vol. 2. Kaohsiung: Foguang.
———, ed. 1988a. *Foguang da cidian* [Foguang encyclopedia (of Buddhism)]. Kaohsiung: Foguang.
———. 1988b. *Foguangshan 20 zhounian jinian tekan* [Foguangshan twentieth anniversary commemorative album]. Kaohsiung: Foguang.
———. 1988c. "The 16th General Conference of the World Fellowship of Buddhists; the Grand Opening of Fo Kuang Shan Hsi Lai Temple, U.S.A." Los Angeles: Hsi Lai. Souvenir magazine.
———. 1994. *Xingyun riji* [Xingyun's diary]. Vols. 1–20. Kaohsiung: Foguang.
———, ed. 1995a. *Fojiao congshu* [Anthology of Buddhism]. 10 vols. Kaohsiung: Foguang.
———, ed. 1995b. "*Youposai Jie Jing* shoujiepin" [Receiving the precepts of the *Upasaka Precept Sutra*]. Kaohsiung: Foguang Religious Affairs Committee.
———. 1996a. "Pingdeng yu heping" [Equality and peace]. Kaohsiung: Foguang. Lecture

first delivered at the fifth annual general conference of Buddha's Light International Association, Paris, 4 August.
———. 1996b. "Press Conference." Foguangshan, 27 September.
———. 1996c. "Shifu bei nüren" [A monk carries a woman]. *Jueshi* [Awakening the world] 1366 (20 November): 2.
———, ed. 1997a. *Foguangshan kaishan 30 zhounian jinian tekan* [Foguangshan thirty-year-anniversary commemorative album]. Kaohsiung: Foguang.
———. 1997b. "A Letter to Members of the BLIA." Translated by Tom Graham and Shi Yiri. Kaohsiung: Foguang.
———. 1997c. *Xingyun riji* [Xingyun's diary]. Vols. 21–40. Kaohsiung: Foguang.
———. 1997d. *You qing you yi* [Noble sentiments]. Kaohsiung: Foguang.
———, ed. 1997e. *Zhongguo Fojiao jingdian baozang jingxuan baihua ban* [Vernacular edition of selections from the Chinese Buddhist canon]. Kaohsiung: Foguang.
———. 1998a. "Financial Resources for Buddhist Temples." Lecture given as part of the "Taiwan Buddhist Administrative Management Seminar," Foguangshan, 7–11 January 1998.
———, ed. 1998b. *Foguangxue* [Foguang studies]. Kaohsiung: Foguang.
———. N.d.-a. "Give Protection to All Sentient Beings." In "To Love Is to Treasure." Typescript. A copy is held by the office of the International Buddhist Progress Society, Foguangshan.
———. N.d.-b. "Zenyang zuo ge Foguangren" [How to be a Foguang Buddhist]. Pamphlet 7502. Kaohsiung: Foguang.
Shi Yifa. 1998. "A Proposal for Researching the Vinaya." Presentation given at the Fifth Annual International Monastic Seminar, Toronto, 29 September.
Shi Yikong. 1994. *Foguangshan lingyi lu* [Record of Foguangshan's miraculous occurrences]. Kaohsiung: Foguang.
Shi Yinguang. 1991. *Yinguang Dashi quanji* [The complete works of Master Yinguang]. Edited by Shi Guangding. 7 vols. Taipei: Fojiao Chubanshe.
Shi Yinshun. 1992. *Jingtu yu Chan* [Pure Land and Chan]. Taipei: Zhengwen Chubanshe.
———. 1993. *Huayu ji* [Resplendent rain anthology]. Vol. 4. Taipei: Zhengwen Chubanshe.
Shi Zhuyun. 1991. *Huangdi yu heshang* [Emperor and monk]. Kaohsiung: Foguang.
Shijie Fojiao tongxun lu [Directory of Buddhist associations worldwide]. 1998. Taipei: Falun zazhi she.
Shils, Edward. 1981. *Tradition*. Chicago: University of Chicago Press.
"Short-Term Monastic Retreat." 1997. Nan Tien Temple, Wollongong, 27 September–4 October.
Snow, Philip. 1988. *The Star Raft: China's Encounter with Africa*. New York: Weidenfeld & Nicolson.
Stainton, Michael. 1999. "The Politics of Taiwan Aboriginal Origins." In *Taiwan: A New History*, ed. Murray A. Rubinstein, 27–44. Armonk, N.Y.: Sharpe.
Sullivan, Kevin. 1996. "Taiwan Knows Monk at Issue in U.S.: With Knack for Promotion, Buddhist on Mountain Disdains Conflict." *Washington Post*, 25 October, A1, A22.

Sun, Lena H., and John Mintz. 1997. "Nuns Tell of Panic about Fund-Raiser," *Washington Post*, 5 September, A1.
"Suspects Say They Too Were Conned." 1996. *China Post*, 19 October, 15.
"Taipei Buddhist Master Allegedly Cheated Followers." 1996. *China Post*, 19 October, 1, 15.
"Taiwan Buddhist Administrative Management Seminar." 1998. Foguangshan, 7–11 January.
Tamney, Joseph B., and Linda Hsueh-Ling Chiang. 2002. *Modernization, Globalization, and Confucianism in Chinese Societies*. Westport, Conn.: Praeger.
Thien Tam, Thich. 1991. *Buddhism of Wisdom and Faith: Pure Land Principles and Practice*. New York: Sutra Translation Committee of the United States and Canada.
———. 1992a. *Pure Land Buddhism: Dialogues with Ancient Masters*. New York: Sutra Translation Committee of the United States and Canada.
———. 1992b. *Pure-Land Zen, Zen Pure-Land*. New York: Sutra Translation Committee of the United States and Canada.
"Thousands Mourn Dead Gangsters: Political Dignitaries Attend Funeral." 1996. *China Post*, 20 January, 1.
Thurman, Robert A. F., trans. 1976. *The Holy Teaching of Vimalakirti: A Mahayana Scripture*. University Park: Pennsylvania State University Press.
"Tien Fo Believers Attempt to Stop Shrine Demolition." 1996. *China Post*, 8 November, 1.
Tien Po-yao. 1995. "A Modern Buddhist Monk-Reformer in China: The Life and Thought of Yin-shun." Ph.D. diss., California Institute of Integral Studies.
Ting, Jen-Chieh. 1997. "Helping Behavior in Social Contexts: A Case Study of the Tzu-Chi Association in Taiwan." Ph.D. diss., University of Wisconsin.
"Triple Platform Ordination." Foguangshan, 10 October–6 November 1996.
"Triple Refuge Ceremony." 1996. Foguangshan, 31 October.
Tu Wei-ming. 1988. "A Confucian Perspective on the Rise of Industrial East Asia." In *1687th Stated Meeting Report. Bulletin of the American Academy of Arts and Sciences* 42, no. 1 (October): 32–50.
———. 1989. *Centrality and Commonality: An Essay on Confucian Religiousness*. Albany: State University of New York Press.
———. 1991a. "The Living Tree: The Changing Meaning of Being Chinese Today." *Daedalus* 120, no. 2 (spring): 1–32.
———. 1991b. "The Search for Roots in Industrial East Asia: The Case of the Confucian Revival." In *Fundamentalisms Observed*, ed. Martin E. Marty and R. Scott Appleby, 740–781. Chicago: University of Chicago Press.
———. 1992. "Core Values in Economic Culture: The Confucian Hypothesis." Harvard University. Typescript.
Tumulty, Karen. 1997. "Gore's Turn to Squirm." *Time*, 15 September, 86–87.
Vogel, Ezra F. 1991. *The Four Little Dragons: The Spread of Industrialization in East Asia*. Cambridge, Mass.: Harvard University Press.
Wallerstein, Immanuel. 1974. *The Modern World System: Capitalist Agriculture and the Origins of the European World-Economy in the Sixteenth Century*. New York: Academic.

---. 1980. *The Modern World-System II: Mercantilism and the Consolidation of the World Economy, 1650–1750*. New York: Academic.
---. 1984. *The Modern World-System III: The Second Era of Great Expansion of the Capitalist World-Economy, 1730–1840s*. New York: Cambridge University Press.
---. 1990. "Culture as the Ideological Battleground of the Modern World-System." In *Theory, Culture, and Society* (vol. 7), ed. Mike Featherstone, 31–55. London: Sage.
Wang Horng-luen. 1999. "In Want of a Nation: State, Institutions, and Globalization in Taiwan." Ph.D. diss., University of Chicago.
Wang I-shou. 1980. "Cultural Contact and the Migration of Taiwan's Aborigines: A Historical Perspective." In *China's Island Frontier: Studies in the Historical Geography of Taiwan*, ed. Ronald G. Knapp. Honolulu: University of Hawai'i Press.
Wang Jianchuan and Li Shiwei. 1999. *Taiwan de zongjiao yu wenhua* [Taiwan's religion and culture]. Taipei: Boyang Wenhua Shiye.
Weber, Max. 1951. *Religions of China*. New York: Collier-Macmillan.
---. 1958. *The Protestant Ethic and the Spirit of Capitalism*. New York: Scribner's.
---. [1968] 1978. *Economy and Society: An Outline of Interpretive Sociology*. Reprint, Berkeley and Los Angeles: University of California Press.
Weisskopf, Michael, and Lena H. Sun. 1996. "Gore Community Outreach Touched Wallets at Temple: April L.A. Event Raised Funds and Questions." *Washington Post*, 25 October, A1, A20–A22.
Welch, Holmes. 1967. *The Practice of Chinese Buddhism, 1900–1950*. Cambridge, Mass.: Harvard University Press.
---. 1968. *The Buddhist Revival in China*. Cambridge, Mass.: Harvard University Press.
Weller, Robert P. 1999. "Identity and Social Change in Taiwanese Religion." In *Taiwan: A New History*, ed. Murray A. Rubinstein, 339–365. Armonk, N.Y.: Sharpe.
---. 2000. "Living at the Edge: Religion, Capitalism, and the End of the Nation-State in Taiwan." *Public Culture* 12, no. 2:477–498.
Wells, Mariann Kaye. 1962. "Chinese Temples in California." M.A. thesis, University of California. A reprint is available through R&E Research Associates of San Francisco.
Welter, Albert. 1992. *The Meaning of Myriad Good Deeds: A Study of Yung-ming Yen-shou and the Wan-shan t'ung-kuei chi*. New York: Lang.
Williams, Paul. 1989. *Mahayana Buddhism: The Doctrinal Foundations*. New York: Routledge.
Wills, John E., Jr. 1999. "The Seventeenth-Century Transformation: Taiwan under the Dutch and the Cheng Regime." In *Taiwan: A New History*, ed. Murray A. Rubinstein, 84–106. Armonk, N.Y.: Sharpe.
Women de baogao [Our report]. 1995. Kaohsiung: Foguang.
Wright, Arthur F. 1959. *Buddhism in Chinese History*. Stanford, Calif.: Stanford University Press.
---. 1971. "Buddhism in Modern and Contemporary China." In *Religion and Change in Contemporary Asia*, ed. Robert F. Spencer, 21–30. Minneapolis: University of Minnesota Press.
Wu Jianxiong. 1994. *Yigong de xile* [The joy of volunteering]. Taipei: Wenhua.
Yamada, Meiji, and the Ryukoku University Translation Center. 1984. *The Sutra of*

Contemplation on the Buddha of Immeasurable Life as Expounded by Shakyamuni Buddha. Kyoto: Ryukoku University.
Yang, C. K. 1967. *Religion in Chinese Society.* Berkeley: University of California Press.
Yang Huiqing. 1996. "Wu Jing: Foxue huikao ge xuexiao liji tingban" [Wu Jing: All schools must immediately stop holding Buddhist examination]. *Lianhe bao,* 18 December, Living section, 6.
Yap, Melanie, and Dianne Leong Man. 1996. *Colour, Confusion, and Concessions: The History of the Chinese in South Africa.* Hong Kong: Hong Kong University Press.
Yu Chun-fang. 1981. *The Renewal of Buddhism in China: Chu-hung and the Late Ming Synthesis.* New York: Columbia University Press.
Zhang, Wei-Bin. 1999. *Confucianism and Modernization: Industrialization and Democratization of the Confucian Regions.* New York: St. Martin's, 1999.
Zhen Yishen. 1991. *Zai renjian zaocheng zhi jingtu* [The pure land established on earth]. Taibei: Daoxiang chuban she.
Zheng Zhiming. 1998. *Taiwan dangdai xinxing Fojiao: Chan jiao bian* [Modern new Buddhism of Taiwan: The Chan tradition]. Jiayi: Nanhua Guanli Xueyuan.
Zurcher, E. 1959. *The Buddhist Conquest of China: The Spread and Adaptation of Buddhism in Early Medieval China.* Leiden: Brill.

Index

Abhijña (shentong), 38–39, 153–154, 155
Africa: Foguang activities in, 265, 292, 296, 298; history of Buddhism in, 262–263. *See also* South Africa, Foguang activities in
alms procession, 229
Ambedkar, Dr. B. R., 78, 81, 268
America. *See* United States of America
Amitabha Buddha (Amituo Fo), 52–53, 55, 57, 96, 101; statue of, at Foguangshan, 8
Amitabha Sutra, 55, 60
Ariyaratne, Dr. A. T., 78
art, 185–186, 189, 236–237
Aung San Suu Kyi, 78
Australia: Foguang activities in, 107, 264, 265, 286–292; history of Buddhism in, 262, 264
Awakening the World magazine, 91, 266

Baizhang, Master, 46
Baohuashan, 178, 180
Baumann, Martin, 94–95
benefactors, Foguang, 100
Berger, Brigitte, 301–302, 305
Berger, Peter, 3, 25–26, 301–302, 305
Bhabha, Homi K., 283
bhikshu. *See* monks
bhikshuni. *See* nuns
blessings, 45, 55
Bodhgaya, Foguangshan triple altar ordination in, 86, 159, 163–165, 274, 297
bodhisattva, 51, 59
Bodhisattva of Compassion. *See* Guanyin
bodhisattva path, 99, 122, 124, 131, 147, 210, 284–286
bodhisattva precepts. *See under* precepts
Buddha, the. *See* Shakyamuni Buddha
buddha field, 51

buddha nature, 50, 81, 186, 284, 292, 304
Buddha Tooth Welcoming Ceremony, 250–251
Buddha's Light International Association (BLIA), 65, 76–77, 90, 127, 135, 165, 192–194, 219, 271, 272–273, 277; chapters of worldwide, 192, 265; compared with Ciji Gongde Hui, 77, 194; estimate of membership in, 264–267; history of, 107, 192
Buddhadasa Bhikkhu, 81–82, 94
Buddhism: Hinayana, 47, 73–74, 142, 163–164; Mahayana, 59, 70, 73–74, 100, 142, 163–164, 284–285, 305–306; Theravada, 86, 163–164
Buddhist Association of the Republic of China (BAROC), 65, 107, 157, 160, 162
Bush, President George H. W., 277
bushi. *See* dana

campaigns of social regeneration, 116–117, 135, 238
camps, Foguang, 150
capitalism: and Buddhism, 92–94; and Foguangshan, 92, 95–104; and religion, 92–93
carefree attitude *(zizai)*, 24, 82, 100
Carter, Paul, 301, 302, 303
cause and effect *(yinguo)*, 40, 99–101, 143–145, 147–149
Central and South America, Foguang activities in, 107
Chambers, Iain, 301, 302–303
Chan, 36, 54–55, 215–216; action *(dongzhong chan)*, 46, 97; practice of, at Foguangshan, 12, 15–16, 35, 45–46, 50, 97, 98, 121, 145, 216–217, 236
charisma, 41–42, 218
Chen Cheng, 9

Chen Lü'an, 9, 20–21, 105, 112–113, 125, 249
Chen Yonghe, 20
Chiang Kai-shek, 108
China, mainland. *See* People's Republic of China
Chinese Buddhist revival, 63–66, 69–73; role of youth in, 71–72
Chinese identity, as motivation to renounce, 152, 155
Chinese New Year, 18, 19, 21, 30, 156, 172, 188, 228–229, 238, 277
Christianity, 109, 114, 116, 129, 131, 132, 133, 141, 142, 172, 192, 268, 270, 275, 282, 292, 297
Chung Tien Temple, 107, 288
Cihui, Ven., 33, 72, 73, 122, 126, 179, 194, 196, 213, 214, 219
Ciji Gongde Hui, 64, 65, 71, 74–77, 193–194, 232, 267, 281
Cirong, Ven., 194, 196, 213, 218, 219, 278, 282
Cizhuang, Ven., 72, 184, 195, 196, 213, 219, 223
clerics, Buddhist. *See* monasticism; monks; nuns
Clinton, President Bill, 107, 277–278, 281, 282
clothing. *See* possessions, Foguang view on
Cole, Alan, 245–247
Communism, 253
Confucianism, 75, 76, 93, 132, 134, 141, 142, 162, 237–252. *See also* post-Confucian hypothesis
cosmic resonance (*ganying*), 40–41
culture and identity, 290–292, 300, 306. *See also* Foguangshan as carrier of traditional Chinese culture; globalization, and culture
Culture Council, 33, 125, 219

dalai lama, 78, 81, 86, 94, 164, 258
dana (bushi), 29–30, 99, 100–101, 134, 172, 226
Daochuo, Ven., 52, 53
Daoism, 114, 116, 132, 141, 142, 261–262
Democracy: Buddhist views on, 81–82; Foguang view on, 48, 71, 133, 213–214, 217–218, 256–257
Democratic National Committee, 276–280, 281, 282, 283, 293
dharma, 59, 142–143, 186, 188, 189, 284–285, 306
diligence (*jingjin*), 46, 97–99

education, Foguang system of: monastic, 14, 118–124, 156, 187, 204, 219, 229, 238, 293, 296–298, 298; lay, 124–131, 238; moral, 135–136; secular, 131–134. *See also* worldwide Buddhism examination; Xingyun, Master, as teacher
Eisenstadt, S. N., 4
Eliade, Mircea, 24
engaged Buddhism, 78–80, 306
entertainment, Foguang view on, 17–18, 22, 34, 184–189. *See also* Foguang headquarters, as tourist site; sports, Foguang view on
equality: Buddhist views on, 81, 83; Foguang view on, 48, 83–85, 91–92
establishing a pure land on earth (*renjian jingtu*). *See under* pure land
ethics, Foguang, 40, 44–45, 62, 84, 96, 237–252. *See also* filial piety; precepts; ritual; vinaya
Europe, history of Buddhism in, 95, 263; Foguang activities in, 107, 264–265
expedient means (*fangbian, upaya*), 22, 26, 148, 184–186, 188–189

Fagushan, 71, 77, 176
fair dinkum Buddhism, 289, 290, 292, 299
faith, 40, 55–56, 138, 251; types of, 131, 134, 140–143
Family Reunion Day, 242, 243
fangbian. *See* expedient means
filial piety, 55, 57; monastic, 238–248
five precepts. *See under* precepts
Foguang headquarters, 103; as sacred place, 21–23, 26, 27, 76; as tourist site, 17–18,

21, 24, 26, 184–185, 189, 225, 228; cloistering of, 10–11, 17–27, 76, 179, 189, 225, 228; entry section of, 8–11; history of, 8, 17–18, 105, 118; housing, 13, 14, 16, 71, 176–178, 183; lay residents of, 200–201; meditation facility of, 15–16; relations with neighbors, 9–10, 17, 18, 19–20, 23; religious section of, 13–17; social-service section of, 11–13
Foguang Satellite Television, 185, 220, 227
Foguang University, 122, 131–134, 219, 226, 227, 228, 237
Foguangshan: abbotship of, 213–214; art galleries of, 15; as carrier of traditional Chinese culture, 236–259, 269, 271–272; as family, 140, 241–243; as hereditary public monastery, 200; bylaws of, 155, 166, 172, 191–198, 200, 203, 214, 223, 298–299; finances of, 21, 23, 133, 139–140, 192, 224–235, 266, 279, 296; globalization of, 1, 6, 107, 120, 128–129, 161–162, 163–165, 189, 219–220, 260, 264–274 (*see also under* Africa; Australia; South Africa; United States); institutional structure of, 213–224; interfaith activities of, 275; lay members of, 191–194, 201–202, 224, 227, 299; monastic members of, 99, 171–190, 183, 194–212, 223–224, 229, 239–243; outreach to non-Chinese of, 120, 269, 272–280, 286–300. *See also* Foguang headquarters
Foguangshan Meditation College, 16, 177
Foguangshan Monastic Academy: Foguang headquarters' men's campus, 17, 177; Foguang headquarters' women's campus, 14, 23. *See also under* education, Foguang system of
Foguangshan Tripitaka Editing Committee, 126, 220
food: eating arrangements of, at Foguangshan, 178–183; ethics of, 168–169, 181–182; eating meditation, 11, 180. *See also* vegetarianism

Fotudeng, Ven., 116
freedom: Buddhist views on, 81; Foguang view on, 82
Friedman, Jonathan, 3
Friends of the Western Buddhist Order (FWBO), 94–95, 267–268
funerals, 9, 230–231
Fusang, 260–261, 286

Gandhi, Mohandas, 68, 81
ganying. See cosmic resonance
gender roles, Foguang view on, 85–91, 96. *See also* triple altar ordination; nuns
globalization (*guojihua*): and citizenship, 283, 305; and culture, 2–5, 299–300, 304–306; and religion, 4–5; history of, 1–2; of Chinese Buddhism, 260–264. *See also* Foguangshan, globalization of
Gong Pengcheng, 125, 131, 132–133, 249, 250
gong'an practice, 55
Gore, Vice President Al, 107, 276–285
Great Heroes Hall, 10, 14, 156, 228, 239
Great Mercy Children's Home, 12–13, 201
Guanyin, 40, 152, 269

Hall, Stuart, 303
heaven(s), 48, 289
Heidegger, Martin, 6, 301
Herberg, Will, 269–270
Hinayana. *See* Buddhism, Hinayana
history, Foguang view on, 48–50, 60, 69. *See also* Chinese Buddhist revivial
homelessness, 6, 301–305
housing. *See* Foguang headquarters, housing
Hsi Lai Temple, 161, 182, 183, 221, 224, 230, 244, 256, 260, 266, 268–269, 276–286, 293, 299
Hsi Lai University, 131, 219, 234
Hsia, Maria, 276, 277, 279
Hu Shi, 252, 253
Huang, John, 278
Huikai, Ven., 121, 122, 123, 124, 213
Huili, Ven., 296–298

Huiri, Ven., 213, 214, 217
Huishen, Master, 260–261, 272, 285–286, 304
Huiyuan, Ven., 53, 116
human rights, Foguang view on, 48–49, 82
Humanistic Buddhism (Rensheng Fojiao, Renjian Fojiao), 43–50, 75–77, 248, 305–306; as practiced at Foguangshan, 22, 28, 74, 179, 188, 194, 209, 215, 242, 273; history of term, 44; parallels with engaged Buddhism, 80

Ikeda, Daisaku, 94
impermanence, Foguang view on, 98–99, 102–103, 145, 175, 223, 303, 305
industriousness. *See* diligence
inheritance, Foguang view on, 96–97, 114–115
interfaith dialogue, 80, 275

James, William, 61
Japan: Buddhism in, 108; Foguang activities in, 123
Jiang Canteng, 20, 21, 42, 64, 188, 227, 234
Jiang Jingguo, 105
jieyuan. *See* links of affinity
Jinshan, 178
Jodo Shinshu, 270

karma, 29, 99–100, 143–145, 147–149, 155, 184
Kellner, Hansfried, 302, 305
King, Sallie, 79
Kuomintang (KMT), 20, 104–106, 107, 110–111, 196

laicization, 76–77
Lamp Transmission Committee, 156, 197, 203, 204, 205, 219
land and sea dharma function (*shuilu fahui*), 17, 227–228, 249
lay monastics, 201, 204, 213, 230, 299
Leiyin Temple, 32, 184, 201
Li Denghui, President, 20, 105
Lian Zhan, 135, 249, 250

Liliu Yuying, 9, 243–248, 255
Lingyanshan, 178
links of affinity (*jieyuan*), 28–32, 110, 114, 116, 134, 152, 210, 258, 277, 278, 283–284
localization (*bentuhua*), 64, 293–300, 306
Longevity Funerary Complex, 8–9, 192, 193, 230

Mahayana. *See* Buddhism, Mahayana
mainland complex, 253
Maiteya Buddha (Mile Fo), 47, 57; statue of at Foguangshan, 10, 23
meditation. *See* Chan
merit, 29, 30–31, 45, 55, 100–101, 138, 172, 210, 226, 227, 230, 244, 245
Merit Times, 126, 226
Miao Tian, Master, 114, 115
middle path, 44, 45, 96, 181
mind-only pure land. *See under* pure land
modernism: Buddhist, 79, 81–83; and religion, 68, 79
modernization, 49, 93–94; Foguang view on, 69, 70–73, 253, 306; and globalization, 1–5; traditionalist and modernist understandings of, 66–68
monastic filial piety. *See under* filial piety
monasticism: motives for renouncing, 151–155; reasons for returning to lay life, 209, 210; Republican-era Chinese, institutional leadership in, 215–216, sources of revenue of, 230–232, types of monasteries in, 198–200. *See also* Foguangshan, monastic members of; monks; nuns; tonsure; triple altar ordination
money. *See* wealth
monks: Chinese, 155, 209, 238; Foguang, 17, 161–162, 177, 197–198, 208, 210, 213. *See also* Foguangshan, monastic members of; monasticism
multiple modernities, 3, 4, 306
music, Foguang view on, 184, 188, 237–238

Nan Tien Temple, 221, 224, 234, 286–292
Nanhua Temple, 183, 234, 294–298

Nhat Hanh, Thich, 78, 164, 267
nuns: Chinese, 153, 166–167, 202, 238; Foguang, 14, 161, 163, 208, 210, 216, 242, 299; vegetarian, 202. *See also* monasticism; triple altar ordination, for nuns

orphanages: Foguangshan (*see* Great Mercy Children's Home); in mainland China, 12; Nanhua, 298
other-power, 52, 55, 60, 62
own-power, 52, 55, 60, 62

panyuan, 31
paramitas, 29, 45, 97–98, 99, 175
patience (*ren, renru, rennai*), 97–98
peace, Foguang view on, 48, 84
People's Republic of China, 271, 272; Buddhism in, 43, 63, 109; Foguang activities in, 125, 254–259
politics, Foguang view on, 107–117, 237, 251, 283–284. *See also* Xingyun, Master, as "political monk"; Xingyun, Master, relations with political figures
posadha ceremony, 165, 170
possessions, Foguang view on, 96, 173–178, 187
post-Confucian hypothesis, 93, 249–252
postmodernity, 6, 300, 304–305
pratimoksha, 158, 165, 167, 171, 181
Prebish, Charles, 289–290
precept scars, 147, 158
precepts, 55, 82, 138, 204, 209; bhikshu, 158, 159; bhikshuni, 158, 159; bodhisattva, 146–149, 158, 164; eight, 149–150; five, 143–146; Foguang view on, 165–171, 181, 183, 184, 189–190; *gurudharma*, 167; shramanera, 150, 157, 158, 296–297; shramanerika, 157, 158; *siksamana*, 150. *See also* short-term monastic retreat; triple altar ordination
profane, the, 24–25, 26. *See also* sacralization and secularization
progress, Foguang view on, 102–103
propriety. *See* ritual

pure land(s), 57; Chinese Buddhist understandings of, 46–47, 51; establishing in the human realm, 47–49, 62–63, 76, 99, 194; mind-only, 46, 51, 53–54; recitation, 45, 53, 55, 57, 58, 101, 230, 241; teachings as practiced at Foguangshan, 46, 50, 58–60, 295. *See also* United States of America, as a pure land
Pure Land, the. *See* Sukhavati Pure Land
Pure Land school, 51–54, 62, 75
pure wealth (*jingcai*), 96

Qing Hai, 114, 141
Qixiashan, 216, 246, 255–256
Queen, Christopher, 79–80

Reagan, President Ronald, 277
recitation. *See under* pure land
recreation. *See* entertainment
Redding, Gordon, 93
religion, academic concept of, 25–27
Religious Affairs Committee, 72, 205, 213–215, 217–219, 234
ren (rennai, renru). *See* patience
Renjian Fojiao. *See* Humanistic Buddhism
renjian jingtu. *See* pure land, establishing in the human realm
Republic of China (Taiwan), 253–254, 271, 304; Buddhism in, 21, 64–65, 109, 114, 176, 193, 202, 231, 264–265
resonance (*ganying*), 40, 55
ritual (*li*), 121, 170–171, 248–252
Robertson, Roland, 3, 4

sacralization and secularization, 5, 24–27, 75–76, 79–80, 188, 302, 306. *See also* Foguang headquarters, as sacred place
Said, Edward, 302
Sangha. *See* Foguangshan, monastic members of; monasticism
Sangharakshita, 267–268
science, Foguang view on, 39, 40, 61, 142
secular, the. *See* sacralization and secularization
secularization. *See* sacralization and secularization

Sengzhao, Ven., 53
Shakyamuni Buddha, 33, 44, 51, 56, 69, 72, 108, 109, 113, 142, 144, 149, 167, 170, 181, 197, 215, 250, 252, 303
Shandao, Ven., 53, 58
Shengyan, Master, 43, 75, 77, 80, 132
Shils, Edward, 66
short-term monastic retreat, 150–151
shramanera, 186, 195, 196, 208. See also under precepts
shramanerika, 195, 196, 208
siksapadha, 170
socialism, and Buddhism, 94
Soka Gakkai, 267
Song Qili, 66, 114, 141
Song Zhuyou, 18
South Africa, Foguang activities in, 264, 265, 294–298
sports, Foguang view on, 17, 186–187
Sri Lanka, Buddhism in, 86, 179
Sudatta, 59
suffering, Foguang view on, 61
Sukhavati Pure Land, 46–48, 51, 52, 53, 54, 55, 57; as portrayed in Foguang headquarter's Pure Land Cave, 11
Sulak Sivaraksha, 78
Sutra of the Teaching of Vimalakirti, 47, 51, 53
Sutra on the Contemplation [of the Buddha] of Immeasureable Life, 55, 58

Taiwan. See Republic of China
Taixu, Master, 43, 45, 63, 69, 70, 74, 94, 108–109, 191, 216, 231, 263
Tang Degang, 260–261, 285–286
Tanluan, Ven., 52, 53
technology, Foguang view on, 48, 49, 69, 70–71, 121, 177, 183–184
Thailand, Buddhism in, 86, 108, 150, 179, 229, 250, 272
Theravada Buddhism. See Buddhism, Theravada
three periods of the dharma, 51–52
Tiananmen Incident, 256–258

Tibet, Buddhism in, 209
ties of affinity. See links of affinity
tonsure, 150, 155–157, 197, 199, 200, 202, 216, 238–239
tourism. See entertainment
tradition: and modernity 1, 253; traditionalist and modernist understandings of, 66–68
triple altar ordination, 157–165, 199, 228, 296, 330nn.14, 16, 19; for nuns, 85–86, 274
triple refuge, 55, 137–143, 291
Tu Wei-ming, 93–94, 253, 291
Tushita Heaven, 46–47, 57

upaya. See expedient means
United States of America: as a pure land, 97–98, 284–286; Foguang activities in, 265, 268–269, 276–286, 292–293; history of Buddhism in, 260–262, 263–264, 270–271
Universal Gate, 35, 126, 226, 236
Universal Gate school system, 12, 187, 200–201
Upali, 85

vegetarianism, 101, 138, 147–148, 163–164; among nuns, 202
Veterans Council, 72, 219
vinaya, 44, 86, 155, 159, 165–171, 175, 179, 187, 189–190, 199, 200. See also ethics, Foguang; pratimoksha
vows, 40, 55–56, 62, 153, 155, 156, 178–179. See also precepts

Wallerstein, Immanuel, 1
wealth, Foguang view on, 49, 91–92, 95–104, 171–173, 223, 234–235, 236,
Weber, Max, 92, 103
Wei Zhuxian, 261
Weijue, Ven., 44, 162, 238–239
Welch, Holmes, 6, 63, 153–154, 199, 205, 215, 231–232
Western Buddhist Order, 267–268
Westernization, 2, 93

women's roles, Foguang view on. *See* gender roles; triple altar ordination, for nuns
World Federation of Buddhists, 272
worldwide Buddhism examination, 106–107, 127–129, 135
Wright, Arthur, 6, 76
Wu Boxiong, 105, 110, 194, 250

Xinding, Ven., 32, 124, 169–171, 177, 178, 194, 195, 196, 213–215, 219, 223, 234, 249, 292
Xingyun, Master: as bodhisattva, 38–42; as Chan master, 216; as "commercial" monk, 224–225; as global monk, 1, 275, 304–306; as grandfather figure, 37–38; as incarnation of Guanyin, 38, 41; as institutional leader, 218–219, 223; as link to mainland China, 152, 254–259; as paradigm of monastic filial piety, 243–248; as parent figure, 36–37, 241; as "political monk" (*zhengzhi heshang*), 21, 108; as teacher, 32–36; childhood of, 41, 98, 243, 246; early years in Taiwan of, 9, 105, 123, 160, 168, 184, 187, 196, 231; monastic training of, 152, 246; relations with political figures, 18, 20–21, 31, 104–107, 214, 249–251, 257–258, 276–286; relationship with matrilineal family, 243–248; relationship with monastic disciples, 16, 34, 35–38, 42; relationship with patrilineal family, 152, 246; residence of, 17; view on homelessness, 6; view on social change, 84; visits to mainland China of, 254–258, 304
Xinping, Ven., 8–9, 17, 174, 213–214, 216
Xu Jiatun, 256–258
Xuanhua, Ven., 264

Yanshou, Ven., 54–55
Yifa, Ven., 123, 167
Yiguandao, 64, 116, 202,
Yikong, Ven., 30, 124, 213, 242
Yinguang, Ven., 50, 56–57, 58, 168, 231
Yinshun, Ven., 43, 50, 57–58, 60, 63, 212

Zhengyan, Ven., 43, 64, 74–77, 80, 194
Zhikai, Ven., 152, 246, 255–256
Zhiyi, Ven., 53–54, 61
Zhongtaishan, 16, 44, 65–66, 71, 162, 176, 177, 238–239, 240
Zhuhong, Ven., 54–55

About the Author

Stuart Chandler received his Ph.D. in the study of comparative history of religion at Harvard University. In addition to writing on contemporary Chinese Buddhism, he is involved in the efforts of the Pluralism Project of Harvard University to track the increasing presence in the United States of such religions as Buddhism, Hinduism, Jainism, Sikhism, and Islam. Professor Chandler is on the faculty of the Department of Religious Studies at Indiana University of Pennsylvania.

HAWAI

Production Notes for Chandler/*Establishing a Pure Land on Earth*
Cover and Text design by Elsa Lee. Text in Goudy Old Style with display in Hiroshige
Composition by Tseng Information Systems, Inc. in Buffalo TEX
Printing and binding by The Maple-Vail Book Manufacturing Group.
Printed on 60 lb. Sebago Eggshell, 420 ppi